COMMUNITY OF FATE

*German-Soviet
Diplomatic Relations
1922–1928*

KURT ROSENBAUM

COMMUNITY
OF FATE

German-Soviet
Diplomatic Relations
1922-1928

SYRACUSE UNIVERSITY PRESS

*Manufactured in the United States of America
by Vail-Ballou Press, Inc., Binghamton, New York*

TO SHIRLEY, BETH ELLEN
AND JONATHAN DAVID

ACKNOWLEDGMENTS

While the researcher labors primarily in solitary seclusion, his work is facilitated by the support, intellectual as well as financial, which he receives from understanding friends. Dr. Warren B. Walsh supervised the dissertation on which this study is based. He contributed unstintingly of his knowledge, time, and advice. Both he and Dr. Kenneth I. Dailey guided my studies in Russian history and inspired me with their splendid teaching. I wish to express my appreciation to the faculty of the Department of History at Syracuse University, especially to its former chairman, Dr. Oskar T. Barck, Jr., for the support which resulted in a University Fellowship. I am also indebted to Mrs. Charlotte Cobb, Miss Marion Mullen, and Mr. Joseph Dosa, all of Syracuse University.

The purchase of the materials and microfilmed documents needed to expand the dissertation was facilitated by a grant from the Central University Research Fund of the University of New Hampshire. I wish to acknowledge my gratitude to the Committee on Research of that institution, especially Dr. Stuart H. Palmer, for the support I received.

Funds for the typing of the manuscript were provided by Dr. Carl M. Frasure, Dean of the College of Arts and Sciences at West Virginia University. Dr. William T. Doherty, Chairman of the Department of History, arranged my teaching schedule to provide a maximum amount of time for work on the study. A special debt of gratitude is due Lee Golay, who typed most of the manuscript from my handwritten drafts, and Mrs. Jeannette Metz, who typed the revised manuscript in record time.

I wish to express my thanks to the Georgetown University Press for permission to use material from *Soviet Treaty Series: A Collection of Bilateral Treaties, Agreements, and Conventions, Etc., Concluded Between the Soviet Union and Foreign Powers*, volume I, 1917–1928, compiled and edited by Leonard Shapiro; to the Macmillan Company for permitting the incorporation of material from Gustav Hilger and Alfred G. Meyer, *The Incompatible Allies: A Memoir-History of German-Soviet Relations, 1918–1941*, Copyright, 1953, by the Macmillan Company; and to the Oxford University Press for allowing me to quote passages from volumes I and II of *Soviet Documents on Foreign Policy*, edited by Jane Degras and published under the auspices of the Royal Institute of International Affairs.

It goes almost without saying that my very sincere gratitude goes to my wife for her intelligent support and her understanding attitude.

CONTENTS

I

Introduction: From Brest-Litovsk to Rapallo

Germany's diplomatic relations with Russia, disrupted by the war, were resumed after the Treaty of Brest-Litovsk had been signed on March 3, 1918. The terms of the treaty were extremely harsh, robbing the Soviet state of one-third of its population and agricultural land and over one-half of its industrial capacity. Russia no longer had an army able or willing to fight. Lenin persuaded the Seventh Party Congress of the Russian Communist Party (B) that a breathing spell was of the utmost importance to revitalize the country so that it could withstand the imperialists' attacks intent on destroying the proletarian state. "In any case," Lenin argued, "and in whatever conceivable circumstances, we are doomed if the German revolution does not break out. . . ." That revolution would probably take more time to develop.[1]

The Fourth All-Russian Congress of Soviets, to whom Lenin's appeal was directed, ratified the treaty on March 15. In April, Adolf A. Joffe went to Berlin to occupy the former Imperial Embassy at 7 Unter den Linden. He immediately set to work to aid in the promotion of revolution. He also tended to his diplomatic business, negotiating with the Imperial government regarding the resumption of trade and the normalization of relations.

Germany's Ambassador, Count Wilhelm von Mirbach, arrived in Petrograd on April 23. His stay lasted seventy-four days, when he fell victim to two left Social Revolutionaries. The bullets fired at Mirbach were the opening shots in an insurrection planned by the Social Revolutionary leaders, who opposed Brest-Litovsk and wanted to overthrow the Bolsheviks by drawing the German army down upon them. To forestall such a contingency, Lenin and three of the leading members of the Soviet government went to the German Embassy to express regrets about the assassination. Joffe transmitted his government's sympathy and regrets to the German Foreign Office in Berlin.

The diplomatic quarter in Moscow was immediately surrounded by

1

troops, but the assassins escaped. The chief of the Cheka, Felix Dzerzhinsky, took charge of the investigation, and by July 19 over 200
persons implicated in the plot had been shot, according to official
announcements. The leader of the Social Revolutionaries, Maria
Spiridonova, acknowledged planning the assassination and insurrection. The Soviet government did not give public satisfaction for the
murder of Mirbach despite prolonged negotiations between the
Wilhelmstrasse and Joffe.[2]

The Fifth All-Russian Congress of Soviets passed a resolution on
July 9 condemning the deed in harsh words:

> The assassination of the German Ambassador is a crime all the
> more shameful since its organizers and executors took advantage
> of their position . . . to undermine by treachery and stealth the
> firm determination of the Soviet Government to safeguard for the
> workers and peasants of Russia the peace bought at so high a
> price.[3]

The rulers of Russia obviously feared military actions by the German army. Their relief was immense when Karl Helfferich arrived on
July 28 as the new emissary, despite the fact that he was an outspoken
anti-Bolshevik. He stayed exactly two weeks, during which he tried to
engineer an anti-Bolshevik coup, despite instructions to be conciliatory.
Helfferich returned to Berlin, followed by the whole staff of the Embassy, convinced that the new Russian regime could not possibly last.[4]
One official remained behind to continue the necessary contacts. The
Russian fears that the death of Mirbach would lead to stringent actions
by the Germans had proven groundless. Diplomatic relations were not
broken off.

In Germany, the domestic situation progressively deteriorated as
the war continued into autumn. By the end of September, the Supreme
Command of the German army had decided that the war could no
longer be won and proposed to the Emperor that negotiations for an
armistice be started. The man selected for the job was Prince Max von
Baden, who became chancellor during the first days of October. His
government included the leaders of the Social Democratic Party
(SPD), Friedrich Ebert and Philipp Scheidemann.

The difficulties of the Germans led to rejoicing among the Bolsheviks. The All-Russian Executive Committee declared its eagerness
to aid in the destruction of a government with which it maintained
diplomatic relations. Because the

> German working class [was] moving irresistibly towards
> power . . . the Central Executive Committee declares that in

this struggle the whole of Soviet Russia will, with all its forces and all its means, support the revolutionary power in Germany against all imperialist enemies.

In Berlin, Joffe expended considerable sums of money, by his own later acknowledgment in excess of 10,000,000 rubles,[5] to bring about the much-desired German revolution. The incessant propaganda and blatant activities of the Russian diplomatic mission led the German government to consider ways and means to remove Joffe and his cohorts. Porters at the Friedrichstrasse Railroad Station in Berlin "accidentally" dropped a few boxes of Russian diplomatic properties containing pamphlets designed to arouse the German proletarians to revolution. Joffe was ordered out of Berlin on November 5. Although he remained two weeks longer, *de jure* diplomatic contacts between the Imperial government and Soviet Russia had ended.

Revolution in Germany came from an unexpected quarter. The Kaiser's beloved navy refused to follow orders to steam out and meet the enemy in one last gigantic battle. Red flags appeared on the masts of the ships of the High Sea Fleet on November 4, and the sailors debarked to spread the revolution on land. Prince Max was confronted with demands from the Social Democrats to turn the autocratic Reich into a true parliamentary state. This, the Socialists felt, could be accomplished only if the Kaiser abdicated and the Crown Prince renounced his right to the succession. If this was not done, Ebert and Scheidemann would leave the Cabinet.

Prince Max rejected the ultimatum on November 7 and threatened his own resignation. The Emperor was persuaded to abdicate by the Supreme Army Command on November 9; Prince Max announced the abdication at noon. At that very hour the Social Democrats arrived at the Chancellery to inform the Prince that they were taking over the government. Prince Max turned his office over to Ebert to assure an orderly transfer of government to the newly-formed Council of People's Deputies. Two days later the German Armistice Commission signed the armistice which ended the war.[6]

The Soviet government lost no time in announcing to the world "that the terms of the peace with Germany signed at Brest-Litovsk on March 3, 1918, are null and void. . . ."[7]

The incumbent Secretary of State for Foreign Affairs continued in office. No protests were lodged against the unilateral abrogation of the German-Russian peace treaty. On December 9, the Foreign Office was offered to Count Ulrich Karl Christian von Brockdorff-Rantzau, Minister (*Gesandter 1. Klasse*) to Denmark, where he had served since 1912.[8]

The Count, born in 1869, was a proud, haughty, and arrogant

member of an old Holstein family which had been noble since the twelfth century. He was excessively proud of his family background and possessed of a rather condescending attitude toward lesser mortals. His sarcastic, often sardonic wit and overwhelming arrogance are best exemplified by the following anecdote: A French reporter approached the Count at Versailles and attempted flattery by referring to a story according to which an ancestor, Marshal Josiah Rantzau, had been the father of Louis XIV. The Count retorted that family tradition recorded this story. What pleased him was the fact that the Rantzaus were not illegitimate Bourbons "but the Bourbons were bastards of the Rantzaus."[9]

The Count was well-prepared for his new position. He had started his diplomatic career, after receiving a doctor of laws degree, as an attaché, the lowest rank in the foreign service. He served in that capacity at Brussels, and, after his promotion to Secretary of Legation, had been posted to St. Petersburg in 1897, where he spent the next four years moving only in the best of circles. He made no attempt to learn Russian because there was no need for it; everybody the Count met spoke French as fluently as he himself. His next assignment, lasting for almost nine years, was at another Eastern court, Vienna, where he advanced to Counselor of Legation. His first independent assignment came in 1910, when he was appointed Consul General at Budapest. Three years later he left, and with his undoubted diplomatic talent recognized, was appointed Minister to Denmark. Copenhagen was generally considered as preparation for the ambassadorship at St. Petersburg, and Brockdorff-Rantzau considered it as such.

During the war the Count maintained a steady flow of Danish foodstuffs to Germany in exchange for coal, on which Denmark was entirely dependent. He came in close contact with the leaders of Danish and German unions and developed a close relationship, based on mutual respect, with Ebert. Brockdorff-Rantzau was instrumental in facilitating the passage of Lenin and his companions across Germany to the Finland Station. In July of 1917, he had been offered the position of Secretary of State in the Foreign Office, but had refused to accept it because he was convinced that he would be unable to pursue a policy independent of military interference and would not be granted the right to influence military decisions. Military leadership, he was convinced, would lead to political disaster. War, he wrote in a secret memorandum for his private files, should never be an end in itself, but only be used to support an intelligent foreign policy. "*Ultima ratio regis* does not mean that the sagacity of the king ceases to exist."[10]

After Prince Max formed his coalition Cabinet, Brockdorff-Rantzau was again considered for the Wilhelmstrasse. The Count refused because the situation in Germany was so critical that he would accept only the chancellorship, and he did not think that a change was advisable. Because of the critical domestic situation only a chancellor, supported by the absolute trust of the people and given complete freedom of action, could possibly achieve something decisive against the military. Finally, and most importantly, he was not willing to take responsibility, before history, for the crimes which had been committed by the old regime.

The concern for the judgment of history was also foremost in Brockdorff-Rantzau's mind when Scheidemann inquired on December 8 whether he would be willing, now that the old regime was no more, to take the extremely important assignment of Foreign Secretary. Brockdorff-Rantzau made his acceptance dependent on five conditions:

1. Convocation of a national constituent assembly should take place before February 16, 1918, so that the Council of People's Deputies, based on revolutionary right, could receive constitutional approval and create a parliamentary regime.

2. Germany's credit had to be restored and based on a solid foundation so that foreign loans, especially from the United States, could be secured.

3. A republican army should be created immediately so that Germany could appear at the Peace Conference as a state of some consequence. President Wilson could be counted upon to pursue his program, which meant that he did not want the destruction of Germany. An army would help Wilson to make his point with his allies. Most importantly, the army was necessary to prevent attempts to bolshevize Germany. Otherwise Germany might be plunged into a terrible bloodbath which could destroy her.

4. Everything possible should immediately be done to remove the Workers' and Soldiers' Councils from participation in the governing of the state.

5. Finally, the Count stipulated that he be given the right to participate in the solution of domestic problems, because a successful foreign policy depended on domestic development. He asked to be permitted to reject a dictated peace, if it was so constituted that it would make Germany's continued existence practically impossible.

Ebert, for the SPD, and Hugo Haase, for the Independent Socialists (USPD), accepted the first four conditions, and Brockdorff-Rantzau was appointed State Secretary for Foreign Affairs on December 18. The Count arrived in Berlin on January 2, 1919, to take over his new duties. He immediately called together the remaining personnel of the Wilhelmstrasse and told them that he would "try to save what could still be saved."[11]

Brockdorff-Rantzau decided to secure a just peace for Germany based on President Wilson's note of November 5, 1918, in which he had notified Prince Max of the willingness of the Allies to conclude peace on the basis of the Fourteen Points. Brockdorff-Rantzau, who had no desire to play the German Talleyrand, continued to base his labors for a just peace on the Points and coupled it with veiled threats about a *rapprochement* with Bolshevik Russia should the Allies decide to deal harshly with Germany.

Even before Brest-Litovsk, Brockdorff-Rantzau had advised against annexations because he did not want to alienate Russia, which he considered as a counterweight against the British, with whom difficulties could be expected even after the war was over.

The rulers in the Kremlin did nothing to repay the Count for the aid he had given them in 1917. Instead, they sent expert advice to the Spartacists, who converted themselves into the Communist Party of Germany (KPD) in January of 1919. The fledgling KPD, led by Rosa Luxemburg and Karl Liebknecht, attempted to seize power in Berlin. The Communists suffered a disastrous defeat at the hands of the Free Corps, directed by Gustav Noske, who was entrusted with the job by Ebert. Luxemburg and Liebknecht were arrested and murdered on January 16. The new party was thus bereft of its most important leaders, a loss which in subsequent years was to be of decisive importance.

During the Spartacist uprising, Brockdorff-Rantzau had threatened to resign unless the insurgents were brought to heel without conditions. No quarter was given, and he continued in office. Brockdorff-Rantzau, who was a disciple of Bismarck in foreign relations, used the Iron Chancellor's threat of resignation repeatedly throughout his career to achieve his ends. He also carried grudges against real and imagined insults to extreme lengths. One example was his dislike for Matthias Erzberger, who had been a member of the German Armistice Commission. During the Communist rising, Karl Radek had been arrested. Erzberger, without consulting Brockdorff-Rantzau, advocated that the revolutionary be delivered to the Entente. The Count was furious about this disregard of political consequences.

Karl Radek[12] had been the Russian expert sent to Germany to give practical advice to the Spartacists. Radek was well known to the German authorities and the labor movement because he had been a member of the SPD from 1908 until he was expelled from the party in 1915. He had joined Lenin in Switzerland and journeyed with him across Germany in April, 1917. After the November Revolution in Russia he had been Trotsky's assistant, spending most of his time spreading revolutionary propaganda directed at German soldiers. At Brest-Litovsk he had infuriated the German negotiators by distributing propaganda to the soldiers. Radek became director of the Central European desk of the Foreign Commissariat when George V. Chicherin replaced Trotsky. His close association with the Narkomindel continued even after he was elected secretary of the Communist Third International, which was founded in March of 1919 to carry forward the task of world revolution. The Chairman of the Comintern, Grigori E. Zinoviev, was a gifted orator and very close associate of Lenin. By the time he was elected secretary of the Comintern, Radek was in Moabit Prison because he had been arrested on February 12 for his suspected part in the Spartacist rising, despite inconclusive evidence. He remained in prison, although under extremely comfortable conditions for most of the time he spent in Berlin. He returned to Russia in January of 1920.

After the defeat of the KPD, preparations for country-wide elections for the Constituent Assembly proceeded apace. Elections were held, and on February 6, 1919, 421 delegates assembled at Weimar, because Berlin was not considered safe enough, to give Germany a new constitution. The SPD, with 163 seats, had the largest bloc of representatives. Ebert was elected President of the provisional government. Scheidemann formed a new ministry, in which Brockdorff-Rantzau continued as Minister for Foreign Affairs; the old designation *Staatssekretär* now applied to the permanent undersecretaries in each ministry. On February 14, the new Minister appeared before the National Assembly at Weimar and presented his program in a long, ponderous address. Brockdorff-Rantzau, who had an excellent command of German, could compose fine state papers and was somewhat a raconteur, but was not an accomplished public speaker. Brockdorff-Rantzau declared that Germany was willing to make peace but refused to acknowledge that she alone was responsible for the war and alone had committed acts of barbarity. The decision could best be left to an impartial judge; in the meantime, Germany would maintain its adherence to the Wilsonian principle of no indemnities or territorial cessions to the victors. Germany was willing to reimburse civilians for damages caused them and to rebuild what she had destroyed, but voluntarily and not by slave labor forced on prisoners of war.

The speech followed Wilson's ideas step by step, and Brockdorff-Rantzau continued to act as if he were the only sincere believer, aside from the President, in the feasibility of all these ideas.

After he had lauded the Wilsonian principles wherever they fitted into his nationalistic conception of the future, Brockdorff-Rantzau turned to Russia and the infamous peace forced on the Bolsheviks at Brest-Litovsk. "Such treaties," the Count told the delegates, "are today a danger for every victor." Obviously, the new Germany should be spared such a peace treaty.

Relations with Soviet Russia he felt, should be based on a cessation of Bolshevik interference in the domestic affairs of other nations and the end of foreign intervention in Russia. As for his own service to the nation, he

> hoped to prove that one could be a Count and at the same time a democrat. Democracy did not mean the rule of the masses as such; only the very best men should rule and lead.

When a democratic people made a mistake in its choice of leaders, it could use the processes of democracy to remove them.[13]

The speech was as much directed toward the victorious Allies assembled in conference at Paris as it was to the delegates of the Constituent Assembly. Brockdorff-Rantzau demanded a fulfillment of Wilson's Fourteen Points, at the same time reminding the Allies that even a defeated Germany, harassed by Bolshevik attempts at revolution, could renew the traditional relationship which had bound Germany and Russia for so many generations.

It was exactly that kind of alignment which gave the statesmen at Paris nightmares. The creation of the Comintern had been the outward expression of the world revolution which was to issue from Moscow. On March 21, Bela Kun established a Soviet Republic in Hungary, and this event gave renewed life to the specter which had haunted Europe, albeit for generations only in the imagination of its creators. On March 25, David Lloyd George, the English Prime Minister, presented a secret note to Wilson and Clemenceau in which he implored them to use their influence to procure a lasting peace. Revolution was at large in Russia and in Germany; it could easily spread, because there was unrest in France, Italy, and Great Britain. Lloyd George saw the greatest immediate danger in an alliance between Germany and Russia, because then the Bolsheviks could conceivably complete their design for the control of the world.[14]

> The greatest danger that I can see in the present situation is that Germany may throw in her lot with Bolshevism and place her resources, her brains, her vast organizing power at the disposal of the revolutionary fanatics whose dream it is to conquer the world for Bolshevism by force of arms. The danger is no mere chimera.[15]

Since revolution had not yet been successful in Germany, Russia turned again to diplomatic maneuver. On April 22 a Russian radio announcement was received in Germany which expressed the desire of the Soviet government to re-establish diplomatic relations. On the next day Brockdorff-Rantzau told a Cabinet session that no official negotiations should take place until after peace had been concluded with the Allies. If the peace was unbearable, official negotiations could be started. In the meantime, talks by private persons about economic relations could continue.

The German delegation, headed by Brockdorff-Rantzau, arrived at Versailles late in the evening of April 29. The Allies made no move to get in touch with them. After five days of waiting, Brockdorff-Rantzau informed the Conference that the Ministers Landsberg and Giesberts would return to Berlin. Thereupon the information was conveyed to the German delegation that the conditions of peace would be handed to Brockdorff-Rantzau on May 7, at 3:00 P.M. at the Trianon Palace.[16] The French papers maliciously proclaimed that the day had been selected by the Americans because the *Lusitania* had been sunk on that date a few years before. A diagram of the hall in which the session was to be held also appeared in the French press, the German table labeled *banc des accuses*. Brockdorff-Rantzau's sensibilities were aroused. He considered the label a deliberate insult. He was further incensed when he was informed that there would be no oral negotiations on the draft treaty, as he had expected. The German delegation was to have fifteen days, subsequently twenty-two, to submit written replies to the 440 articles which it had taken several committees more than four months to complete.

May 7, Brockdorff-Rantzau later recalled, was a beautiful day. A brilliant spring sun bathed all of Versailles; the air was filled with the song of birds and the smell of lilac—not the kind of day that would fit the occasion.

After Brockdorff-Rantzau had taken his seat at the table facing the half-circle formed by the Allies, Clemenceau rose and addressed the German delegation. The time had come to settle accounts. "You have asked for peace. We are willing to grant you peace." He departed from the prepared text and accused Germany of being responsible for the war. He almost immediately controlled himself and returned to his text, concluding his short speech by emphasizing that the Conference was determined to construct a lasting peace.

After Clemenceau finished, the Secretary of the Conference brought the big, white volume in which the draft treaty was bound to the German Foreign Minister. The Count received it, rising ever so slightly, and placed it on the table. As if occupied in deep thought, he carelessly dropped his black gloves on top of the white cover.[17] Adjusting dark-rimmed glasses on his nose, he read his prepared reply, in stark contrast to Clemenceau, seated.

"Gentlemen!" Brockdorff-Rantzau began, his voice vibrating. He clearly enunciated each word as he went into his speech.

We are deeply impressed with the lofty aims which have brought us together with you: to give to the world quickly a permanent peace. We have no illusions about the extent of our defeat, the degree of our impotency. We understand that the power of German arms has been broken; we know the weight of hatred which confronts us here, and we have heard the vehement demands that the victors are supposed to let us pay because we are vanquished and punish us because we are guilty.

It is demanded of us that we acknowledge that we are the ones solely responsible for the war; such an avowal, coming from me, would be a lie.

After this introduction, Brockdorff-Rantzau told the assembled representatives of the Allied and Associated Powers that he was aware of the failings of the old regime. But he emphatically rejected Germany's sole responsibility.

The assassination of the Austro-Hungarian heir to the throne was not the first act in the drama. Fifty years of imperialistic adventures had poisoned the international atmosphere, and the

policy of revenge, as well as the policy of expansion in disregard of the right of peoples to determine their own affairs contributed to the sickness of Europe, which reached its crisis in the World War. Russian mobilization took the possibility of curing the disease out of the hands of statesmen and placed the decision into the hand of military force.

Public opinion the world over held Germany responsible for crimes, especially against Belgium. The new Germany was willing to atone for this wrong committed by the fallen leaders. But other nations too "knew of deeds and persons" which they would rather not recall.

Guilt should be determined by an objective commission which would hear the main actors in the tragedy and which would have access to all archives. Peace, Brockdorff-Rantzau insisted, should be based on Wilsonian principles. If such a peace were granted, Germany would fulfill the obligations placed upon her. A peace not based on justice could not be defended or signed by anyone in good conscience because the demands of an unjust peace could not be fulfilled. The

German delegation would inspect the draft treaty in the hope that the final version could be signed by all.

After completing his speech, Brockdorff-Rantzau rose, moved slowly toward the exit and out to the stairway; while waiting for the rest of the delegates to join him he lit a cigarette. The gesture caused another sensation. Brockdorff-Rantzau, a chain smoker, was unaware of the stir among the newspaper and cameramen who crowded around him.

Brockdorff-Rantzau had, however, been deliberate in the choice of his words and their deliverance. Throughout the Count's response, Clemenceau looked as if he were going to interrupt, his face turning red with anger. Wilson listened attentively, but obviously was appalled by what he heard. Lloyd George, feigning indifference, was smiling, and Bonar Law yawned. Obviously, after the opening words, the other relatively reasonable proposals did not remove the earlier impression of cold arrogance in the face of overwhelming defeat.

The Count was perfectly aware of the impression he was creating, but he was incapable of acting as if he had been defeated. He, personally, had not wished the war, nor had he approved of the methods used by his compatriots. As an aristocrat, he was not going to grovel before the victors. Germany had fought well and deserved to be treated with magnanimity. Understandable as such feelings are from a human point of view, under the circumstances they were a tremendous blunder. What good will had existed was crushed during the few minutes it took for the Count's contemptuous address, delivered with icy irony.

The speech was prepared in advanced, drafted and redrafted by various members of the delegation. Walter Simons, Commissioner General of the German delegation, advised Brockdorff-Rantzau to consider the manner of delivery carefully so that the door to reconciliation would remain open, without relinquishing insistence on a just peace. For years afterwards, Brockdorff-Rantzau resented the courtroom atmosphere which, he remained convinced, was designed to humiliate the German delegates. He remained seated because in his mind he could hear the words, "Prisoner at the bar, rise and face your judges." To him the three statesmen appeared to be Minos, Aeacus, and Rhadamanthys, the judges of the dead in Hades.[18]

The experts of the German delegation labored over the 440 articles of the treaty draft in an effort to deliver their counterproposals by the appointed date. Realizing that the time was insufficient, they requested, and were granted, a seven-day extension.

In Berlin, the Cabinet had declared on May 8 that the treaty as it stood was unacceptable. Four days later, Scheidemann addressed the National Assembly in the *Aula* of the University of Berlin.

I ask you: who can, as an honest man, I will not say as a German, but only as an honest, straightforward man, accept such terms? What hand would not wither that binds itself in these fetters?

There was applause and cheering from the representatives, all of whom agreed that the draft was not acceptable.[19]

In Versailles, the delegation completed the counterproposals by the last day allotted and turned them over to the Conference. Neither the popular clamor, nor the solidarity exhibited by the National Assembly, nor Brockdorff-Rantzau's continued public espousal of Wilsonian principles impressed the Allies. The draft treaty was returned to the delegation on June 16, with a few changes indicated in red. The conferees gave the Germans an ultimatum: sign within five days or the armistice ends. Simons succeeded in getting a two-day extension of the ultimatum. The six chief delegates left for Weimar and on the train, after perusing the revised draft, decided that they would recommend that their government refuse to sign the treaty.[20]

When the delegates arrived at Weimar on June 17, Gustav Stresemann, leader of the German People's Party (Deutsche Volkspartei), "dashed up to [Brockdorff-Rantzau], though I had only known him slightly, and shook his hand in gratitude for his behavior at Versailles. . . ."[21] The Cabinet met to discuss the ultimatum. Brockdorff-Rantzau called for resistance. The Cabinet then called Field Marshal Paul von Hindenburg, who informed them that resistance was useless, "but as a soldier I prefer honorable destruction to an ignominious peace." Brockdorff-Rantzau insisted that a rejection of the ultimatum would at worst lead to a resumption of hostilities, at best to occupation. All the German people had to do was wait, and the cost of war or occupation would lead to problems among the victors. When that happened, Germany could again negotiate. Erzberger accused Brockdorff-Rantzau, who was supported by Scheidemann and Otto Landsberg, of playing a dangerous game (*Vabanquespiel*).[22]

The Cabinet voted at 3:00 A.M., eight to six, for signing. Ebert, who was among those in opposition, ruled that the final decision be left to the National Assembly. An acute domestic crisis developed; the unanimity exhibited by the delegates on May 12 had disappeared. Scheidemann's Cabinet resigned, and, on June 20, Brockdorff-Rantzau retired into private life. After prolonged debate, the National Assembly decided that resistance was not feasible. On the fifth anniversary of Sarajevo, a new German delegation signed the Treaty of Versailles.

Brockdorff-Rantzau no longer had an active part in the shaping of German foreign policy. In an article he wrote for the *Berliner Tageblatt* which appeared on July 12, the Count counseled his countrymen, to many of whom he had become a hero because of his defiant attitude, that nothing should be done which would let the suspicion arise that Germany intended to sabotage the treaty. It should be proven to the victors that some of the articles could not possibly be fulfilled. Privately he continued to suffer from the thought that only "stupidity and vileness" had prevented his policy from being successful.[23]

Brockdorff-Rantzau remained in close touch with the Wilhelmstrasse, where he had found many admirers who agreed with him that closer relations with Soviet Russia would provide a means for revising the more onerous clauses of the treaty. Foremost among these was Baron Ago von Maltzan, who looked upon the Count "as a proud, upright pioneer of our national honor." He had written to Brockdorff-Rantzau, whom he had never met, asking him for a photograph so that he could have a memento of the time during which he had been privileged to work under his direction.[24]

Lord Edgar Vincent D'Abernon, who became British Ambassador to Germany in 1920 and who remained in Berlin for six years, considered Maltzan "perhaps the cleverest man who worked in the Wilhelmstrasse since the War. In diplomacy and politics a pupil of Kiderlen-Waechter, who in turn was a pupil of Bismarck. . . ." Maltzan was determined to use an alignment with Russia because he believed that "friendship with Russia was indispensable even if expensive. . . ." Maltzan gave the impression of trickiness, although he "was fundamentally trustworthy."[25]

In addition to Maltzan, there were two men in Berlin in 1919 who had already begun to renew contacts with Soviet Russia. In January, 1919, the German government had established the Reich Central Office for Military and Civilian Prisoners, which was directly responsible to the Cabinet. The *de facto* head of the organization was Moritz Schlesinger:

> a democratic Socialist by conviction, and therefore opposed to communism, he was nevertheless an untypical representative of the Social Democratic Party because of his acute feeling for political constellations and exigencies, unhampered by the doctrinairism hampering so many of his party comrades.

The other was Gustav Hilger, a German born in Moscow, who spoke Russian fluently and knew the country extremely well, and was attached to it "with affection and nostalgia." In the beginning of 1918, he had returned to Moscow, after spending the war years in a Russian internment camp, and had taken over the supervision of the repatriation of German prisoners of war. After the break of diplomatic relations in November of 1918, Hilger returned to Germany and in the spring of 1919 joined the Reich Central Office, where he supervised the camps that held Russian prisoners.

In the course of time, both Schlesinger and Hilger became acquainted with Brockdorff-Rantzau, with whom they formed a close friendship.[26]

The prisoner of war exchange provided a convenient, although narrow, road across which German and Russian representatives traveled on their way to re-establish closer diplomatic contacts. In November of 1919, Victor Kopp arrived in Berlin to take over the care of Russian prisoners. Kopp began negotiations which were designed to convince the Germans that the prisoner of war commissions could be converted into *de facto* consular missions. The talks, supported by Schlesinger, Hilger, and the Easterners in the Wilhelmstrasse, proceeded cautiously and slowly. One of the main concerns was the position of the Allies. Action was further delayed because of the grave domestic problems brought about by the rightist attempt, led by Dr. Wolfgang Kapp, to seize control of the government on March 13, 1920. A general strike, called by the unions and totally successful, led to the collapse of the Kapp *Putsch* four days later. No sooner was the danger from the Right removed when the Communists decided that the time was ripe for revolution. Risings took place in the Ruhr industrial area which were put down with great severity by troops.

With the restoration of a semblance of order, and despite the Communist activities, an Agreement on the Repatriation of Prisoners of War and Civilian Internees was signed on April 19. It was presented to the Reichstag by the Foreign Minister, Dr. Adolf Köster, exactly one month later for ratification. The first seven articles dealt with the details of repatriation. Article VIII provided that each country could maintain a welfare center in the other party's territory.[27] The agreement was ratified by Moscow on May 31, and the first step toward the resumption of normal relations had been taken. Victor Kopp became the official representative in Berlin, and Hilger was appointed to head the German Welfare Center in Moscow.

When the incumbent Cabinet resigned toward the end of March, President Ebert approached Brockdorff-Rantzau about his willingness to take the Foreign Ministry again. The British objected, informing the German Ambassador, Dr. Friedrich Sthamer, that such an appointment would be considered as an "unfriendly act." Brockdorff-Rantzau had already refused to accept the position, because he did not want to join a transitional cabinet. After his experience at Versailles, he would come out of retirement only if and when a situation existed which would make it possible to achieve something positive.[28]

In June there was yet another change of Cabinet. Dr. Walter Simons became Foreign Minister. He actively supported better relations with Soviet Russia. The Red army, involved in war with Poland since the end of April, was advancing rapidly across Poland; by July its right wing was approaching the borders of East Prussia. Brockdorff-Rantzau was watching the amazing progress of the Red forces with great care. Considering the very friendly relationship with Simons, it is quite probable that the Count shared his views with the Foreign Minister. Brockdorff-Rantzau advocated the resumption of economic and political relations with Soviet Russia to forestall a continuation of the Red advance into Germany after the collapse of Poland.[29]

With the victories of the Red army, Victor Kopp's status in Berlin improved considerably. He extended his activities into negotiations with private business firms and was a frequent visitor at the Wilhelmstrasse. During the last third of July, he returned to Moscow carrying with him a letter from Simons to the Commissar for Foreign Affairs, Chicherin. Simons thought that the time had arrived to start negotiations about the "resumption of normal relations." Talks could commence as soon as formal amends had been made for the assassination of Mirbach. Germany would be satisfied if the German flag were raised over the building in which the murder had occurred and if a company of Red army soldiers, led by an officer giving a solemn salute, paraded past. Simons also offered to send Schlesinger to Moscow to discuss ways and means by which the "Society for the Resumption of Trade with the East" could supply medicines to fight the "danger of an epidemic" which was approaching the German border.

Kopp had indicated that the Red army would respect the German borders, and Berlin had informed Moscow on July 20 of its intention to remain neutral in the Russo-Polish conflict. It might still be a good idea, Simons wrote, if a German liaison officer were attached to the right wing to advise on problems concerned with Germany's borders. If Chicherin wanted to reply to these ideas, he could do so directly by radio or via Hilger.[30]

Maltzan, who now handled the Russian desk in the Wilhelmstrasse, informed Brockdorff-Rantzau about the attempt at a *rapprochement*. A German officer had established contact with the Red army. The Entente Powers had approached Germany about giving up her neutrality. Maltzan assured the Count that this would not happen. The

Russo-Polish conflict was beginning to have beneficial effects on Germany's diplomatic stock. Maltzan was convinced that England would approach Russia as soon as Warsaw had fallen. The English move would make it easier for Germany to resume *de jure* relations, because the moral odium would fall on the British for having taken the first step.[31]

Kopp returned with Chicherin's reply on August 12. The Foreign Commissar wrote that Simons'

> allusions agreed in principle completely with the wishes and opinions of our Government. Public satisfaction for Mirbach's murder was given at the time. The murderers themselves could not be punished, as the German Government had demanded, because both had escaped into the German-occupied Ukraine. In any event, this matter was in the past. Discussions on the resumption of relations should take place in Berlin.[32]

Maltzan asked Brockdorff-Rantzau to hold himself available because the sending of a commission to Russia was being considered. Chicherin's reply had been friendly and agreeable. Maltzan had proposed the commission to Simons, who agreed. It would have a threefold task:

a. Atonement (overt reason);
b. Resumption of diplomatic relations by the fact of its presence [in Moscow];
c. Drafting of a skeleton agreement [*Rahmenvertrag*] regarding economic and political relations;
d. Recognition of Kopp as temporary chargé d'affaires in Berlin.[33]

With Russian troops approaching Warsaw, the collapse of Poland imminent, and the possibility of re-establishing the prewar border with Russia before their eyes, the Easterners in the Wilhelmstrasse were eager to reach an agreement with Moscow to prevent an inundation by the victorious Red tide. However, the Red army was repulsed before the gates of Warsaw and driven out of Poland. In October an armistice was concluded.

Now it was the turn of Soviet Russia to court Germany. Kopp's stock fell in Berlin. The refusal of public satisfaction for Mirbach became a convenient excuse with which to repulse Russian overtures. Moscow, which had not been overly eager to come to an agreement with the "bourgeois" German government while an excellent opportunity existed to create a Soviet state with the aid of the Red army, was now willing to resume diplomatic moves and make the best of what it considered a transitory situation.

On November 7, the third anniversary of the Bolshevik Revolution, Hilger attended the celebration dinner given for the foreign missions accredited in Russia (Afghanistan, the Baltic States, Persia, and Turkey). He was treated as the guest of honor and seated at the head of the table at Chicherin's right. Afterwards, the Soviet government announced the event to the world by radio, giving a list of the persons who had been present, prominently headed by Hilger.[34]

On the basis of a Cabinet decision, Simons informed the Reichstag that the resumption of diplomatic relations depended completely on an absolute assurance that the Soviet Union would not sanction interference in Germany's domestic affairs and would make amends for Mirbach's murder. Economic relations were already developing. Kopp had been authorized to pursue business contacts besides his regular job. A Russian representative was already in Germany trying to purchase locomotives. The major problem was the inability of the Russians to pay in the raw materials Germany needed in return. Furthermore, there were difficulties in economic relations resulting from the differences between the communist and capitalist way of doing business. Sending an economic expert of the Foreign Office to advise Hilger was contemplated. The Russians had accepted the proposal.

Simons also pointed out that Germany was not the only one interested in Russian markets. Anglo-Soviet economic negotiations had reached a point where a treaty was almost completed.[35]

Germany and Russia were rapidly moving closer together because each could use what the other had to offer. Russia needed Germany's skilled, now idle, industrial workers, its engineers, and general knowledge of advanced industrial methods. For Germany, Russia provided an outlet for its energies, a market for its products, and a source of raw materials. The Bolshevik regime was facing mounting discontent among the peasants, who were bled white by the policy of forced requisitions.

Schlesinger went on a special mission to Moscow toward the end of January, 1921, to discover what hopes there were for economic relations. He reported that it would be extremely difficult to make economic agreements with the Soviets because the people he had contacted did not have an understanding of even the most fundamental economic concepts. He advised that negotiations should take place in Moscow because that would reduce problems. Schlesinger was amazed at the successes Hilger achieved under most excruciating conditions.

Hilger was given to optimism; he was sure that the Bolsheviks would survive their troubles and remain firmly in control of the government. Schlesinger, given to pessimism, felt as if he had awakened from a beautiful dream. "Soviet Russia, it appeared, could no longer become a paradise, although the people eat only apples and have nothing to wear. I, for one," he wrote to the rather Russophobic Director of the Eastern Department, Behrendt, "have lost all hope."[36]

Despite Schlesinger's hopeless tone, he and Hilger, in negotiations with Kopp and other Russians, succeeded in reaching agreement on a draft protocol for the resumption of economic and political relations.[37]

While the two Germans were negotiating, a revolt erupted at the Kronstadt Naval Base off Petrograd in the Gulf of Finland. Kronstadt had supplied some of the staunchest supporters for the Bolsheviks during 1917. Now most veterans were gone, replaced by peasant boys who brought with them the discontent of the villages. It looked as if the crisis of the Communist regime had arrived. The revolt was drowned in blood by March 18, ten days before the Tenth Congress of the All-Russian Communist Party (B) convened. It was to be a momentous meeting. At the opening session, Lenin told the Congress in so many words that communism had not worked because of the war. New methods had to be found to feed the people and assuage the discontent of peasants and proletarians. After much discussion, the Congress accepted Lenin's New Economic Policy (NEP), which for him was two steps back to capitalism, so that at some future date he could take one giant step toward communism. Forced requisitioning was replaced by a tax on agricultural products. After the tax was paid, the peasant could sell the surplus in the open market. In industry, consumer goods could once again be manufactured by private enterprise. There was a catch: transportation, finance and banking, heavy industries, and foreign trade remained a government monopoly.

In the West, the NEP gave rise to the hope that the Communists had seen the folly of their ecomomic principles and had returned to capitalism. For many in the West, it meant that the revolution had come full circle.

In London, economic negotiations were completed, and the Anglo-Russian Trade Agreement was signed on March 16. In Germany, discussions were still underway in the Wilhelmstrasse on the best way to proceed. The Anglo-Russian agreement provided a welcome opening. The German Communists chose this most inopportune time, from the point of view of the Foreign Office, to start an armed uprising in the industrial areas of Saxony and Thuringia about March 22 in response to police occupation. Behrendt, never overly enthusiastic about co-

operation with Russia, saw an opportunity to end the economic negotiations because there were strong rumors that the rising had been
ordered by Moscow. Simons instructed Behrendt not to break off negotiations. Simons also wrote to Undersecretary Edgar von Haniel that
the

> agreement with Russia had, of course, to be placed in the back-
> ground during the Communist rising. It really takes a considera-
> ble dose of self-control to negotiate with these people, while they
> are trying to burn one's house down over one's head. Despite this,
> I am for bringing the negotiations to their conclusion.[38]

The repatriation of Russian prisoners of war and civilian internees
was about to be completed. Therefore, the time to expand the func-
tions of the mutual delegations was quickly running out. The Russian
government had not indicated that it accepted the draft initialed by
Kopp and Hilger. However, Boris Stomoniakov, Director of the Soviet
Trade Department, who had joined the Kopp mission at the time that
the German economic expert, Stähler, had gone to Moscow early in
1921, had initiated discussions with a large number of German businessmen introduced to him through the good offices of the Wilhelmstrasse.

German policy vis-à-vis the Allies had not resulted in alleviation of
the reparation demands. In January, the Allies decided that Germany
must pay 226 billion gold marks, spread over a period of forty-two
years. Early in March, Simons had offered fifty billion, including
twenty billion on account for payments already made. The Allies refused to accept the proposed payment and issued an ultimatum,
threatening occupation of the Rhine ports. The threat was fulfilled on
March 8, when French troops moved into Düsseldorf, Duisburg, and
Ruhrort. Additional sanctions were to be employed unless Germany
accepted the Allied demands.

On April 25, Brockdorff-Rantzau discussed the situation with Ebert,
advising the President that the time had now arrived to break the
stranglehold applied by Germany's enemies. Said Brockdorff-Rantzau:
"To pursue an active policy of catastrophe is a crime. To let oneself be
driven into a policy of catastrophe is a double crime, because it is at
the same time stupidity."

The policies pursued by the victors, especially France, left no alternative to Germany but to move closer to Russia, despite the obvious
pitfalls inherent in cooperating with the Soviets. One possibility would
be economic and political relations, but not an alliance. The Bolsheviks
were split among themselves, their army in disarray, and general con-

ditions chaotic. As far as the danger of Bolshevik propaganda in Germany was concerned, he did not think that this would become any worse by normalizing relations. He would be willing to go to Moscow, as a prominent member of the Red Cross, to ascertain whether it was possible to resume relations.

Ebert was not interested for two reasons: he did not want negotiations with Washington, designed to get American arbitration in the matter of reparations, jeopardized; secondly, he did not think that one could deal with the Soviets. Their aim was world revolution, and therefore they could not be trusted.

Brockdorff-Rantzau agreed that the Washington talks should not be jeopardized, but he expressed his conviction that the choice was between ruination through the Entente or infection with bolshevism. The latter was the lesser evil, because chaos in Germany would open the gates to Communism. This could be prevented by resuming relations with Moscow which would give Germany room to maneuver and forestall internal chaos. Brockdorff-Rantzau warned that he would not remain passive in the face of Allied attempts to destroy Germany. If necessary, he would pursue an independent course. Ebert assured the Count that his ideas would be discussed with other members of the government. On the following day, the Cabinet, on Ebert's suggestion, tabled discussion of the Hilger-Kopp agreement for eight days.[39]

The delay was agreed upon to await the American reply. On May 2, the United States government rejected the German request because the proposed compromise on payments was insufficient. The Allied Supreme Council met in London at the end of April and on May 5 issued an ultimatum with a six-day time limit; Germany had to pay one billion gold marks by the end of the month or the Ruhr industrial area would be occupied. The total reparation bill had been reduced to 132 billion gold marks.

On the day after the London ultimatum, Simons authorized the signature and publication of the Supplementary Agreement to the Agreement on the Repatriation of Prisoners of War and Civilian Internees of April 19, 1920. Simons shared Brockdorff-Rantzau's belief that the Allies were determined to bring about a catastrophe in Germany so that Berlin, fearful of bolshevism, would turn to the West for succor, thus becoming a pawn in the Western anti-Bolshevik game. The Supplementary Agreement was designed to give Germany a modicum of independent action, because it opened the way, via the economic mission, to de jure recognition. Simons' tenure at the Foreign Office was almost over, because it became clear that a new cabinet, willing to fulfill the Allied ultimatum, would have to be formed. The Supplementary Agreement was his last major act in the service of better German-Soviet relations.

The Supplementary Agreement extended the sphere of competency of the Welfare Missions to the care of all nationals within the country they served. Commercial representatives were to be attached to the missions, although in fact such representatives had already functioned since the placement of Stähler and Stomaniakov. These persons, as well as the heads of missions and six additional members, were given "rights and privileges of accredited missions." No search of premises was to take place without prior notification of the Foreign Office or the People's Commissariat for Foreign Affairs (Narkomindel), unless a clear and present danger existed. In the case of arrests or detentions, the Foreign Offices were to notify the head representative within twenty-four hours. Most importantly, from the point of view of *de facto* diplomatic recognition, was the provision in Article I which gave the plenipotentiary of the RSFSR the sole right to represent Russia in Germany. This ended the semiofficial status of the various White Russian organizations in Berlin with whom the Wilhelmstrasse had at various times carried on conversations. The chiefs of the delegations were accredited with the respective Foreign Offices, given the right to dispatch couriers who enjoyed diplomatic immunity, and the privilege to communicate directly with their governments in clear and code. Finally, both parties pledged not to interfere in the domestic affairs of the host countries in any form whatsoever.[40]

The last pledge was not given in good faith by Moscow; the Comintern, nominally independent, continued to use its facilities and agents to bring about a Communist seizure of power in Germany.

In the summer of 1921, Soviet Russia faced famine. On June 16, *Pravda,* the official newspaper of the All-Russian Communist Party (B), admitted that twenty-five million people were starving. Two weeks later the celebrated writer, Maxim Gorki, appealed to the world for food.

Lenin called upon the world's proletarians to save the Soviet state, and Chicherin addressed a note to the various governments of Europe and of the United States informing them of the extent of the catastrophe, urging them not to hinder the flow of private assistance. Herbert Hoover, Chairman of the American Relief Administration, replied to the Gorki appeal, making the stipulation, speedily accepted by the Soviet government, that all United States prisoners held by Russia be released and that free movement be guaranteed to the Relief Administration. An agreement was signed by Maxim Litvinov, Deputy Commissar for Foreign Affairs, and Walter Lyman Brown, European Director of the ARA.[41]

Under these circumstances, it is not surprising that the Third Congress of the Comintern announced that the world revolution was receding. Like Lenin's NEP, Comintern pronouncements were tactical moves; the strategy remained unchanged.

The German Foreign Office had no illusions about immediate beneficial results of the agreement; it looked upon Russia as the one area in Europe which held the greatest potential possibilities for active political and economic work. That a larger Russian mission would try to expand its propaganda activities was to be expected, but the danger of bolshevizing Germany was not immediate, because there was no immediate advantage to be gained by Russia from chaos. Economically, Russia had become more attractive to German business; whether or not Lenin's NEP was opportunistic did not alter the fact that concessions could be obtained and conditional freedom of trade existed.

The Commissar for Trade, Leonid Krassin, had made a number of visits to Germany to get people to take up concessions and invest in Russia.[42] The blossoming economic relationships, as well as the political connection, was subjected to a few rude shocks, because, when it became obvious that the Reichstag would accept the London ultimatum, the Fehrenbach Cabinet resigned. A new cabinet was formed, headed by Dr. Josef Wirth, who had been Minister of Finance in the preceding cabinet. The new cabinet announced its willingness to fulfill the Treaty of Versailles and pay reparations to the limit of the economic possibilities. The new Foreign Minister, Dr. Friedrich Rosen, was not particularly enamored of the Russians, and his attitude was reinforced by Behrendt. Instead of giving Hilger greater status by making him an officer in the foreign service, it was decided early in July to send Dr. Kurt Wiedenfeld, a Westerner in orientation, to Moscow.[43]

Moscow appointed Nikolai N. Krestinsky as plenipotentiary. Krestinsky was an old Bolshevik; he had been a member of the first Politburo, with Lenin, Trotsky, Kamenev, and Stalin, and functioned as General Secretary of the party until Stalin was appointed to the job. Immediate objections were raised by Bavaria, which had just expelled Krestinsky,[44] and the Wilhelmstrasse refused to give its consent. Thereupon Moscow, which had accepted Wiedenfeld, refused an entry visa to the representative, and it appeared as if the newly established relations were about to end.

Hilger, despite the intrigues against him, succeeded in getting Radek, who was Lenin's "special confidant" to intercede.[45] The Kremlin gave permission for Wiedenfeld to take up his position in Moscow. Before he could do so, he was subjected to a number of petty annoyances. When Wiedenfeld arrived at Reval on September 7, it took two days for the special railroad car promised him to arrive. In Petrograd the car was not attached to the Moscow train on the direct orders of Zinoviev. Wiedenfeld telephoned Zinoviev, and the car was coupled to the Moscow train, which left quite a bit behind schedule. On Wiedenfeld's arrival in Moscow, no official of the Foreign Commissariat was there to greet the German representative.

On September 14, Wiedenfeld, during an interview with Litvinov, insisted that President Mikhail I. Kalinin receive him. Litvinov made it clear that this would necessitate the reception of Krestinsky by the German President. Wiedenfeld assured Litvinov that negotiations were in progress to remove Bavarian objections to the *agrément*. He inquired, why had Russia insisted on Krestinsky? Litvinov replied that there were few trained diplomats of a stature sufficient to fill the very important Berlin post. Krestinsky was not only a staunch advocate of good relations with Germany, but he also had great influence in the Russian government. If Krestinsky was not accepted, the Berlin post would remain open.

Five days later, despite the fact that Krestinsky's status remained unclear, Kalinin received Wiedenfeld and expressed his personal pleasure at the establishment of good relations. Wiedenfeld made a point, in his reply, of his own delight that German-Russian relations had once again assumed an official character.[46]

Bavaria remained adamant and refused to accept Krestinsky. Thereupon Radek entered the fray with a vitriolic article in *Pravda*. Radek castigated Germany for its helpless position vis-à-vis the Allies. Only strong relations with Russia would alter this situation. The way German-Russian relations were handled led one to believe "that all the cows have been exported to France, and all the donkeys left in the Foreign Office."

Radek displayed a keen insight into German motives. During the Civil War, all the "wise men" in the Wilhelmstrasse had counted on the victory of the Whites. When this did not take place, Maltzan considered such an attitude as "madness." Simons supported Maltzan and was willing to resume normal relations when the Red army stood before Warsaw. After the retreat of Russian troops, Simons concluded only a trade treaty.

Rosen stood for allied intervention in Russia. Whether Rathenau, the Minister for Reconstruction, supported the Foreign Minister was not known. In any event, Rathenau had visited Radek while the latter was incarcerated in Moabit Prison and discussed "conditions for the resumption of relations."

There was one group in the Wilhelmstrasse which preached a Franco-German attack on Russia; another danced to the English tune, hoping for cooperation with Winston Churchill.

Radek referred to the appointment of Maltzan as Minister to Greece as evidence of the anti-Soviet attitude of the leading men in the Foreign Ministry, which included Behrendt, the "friend of White guardists." Undersecretary Haniel instructed Wiedenfeld to lodge a strong protest against Radek's innuendo, which "passed the limits of permissible polemic and poisoned relations." Haniel made representations directly to Stepan J. Bratman-Brodovsky, who was functioning as temporary Russian representative in Berlin.

This was not to be the last official protest against journalistic attacks lodged at Moscow. Chicherin's reply to Wiedenfeld's protest was also to become a stock excuse. The Narkomindel had no influence over Radek, who was endowed with "the insolence of the gods."[47]

Maltzan never left for his assignment, because the Wirth Cabinet fell toward the end of October over the furor created by the Allied decision, despite extremely strong German opposition, to partition Silesia. Wirth formed a new cabinet and reversed the fulfillment policy. Wirth personally had always based his hopes for Germany's recovery on close relations with Russia. He now retained the portfolio of foreign minister and rescinded Maltzan's assignment to Athens. He appointed him Director of the Eastern Department in place of Behrendt.

This change of events was greeted in *Izvestia,* the official newspaper of the Soviet government, as evidence that good relations between the two countries would now speedily materialize. Radek, in *Pravda,* exulted over the new course.[48]

Kestinsky finally arrived in Berlin after the objections to his *agrément* had been removed. The documents yield no evidence when this took place, but Krestinsky had a discussion with Wirth on December 6. Bratman-Brodovsky translated; although Krestinsky understood some German, he was not yet fluent in the language. In later years, Krestinsky, who tried to improve his German, still appeared with an interpreter when important matters were under discussion. During this first talk, Krestinsky spoke about a resolution of a number of economic problems. He also conveyed the impression that he was interested in restoring conditions as they had existed between the two countries in the past. However, he never directly mentioned a resumption of diplomatic relations.

Six days later another conversation took place. This time Krestinsky talked with Wirth, the Undersecretary in the Chancellery, von Simson, Maltzan, and Herbert Hauschild, who had taken over the Russian desk. Krestinsky was returning to Moscow to attend the Ninth Congress of Soviets and wanted to know whether he could report that there was great interest in raising political relations to the level of the economic ones. Wirth expressed his pleasure over the fact that there was a chance to talk. He was of the opinion that the economic relations would eventually improve political relations. Krestinsky stated that his government had taken the position, even before May 6, that *de jure* diplomatic relations should be resumed.

Wirth replied that this was not possible unless the preliminary steps, such as developing a consular system, had first been taken. Krestinsky indicated that his government was interested in resuming full consular relations. But if this was all Germany wanted, then he would report that the diplomatic question was "not yet ripe." Thereupon Wirth said, "I place great value on immediate discussions regarding normal diplomatic relations; if you wish it, immediately." Krestinsky was obviously pleased with this retort.

The Chancellor now said that matters of German property in Russia should also be discussed and that Russia should forward proposals as to the points she wanted discussed. Krestinsky stated that he personally would return with proposals or send them ahead.[49]

During the opening session of the Ninth Congress of Soviets, Lenin told the assembled delegates that the "advanced capitalistic states" had begun to trade with Soviet Russia, although they still refused to resume diplomatic relations. Radek, in an article in *Pravda* on December 27, declared that Germany simply had to accept the fact that there would not be a change of government in Russia and let the ghost of Mirbach rest; after all, satisfaction had been given for his murder.

> If Germany really wants to turn a new page in the history of relations with Russia—and she needs this no less than does Russia—one must proceed. . . . After all, communism was an ideology which would spread its influence whether there was a Russian representative in Berlin or not.

It mattered little whether Comrade Krestinsky called himself "plenipotentiary, minister, or ambassador." Relations would improve. After all, the Soviet Republic also took a chance when it allowed capitalists to do business in Russia, since these gentlemen had certainly not come to aid in the development of communism.[50]

On the last day of December, Radek told Secretary of Legation Schmidt-Rolke, who functioned as Wiedenfeld's political collaborator, that there was a chance that England and France intended to draw Germany into their anti-Soviet front. Should this design be completed, Russia would proceed against the weakest link. In that case, the Treaty of Versailles would provide Russia with a fine lever to pry the partners apart—and avoid isolation. He declared that the Soviet government did not want to use the treaty, but had to threaten that it would because of Germany's "puzzling and reticent" behavior.[51]

Radek's blunt warning did not exactly quiet Maltzan's concerns. He was afraid that the French would try to bring about a *rapprochement* with Russia by convincing the Soviets to pay the Tsarist debts due France by claiming the Russian share of German reparations under Article 116 of the Treaty of Versailles.

On January 6, 1922, the Allied Supreme Council, meeting at Cannes, invited both Germany and Russia to attend a conference at Genoa "to discuss measures for the economic reconstruction of Central and Eastern Europe."[52]

Chicherin sent a telegram of acceptance two days later. On January 9, Maltzan wrote to Brockdorff-Rantzau that the French maneuver on Article 116 had met resistance from England and the United States. He expected an authorized person from Moscow to arrive soon in Berlin for discussions on the intensification of German-Russian relations. He hoped that agreement could be reached on a common policy at Genoa. Consulates in Petrograd and Kharkov would probably be reopened within a short time. "Slowly but surely one places one stone upon another." To achieve good relations with the Russians was akin to the labors of Sisyphus. He hoped that Brockdorff-Rantzau would soon come to Berlin so that Maltzan's "Russian psyche could recharge itself."[53]

Brockdorff-Rantzau, who had worked toward a direct understanding with Russia for the past eighteen months without success, thought that the best opportunity for getting the most out of resuming direct relations had been missed.[54]

Maltzan did not share the Count's pessimism. In January Radek arrived in Berlin and during talks with Maltzan revealed that the French had approached Russia and offered *de jure* recognition as well as credits, in return for a Soviet endorsement of Versailles and a demand for payments under Article 116.

Radek also held conversations with Walter Rathenau, who became Foreign Minister on January 31, representatives of Krupp, Stinnes, and the German General Electric Company (A.E.G.). With all of them

Radek emphasized that German credits and full diplomatic recognition would prevent Russian acceptance of the French proposals. He also emphasized that the Soviet government was willing to give economic concessions to individual countries to aid in her reconstruction, but did not want to deal with a European consortium organized for that purpose.[55]

The Russians were quite upset about the appointment of Rathenau because they considered him the originator of the idea of reconstructing Russia through an international consortium. Chicherin told Wiedenfeld on February 5 that Russia opposed Rathenau's plan because it would turn Russia into a field for colonial exploitation.[56]

It was quite true that Rathenau favored international financial cooperation, since Germany did not have the resources, to rehabilitate the Soviet economy. Neither Maltzan nor Schlesinger thought this a good idea. Both men—and their opinions were shared by Brockdorff-Rantzau—thought that Germany should attempt to gain a major share in the economic reconstruction unilaterally. Maltzan almost certainly tried to change Rathenau's mind. In that task he continued to have Radek's valuable assistance, for the revolutionary intellectual and the refined, educated Rathenau had much in common. After a luncheon, Rathenau sent his old acquaintance a number of books in which Radek had shown some interest.[57] During February, Krassin and Christian Rakovsky, Chairman of the Council of People's Commissars of the Ukrainian SSR, appeared in Berlin to aid Radek in swaying German opinion.

All of these Russian moves began to have an effect. Evidence of this change is provided by the fact that Dr. Friedrich Gaus, Director of the Legal Department, circulated a memorandum in the Wilhelmstrasse on February 20. Gaus held that despite the abrogation of the Treaty of Brest-Litovsk, the diplomatic recognition afforded Russia by its terms remained valid. Furthermore, the Treaty of Versailles (Article 117) did not prevent a new recognition of Soviet Russia. The various German agreements with Russia now in force rested "beyond a doubt" on the recognition of the Soviet government.[58]

Chancellor Wirth needed little convincing. His policy of fulfilling the demands of the Allies had not saved Upper Silesia, and he now determinedly turned to the East. In a speech to the Reichstag, Wirth reassured Moscow that Germany had no intention of exploiting Russia in company with the West. While Germany greeted the cooperation of those third powers with whom Russia was also willing to deal, Germany "would have the strongest reservations against a policy which looked upon Russia as a colony and was designed to treat her as such."

Emphasized Wirth, "We do not want a colonial policy, but instead combine our efforts in league with defeated peoples who bleed and starve as we do."

Rathenau also assured the Russians, in a Reichstag speech, that he did no longer believe that syndicates were the best way to rebuild Russia. Germany's part in the reconstruction of Russia was a matter to be discussed between the two states alone. He declared, as Wirth had done, that Germany had no intention of playing the role of colonialist. The Reichstag members agreed.[59]

The German overtures delighted the Russians, who were fearful of the results continued isolation might bring and extremely concerned that Germany would join the Western bloc. The Russian delegation, headed by Chicherin, arrived in Berlin ready to come to an understanding. Rathenau welcomed Chicherin and the delegates in a personal letter delivered by Maltzan on the first day of April, a Saturday. Rathenau invited Chicherin for a meeting the following Monday. During that day, Chancellor Wirth apprised Chicherin and Litvinov of the decision to return the former embassy building so that German-Russian diplomatic relations could "be put on the right track." *Pravda* printed the Chancellor's remark verbatim, and *The New York Times* reported that the return of the premises constituted *de facto* recognition of the Soviet Union.[60]

Rathenau, despite his withdrawal from the consortium in his Reichstag speech, returned to the idea during his official talks with Chicherin. However, the Commissar and Maltzan worked out a protocol which became the basis for the now famous Treaty of Rapallo.[61]

Once arrived at Genoa, the German delegation, headed by Chancellor Wirth and including Rathenau and Maltzan, found itself in relative isolation while the Russians held long discussions with the representatives of France, Belgium, and Italy in Lloyd George's Villa d'Albertis. The German suspicion that Article 116 was being used to draw Russia away from Germany became a powerful weapon for Maltzan and Wirth in their attempts to get Rathenau to agree immediately, even before the conference had adjourned, to sign the protocol drafted in Berlin. Rathenau was swayed sufficiently to allow Maltzan to discuss the resumption of the Berlin talks with Rakovsky and Joffe.

During these discussions, Maltzan tried to prove to the Russians that German aid in the reconstruction of Russia's industries would not be available if the Soviet delegates made agreements with the Allies. The two Russians indicated willingness to sign a treaty with Germany.

Rathenau still needed convincing that a separate treaty was wise, but his resistance collapsed under the combined persuasion of Maltzan and Wirth. On April 16, the German delegation, after an invitation from the Russians, drove out to Rapallo and there signed a treaty based on the protocol which had been reworked by Maltzan and Litvinov.[62]

Under the terms of the Treaty of Rapallo, both countries renounced compensation for war expenditures, war damages, requisitions, and damages incurred by civilians because of martial laws or forcible measures. Germany, under the terms of Article 2, renounced compensation arising from confiscations unless the RSFSR satisfied claims of third states at some later date.

Diplomatic and consular relations were to be resumed immediately, the admission of consuls to be regulated by special agreement. Economic relations were to be based on the most-favored-nation principle, not to extend to easings granted to those states which had been an integral part of the Tsarist Empire. Should the economic needs of both countries become the subject of international regulation, then mutual exchange of views was to precede any such action. The German government pledged to support, as far as possible, the attempts of private enterprise to enter into economic agreements with Russia.

Chicherin presented a confidential explanation of Article 2 to Rathenau. Any negotiations regarding the recognition of claims by third parties was to depend on previous discussions between Germany and Russia on the basis of equal treatment for German claims. Germany, for her part, obliged herself not to participate in any economic consortium without previous agreement with the RSFSR. Germany retained complete freedom of action in regard to "industrial and trade undertakings in Russia outside the framework of the international economic consortium."[63]

The Russians had not offered satisfaction for the murder of Mirbach, but that particular demand had never been a major obstacle to the resumption of diplomatic relations. Thus, with the signature of the Rapallo Treaty, the choice of an ambassador became a matter of urgent discussion. The person selected had to be acceptable to the German governmental parties and to Soviet Russia, and had to have the kind of diplomatic experience necessary to deal with the Russian situation. The choice rapidly narrowed to former Admiral Paul von Hintze, who had been naval attaché at St. Petersburg and Secretary for Foreign Affairs in July, 1918. He was unacceptable to the Socialists. Another candidate was Rudolf Nadolny, who had been Vice-Consul in St. Petersburg in 1905, spoke Russian fluently, and had been one of Ebert's advisors in 1921. The Russians agreed to Nadolny, on the condition that Joffe be received in Berlin. This was clearly an impossible and impertinent demand. Ebert decided to leave Nadolny in Stockholm, where he was serving as German minister.[64]

On May 10, Ebert invited Brockdorff-Rantzau in order to sound him out on his willingness to serve in Russia. Ebert had strongly objected to the conclusion of the Rapallo Treaty and agreed with Brockdorff-Rantzau, who declared that such a treaty should have been concluded at the time of the London ultimatum a year before. The signature had been an affront to the West. As the Count put it, somewhat inelegantly, the German delegation had behaved "like the man who has been invited into the living-room and who spits on the carpet." Now that the treaty had been concluded, there was nothing left to do but fulfill its terms and make the best of it. He would be willing to accept the nomination if he were granted complete independence from any given incumbent foreign minister; Rathenau, a man given to sudden changes of mind, was an example of the kind of superior to whom the Count had no intention of being subordinated.

Brockdorff-Rantzau told Ebert that he would submit a detailed program about the strategy he intended to follow in Moscow. When that program had been approved, he would go to Moscow, ascertain whether positive results could be accomplished, and only after he had convinced himself of the feasibility of his program would he accept a permanent appointment. He had absolutely no intention of exposing himself to another personal Versailles. After all, one never called upon his services until conditions were in a "real mess." Despite the last remark, Ebert told Brockdorff-Rantzau that he was the only candidate he would consider.[65]

On June 23, Brockdorff-Rantzau, in a move as unconventional as it was characteristic, visited Chicherin at his apartment. With a frankness that must have quite surprised and pleased Chicherin, the Count developed his strategy for the furtherance of good political relations between Germany and Russia. His belief was, he told the Commissar, that "Germany was needed for the reconstruction of Europe, and Russia for that of the whole world." The Count wanted it clearly understood that he had no intention of being used as a pawn in any Russian game with the Entente. He told Chicherin that he opposed a European syndicate for trade with the Soviet state because he wanted to prevent the English government from using Germans as colonial shock troops in Russia.

Chicherin listened with great interest to these revelations. At the conclusion of their illuminating conversation, Chicherin apologized for having used his bedroom for their talk. Brockdorff-Rantzau graciously assured him that he had found the place well chosen, especially since he assumed the bedroom to be "virginal [*jungfräulich*]." This was not only an obvious reference to the fact that Chicherin, like Brockdorff-Rantzau himself, was a bachelor, but also an example of the Count's caustic sense of humor.[66]

From their first meeting onward, the two men developed a very intimate personal relationship which survived the many disappointments and "the feeling of acute despair caused by the intransigence of the Soviet government and the recklessness of its methods. . . ." The Count did not form friendships easily.

> In distributing his favors, he was less guided by his intellect than by his emotions. . . . To be shifted from one category to the other amounted to an impossibility. Whoever was classified among the unreliable ones was persecuted by his untiring hate, by a biting irony, till the elimination at least from his sphere of influence was attained. Just as firmly seated were those classified as reliable.[67]

Chicherin now joined the select circle of Brockdorff-Rantzau's close friends. The two had much in common. Both were of aristocratic background, cosmopolitan in their tastes, which included a gourmet delight in fine wines and liquors. Throughout their relationship, Brockdorff-Rantzau supplied Chicherin with wines and champagnes and regaled him with excellent dinners. Both of them were bachelors, unburdened by family obligations; both spoke French with excellence, and Chicherin in addition commanded a fluent German. They liked to work at night and almost always met after dark, continuing their talks into the small hours of the morning. Their work habits were similar. Chicherin, as well as Brockdorff-Rantzau, attended to the details of diplomatic labor with the greatest attention, doing most of the important work himself. The Count spent hours on the drafting and redrafting of important papers, which he did not send off until they were polished to a fine sheen.

In some ways they were quite dissimilar. Brockdorff-Rantzau chain-smoked cigarettes, loved French cognac, and disregarded his health. He was an immaculate dresser, given to old-fashioned garb, and meticulous in all his personal habits. Chicherin cared little about his appearance, mislaid important papers, and was hypersensitive about his health, taking extended cures in German resorts and clinics and absenting himself from Moscow at the most inconvenient times. Despite these differences, the two men were united in their desire to restore their respective countries to great power status, break out of their diplomatic isolation, and discuss with utter frankness the problems which confronted them.

There were also differences due to their relative positions in the political scheme of their respective countries. Chicherin, who had joined the Bolsheviks late, was valued by them for his diplomatic skills, but in the party councils the voices of his deputy, Litvinov, and of Krestinsky carried more weight. Even in the Foreign Commissariat, decisions had to have the approval of the whole Collegium, which, in turn, was bound by directives issued by the party. The real power in Soviet Russia lay not in the Council of People's Commissars but in the Politburo of the party. Furthermore, the militancy of the Comintern, dedicated to world revolution, frequently created problems for the normal functioning of diplomatic relations.

Brockdorff-Rantzau represented a country where control of affairs was concentrated in an elected legislature whose support was necessary for any cabinet. Because of the multiparty make-up of the Reichstag, cabinets consisted often of shaky coalitions. Since February, 1919, there had been six different foreign ministers, who served an average of seven months. Brockdorff-Rantzau, who did not belong to any of the major parties, had to rely on his personal influence, which, in 1922, was admittedly great because of his stand at Versailles and his intimate personal relationship with Ebert and many other leading men in Germany. Despite this, he found it extremely difficult to get even conditional acceptance for his demand to be independent of the Foreign Minister, so that his long-range policy would not be subject to change.

On July 3, Brockdorff-Rantzau explained this again to Ebert, who listened sympathetically. The Count advised Ebert that the reconstruction of Russia should be aided by German workers employed directly in the Soviet Union. This procedure would have the immediate benefit of relieving unemployment and would be more advantageous than concessions to the big industrialists, like Stinnes and Krupp.

Rathenau was assassinated on June 24 by right-wing fanatics, and Wirth again took over the portfolio of foreign affairs. He made no move to get in touch with Brockdorff-Rantzau, and when Maltzan tried to persuade him to do so objected that, according to certain allegations, the Count was addicted to morphine and had the habit of working during the night, when most people slept. Maltzan assured Wirth that the first was a vicious, unfounded rumor, and the second a positive asset. Chicherin also favored the depth of night for serious work.

Wirth agreed to talk with Brockdorff-Rantzau on the following day, July 11. When the Count arrived, Wirth talked about domestic problems, irritating the Count more with every passing minute. After half an hour, he stopped Wirth with the blunt interjection that he had not come to discuss the domestic situation, but his candidacy for the Moscow job. Wirth refused to commit himself, telling the irate Count that he would be duly informed about any final decision regarding the appointment.

Brockdorff-Rantzau fairly sizzled with indignation about the treatment Wirth, whom he considered socially and intellectually below himself, had given him. He did not "belong to the class of people with whom the Herr Chancellor has been associated with up to now and with whom he was accustomed to make political deals."[68]

After four days passed without a decision, Brockdorff-Rantzau, who badly wanted the appointment, went to Undersecretary Haniel, who had headed the Political Commission in the German Delegation to Versailles and was one of the Count's friends. He impressed upon Haniel that Ebert would hear about the Chancellor's addiction to rumor-mongering. Wirth seemed to misunderstand their relative positions. If he

> believed that he could test my personal, moral, and professional ability for a public office, then it was time to show this back-thumper [Steisstrommler] uncontrovertibly that it was after all I who, in the critical hour in the year 1918, responding to the urgent pleas of Ebert, Scheidemann, and Haase, jumped into the breach to take the job of Minister for Foreign Affairs when nobody else could be found to take it. Also that I not only cofounded the Republic, but saved it from the Communists in January, 1919; that I exposed myself, at the side of Scheidemann and Ebert, in the Reichschancellery to hand grenades, while Herr State Secretary Erzberger and the other gentlemen had disappeared. Finally, that I saved the prestige of the young Republic in Versailles as nobody else could have done. All this happened at a time when nobody knew anything about Herr Wirth, except for his third-form students [Quartaner] in Baden. I will therefore tell the President that I am sick and tired of this bloody scandal. . . .

Haniel agreed that the time had come to be frank with the people in charge. However, there was probably nothing personal in Wirth's attitude. Just the other day he had mentioned to the President that the Count might be too big a man for the job, that his appointment might give the impression that Germany had greater plans in Russia than was the case. The Count was not mollified, but told Haniel that the Chancellor should have thought of all that before. He would talk to Ebert as soon as possible to settle the whole matter once and for all.[69]

Wirth evaded another meeting with Brockdorff-Rantzau, who visited Ebert for the third time on July 19. The Count made no attempt to conceal his anger about Wirth's evasion of a direct and definite commitment. He informed the President about the Chancellor's remarks to Maltzan. Ebert declared that it was nothing less than despicable for Wirth to spread such unfounded rumors. The President again assured the Count that he had every intention of exercising his constitutional right to appoint an ambassador. Ebert's firmness was a relief to the Count. Before he left he handed the President a memorandum dated July 17, 1922, entitled "Political Instructions for the Ambassador to Moscow."[70]

In the introductory paragraph, Brockdorff-Rantzau explained that he had purposely kept the whole memorandum in general terms, but that anyone reading between the lines could recognize his program. The Count wrote that he agreed with Dr. Otto Landsberg (SPD Reichstag deputy who had been one of the chief delegates to Versailles) that the debts Germany owed her former enemies could not be paid in gold and silver but, in the final analysis, had to be settled with iron. From Landsberg's remark, the Count drew the conclusion that this feeling reached deep into the Socialist party and that it was proof that his own policy was correct. Should it come to the final decision, the broad masses of the people would support such a policy. The Count made it immediately clear that he did not favor any kind of military alliance with Russia because such a move would deliver Germany helplessly into the hands of Moscow. The Soviet government would never hesitate to use the alliance to blackmail the German government into possibly detrimental actions with the threat of revealing the military cooperation to the Entente.[71]

While the Count worked on Ebert, Maltzan and Haniel continued to place pressure on Wirth to get the Chancellor to acquiesce in the appointment of Brockdorff-Rantzau. This pressure, combined with Ebert's support, resulted in another interview between the Count and Wirth on July 24.[72] Wirth declared that he would now speak openly, but in the strictest confidence, about certain ideas he had regarding a constructive Eastern policy. He had concluded the Treaty of Rapallo to bring Germany and Russia closer together. He agreed with General Hans von Seeckt, Chief of the German army, that the Polish situation had to be resolved even if the use of force was required. "Poland had to be finished off." He wanted to work with the Russians, but Ebert considered them "unscrupulous criminals." Did the Count care to express his own views on the matter?

Brockdorff-Rantzau, who had agreed with Ebert that the Bolsheviks were indeed criminals, now disclosed that he had been eating his heart out ever since Versailles. He was willing to use any means "with the dear Lord, [or] if necessary with the devil" to save Germany. He handed Wirth the "Political Instructions for the Ambassador to Moscow," which the Chancellor read immediately. Wirth then offered the ambassadorship to Brockdorff-Rantzau. The Count immediately repeated his two demands: absolute freedom from the foreign minister (which portfolio Wirth still held), and agreement that he would have six months in Moscow before deciding whether he would stay on.

Wirth agreed to these conditions. He also told the Count that the formal announcement could not be made until the pending reparation negotiations, necessitated by the runaway inflation which plagued Germany, had been successfully concluded. The Count had no objection to this procedure.[73]

For some reason not made clear in the documentary evidence, Brockdorff-Rantzau decided to see Wirth once more on August 1. About five minutes before he went into the Chancellor's office, Haniel told the Count that Wirth had shown him a letter by Seeckt in which the Chief of the German army brought to Wirth's attention the idea that the Count had conducted negotiations at Versailles in an unpatriotic manner, and therefore should not be appointed to Moscow.[74] The Count, who had won his battle with the civilian authorities, now was confronted with an entirely new and dangerous obstacle on his road to Moscow. His dislike of military men in politics was well known. He stormed into Wirth's office and demanded that the Chancellor tell him about Seeckt's accusation.

Wirth side-stepped the question, but insisted that any differences between the Count and the General would have to be resolved, because, Wirth said, he intended to expand the Treaty of Rapallo. This might bring up military matters involving Poland. Wirth informed the flabbergasted Count that clandestine military collaboration between the German army and Soviet Russia was already in full swing. Ebert had not been informed, because the President was opposed to such a policy.

After the Count had overcome his initial shock, he expressed the opinion that it was unwise for Germany to approach the Russians. No odium would attach to Germany if the Russians made the first move. This would also eliminate the chance that they might inform the Entente if Germany attempted to make a military agreement. The

Count warned that premature action was downright dangerous. In her weak condition, Germany could not gain anything from a military alignment with Russia. The Count, in an attempt to place Seeckt's objection on a personal basis, went into a polemic about his association with the General which dated back to the time when they both had been young lieutenants. In Versailles he had been on the best of terms with Seeckt. About eight days before the 100,000-man army had come up, they had had some cognac together. At that time, Seeckt had confided a secret ambition: he wanted to enter the Foreign Office. Brockdorff-Rantzau told Wirth that he had promised Seeckt a job, should he remain Foreign Minister. Then Seeckt had written an impertinent letter, in which he asserted that the delegation, under Brockdorff-Rantzau's leadership, had sacrificed the last thing which remained for Germany, her honor. After this, Seeckt, on the basis of a unanimous decision by the delegation, had been relieved of his position as the expert on army matters.[75]

Wirth tried to smooth the Count's feelings by telling him that the Soviet government had forwarded its *agrément* for his appointment. Brockdorff-Rantzau insisted that he would not leave Berlin until Seeckt's intervention had been eliminated.[76]

On August 2, 1922, Krestinsky presented his credentials as plenipotentiary of the RFSFR to President Ebert, who told him that this act re-established ". . . full diplomatic relations between our two countries.[77] The time had obviously arrived for Germany to send her own ambassador to Moscow. Brockdorff-Rantzau apparently felt that Seeckt's interference would soon be removed. As far as he was concerned, everything but his departure date was settled.[78] The Count now went to Annettenhöh, his private estate in Schleswig, as he had previously planned, in order to prepare for his trip to Moscow.

While at Annettenhöh, Brockdorff-Rantzau wrote a number of drafts for a memorandum which he considered an exposé of Wirth's revelations. The final product of these labors, dated "Annettenhöh vor Schleswig den 15. August 1922," contained the demands that the Count had already presented to Ebert and Wirth, as well as an attack on the military ideas of Seeckt and the Chancellor. The memorandum was Brockdorff-Rantzau's insurance policy against future attacks from any quarter and a defense against the military, or any other individual or group who might try to interfere in the province of the ambassador to the Soviet Union. It was also an attempt to checkmate the military experiments of Seeckt, which the Count considered as "madness" under the given circumstances.

The contents of the memorandum were as follows: The Count pointed out that Germany could no longer pursue an exclusively Eastern or Western policy. Bismarck made Germany the balancing force in European politics, but those who succeeded the Iron Chancellor dissipated his legacy, and disastrous consequences followed. Now Germany was confronted with an impossible situation because the West was a neighbor bent on revenge, while the East wanted an ally for chaos. Neither the West nor the East had any doubts about Germany's powerless condition, and any foolish move could easily lead to a world conflagration during which Germany would be completely destroyed. Therefore, an active policy of alliance with either side was precipitate. That possibility should be left for later. The most important thing Germany represented to the Russians was an opportunity to sell her out. This consideration should not preclude listening to what Moscow had to say about military questions, but it was equally important to find out if they had already negotiated with the West. Even the hint of a military alliance with Soviet Russia would have a detrimental effect on Germany's relations with the West, and these could not be ignored. England was no longer an island in military terms and would have to look around for allies. Normally she would not look to France, but, in the event of a German-Russian alliance, England would be driven into French arms. Once again it was most important to realize that political relations are based on intellect, not feeling. Therefore, an alignment of Germany with England had to be considered. England would see in Germany a counterweight to the threat presented to her by France. German policy in the military field should be such that England would be looking toward Germany as an ally.

One of the disadvantages of the Treaty of Rapallo was the belief that it contained secret military clauses. The British Prime Minister, David Lloyd George, had only recently (March 25) referred to the danger that Germany, bent on revenge, presented to the world. This danger would be enhanced if Germany received aid from Russia. The Count again emphasized that such an alliance could be defended only if it had the possibility of success, which it did not. In Germany the Social Democratic Party, and thus the widest range of classes, would object to an alliance with Russia. This could lead to domestic upheavals which would endanger the existence of the Reich. Furthermore, Russia was no longer the country of Tsar Alexander I or Nicholas I; there, too, the voice of the people had become an important factor. German-Russian relations had to be based on peaceful pursuits, but not to the exclusion of other political combinations:

It should be hoped that a really close relationship with Russia will be sufficient to expiate the crime of Versailles, and that a peaceful development will rectify what has been sinned against Germany. I personally judge this possibility with scepticism.

Despite his scepticism regarding the possibility of a peaceful rectification of Germany's conditions, the Count considered an exclusive military alignment with Russia premature and dangerous. He felt that neither she nor Germany was in an economic position which would allow such a policy. It would be dangerous because the Russians could get more from the Entente than from Germany and would not hesitate for one moment to use any military collaboration to blackmail Germany. Even if the Russians should someday overrun Poland, it would not be possible for Germany to hold France long enough for the Reds to arrive to aid Germany. There was also the danger that the Red army would not come to liberate, but to push the borders of Asia to the Rhine. In any case, Germany should prevent Russia from going to war. If Russia were intractable, Germany should remain neutral. This might present the opportunity to regain the lost territories from Poland. Brockdorff-Rantzau concluded the *Promemoria* by pointing out that he did not advocate a resigned attitude in the face of provocations from the West, but again warned against premature acts.

> Since Versailles I have had no other thought but that we should find justice or if necessary take it. The dragon seed of revenge has been sown at Versailles, and our enemies bear the guilt which cannot be expiated, if they do not destroy this seed. Should the gentlemen in Paris and London really call forth disaster and attempt to destroy Germany, they will find out that a people of sixty million will not voluntarily deliver itself to the executioner; they will then have chaos and will themselves be drawn into it.[79]

A few days after the completion of the *Promemoria*, Brockdorff-Rantzau returned to Berlin. The Count considered it his most important job to eliminate Seeckt's opposition to his appointment. In order to accomplish this, the Count skilfully exploited the existing rivalry between the Army High Command and its navy counterpart. On August 24, he had an illuminating talk with the very frank head of the navy's Sea Transport Service, Captain Walter Lohmann. The Captain had been in Petrograd and Moscow from the end of May until the middle of June. He had been accompanied by a sixteen-man "study group" especially selected from industry, commerce, and the press; and the group had been accompanied by the Consul General at Petrograd, von Kessler. The trip had been undertaken with the approval of the Navy High Command, the Ministry of Defense, and the Russian Department of the Wilhelmstrasse. The Count listened with undisguised pleasure when the Captain told him that he felt that "Seeckt as a personality was even below Hintze and politically even more dangerous." Lohmann then became quite specific about German military collaboration with Russia. He himself, he told the Count, had negotiated with Trotsky in 1921. Just when positive results had been in sight, Seeckt sabotaged them. Lohmann agreed to talk to Chancellor Wirth, and did so on August 29. The Captain, mindful of Brockdorff-Rantzau's attitude, emphasized to Wirth that all military deals with the Russians should be subordinated to political experts. The Navy High Command acted only as an instrument of policy, and there was absolutely no reason why the Army High Command should carry on independent relations with the Red army.

Brockdorff-Rantzau also attempted to get the support of Admiral Paul Behncke, Chief of the Navy High Command, against Seeckt, but failed. However, Behncke agreed that the ambassador to Moscow should receive information about all actions undertaken by the military in Russia.[80]

Now that Brockdorff-Rantzau was beginning to see the extent of the military involvement with Russia, he began to probe more deeply into the situation. Captain Lohmann introduced a German journalist by the name of Bernhard Waurick to the Count. Waurick had traveled extensively in Soviet Russia. He had the confidence of many of the leading Bolsheviks and was well informed about the collaboration between the Reichswehr and the Red army. Waurick told Brockdorff-Rantzau on September 5 that the political ineptness of the German military had led to the complete bankruptcy of their enterprise in Russia. The Soviet government was particularly upset about a number of extravagant promises by Seeckt's representative in Moscow, Major (ret.) Oskar von Niedermayer. During a severe coal shortage in 1921, Niedermayer had promised the Russians all the coal they could use. He had never made good on the offer. (Niedermayer later assured Brockdorff-Rantzau that the story was a malicious fabrication.) The Soviet government had told Waurick that it wanted to continue negotiations concerning military matters, but only with the duly appointed ambassador. It did no longer care to deal directly with the Reichswehr. According to Waurick, the military representative in Moscow had reported this to Seeckt and to Colonel Otto Hasse of the

Truppenamt (*i.e.*, the department which functioned in place of the General Staff prohibited by the Treaty of Versailles), who was in control of all military dealings with Russia.

On Brockdorff-Rantzau's inquiry, Waurick informed him that Seeckt opposed his appointment because he did not think that Brockdorff-Rantzau would take proper care of military interests.[81]

With all this information at hand, Brockdorff-Rantzau prepared for a showdown talk with Wirth. He met the Chancellor on September 7. After a few words about the domestic situation and a hint that he had heard more about the military collaboration than Wirth had indicated at their last talk, the Count abruptly threatened to resign unless all intrigues by the military against him were stopped. Wirth became quite agitated and implored the Count not even to mention such a possibility because matters had gone too far for such actions.

Brockdorff-Rantzau, who had banked on the nonacceptance of his resignation, demanded that all negotiations with the Soviet government be handled by himself. The Count informed the Chancellor that he had discovered that the military had carried on direct negotiations with Trotsky since 1920. Even before Wirth had taken office, Major Niedermayer had negotiated with Kopp. Not only had the Krupp concern been involved in these negotiations, but the Russians had received more than 100 million marks ". . . from the illegal fund of the Army High Command for the building of airplanes and arms factories . . ." in Russia. Brockdorff-Rantzau was concerned about the possibility that this collaboration would become known to Germany's enemies. In fact, Lloyd George was already in possession of a letter written by Niedermayer which contained information about the military deals with Russia. All the British Prime Minister had to do was to wait for the opportune moment to publish it and demand the destruction of Germany as a perennial troublemaker. Brockdorff-Rantzau wanted to know where the money for this collaboration had come from and whether Wirth knew about the collaboration and sanctioned it. Further, the Count insisted on being told whether Ebert, the Cabinet, the Vice-Chancellor, and the Minister of Defense had been informed about these military agreements.

Wirth replied that he knew about Seeckt's actions only in a general way (which was not true), but that neither the President nor the Cabinet had been informed. To the regret of the military, they did not have an illegal fund. Krupp, it was true, was interested in agricultural concessions. It was not known to him whether the company had spent money for other purposes in Russia. Wirth readily admitted that he supported the participation of German industry, including the production of airplanes, in any country, because such work aided in the economic reconstruction of Germany. Brockdorff-Rantzau agreed that German industry should be supported but warned the Chancellor against undue haste in this matter. The Count repeated his earlier threat that he would resign at the least hint that his own work in Russia would be subjected to sabotage at home. Wirth agreed that the interference of Seeckt would have to be settled. Brockdorff-Rantzau, pressing his advantage, demanded that the Minister of Defense, Otto Gessler, transmit a written statement promising not to interfere in the domain of the ambassador to Moscow. Then the Count planted a time bomb: he might have to inform President Ebert about the extent of military collaboration. Wirth, as the Count had expected, almost fainted.[82] Before he left the stricken Chancellor, Brockdorff-Rantzau gave him a copy of the *Promemoria*, the perusal of which would show Wirth that the Count could easily make good on his threat to inform Ebert about the clandestine relationship with the Bolsheviks.

On the next day, Brockdorff-Rantzau visited Ebert again. He told the President that Wirth still preferred discussing domestic matters and avoided talking about foreign affairs. Despite this, he had given the Chancellor an extensive memorandum on the strategy that he intended to follow in the East. After Ebert had received his copy of the *Promemoria*, he assured Brockdorff-Rantzau that he would read it immediately and then talk with Wirth. Brockdorff-Rantzau asked Ebert to refrain from talking with the Chancellor. The Count emphasized that he would accept the Moscow appointment only if definite permission was granted to him to follow his own self-determined course, depending only on previous agreement with the President and the given incumbent chancellor. Ebert appeared to be confused by this new memorandum. Brockdorff-Rantzau explained that the earlier one was a "general political instruction for any German ambassador to Moscow." The *Promemoria* was designed exclusively for his own actions. Ebert, less confused, told his visitor that he thought that the time had come to make the official announcement of the appointment.[83]

With the Navy High Command on his side, Wirth apparently in his place, and Ebert's support absolutely assured, the Count utilized a dinner on September 9, to which Chicherin had been invited, to further impress the People's Commissar with his ideas and charm. Chicherin wanted to know when the Count could be expected in Moscow, where his arrival was impatiently awaited. Brockdorff-Rantzau advised him that he intended to leave in about a fortnight. When Chicherin mentioned that the Russians wanted someone with authority, the Count asked what the Russians wanted to negotiate. To this Chicherin replied ". . . we want *peace* and we want to make great international politics, unhampered by internal questions. This seems not to be understood here, and also not wanted."[84]

On the day on which Brockdorff-Rantzau had his talk with Chicherin, Chancellor Wirth provided Seeckt with the Count's *Promemoria*. The General's reply was transmitted to the Chancellor on September 11; it showed that both he and Brockdorff-Rantzau thought along similar lines. Both wanted to destroy the Treaty of Versailles, and both thought that this could best be accomplished through cooperation with the Russians. Seeckt desired an active policy for Germany. He saw in the Rapallo Treaty not only a possibility for economic and political cooperation, but also a chance for a military alignment. The General thought it a positive advantage that foreign governments believed military clauses to be attached to the Rapallo Treaty. Both countries had one thorn in their sides: Poland. Removal of it could be the basis for common action. Any man who saw in the Treaty of Rapallo a political mistake could not represent the Reich in Moscow. Seeckt wanted the Russian armament industry rebuilt with German aid so that it could serve as a reserve should the Reich require it. While Brockdorff-Rantzau demanded that he handle all negotiations with Russia, Seeckt warned against the official participation of the German government in the military collaboration. This should be left entirely to the military. As a safeguard, no politically binding agreements should be entered into by the military unless the German government had been informed and had given its approval. However, the General insisted that anyone who "still lives in the days of Versailles . . . was of no use in the representation of German interests in Russia. Possibly nowhere."[85]

In the meantime, Ebert had read Brockdorff-Rantzau's *Promemoria*. He invited the Count and immediately asked him to explain what he meant by his hints about "a certain possibility," and whether he really thought that such an exigency existed. Now that the opportunity for which the memorandum had been written had arrived, and the Count had the chance to deal with the military collaboration, he evaded the issue. Instead he sought refuge in the remark Chicherin had made to him on September 9 about the Russians' intention to proceed to important matters unhampered by Germany's internal affairs. Because of that remark, Brockdorff-Rantzau told Ebert, he wanted to be prepared for the eventuality that the Soviets would bring up military questions.

Ebert, somewhat reassured, told the Count that he completely agreed with the views presented in the memorandum. He had expressly forbidden such insane moves even before Genoa. He had heard nothing since. Did the Ambassador know something? Brockdorff-Rantzau replied that he would not have written the memorandum if he did not think a tendency in that direction possible. He also told Ebert again that he had given the Chancellor a copy of the *Promemoria* and that he had told him that he would resign should it be refused as the basis for his policies in Moscow.[86]

The Count avoided telling Ebert what he knew about the secret military deals because he had made up his mind to stand behind the agreements already made and to take charge of those to come. He felt that it would be a diplomatic blunder to terminate the military collaboration now, because it would antagonize the Russians and force them to deal with other countries, possibly France. If this should revive the old Russo-French alignment, Germany would be faced by an almost impossible situation. Brockdorff-Rantzau was not opposed to changing the provisions of the Treaty of Versailles by force, if necessary. He simply wanted to control all aspects of German relations with Russia in order to receive political *quid pro quos* for any offers made to the Soviets. He was thinking about an arrangement by which Russia would come to the aid of Germany in case she was attacked. In return, Brockdorff-Rantzau was willing to offer economic aid provided by private enterprise, designed to support Russia's economic revival. Aid in military reconstruction should not go beyond the power needed to keep Poland and the Little Entente in check and make it possible for Russia to seek an outlet for her ambitions in the direction of India.

During the course of the day, following his discussion with Ebert, Brockdorff-Rantzau was informed by Waurick that Wirth had requested Seeckt to submit proofs for his allegations against the Count. With support developing in the lion's den, Brockdorff-Rantzau now tried to consolidate support for the policies he had in mind among the leaders of the important German parties. On September 15, he and his brother Ernst von Rantzau gave a formal dinner for Chicherin to which leading representatives of German industry and commerce, and a few Reichstag deputies who favored closer relations with Soviet Russia were invited. After the meal, the Count had a very satisfying talk with Stresemann, who told him that Wirth was losing the respect of more and more people; even his very words were becoming suspect. Only the other day, he had said to someone, in reference to Upper Silesia, "Just wait until we take it back through war." Brockdorff-Rantzau agreed wholeheartedly that Wirth had no feeling for nuances. Stresemann mentioned that Wirth wanted to work with the Russians and apparently had very close personal contacts with Seeckt. Since the matter had come up, the Count felt justified in acquainting Stresemann, in the very strictest confidence and in general terms, with the occurrences of the past weeks. Stresemann found the accusation that Brockdorff-Rantzau was a pacifist

unheard of and laughable, since [Brockdorff-Rantzau] had been the one who rejected the infamous peace of Versailles first, and in the most rigorous form.

The Count now insisted that he would never countenance

military actions behind [his] back and felt no notion to have the already delicate and difficult position in Moscow undermined by the unscrupulous wantonness of ambitious military people.[87]

Brockdorff-Rantzau had expected that Wirth would take some definite action in the Seeckt matter. When the days passed without a word from the Chancellor, the Count went to Haniel and read the *Promemoria* to him. He also told Haniel about the Niedermayer letter that Lloyd George had in his possession, giving proof of the military relationship with Russia. The Count emphasized that, should the English Prime Minister reveal these machinations to the world, the Germans "would be beaten to death like rabid dogs." The Count once again asked the Undersecretary to intercede in his behalf. Haniel urged the Chancellor to make the official announcement of the Count's appointment. Wirth acquiesced, and the announcement was made on September 29.[88]

Almost two months had now passed since Krestinsky had presented his credentials in Berlin, but the German Ambassador still remained far from his post. The chargé d'affaires was already in Moscow. The Count refused to leave for Russia, even after he had received assurances from Haniel that Seeckt had promised Wirth not to interfere in the Count's ambassadorial domain.

Brockdorff-Rantzau did not trust these oral commitments but demanded written guarantees. Since these were not forthcoming, the Count composed a letter to Wirth in which he thanked the Chancellor for having made the official announcement of the appointment. The Count wrote that this action indicated that his *Promemoria* had been accepted as the basis for his policies in Russia. He also expressed the hope that the still unfinished business with Seeckt would now be settled. Should he receive no satisfaction, he would resign. The Count requested another appointment to discuss the matters still pending.[89]

Without waiting for Wirth's reply, the Count wrote to Simons, who was now President of the Supreme Court (Reichsgericht), asking him to intercede with Seeckt. In deference to Brockdorff-Rantzau's wish, the judge wrote to Seeckt asking him to find a way congenial to himself to take back the reproach about Brockdorff-Rantzau's lack of patriotism. Germany could ill afford to have her "two ablest political minds work against each other." He should also discuss the whole Eastern problem with the ambassador to Moscow, because that person certainly had a right, not only to have the backing of the Chancellor, but also of a man as important in politics as Seeckt.[90]

On the morning of October 16, Haniel gave Wirth a letter which Brockdorff-Rantzau had drafted on the day before. The Count had taken considerable pains with his communication because once it was signed and mailed to him by Wirth it would constitute his Magna Carta and make him independent of interference from Berlin, especially from the military. It read:

> In reply to your kind letter of the 4th instant, I declare that I agree with the program of August 15 of this year which you submitted to the President and me. At the same time, I order, in response to the wish your Excellency presented to me orally in addition to your program, that the conduct and care of our relations with the Russian government are exclusively entrusted to you or to your deputy. Any direct or indirect activity in Russia by organs of the German government shall have to have the specific approval of your Excellency.[91]

In the afternoon, Brockdorff-Rantzau had his long-requested talk with the Chancellor. Wirth declared that Germany had to try to become once again the direct neighbor of Russia and, if need be, destroy Poland to achieve that end. In any case, Germany should never be forced to fight for Poland against Russia. Besides this, the "fringe and robber states" in the East "behaved in such a way that he would rather knock them over today than tomorrow." Wirth then assured the Count that he agreed with his program. He also promised that no special operations would be carried on in Russia unless Brockdorff-Rantzau was informed about them. Wirth then begged the Count to let bygones be bygones as far as Seeckt was concerned because the General agreed with his own point of view in this matter. Brockdorff-Rantzau replied that the Chancellor's assurances were "essentially sufficient" and that he was pleased about the prohibition against military interference in political matters. However, had Seeckt given his personal word to that effect? Wirth assured the Count that the General had done so. Then, to the Count's "great surprise," Wirth added that Seeckt had never protested against the appointment.

This reopened the whole matter as far as Brockdorff-Rantzau was concerned. He told Wirth "very quietly" that all difficulties of the past eight weeks had been unnecessary. He really could have left for his assignment two months ago had Wirth not informed him, in a way which left no doubt, that the Army High Command objected. The existence of these objections had been confirmed by unimpeachable sources, including an officer of Seeckt's entourage. Wirth listened in silence, but his face revealed his inner agitation. Finally, the Count continued, a high German military personage had apparently attempted to get Chicherin to rescind the Russian *agrément*. Chicherin had refused to listen to such a suggestion.[92]

Despite the Count's irritation, Wirth told him that he did not think anything had been done to undermine his own confidential relationship with Seeckt. Wirth reiterated that all dealings with the Soviets would be carried on by the Count, to which the latter remarked, "Yes, or over my dead body!" After this aside, the Count pressed Wirth to sign the letter which he had sent to him in the morning. He was eager to have the letter so that he would be covered against "all future eventualities." Wirth evaded a direct commitment and told the Count that he would compose a letter of his own after he had consulted the President. Wirth promised to speak to the military, especially Seeckt. Brockdorff-Rantzau insisted that the Chancellor also talk to the Minister of Defense, Gessler, who, after all, was responsible for military matters. Wirth agreed to have a talk with his cabinet colleague. Brockdorff-Rantzau declared himself satisfied with the assurances, especially since Admiral Behncke had already given his word that the Navy High Command would do nothing in Russia without the Ambassador's knowledge. "The 'wet' comrade was already on his side, the Chancellor needed only to win the 'dry' one over." Wirth appreciated the pun on Seeckt's rather spare appearance.[93]

Immediately after his argument with Wirth, Brockdorff-Rantzau visited Haniel's office. The Undersecretary repeated that Wirth had read Seeckt's "nonexistent" letter to him. The Count now had positive proof that Wirth agreed with the position taken by Seeckt. On October 19, Brockdorff-Rantzau went to Gessler's office in the Bendlerstrasse demanding that the Minister of Defense submit a written declaration to the effect that the Ministry of Defense would neither directly nor indirectly deal with the Russians unless he, as the ambassador, agreed. He threatened to resign unless this agreement was given. The threat did not impress Gessler. He simply said that he would discuss the request with his staff. After all, the most important thing right now was to settle the disagreement with Seeckt amicably. The Count urged the Minister to expedite the case and told him that the Navy High Command had already agreed with his proposals and course of action in regard to German relations with Russia.[94]

During the evening of the nineteenth, Brockdorff-Rantzau telephoned Haniel and asked him to make an appointment with Wirth. The Chancellor received the Count the next forenoon, and the latter told him briefly about his talk with Gessler. Wirth appeared preoccupied and hardly listened. The Count asked Wirth to sign the letter he had forwarded on October 16, so that he could either leave for Moscow or resign from the post. The Russians were clamoring for his arrival because of the celebration of the anniversary of the Bolshevik Revolution. In any event, the present situation was impossible. Wirth promised that the Count would receive something positive in two days, but refused to sign the letter. In fact he never signed or sent a letter of his own in affirmation of the Count's demands.

After his failure to get a written commitment from Wirth assuring his independence from the Foreign Office, the Count accepted a telephoned invitation by Gessler to come to the Bendlerstrasse during the afternoon. Upon his arrival in Gessler's office, the Minister assured him that the military had not intended to interfere in diplomatic affairs. But Gessler also sidestepped any written agreement that the military would not continue their work in Russia independent of the Ambassador. After this totally unsatisfactory meeting with Gessler, the Count wrote another insurance note for his personal files.

> Now that the matter regarding the regulation of the official relations between the Ministry of Defense and the Embassy in Moscow has been settled in a satisfactory way, on the basis of direct negotiations between me and the Minister of Defense, there remains only the affair of General von Seeckt which might possibly lead to later attacks on my honor. In view of the seriousness of the political situation and the necessity to take up my post immediately, I will not now insist that the Seeckt case be settled. I retain, however, the right to return to it in a manner of my choosing, should the matter be touched upon by anyone whomsoever.[95]

The Count's decision to be satisfied with the status quo was supported by Simons in a letter in which he informed Brockdorff-Rantzau of Seeckt's reply to his intercession. The General had declared that he would place no obstacle in the Count's way as long as the latter pursued policies which were in the interest of Germany. Should he do so, Seeckt would support these policies whenever he had the opportunity.[96]

After the receipt of Simons' letter containing the General's ambiguous assurance, Brockdorff-Rantzau informed Gessler that he had thought about the business with Seeckt and would be satisfied if the General officially declared that he had not reproached him about his lack of patriotism.[97] Certain that not much more could be done to checkmate interference by the army or to get more than oral assurance in response to his unconventional demands, Brockdorff-Rantzau left Berlin on the evening of October 30. Despite the rather cool temperature, many friends of the Count's had assembled at the Friedrichstrasse Railroad Station to bid farewell to the Ambassador. When the signal for departure was given, Maltzan handed the Count a bottle of his favorite old French cognac. He took it and said: "You seem to want to say with this: *In hoc signo vinces!*" All those who had crowded around the railroad car laughed.[98]

Then the train pulled out for the East, where Brockdorff-Rantzau confidently expected that Germany's sun would rise again. It was in and with Russia that he would attempt to wipe the stain left by Versailles from his own escutcheon and restore Germany to her former world position. He had come out of retirement only

because I believe and hope to be able to fight the consequences of the ignominious *Diktat* of Versailles successfully from Moscow and possibly throw the whole infamy overboard.[99]

II

A Year of Crisis

Brockdorff-Rantzau arrived in Moscow on November 2, 1922. The Soviet government had provided him with a luxurious salon car for the rail trip from Riga. As he looked out the window at the station platform he saw the staff of the Embassy—not a glimpse of any high-ranking member of the People's Commissariat for Foreign Affairs, but only three junior members of its staff. He had confidently expected to be received with the military honors due his position and felt as if he were "being unloaded like a better class profiteer." Shortly after his arrival Brockdorff-Rantzau received an invitation from Chicherin for nine o'clock in the evening. The Count lost no time in venting his anger about the insulting and shabby reception after he arrived at the Commissar's. Despite Chicherin's protestations that in revolutionary Russia formalities had been abrogated, the Count insisted that Germany and Russia could ill afford to ignore internationally approved procedures. With typical arrogance, he told Chicherin that he would never allow any greater ceremony for a future French or British ambassador. This sally apparently impressed the Russians sufficiently to have President Kalinin forward a personal invitation for a formal reception on November 4.

On the appointed day the Count was greeted by an honor company of the First United War School when he arrived at the Kremlin. This was certainly in sharp contrast to the "unloading" two days before. Brockdorff-Rantzau's short speech, at the presentation of his letter of accreditation, expressed his formula for a better world through German-Russian cooperation.

I shall use my ability and person to prove that the Treaty of Rapallo inaugurated a new era for the German and Russian people and thereby not only for Europe but for the whole world.
The Treaty of Rapallo drew a line under the past. . . .

49

We greet honest cooperation gladly, from whichever side it might come. We reject pity and tutelage. We want to work together in confidence, independently and purposefully, not only to reconstruct that which has been thoughtlessly destroyed but also to provide new cultural values for mankind.

In the unshaken belief in the future of the German and the Russian people, without whom the world cannot recover its health, we proceed in this peaceful work, in which nobody shall disturb us.

After Kalinin's reply, expressing pleasure at the Ambassador's desire to work in Russia according to the "spirit of Rapallo," Brockdorff-Rantzau proceeded to the courtyard of the Kremlin in the company of Kalinin, members of the Central Executive Committee, and nine members of the Narkomindel including Chicherin, Litvinov, Karakhan, second deputy commissar and the economic expert Ganetzky. The Count extended a brief greeting to the troops who were drawn up in front of him and they replied with an approving shout. The band struck up "Deutschland Über Alles," and then the "International." The commander of the honor company and the commandant of the Kremlin reported to the Ambassador. The ceremony concluded with the trooping of the honor company past the dignitaries, to the tune of the Count's favorite march, the "Hohenfriedberger." Motion pictures were taken of the whole ceremony except the review of the troops. Copies were made available to Brockdorff-Rantzau for showing in Germany. The Wilhelmstrasse interpreted the ceremonious reception as the Russians' way of offering satisfaction for the assassination of Mirbach, as well as an honoring of the new Ambassador.[1] Shortly after his arrival Brockdorff-Rantzau informed Maltzan that the Russians were in a very precarious economic position and since the expected aid from Germany, for which they were willing to make political concessions, had not materialized, they would probably look for a more reliable partner. He warned, as he was to do often thereafter, that "Russia will be lost to us if we do not arrive at the last hour with a strong political deed."

The possibility that Russia would be forced, by German diplomatic ineptitude, into an alignment with the West, especially France, remained one of the predominant fears of Brockdorff-Rantzau. Another was the possible alignment of Germany with England. Such an eventuality constituted the acceptance of the hated *Diktat* of Versailles and thus a personal defeat. The Count's fears were enhanced by a cabinet crisis in Germany which held the possibility that the new ministry would swing toward England. On November 18, Maltzan reported with relief that the new Chancellor, Wilhelm Cuno, and his Foreign Minister, Frédéric von Rosenberg, would support his policy in regard to Russia.

The same sentiments were expressed by Cuno and Rosenberg to Chicherin, who used a stopover in Berlin on his way to the Lausanne Conference to get acquainted with the new Chancellor and Foreign Minister. Wirth was also present to assure the Commissar for Foreign Affairs of the continuity of German-Russian relations, in all their varied aspects. During their two-hour discussion Rosenberg and Chicherin agreed to exchange views before all important international discussions and to maintain a reserved attitude toward the League of Nations. Chicherin proposed the preparation of a common project to enter a League of Nations but not the existing one. Rosenberg listened but did not commit himself to any agreement, however tentative.[2]

Brockdorff-Rantzau's immediate fears about a realignment of German foreign policy were somewhat calmed. At the same time he had the first of his many encounters with the Comintern. The position of the Comintern in relation to the Soviet government was bluntly put by Trotsky in the following way: The government of Russia is the proletariat which is also "the most important constituent part of the Third International. The working class throughout the world is interested in the strengthening of Soviet Russia, and has given proof of this on several occasions." On November 24, Radek characterized the new German Cabinet, in a *Pravda* article, as a transition stage to the takeover by the right. Radek advised the Communist Party of Germany (KPD) to train its worker battalions and prepare for fighting in January or February of 1923.

Maltzan instructed the Ambassador to take the first opportunity to point out to the Foreign Commissariat that Radek's remarks were not helping in the creation of a pro-Russian atmosphere in Germany. Brockdorff-Rantzau spoke to Radek and was impressed with his great intelligence. On December 8 Radek arrived in Berlin, and had a long discussion with Maltzan. Radek told Maltzan that he liked Brockdorff-Rantzau. As to politics, Radek explained that Russia would have to approach France. This would in no way change the traditional Russian policy toward Germany.[3]

Brockdorff-Rantzau was perfectly aware of the peculiar role played by the Comintern, but, as a diplomat of the old school and a realist, preferred to act as if the People's Commissariat for Foreign Affairs was the only branch of the Soviet government directly concerned with foreign relations. He dealt with the Narkomindel as if it were a policy-making body and not just the mouthpiece of the Politburo which controlled it.

The Count was convinced that Russia depended as much on Germany as did his own country on the Russian relationship to play a part in international politics. He sent a long report entitled "Germany's and Russia's Community of Fate [*Schicksalsgemeinschaft*]" to the Foreign Office, requesting that the report be treated as "extremely secret," be shown only to President Ebert, and under no circumstances be circulated among German diplomatic missions abroad. Maltzan showed the report to Ebert, Cuno, and Rosenberg.

Quite obviously the Count had already decided that he would be able to accomplish great things in Russia. He made no further mention of the possibility that he would leave after the trial period had passed. But he made it perfectly clear that he would only remain in Moscow "*as long as I have the confidence of the Russian government and have the influence in Berlin, which I demanded for my policies.*"[4]

Fortunately for the Count and all other advocates of close relations with Soviet Russia, Maltzan took over the post of Undersecretary on December 22, when Haniel vacated that position. Maltzan assured Brockdorff-Rantzau that even in his new position he "would first and foremost live for my Russian child" even if it would appear as if he favored the West. The Russians utilized the promotion of Maltzan, which they rightly interpreted as an indication that the "Easterners" had the upper hand in the Wilhelmstrasse, to request that Berlin send an outstanding military expert to Russia for a discussion. For tactical reasons Maltzan wanted the Soviets to send someone, preferably Marshal M. N. Tukhachevsky, to Berlin, and he instructed Brockdorff-Rantzau to work toward that end. The Count agreed and advised Maltzan to wait until he, the Count, had spoken with the Commissar for War, Trotsky. Brockdorff-Rantzau still opposed an outright military alliance but had accepted Seeckt's view that it would be beneficial if the West thought that the relationship held the possibility of a military alignment.

Trotsky visited the Ambassador on December 27. The Commissar saw no need to hurry the military talks. He assured Brockdorff-Rantzau of Russian support should the French attempt to occupy the Ruhr. He went further, promising that the Red army would interfere should the Poles, acting on French orders, use the opportunity to occupy Upper Silesia. Chicherin also told the Count that Russia wanted the most cordial relations with Germany. Nikolai I. Bukharin, candidate member of the Politburo, the party's ideological expert, and editor of *Pravda*, wrote to the French Communist Boris Souvarine, in the name of the Comintern, that Russia would probably take action if the German revolution started and Poland attacked Germany.

The assurances of Soviet aid came at the right moment because the occupation of the Ruhr, long expected by the Wilhelmstrasse, was begun by the French and Belgian troops on January 11, 1923. The British government refused to participate in this action, designed to force the Germans to pay the reparations due France, because it considered the occupation unauthorized by the Treaty of Versailles. Maltzan rejoiced at the evidence of a split among the victors. He saw in it the psychological moment he had been waiting for.[5]

If he had hoped that the divergence of opinion among the Allies would mitigate the effect of the occupation, Maltzan was to be disappointed. The Cuno government decided on passive resistance and subsidized the workers of the Ruhr by grants from the national treasury. This flow of gold to the Ruhr worsened an already bad economic situation and multiplied the problems facing the Weimar Republic. Internally it led to an inflation which brought the young republic to its nadir by creating an atmosphere in which political extremism, particularly communism and nazism, saw the opportunity to end democracy. Externally it encouraged Poland, France's Eastern ally, to think of acquiring more German territory. It became of the utmost importance to Germany that the Poles be kept in check by Russia. For that purpose the Wilhelmstrasse wanted the private assurances given by Trotsky and Chicherin to result in some public demonstration of Russian support for Germany.

In Moscow and provincial cities sympathy demonstrations were held. The demonstrators carried banners with such slogans as "Down with the French Imperialists," and "Long Live the German Revolution."[6] *Pravda* advised the German government to overcome its scruples and conclude "an intimate economic and political alliance with Soviet Russia" in order to resist the French. The article contained the thinly veiled threat to Paris that an alliance between Berlin and Moscow could become a reality if conditions in Germany became really desperate.[7]

As early as January 6, Maltzan had asked Brockdorff-Rantzau to return to Germany for consultation. He had advised the Ambassador to surround his departure from Moscow with an air of secrecy and importance. Such behavior would prompt rumors that something sinister was under way. The Count left Moscow on the day after the occupation of the Ruhr had actually begun, and he arrived in Berlin during the evening of January 15. On his arrival he was greeted by Krestinsky and the entire staff of the Russian Embassy with an effusive show of cordiality. Walter Duranty, the Moscow correspondent of *The New York Times*, wrote that the Ambassador's recall was particularly important because he had defied the Allies at Versailles and believed that Germany's salvation lay in Russia. This did not mean that the Count favored a Communist revolution in Germany, or that he gave credence to the French bogey about the irresistible march of a million-strong Red army to the Rhine. He knew that such an army did not exist. On January 17, Brockdorff-Rantzau was reported as having assured the Foreign Office, at a meeting of German ambassadors from the countries bordering on Russia, that he had been promised by the Kremlin that nothing would be done to weaken Germany's position. Dark hints emitted from the Wilhelmstrasse about military aid from Russia. Despite repeated denials that the Treaty of Rapallo did not contain any secret military clauses, rumors did not die that the Germans knew all about the details of Soviet military plans.[8]

Besides discussing German-Russian relations in Berlin, Brockdorff-Rantzau also settled a still outstanding score. Gessler had refused to comply with the demand that he, as Seeckt's superior, see to it that the General officially withdraw his objections to the Count. After a number of the Count's letters on the subject, the exasperated Minister of Defense finally advised Brockdorff-Rantzau to make an official complaint to the Chancellor. The Count first went to his friend, Foreign Minister Rosenberg, and gave him the details of the feud with Seeckt. Rosenberg advised the Count to formulate his request for a withdrawal of Seeckt's objections in a conciliatory form, so that it would be easier for the General to make amends. Brockdorff-Rantzau was not satisfied with Rosenberg's attitude. He went to Chancellor Cuno, who also happened to be a good friend of his, and gave him the complete correspondence with Gessler. Cuno promised to settle the matter immediately.

Brockdorff-Rantzau left Berlin for his estate in Schleswig, and when he returned to the capital Cuno told him that Seeckt had declared that he no longer upheld the reproach that Brockdorff-Rantzau lacked patriotism. The Chancellor made it absolutely clear that this closed the matter as far as he was concerned. The Count quickly agreed, and expressed the wish that Cuno arrange a meeting with the General, at which Brockdorff-Rantzau could discuss the possibility of fruitful cooperation in Russia. The Chancellor proposed a dinner at his residence and left the guest list to Brockdorff-Rantzau. The dinner took place on January 27, and the Ambassador made sure that he would arrive at Cuno's before Seeckt. This minor stratagem required the General to greet Brockdorff-Rantzau. After dinner, the two discussed their common labors in Russia without referring to their lengthy, though one-sided, feud. The Count noted that they were of one mind on most important questions.[9] Having finally settled with Seeckt, the Count returned to his post.

While the Ambassador was on his way back to Moscow, his chargé d'affaires, Hentig, reported to the Foreign Office that Trotsky, according to the Russian newspapers of January 28, had declared that the Soviet Union wanted peace, and that Poland's preparation for war would not provoke Russia; only a direct attack would get a proper Soviet reply. Hentig had been informed by a very reliable source that Trotsky had declared that Soviet Russia would continue to demobilize about 200,000 men as planned. Trotsky had emphasized that Russia did not have the means to prepare for war, and would therefore withdraw her forces to a line stretching from Moscow to Smolensk. The chargé d'affaires followed his telegrams with the regular political report. After describing the Russian tactics during the past three weeks, he concluded with an incisive evaluation:

> . . . Russia once again reveals herself as a many-sided protagonist who, with an ever changing mask, and with an expenditure of strength determined by her domestic conditions, tries to play as big a role as is possible without risk. Germany is only an object of this policy.[10]

Brockdorff-Rantzau regretted that Hentig had made that last statement because he was sure that it could easily "destroy the last glimmer of hope for positive work" in Russia.

Trotsky's remarks created a rather awkward situation for the Wilhelmstrasse. Germany's desperate economic situation, as well as her disarmed condition, excluded any armed resistance to French force. The implied threat that Russia would come to her aid was one of the few things left to the Foreign Office in its attempts to force the French to abandon the occupation. The statement attributed to Trotsky removed an important diplomatic factor. In addition there were renewed indications of a Russo-French *rapprochement*.[11]

Brockdorff-Rantzau told Litvinov during a frank discussion that he had found a serious situation in Germany. He hoped that the German people would weather this storm and find friends again. Apparently the decision had been made to leave them to their fate. After this transparent allusion to Trotsky's remarks, the Count casually dropped a few hints about the possibility of an Anglo-German *rapprochement*. Just as Brockdorff-Rantzau had expected, Litvinov became agitated and assured him that the remarks attributed to Trotsky had been fabricated out of whole cloth, and had absolutely no foundation in fact. The Commissar would return to Moscow in two days and Litvinov promised to discuss the matter with him immediately. Brockdorff-Rantzau indicated that he would speak to Trotsky himself especially since Radek had told him in Berlin that the Commissar had been extremely pleased with their first conversation.

Litvinov, the Count continued, had once told him that the various components of the Soviet government worked as one. He found it difficult to believe in this much vaunted solidarity. In fact, he suspected that a difference of opinion on the treatment of Germany existed between the Narkomindel and the party leaders. Litvinov denied this vehemently. The Ambassador now explained that he had come to Russia because he was convinced that the two peoples were dependent on each other, not only because of their "community of fate" but also because of the nature of things. He was determined to cooperate with the Communist regime but not if this meant that it would throw Germany to "French imperialistic capitalism in order to prepare Germany's soil for world revolution." Brockdorff-Rantzau underscored this veiled threat at resignation with a bit of blackmail. He told Litvinov that he would not support the reorganization of the Red army with Germany intelligence and industry, just so it could withdraw to the Smolensk-Moscow line and watch while Germany was destroyed by insane Frenchmen.

Litvinov detained Brockdorff-Rantzau as the latter made ready to leave and emphasized that he would clear up the matter. The two then talked about the Lausanne Conference. Litvinov informed the Ambassador that Chicherin would visit in Berlin on his return trip. Brockdorff-Rantzau declared he was delighted to hear that. The Wilhelmstrasse suspected that a Russo-French "understanding" had been reached. He had tried to remove these suspicions and Chicherin could aid in this effort. Litvinov took the cue, giving his word that no meeting between Chicherin and the French delegate Barrière had taken place. Brockdorff-Rantzau received this assurance without any show of enthusiasm.

A week later Litvinov showed Brockdorff-Rantzau a secret letter from Trotsky in which he asked for German understanding for the necessity of making it clear to the world that the Soviet government had only peaceful intentions. Litvinov affirmed Trotsky's assurances to act in case of a Polish attack on Upper Silesia.[12]

During talks with Chicherin in Berlin Maltzan insisted on an unequivocal attitude of the Russians vis-à-vis the French. Otherwise German assistance in Russian reconstruction could hardly be defended. On the following day, February 10, Litvinov made the following oral statement to Brockdorff-Rantzau: "Mr. Ambassador, I give you formal assurances that no approach of any kind took place between Russia and France at Lausanne." Russia had been approached to act as arbiter between France and Germany but had refused.[13] Moscow also informed Warsaw and Paris that any extension of the Ruhr occupation could lead Russia to take a forceful stand.[14]

In a further show of Russo-German solidarity, Chicherin gave an interview to the *Manchester Guardian* on March 3, in which he made it clear that the French activities in the Ruhr created grave problems for the USSR. Continued occupation reduced the possibility of German economic aid and the extensions of credit which Russia needed to reconstruct. Foreign Minister Rosenberg used these remarks before a committee of the Reichstag three weeks later in order to show that the Soviet Union could be counted upon to support Germany.[15]

While the Wilhelmstrasse tried to get a public commitment of Soviet support it took steps to prevent the Communists from using the existing distress to destroy the Republic. The legal entry of known agitators from Russia was discreetly, but absolutely, refused.[16] At this juncture Brockdorff-Rantzau's attention was diverted from the possibility of a Franco-Russian alignment to a more immediate matter. A military mission led by Colonel Otto Hasse arrived in Moscow.[17]

In the beginning it seemed to the Count that Hasse, whom he found charming, would cooperate and keep him informed about the clandestine negotiations. When Hasse told him that all the "salesmen" would leave Moscow with him, Brockdorff-Rantzau used the opportunity to press Rosenberg, Cuno, and Maltzan to influence and convince the Army High Command to send Major Fischer, whom the Count knew from Versailles and whom he liked because he had been on his side during the Seeckt affair, and not Major Fritz Tschunke to Moscow to represent the army.[18] The Navy High Command already had an unofficial representative in Moscow; he had introduced himself to Brockdorff-Rantzau on February 25. But the army refused to send Major Fischer at this time.[19]

The era of good feelings between the Count and military changed abruptly. Brockdorff-Rantzau discovered that Hasse had told some Russians that a war of liberation would be launched in three to five years, and that a regular military attaché would soon be sent to Moscow. The Ambassador considered the whole Hasse mission an absolute fiasco, an opinion which, according to the Count, was shared by Chicherin. The Count forwarded a highly secret memorandum about a talk with P. P. Lebedev, Chief of Staff of the Red army, to Maltzan and asked him to burn it after he had shown it to Chancellor Cuno and Foreign Minister Rosenberg. Maltzan did as he was requested.[20]

Brockdorff-Rantzau's constant concern about the verdict of posterity, and the opinion of his contemporaries forced him to establish an alibi for any unpleasant situation or any development which had poor results. In the case of the Hasse mission he made sure that everyone understood that it was due to Hasse's refusal to confide in him that the fiasco had occurred in the first place. In the future he wanted to be in complete charge of the military negotiations. As matters now stood he could not be held responsible for the results which in his opinion were detrimental to Germany's relations with Soviet Russia.

The unpleasantness caused Brockdorff-Rantzau by the military was mitigated by what the Count considered his first significant diplomatic success. During extended negotiations with Krassin, the Ambassador had succeeded in coming to a preliminary agreement by which the Russians would deliver grain in exchange for German industrial goods. Under this Grain Agreement, as it was to be called, Germany was to advance 50 percent of the money value of about 328,000 tons of Russian grain. The Soviet Union bound itself to use the advance for the purchase of industrial goods in Germany.[21] The preliminary agreement had been sent to Berlin in early March but had encountered difficulties, just as the Count had expected. The various provisions of the agreement were discussed during long sessions between the Foreign Office and representatives of other government departments.

While Brockdorff-Rantzau spent much time on the matter in Moscow, the brunt of these painstaking discussions in Berlin fell on Schlesinger, now in the Foreign Service with the rank of Consul General. He kept the Ambassador current on the progress and disappointments. Maltzan used his influence to overcome opposition to the Grain Agreement in the Foreign Office itself. Following this, Schlesinger fought an uphill fight with the other departments. These were finally convinced that the agreement was of great value to Germany. On April 5, to Schlesinger's consternation, not to say disgust, the negotiations almost collapsed when the Chairman of the Russian Trade Delegation (Handelsvertretung) in Berlin, Stomoniakov, made new demands. After a few minor adjustments the German Cabinet approved the Grain Agreement on April 16, the first anniversary of Rapallo. The date had been chosen by Maltzan for its sentimental value. Schlesinger gave all the credit for this achievement to Brockdorff-Rantzau, who graciously returned the flattery by assuring Schlesinger that the merit belonged to him for having proposed the project in the first place.[22]

A few weeks before the approval of the Grain Agreement Lenin suffered a stroke. Despite the efforts of five German specialists who attended him, his physical condition did not improve. Lenin's sickness gave rise to rumors of impending troubles for the Bolshevik regime. Brockdorff-Rantzau did not think that attempts to overthrow the Soviet government would be successful even if aided from without.[23]

The Ambassador was much more concerned about the effect the Ruhr situation had on the value of Germany's political stock in Russia. The approval of the Grain Agreement had been helpful, but not sufficient to camouflage the weakness of the Reich as revealed by the Ruhr situation. In a detailed and careful report Brockdorff-Rantzau analyzed the possibility of a Russo-French *rapprochement* prompted by the political and economic conditions of Germany. The Ambassador considered such an alignment a most dangerous threat to the very existence of the Reich. He was convinced that in Soviet Russia as in the land of the Tsars, traditional anti-English policies made close relations between Russia and France not just a matter for idle conjecture. He based his belief on the recent trip of the Russian Admiral Behrens to Paris. Chicherin had tried to minimize the importance of the trip and assured the Count that the Admiral had only discussed economic problems. Brockdorff-Rantzau indicated his disbelief by impressing on Chicherin that any *rapprochement* between Russia and France would be detrimental to the continuation of good relations between Germany and Russia. Both Maltzan and Brockdorff-Rantzau discounted the danger of an immediate improvement of relations between the two former allies. If and when such an improvement occurred, Maltzan held, Germany would derive some benefit because France would have to give up Poland which in turn would have to look toward an improvement of her relations with Germany.[24]

A few days later, Brockdorff-Rantzau invited Chicherin to dinner, and remonstrated in the strongest terms against the interference of the Comintern in foreign affairs. Two Russians who accompanied Soviet grain sent to the Ruhr workers had told a rally on April 17 that this was only step one; the second would be the arrival of the Red army once the fighting had started. Everywhere the grain arrived there were propaganda speeches and demonstrations. Chicherin blamed the German Communists, because he could not believe that Russians acted in the manner described. Added to this harassment was the fact that Zinoviev had been quoted by the Soviet press as favoring friendly relations with France. The Ambassador told Chicherin in unequivocal terms that such a speech simply should not be tolerated by the Narkomindel. Chicherin lamely contended that Zinoviev had only addressed a party meeting and the reference had been to economic relations. Brockdorff-Rantzau pointed out that this was too subtle a nuance to be understood by the general public. Clearly, any remarks by a man as important as Zinoviev strengthened France, a country which had just "assaulted Germany in the most shameless manner." Chicherin was impressed. Three days after the dinner he categorically told the German Ambassador that an understanding between Russia and France was out of the question. During dinner at Brockdorff-Rantzau's, Radek repeated Chicherin assurances and added that the Soviet government had discontinued economic talks with France in protest against the Ruhr occupation.[25]

Brockdorff-Rantzau succeeded in showing the Russians that they could not go too far in the direction of France without running the danger of losing Germany, and thus their *point d'appui* in Western Europe. Such a threat was necessary because the Count was known to be personally convinced that Germany would not cut the wire to Moscow. On the other hand he was also known to place the welfare of his country first in all his considerations. Under these circumstances Russia could not take a chance of provoking even the possibility of a break. Germany was still the only major country which had recognized the Soviet regime, and it had thereby received a certain measure of respectability.

Brockdorff-Rantzau became concerned that rumored differences among the Russian leadership, accentuated by the absence of Lenin's authority, would lead to a change in foreign policy detrimental to Germany. The Ambassador assumed that the struggle for power was being waged between the party, headed by Zinoviev, Kamenev, and Stalin, and the Red army, led by Trotsky. Because of the good relations in military matters and because the party represented revolution and interference in Germany's domestic affairs, Brockdorff-Rantzau hoped that Trotsky would emerge victorious. Trotsky had not been available for a discussion of the military arrangement made by Colonel Hasse. A new delegation headed by Lieutenant Colonel Mentzel had arrived on April 27, and Brockdorff-Rantzau had told Mentzel that he was not to negotiate without informing the Ambassador. Mentzel had agreed but Trotsky, in Chicherin's words, "was as unapproachable as the gods of Egypt not only for foreigners but for the most important natives as well." This information disturbed the Count. The continuing deterioration of economic conditions made it imperative for the Soviet Union to get foreign aid. Krassin told Brockdorff-Rantzau with brutal frankness that the Soviet Union needed money and would get it where it could. Chicherin also emphasized that Russia's precarious economic position made it necessary to make foreign policy from the economic point of view and not from the political. All this made good sense to the Count.[26]

Brockdorff-Rantzau considered Germany's own situation desperate enough for a drift to the West to take place. He devoted a whole political report to that possibility. He pointed out that Germany's condition made her rather unimportant in international politics. The time had arrived to benefit from the past mistakes. Anyone in politics had to have the courage to evaluate various courses of action coldly and realistically. It was absolutely impossible to move toward "the West either economically or politically without delivering the majority of the German people into helotism." The only possibility available to prevent such a tragic fate was close political and economic cooperation with Russia.

I hold to the conviction that the Soviet government—one may approve or despise its final aims—can be won for a healthy cooperation with Germany if it is decently treated, because it honestly wants to reconstruct and knows that it can not dispense with Germany's assistance in this work.

It also knows very well that a further weakening of Germany is not in Russia's interest and does not lie in the interest of the final aims which it pursues, because it needs tranquility for these too; chaos in Germany, when it occurs—and this possibility does not appear infeasible—would today come at a most inopportune time.

We should finally stop tearing each other to pieces in domestic dissension, and try to enter the road to the East together in agreement. The West jealously watches every step we take in that direction, because it knows quite well, that once we have found the way, it also must open the door which it so impertinently slammed into our face.

Not fear born of a dark misery and an uncertain future, but cool, clear evaluation, and the unshaking belief in the world mission of the German people points the way to the East, whether the present government of Russia is "sympathetic" or not. I could imagine a more ideal system of government and do not underestimate the dangers which lurk in cooperation with the Soviet government. But I am convinced that this and the ever-repeated danger of Bolshevik contagion—which, incidentally, is not particularly increased by the kind of cooperation I envisage with Russia—is less of a threat to the nation and the existence of the Reich than the revolting violence and shameless humiliations to which the Entente has exposed the German people for the past four years.

In view of the situation in which we find ourselves such objections as exist against closer relations with Russia must, at least for the time being, be placed into the background. We depend on Russia today. We have been and shall continue to depend on her for a long time, if not forever, because of the last World War. This has nothing to do with likes or dislikes, but only with the sober fact that we need Russia, and that *every* other [Russian] government must seek support among the Allies, and what that would mean for Germany is obvious.

The way to the East is open; it has been for years. Let us take it with as little delay and bother as possible. This too will be a difficult and hard road; nobody will dream that it will quickly lead to shining heights.

But one thing at least is assured: We can walk this path with head high and need not crawl along it; and that is what the German nation needs if it does not want to surrender.[27]

This report embodied the Russian policies of Brockdorff-Rantzau. The *Promemoria* had served as a polemic against Seeckt. The Count's major concern was the prevention of a one-sided alignment with the West, because it was a departure from the time-honored Bismarckian policy of isolating France and keeping Russia friendly. For the Ambassador this held a double truth; he hated France and wanted Moscow to be the most important German diplomatic post. Under no circumstances should it become secondary, because his mission was to strengthen Germany with Russia's potential, keep the West in check by threats of a closer relationship than that of Rapallo, and thus destroy the *Diktat* of Versailles. He conceived this policy to be the only tenable one for a weak, demilitarized, and friendless Germany. A withdrawal from the community of fate, initiated by Rapallo, would deliver Germany into the merciless hands of her former enemies, who would once again be able to treat her as a *quantité négligeable*.

While the Count tried to convince the Wilhelmstrasse that salvation lay in the East, Russian interference in Germany's domestic affairs was making it quite difficult to follow a pro-Soviet course. Even people who normally had logical and economic reasons to be friendly were beginning to have a change of heart. Maltzan warned Brockdorff-Rantzau that

a really dangerous, poisonous atmosphere is forming here. The Communist uprisings in the Ruhr and Saxony, which, as even the English have shown beyond a doubt, are traceable to French machinations and French money, are being utilized by the press and various ministries . . . to shove the blame into the shoes of Russian agitators.

There had been demands to stop issuing passports to Russians, and Radek in particular; even Chancellor Cuno had become quite agitated. Maltzan was convinced that there were no agitators in the Ruhr with the knowledge of the Russian government, because it was neither in their political nor in their economic interests.[28] Despite opposition by the Wilhelmstrasse the Cabinet ordered that no entry visas be issued to any foreign Communists. The Moscow Embassy was informed of the decision with the lame advice to explain to the Narkomindel that the order was issued against all foreign Communists, not only those from Russia.[29]

During this period Maltzan saw Radek twice and was very frank with him because Radek knew more about Germany's domestic affairs than Maltzan. Radek was in Germany trying to persuade the right-wing nationalists, many of whom he had met while in Moabit Prison, to act with the Communists in the spirit of "National Bolshevism."

It is interesting, in view of his easy access to the Wilhelmstrasse, that Radek, in a *Pravda* article published on June 8, wrote that the rumor that the Communists in the Ruhr worked with French gold was spread by the English in order to give the German bourgeoisie a chance to accuse the KPD of high treason.[30]

Brockdorff-Rantzau was certain that the Foreign Commissariat was not involved in the agitations in Germany. But he let Chicherin and Litvinov know that Germany could not indefinitely take the separation of the government and the party as an excuse when the Comintern interfered in Germany's domestic affairs. The two Russians, for their part, were very much concerned about a rightist coup and told the German Ambassador about their fears. Brockdorff-Rantzau was convinced that it was not Russia's desire but the intention of the French Premier Raymond Poincaré to drive Germany into anarchy. This policy was designed to prevent a continued improvement of German-Russian friendship by blaming the deteriorating conditions on the Communists. The Count firmly believed that friendship with Germany was the cornerstone of Soviet foreign policy, despite the provocative propaganda and invective spewing from the mouth of the Comintern.

When the Narkomindel continued to flirt with the French in order to force Germany into a closer relationship with Russia, Brockdorff-Rantzau made it perfectly clear to Litvinov that *he* understood these coquettish moves. But, the Count pointed out, others in Germany might not. These people might easily mistake tactics for strategy, and thus become opposed to continued cooperation with the Soviet state.

Brockdorff-Rantzau's major concern continued to be an Anglo-German alignment which for him overshadowed the propaganda of the Comintern in Germany and Russian approaches to the French. He informed Maltzan that he would not cooperate in a policy based on English aid against the French. Maltzan, who had repeatedly given the Count definite assurances that no change in policy was contemplated, now became distinctly irritated with the Count's one-sided attitude. The Undersecretary explained that the Russians were not making things easy. During the past months Germany had bent over backwards to accommodate Moscow, even at the risk of hampering her own advantages in the reparation talks. Finally, a definite answer to some very plain hints from the West about joining the League of Nations had been evaded by making strong counterproposals. However, if a solution of the Ruhr problem was only possible if Germany considered League membership, a change of policy might eventuate. Maltzan promised to consult Brockdorff-Rantzau before anything definite was decided. Maltzan considered Germany's possible entry into the League only as a *quid pro quo* by which Germany might obtain worthwhile diplomatic concessions.[31]

Maltzan's information eased Brockdorff-Rantzau's concern. He now turned again to German military collaboration with Russia. The military mission headed by Lieutenant Colonel Mentzel had concluded an agreement with the Russians which provided for the delivery of thirty-five million gold marks' worth of war materiel to the Red army.

When the Count found out about this renewed evidence of military disregard for political expediency, and the deliberate affront to himself, he strenuously complained to the Foreign Office. As Germany's domestic situation deteriorated further, the Count began to look at the military collaboration with greater favor. By the end of June, he became convinced that the military collaboration constituted the most important aspect of Germany's relations with the Soviet Union. Decisions, deals, and the continued care of the military relationship were much too involved to be left to the Reichswehr; the Count maintained that the political departments, *i.e.*, the civilian authorities, of the German government should take over. What disturbed the Count was positive evidence that Seeckt's subordinates wanted to come to terms with the Soviet Union without regard for the cost. On June 15, he requested authorization to persuade the Russians to send a negotiator to Berlin. Brockdorff-Rantzau was sure, on the basis of repeated complaints by Chicherin about the delays which the negotiations with the Reichswehr had encountered, that the Russians were much more interested in deals than the Germans. This eagerness could be turned into an advantage which could be used to remove the "grave mistakes" made in the past. Chancellor Cuno, on June 20, sent permission for negotiations to continue in Berlin. After some initial reluctance the Foreign Commissariat decided to request that Trotsky send a negotiator to Berlin.[32]

At a meeting on July 11, at which Chancellor Cuno, Minister of Finance Hermes, Minister for Reconstruction Heinrich Albert, and Maltzan participated, it was agreed that the existing military collaboration receive financial support. This support would amount to sixty million gold marks for the ensuing year, 50 percent of which would be made available within the next few months. Maltzan informed Brockdorff-Rantzau about the tentative agreement. Arms production in Russia was to be financed by a government trust company under the direct control of the Minister of Finance. The military were to contribute their professional knowledge to this company while the Foreign Office would supervise the political relations springing from the new arrangement. The negotiations to implement the promises made by Mentzel in April were to take place in Berlin in July. Brockdorff-Rantzau had no intentions "de mettre mon doigt entre l'écorce et l'arbre—ni ailleurs," but had decided that his participation was necessary. In the event that Arkady P. Rosengolts, Chief of the Red air force, the Russian negotiator, arrived in Berlin before Brockdorff-Rantzau, Maltzan should see to it that Rosengolts would talk only with representatives of the Ministry of Defense. Krestinsky would cooperate in this matter because he was on the side of the German Foreign Office.[33]

The Ambassador arrived in Berlin on July 17, to start his furlough and to participate in the impending, very clandestine military negotiations with the Russians. The Count's primary purpose in attending these meetings was to get the control of all military negotiations in Russia into his own hands. He was convinced that only his direction of the negotiations between the Reichswehr and the Red army would result in *quid pro quos* in the political arena. This was a basic difference between Brockdorff-Rantzau and Seeckt, who was satisfied with military benefits and felt that political advantages would follow.

During several conferences under the chairmanship of Minister for Reconstruction Albert, in which Brockdorff-Rantzau, Foreign Minister Rosenberg, Colonel Hasse, Lieutenant Colonel Mentzel, and representatives of the German banks took part, the participation of German industry was discussed, as well as a possible increase of the thirty-five million marks credit promised by Mentzel by an additional forty million. Brockdorff-Rantzau insisted that the thirty-five million credit promised by Mentzel be granted to the Russians because he feared that otherwise dire political consequences would result. Albert's committee agreed with the Count. In subsequent discussions under the chairmanship of Chancellor Cuno, President Havenstein of the Reichsbank categorically refused to grant even thirty-five million because of Germany's precarious economic conditions. It was only after Brockdorff-Rantzau, at Cuno's request, gave a short lecture on German-Russian relations coupled with a threat to resign, that Havenstein agreed to make the money available.

In a secret memorandum for Chancellor Cuno, Brockdorff-Rantzau had insisted that the negotiations had political overtones and should therefore be conducted by the Foreign Office rather than the Ministry of Defense. The military had shown their political ineptitude in November of 1922, when Niedermayer made exaggerated promises, and again in February and April of 1923. The relationship had to be changed so that Germany would no longer appear in the role of "supplicant" before the Soviet government. The Count was convinced that Russia needed Germany to reconstruct its armament industry. The Russian needs could and should be utilized. He advised Cuno to get a number of concessions. Since it was doubtful that Moscow would deliver war materiel in case of serious need, it should be insisted that Germany receive "a sort of monopoly" in the armament factories in which Germans worked and which were financed from Berlin. Some arrangement, other than a political or military alliance should also be negotiated in order to protect Germany against an attack by Poland. Such an agreement would have the additional advantage of being an indirect protection against France which was bound to aid the Poles. The demands had to be made to Rosengolts in Berlin. Then Brockdorff-Rantzau would continue negotiations in Moscow with Chicherin.

The question of Poland had to be brought up because Rosengolts had declared, during an hour-long talk in Moscow, that "the resolution of the question regarding the production of gas and the order of shells was the basis for the further extension of the negotiations." Brockdorff-Rantzau interpreted the last as Russian willingness to come to an agreement about the fate of Poland. In case Rosengolts rejected the monopoly in arms production, which would be of great economic advantage to Germany, promises of financial aid in addition to the thirty-five million gold marks already pledged by Mentzel could be offered.[34]

After the Germans had come to a general agreement among themselves about finances and Cuno had accepted the Count's *quid pro quos* as the basis for the negotiations, it was decided that an unobtrusive meeting with Rosengolts should take place on July 30, in the private apartment of Ernst Rantzau at Viktoriastrasse 32 in Berlin. The Chancellor arrived after dinner because of a previous engagement with some labor union representatives. Besides the Count, Cuno, Rosengolts, and Krestinsky, only Ustinov, a secretary of the Soviet Embassy who acted as interpreter, was present. The talks began at a quarter to ten and continued until well after midnight. From beginning to end a friendly atmosphere prevailed. Cuno started with the remark that "the German and the Russian people, regardless of their governmental forms at any given time, depended economically as well as politically upon each other unconditionally. As the man directing the total policies of Germany he was determined to recognize that fact." He was glad to hear that the first agreement on economic and military matters was due to be signed July 31. Economic cooperation between the two countries was a "matter of life and death" because of the prevailing economic conditions. He considered the thirty-five million as only the beginning of reconstruction and, in view of Russia's gigantic needs, only a pitiful sum. Unfortunately more could not be offered because of Germany's poor financial situation. Germany wanted to secure herself against future competition which might push her out of the Russian field and therefore proposed "that Russia oblige herself not to employ foreigners in the factories where Germans worked without prior consultation with Germany." The same consideration applied to financial aid from additional German sources.

Cuno then talked about the international situation and "unobtrusively dropped the remark that he considered Poland, next to France, the most dangerous disturber of peace not only in Europe but in the whole world." The German-Russian agreements now under consideration were designed to guarantee the peaceful development of their two nations. Rosengolts agreed but remarked that Russia could not take the chance of defeat and therefore had to wait. Cuno replied that the time could always be chosen when the opportunity arose. Rosengolts thought that Germany was not too determined on war and Cuno assured him that it would be foolish to give the impression that Germany was preparing for a war of revenge. But much more was being done for defense than even the best informed circles knew. Rosengolts was pleased to hear the latter and Cuno now proceeded to the matter at hand. They had not come together to exchange pleasantries, he told Rosengolts, and added, "Would you have the kindness to make concrete proposals?"

At the end of the long discussions Rosengolts asked that a representative of the Reichswehr be sent to Russia. At this point Brockdorff-Rantzau interjected that it would be best to let him negotiate in Moscow. The Chancellor agreed and empowered the Ambassador "to negotiate in Russia with the political and military departments in the sense discussed." Rosengolts said he would order the necessary matters in Moscow.[35]

"Following this conference, an agreement regarding the reconstruction of the Russian armament industry and the production of war material for Germany was signed provisionally . . ." between the German military authorities and Rosengolts. Brockdorff-Rantzau was not informed about the details of this agreement. But on the day after the signing, Rosengolts told the Count that the negotiations would be continued in Moscow. The Ambassador felt that Germany had come out rather well.

> We had, instead of sending a German mission for the third time, brought an authorized Russian military personality to Berlin. In the case of indiscretions, Germany was covered because of this. The realization of the military-technical program had been bound up with conditions, on the fulfillment of which we could at any time make our participation in the expansion of the Russian armament industry dependent, and finally, the Russians had bound themselves to make written proposals to us, so that not only they alone, as up to that time (letter of General Hasse to Rosenholtz), were in possession of written proposals on our part. Under these conditions, and only these, did I approve of the whole action.[36]

The agreement, tentatively made during the July negotiations in Berlin, resulted in German financial participation and technical assistance in the production of armaments at the Red army's factories at Zlatoust, Tula, and Petrograd. The contracts provided that part of the armaments produced were to be shipped to Reichswehr depots in Germany. Other agreements between the Red army and the German Ministry of Defense established a school for the training of German pilots at Lipetsk in Tambov Province during 1924. The German Ministry of Defense late in 1921 had founded a company, now capitalized with the seventy-five million gold marks, to finance this collaboration. This firm, with the innocuous sounding name of Gesellschaft zur Förderung gewerblicher Unternehmungen (Association for the Promotion of Professional Undertakings), GEFU for short, had offices in Berlin and Moscow.[37]

After the major business in Berlin had been concluded, Brockdorff-Rantzau repaired to his estate in Schleswig. While he was there, a government crisis put Cuno out of office on August 13, and substituted Stresemann. The new Chancellor kept the portfolio of Foreign Minister. From that time, until his death on October 3, 1929, Stresemann remained Foreign Minister in every succeeding Cabinet. For the next five years the two most important Cabinet posts, as far as relations with Russia were concerned, were held by the same men—Stresemann in the Wilhelmstrasse, and Gessler in the Ministry of Defense in the Bendlerstrasse. Both were perfectly willing to support the Russo-German relationship which Seeckt and Brockdorff-Rantzau developed.

On the day the Cuno Cabinet fell Maltzan informed the chargé d'affaires in Moscow that a military mission including Major Tschunke and Baron von Hagen of the Chemische Werke Stolzenberg in Hamburg could be expected in Moscow on August 22. Director Hagen was going to Russia to put the finishing touches on an agreement to begin the manufacture of poison gas.

Brockdorff-Rantzau was still in Schleswig and apparently was informed by Maltzan about the new military mission. With Cuno's promise that he would be in charge of all negotiations still in mind, Brockdorff-Rantzau insisted that nothing be done in Moscow until his return. Maltzan instructed the chargé d'affaires on August 22 to inform the military, on arrival, not to enter into any binding agreements because the Ambassador had been invested with the "technical as well as the cultural direction of all negotiations."[38]

Radowitz failed in preventing Tschunke from proceeding with his assigned task. This was primarily due to the fact that the German army had established its own headquarters in Moscow, the Zentrale Moskau, or Z. Mo.,[39] which was in charge of all aspects of the secret military collaboration between the German and the Red army. Z. Mo. constituted an agency independent of the Embassy and was designed to eliminate civilian interference in army matters. There is no evidence in the documents that Brockdorff-Rantzau objected to this extradiplomatic establishment. The Count always demanded that he be informed of all deals made by the military so that he could impose the necessary political safeguards and *quid pro quos*.

Before his return to Moscow Brockdorff-Rantzau sent a long protest to the new Chancellor which was designed to get Stresemann's support in the Ambassador's continuing struggle with those in the Reichswehr who were still determined to deal directly with the Red army. The Count gave a detailed outline of the German-Russian secret military collaboration from Wirth's chancellorship to the Rosengolts mission. The Ambassador demanded an unqualified acknowledgment of his

own supremacy in all negotiations between any department of the
Soviet government and Germany. Brockdorff-Rantzau underlined his
demand by pointing to renewed evidence of military ineptness. Director von Hagen had died in a Riga Hotel on his return voyage. His
briefcase, full of secret documents, including notes about negotiations
for the establishment of the poison gas factory, had been found by the
hotel people. Fortunately, they had delivered the unopened briefcase
to the German representative in Riga.[40]

Brockdorff-Rantzau's protest had an immediate effect, because on
the eve of his departure for Moscow, September 15, the Count was
received by President Ebert in the presence of Chancellor Stresemann.
Both declared that

> they rejected all negotiations by the military authorities in Mos-
> cow and demanded that the recent actions in the armament in-
> dustry be transferred to the economic sphere exclusively.[41]

The Ambassador arrived in Moscow on September 20, and on the
following evening went to pay his respects to the Commissar for Foreign Affairs. Chicherin appeared nervous and complained about the
Count's long absence. Brockdorff-Rantzau inquired whether Chicherin
had been informed about the demands made by Cuno during the
conference with Rosengolts. Chicherin only said that he had heard
about them, but did not go into details. Brockdorff-Rantzau, because of
the instructions he had received from Ebert and Stresemann, did not
press the matter of the Rosengolts pledges. He was almost certain that
the Russians did not intend to fulfill the conditions made by Cuno.
Because of this the Ambassador advised Stresemann against imple-
menting the German promises made to Rosengolts.

After Chicherin's refusal to enter into a discussion about the Cuno-
Rosengolts conference, Brockdorff-Rantzau criticized Zinoviev's appeal
for a Red revolution in Germany, which had appeared in the KPD
daily, the *Rote Fahne*, on September 2. The Commissar assured the
Count that Zinoviev's outburst was strictly within the province of the
party. Brockdorff-Rantzau made it clear to Chicherin that it was time
to "ask whether, in the final analysis, the Soviet government or the
Communist party directed the country's policies." Brockdorff-Rantzau,
believing that the Commissar was doing his best to counteract the
chauvinistic attitudes of the Communist party, was willing to wait for
positive results from Chicherin's activities.[42]

A few days after his meeting with Chicherin, Radek visited the
Ambassador and told him that an official answer to the question he had

directed to the Commissar regarding the Rosengolts pledges would be forthcoming within a few days. Brockdorff-Rantzau's retort that his question had not been official, merely academic, highly incensed the sharp-tongued Radek. He shot back:

We are ready for military agreements, but if you only posed an academic question, you shall receive a fitting academic answer. You cannot ask of us that we bind ourselves politically with one side for the few measly millions which you offer. As far as the monopoly, which you demand for German industry, is concerned, we do not have the slightest intention of granting it; on the contrary we take everything which we can use militarily where we find it. Thus we have bought planes in France and will also accept delivery from England.

Brockdorff-Rantzau interpreted Radek's outspoken honesty and implied threat to turn toward the West as an indication that the Russian government had absolutely no intention of honoring the demands made by Chancellor Cuno. This interpretation was supported by the fact that Chicherin did not return to the Rosengolts pledges.

The Commissar's silence did not indicate an end of the military collaboration. The Germans did make the funds available; foreigners were kept away from the German-run arms factories and Tschunke continued as one of the Reichswehr representatives in Moscow. Brockdorff-Rantzau's relations with the Major went quite smoothly. But it was not until April, 1924, that the Count was satisfied that for the time being at least, all phases of military collaboration were under his personal scrutiny. During a meeting with Niedermayer, who headed a new mission to Russia under the name of Siebert, the Major made definite promises that he would refuse to work in Russia unless he would be cooperating with the Ambassador, that Ebert would be informed, and that Seeckt would submit all agreements to the Foreign Minister for expert evaluation. Finally, Niedermayer promised that all GEFU correspondence would now be sent through the German Embassy and no longer through the Foreign Commissariat.[43]

Overshadowing military collaboration were the efforts by Moscow to foment a Communist revolution in Germany through the Comintern. The Wilhelmstrasse received a report from the German envoy to Latvia which asserted that during a high-level meeting on the subject, Trotsky, Radek, who was wrongly identified as the Chairman of the Comintern, Kamenev, Rykov, and Molotov had agreed that the Russians would not interfere in Germany militarily unless such indifference would plunge Russia into a war and then under unfavorable conditions. At that point intervention would be admissible to assure the ultimate victory of the proletariat.[44]

Additional signs that the Communist leadership of Soviet Russia stood ready with advice and aid in the support of those intent on overthrowing a government with which Moscow had the friendliest relations were heralded by the arrival of Heinrich Brandler and August Thalheimer in Moscow. Both men were leading figures in the German Communist party.

On his arrival Brandler found Moscow decked out with signs and slogans in honor of the coming German revolution including one calling on Russia's youth to learn German because the German October was just around the corner.[45] As far away as Siberia newspapers informed their readers that "the fate of the German revolution is our fate, defeat of the German revolution is also our defeat."[46] These ominous rumblings were somewhat quieted by an interview which Trotsky gave to U.S. Senator William H. King and which was published by Izvestia on September 30. Trotsky had told his visitor, who was in Russia on a fact-finding tour, that Russia would only interfere in a German civil war to act against Poland or to stop German monarchists if they attempted to give the Allied Powers a mandate to intervene in the Soviet Union. He did not consider such an eventuality likely, and Russia supported Germany against the exploitations of French capitalism as much as it sympathized with the German proletariat against domestic and foreign exploitation. If Russia could safeguard the revolution in Germany without military actions, all necessary aid would be provided.[47] On September 25, the Vorwärts, official organ of the Social Democratic Party of Germany, published an article in which it was asserted that a certain Petrov, an attaché in the Russian Embassy in Berlin, had purchased machine guns and ammunition. The article went on that documentary evidence also linked Petrov to two large arms caches found on premises occupied by German Communists. The Soviet Embassy issued an immediate denial of any involvement by its personnel, but admitted that several Petrovs worked in the Embassy, and that one of these concerned himself with military matters.[48]

The man involved, despite Embassy evasions, was the military attaché Michael Petrov. Maltzan discovered that Petrov had bought weapons from a German firm, not for delivery to Russia as had been assumed, but in order to provide the KPD with an arsenal for armed insurrection. This new evidence of support for revolutionaries by accredited agents of the Soviet government led the Cabinet to demand stringent actions, particularly against Comintern agents, whatever their disguise. Maltzan, who did not want to upset the Russian government to a point where the Russians would abandon their support in international affairs, instructed Brockdorff-Rantzau to do his utmost to have Petrov recalled. If this was not done the Cabinet would insist on deportation.

Maltzan, as well as Brockdorff-Rantzau, was willing to overlook Russian trespassing in Germany's internal affairs as long as it was not done too overtly. Both men believed that such interference could be controlled, and that the German alignment with Russia was too important to be sacrificed since it presented an effective diplomatic weapon against the West.

The Petrov case generated some nervousness in Moscow. Brockdorff-Rantzau felt the case demanded "discretion as a matter of honor." Radek held a long discourse before the Count about the fact that the *Vorwärts* article had been inspired by the German Foreign Office and thus meant a change of policy. Radek even tried some blackmail by announcing that the Soviet government might be forced to announce that the weapons were part of "officially agreed upon arms deliveries from Germany to Russia." Brockdorff-Rantzau advised Maltzan to proceed cautiously but firmly, because it was quite obvious that the Russians were deeply involved.[49]

On October 6, the first official public reaction to the Petrov case appeared in *Izvestia*. According to the official organ of the Soviet government it had delayed replying to the "obviously inspired communication" in the *Vorwärts* because it had hoped that the German government would take definite actions against the accusations. "Since it had not done so it created . . . the impression that it had encouraged the campaign which has been opened against our Embassy in Berlin. Loyally upholding the terms of the Treaty of Rapallo and deeply sympathetic with the German people in these difficult times, the Soviet Government hopes that its suppositions will prove unfounded."[50]

Brockdorff-Rantzau was furious about this "impertinent article." He demanded an interview with Chicherin despite the fact that the Commissar had been sick for over two weeks with a liver complaint and was unavailable for the conduct of official business. Chicherin received the German Ambassador on October 7, and Brockdorff-Rantzau characterized the article as either a "provocation or a threat." Chicherin tried to retreat and retorted that the article in question was not official but a concession to Russian public opinion. Brockdorff-Rantzau did not think that such a course would keep him much longer in Moscow. Chicherin reminded him that the *Vorwärts* report was at least semiofficial. The Count interrupted and underlined the fact that Maltzan had already assured Krestinsky that this was not true. Chicherin let it go at that and expressed his concern that heavy industry taking advantage of the domestic situation would create a dictatorship, then make common cause with France against Russia.[51]

Chicherin's apprehensions were based on a number of developments in Germany. Passive resistance in the Ruhr had ended on September 26. Two days later, Bavaria declared a state of emergency ostensibly aimed against the Hitler-Ludendorff organizations but interpreted in Berlin as a challenge to the Republic. During the night of the twenty-eighth the Reich Cabinet declared a state of emergency for all of Germany which was not rescinded until March 31, 1924. Brockdorff-Rantzau advised Maltzan not to make the slightest concessions in the Petrov case. The Russians had to learn that Germany would not indefinitely countenance this kind of activity by accredited representatives of the USSR. He advised the Undersecretary to use this opportunity to purify the air. The Count did not think that this would remove the basic problem inherent in relations with the USSR,[52] but it would at least show Moscow that there was a limit to German patience with the gross interferences by the Comintern and the Russian Communist party. That more than words was needed to put a stop to their meddling became obvious on October 10, when the *Rote Fahne* published a letter by Stalin, in his guise as General Secretary of the Communist Party of Russia. Stalin informed the German comrades that their victory in the coming revolution would transfer the center of the world revolution from Moscow to Berlin.[53]

The continued vehement Comintern propaganda persuaded the Ministry of the Interior and some of the leading German politicians to urge that relations with the Soviet Union be terminated. The Wilhelmstrasse did not take a stand. After a long struggle, including the resignation of the first Stresemann Cabinet on October 3 and the formation of a new ministry by Stresemann, delaying actions by the Social Democrats, and attempts by the German Nationalists and the Communists to wreck the new government as well as prevent the necessary two-thirds vote, the Reichstag by a vote of 316 to 24 on October 13 gave the President special powers to deal with the national emergency. At one point during the parliamentary fencing, those around Maltzan had encouraged Stresemann to "govern without the Social Democrats and without Parliament. . . ."[54] The German army was ordered to proceed against the Communists in Saxony, where Brandler, returned from Moscow, had become head of the State Chancellery, and against

Thuringia where Communists had also legally entered the State Cabinet.[55]

These developments confronted the Russians with the dilemma, to interfere or not to interfere in Germany. Brockdorff-Rantzau lost no time at all in pointing this out to Chicherin. During a discussion on the situation the Ambassador told the Commissar that he was well aware of the fact that the Russians "wished for peace, but apparently considered the situation in Germany so critical that they wanted to be prepared for *any* eventuality, even for military assistance to the Communist movement in Germany." The Ambassador told Chicherin that Germany was not an experimental rabbit which Moscow could use for the purpose of testing its ideas for saving the world. If this continued interference did not stop, Brockdorff-Rantzau assured Chicherin, he might suddenly find "that the Moscow climate did not agree with him any more." The Count again was positive that even the contemplation of his resignation as ambassador was very painful for the Commissar.

This belief of the Count's that the threat of resignation would suffice to bring the Russians to heel recurs throughout his tenure in Moscow. It was partly due to Brockdorff-Rantzau's egocentrism and partly to his belief that Chicherin, because of their friendship, would use his influence with the rulers of Russia to secure moderation. The Count could not convince himself that Chicherin was first and foremost a Bolshevik and a gentleman only in his private relations with Brockdorff-Rantzau. The Count continued to flatter himself with the belief that Chicherin would somehow be able to control the demands of the party and of the Comintern and prevent interference with normal diplomatic relations, just because he had the Count's support. Brockdorff-Rantzau acting on this assumption requested permission from Stresemann to threaten the Soviet government with a break of diplomatic relations at his own discretion. Brockdorff-Rantzau was convinced that this course of action would strengthen the Narkomindel "which was honestly trying to keep up appearances and which has in recent days stood in ever sharper conflict with the completely chauvinistic party leadership."

The party certainly had a heyday with the events in Saxony. In a lead article in *Pravda*, Zinoviev attacked Ebert as a Menshevik "who constantly pulled the rope tighter around the neck of the Saxon proletariat." In Zinoviev's words the President was taking the last crust of bread from the workers and then, for full measure, sending soldiers to shoot them in the back. Brockdorff-Rantzau complained first to Litvinov (Chicherin was sick once again), and then continued his stringent denunciations with the ailing Commissar. He told Chicherin that in the face of the insolent attack on Ebert he really had little left to do in Moscow. The Russian government could look around for "a mailman or porter for the transaction of unavoidable contacts." The attacks on the President were a "vulgarity" and a "political stupidity" which would have unpleasant consequences for Russia. Chicherin did not reply to the innuendo but conveyed his official regrets for the article.[56]

Brockdorff-Rantzau assured Stresemann, on October 26, that Chicherin was sincerely interested in the development of German-Russian relations because this course was the only reasonable one to take. Chicherin had promised to speak to his colleagues in the party about the Count's demand for a realistic working arrangement. Brockdorff-Rantzau then threatened Stresemann with his resignation unless something definite was done in Berlin to settle the Petrov affair.[57]

The Foreign Office had inserted a communiqué in the *Vorwärts* which stated that the involvement of Petrov had not been verified. However, the Soviet Embassy had declared that a German employee had been involved in the arms deal. He had disappeared and the Embassy had dismissed him. All employees had been strenuously warned against any future private deals at the expense of the Soviet representation. Brockdorff-Rantzau refused to let the matter rest. He considered the communiqué insufficient. With characteristic perseverance he tried to get to the bottom of the case. On November 29, he found out that Petrov had been a French navy officer. This was confirmed by Krestinsky to Maltzan. The Count wanted the case reopened and used to squelch the interference of the Comintern in Germany's domestic affairs. The worst of the matter was the fact, admitted by Colonel Hasse, that Petrov had been taken into the deepest confidence by the military. Because of the Count's insistence the Wilhelmstrasse, which had not insisted on Petrov's removal after the initial instruction to Brockdorff-Rantzau, objected to the continued employment of Petrov in the Soviet Embassy and urged that he be dismissed and sent out of Germany as quietly as possible. Krestinsky agreed that Petrov would be relieved of duty because the military attaché no longer had the confidence of the German government. Krestinsky made it clear, however, that Petrov's involvement in the arms deals had not been proven and that reasonable doubts still existed. Petrov's removal satisfied Brockdorff-Rantzau and he considered the case closed by the end of January, 1924.[58]

By October 26, Brockdorff-Rantzau thought that relations with Moscow had reached a point where an OGPU raid on the Embassy might become possible. He intended to ship some papers to Germany for safekeeping. The Russians, as Chicherin had confided to him, expected an attack on their Berlin Embassy by chauvinistic (*völkische*) groups. Brockdorff-Rantzau insisted that he be granted permission to return to Berlin.[59]

Maltzan informed the Ambassador that Stresemann and Ebert had decided that even a short absence of the Count from Moscow was not advisable. On orders from the Chancellor, Maltzan had called Krestinsky to the Foreign Office and had told him in the most solemn terms, in the presence of the Director of the Eastern Department, Dr. Erich Wallroth, and Hauschild, that the continued pro-Communist propaganda was untenable. He had also informed Krestinsky that the recall of the German Ambassador was "unavoidable" if these attacks continued. The Russian Ambassador had become very dejected and promised to use his influence in Moscow.[60]

In the meantime the German October Revolution, of which so much had been expected in Moscow, had ended in a great fiasco. A Communist rising, which had started in Hamburg on October 22, had ended in complete disaster. The Reichswehr occupied Dresden, the capital of Saxony, on October 23, ending Brandler's tenure in the State Chancellery. Thuringia was in the process of being occupied. It was obvious that the KPD, even with Comintern advice, was still unequal to the task of overthrowing the Weimar Republic. The disappointment among the rulers of the Soviet Union was great, but it was particularly so in Petrograd where Zinoviev headed the party organization. It was not until November 23, however, that he made a half-hearted acknowledgment in *Pravda* that the revolution had failed, but he warned that it would be resurrected at another time.[61]

Hilger, who had joined the Moscow Embassy as Counselor of Legation in January, and who had excellent lines of communication in Moscow, was certain that Trotsky's "peace under any conditions" was opposed by Stalin. Until October 25, there had been great optimism about the success of the KPD in Germany. This mood had changed by the twenty-seventh.[62] Victor Kopp, now Director of the Narkomindel's department for the Baltic States and Poland, had been on a trip to the capitals in his bailiwick to make sure all governments understood that the Russians intended them to remain neutral should Moscow find it necessary to intervene in Germany to protect a Communist government.[63] Brockdorff-Rantzau was determined to utilize to the utmost possibility the internal dissension created by the disaster in Germany in the highest echelons of the Communist Party in Russia. Maltzan's unequivocal threat that the Ambassador would be recalled unless propaganda against Germany ceased had already been effective. The Count knew that Krestinsky had great influence in the party, and it was apparently due to Krestinsky's intercession that *Pravda* had begun to take a more conciliatory tone toward Germany. The failures of the Communists in Saxony and Hamburg, the Count was certain, would strengthen the "circumspect" policies of the Narkomindel.

In the meantime, unfortunately, the "agitators" of the party, Zinoviev, Bukharin, and Stalin, had the upper hand, although the latter stayed in the background. "It will simply come down to a trial of strength between the party leadership and the Soviet government, and I intend, if possible, to utilize the differences which have clearly come to light to bring about a split."[64] This attempt at *divide et impera* indicates that the Count assumed that there was a good chance, during these October days, to exploit the differences between the party and the government of the Soviet Union. A man of keen powers of intellect and observation, sharpened by thirty years in the foreign service, Brockdorff-Rantzau certainly did not wish for more then a chance to end party interference in the pursuit of old-fashioned diplomatic relations. This is, of course, where the Count's wishes and the *de facto* situation did not match exactly. Brockdorff-Rantzau was therefore delighted to receive Chicherin's assurances during the evening of November 2, that the Soviet "government had taken energetic measures against the press attacks which occurred during the recent past."[65]

The Count's belief that he could exploit the divergence between the party and the Narkomindel was strengthened by a letter from Schlesinger, whom he considered an expert on Soviet conditions, in which his correspondent underlined the importance he attached to a remark Kopp had made to him in Warsaw. Kopp had let it be known that Brockdorff-Rantzau's "position at any given time on particular problems is of decisive importance to the Russians." Unfortunately, to Schlesinger's way of thinking, the same was not true in Germany where "the domestic situation daily brought definite proof that the leading Germans would rather let themselves be driven into a policy of catastrophe, than to exercise such a policy themselves." Schlesinger continued that he would not be surprised if, due to the political attitude of most Germans and the lack of determined leadership, the political situation would become completely mired. The SPD members of the Cabinet had resigned; there was no other course, because of the scandalous interference by the government in the affairs of Saxony. It was extremely doubtful whether Stresemann could continue as chancellor. It looked as if he would move aside for a rightist from the Deutschnationale Volkspartei. This, in Schlesinger's opinion, would clear the way for the "transition to a legal dictatorship of the right." Stresemann, if he wanted to, could instead take the wind out of the extremists' sails and establish a dictatorship run by a directorate lawfully established by presidential initiative.

Brockdorff-Rantzau was pleased to note that Schlesinger agreed with him on his evaluation of the way difficult situations were handled by German politicians. He agreed that the solution Schlesinger proposed was the only correct one for the problem confronting Stresemann's government. Brockdorff-Rantzau recalled the report he had prepared in 1921 in which he had written that "to carry on an active policy of catastrophe is a crime; but to let oneself passively be driven into a policy of catastrophe is twice a crime, because it is at the same time a stupidity."[66]

Maltzan held views similar to those of Schlesinger on the internal situation in Germany. He wrote to the Ambassador that the Deutschnationale Volkspartei was demanding a dictatorship, but no one was in sight for the job of dictator. He had advised Ebert to dissolve the Reichstag if it should prove impossible to form a new cabinet, then to put off new elections as long as possible and leave Stresemann at the helm. In Bavaria the Reichswehr and the organizations headed by Hitler and Ehrhardt were combining to cleanse Saxony and Thuringia of Marxism, take Berlin, and drive all the Jews out of Germany. These rightist machinations boded ill for the hard-won gains in foreign relations. German missions abroad reported adverse effects of these nationalistic excesses. The KPD and the SPD were apparently powerless in the face of these stratagems.

On November 9, Hitler felt that the time had come to start his march to power. Maltzan reported to Brockdorff-Rantzau that the disaster in which this "tragi-comedy" had ended signified a decline of the danger posed by Hitler, at least for the time being. Maltzan felt sorry for Ludendorff because he had let himself be duped by a "scene-painter [Dekorationsmaler]." Brockdorff-Rantzau did not react to the Hitler-Ludendorff Putsch. He did think, however, that the situation in Germany demanded his presence in Berlin. Schlesinger agreed that the situation was very serious. He wrote that

> parliamentarianism to which the hopes of the people were tied has collapsed and buried them. What kind of political life will come forth from these ruins, I do not venture to predict.[67]

Stresemann wrote to Brockdorff-Rantzau that the French militarists were attempting to incorporate the Ruhr into their arsenal as protection against Germany. Since they were afraid of a close relationship between Germany and Russia, they were going to do everything in their power to entice Russia into their own camp. Conditions in Germany were rather depressing and to make matters worse the KPD was being financed by Russian gold. This placed quite a strain on good relations with the Soviet Union. But he was "in general agreement with your attitude to the Russians. . . ." Stresemann exhorted the Ambassador not to be a mere diplomatist like Chicherin, "but a German Count whose determination, energy and character has placed him in a position to represent his country where a strong personality was never more needed than at present."[68]

In Stresemann's acknowledgment Brockdorff-Rantzau found confirmation that his presence in Russia was indispensable for the continuation of good relations between Germany and Russia. He refused to leave Moscow, despite Maltzan's repeated urgings to return to Germany to visit his eighty-year-old mother who was seriously ill. He continued to advise the Wilhelmstrasse to make *tabula rasa* about interference of the Soviet government in the affairs of Germany even if the Russians continued to hide behind the smoke screen provided by the Comintern. Maltzan told Krestinsky, when the latter came to bid farewell, before his regular year-end return to Moscow, that something positive had to be done, and quickly, to rectify the situation. Krestinsky, as usual, insisted that the Executive Committee of the Comintern was not a branch of the Soviet government but added—and Maltzan found this extremely significant in view of the mechanical excuse just proffered—that the Executive Committee could at times be "insubordinate." Maltzan immediately took advantage of the slip and remarked that he for one was pleased to hear this; it made it unnecessary to grant the members of the Executive Committee the prerogatives reserved for governmental officials if, after all, they were private individuals. Krestinsky had nothing to say to that.

Maltzan informed Brockdorff-Rantzau of the annoying fact that the Ministry of the Interior had evidence in its files that Radek was in Germany illegally trying to get the Central Committee of the KPD to shake off its stupor and act. The Ambassador was to protest in the strongest way possible about this renewed interference in German affairs.[69]

On December 3, the Ambassador protested to Chicherin as instructed about the provocation by Radek. Matters could not much longer continue along these lines, he emphasized. The Russian government had to divorce itself unequivocally from the Executive Committee of the Comintern. Now more was needed than mere assurances by the Commissar for Foreign Affairs to the effect that his government did not approve of the Comintern's activities. Brockdorff-Rantzau could assure him that German-Russian relations would definitely suffer and be adversely affected unless the Soviet government formally and sharply drew a dividing line between itself and the Executive Committee of the Comintern.

Chicherin mumbled that it was a "coincidence" that the seat of the Comintern was in Moscow. Nobody had ever complained to the King of the Belgians while the Second International sat in Brussels. Brockdorff-Rantzau was unwilling to let Chicherin off without a few well-placed barbs. He found it quite interesting, said the Count, "that the final aim of the Soviet government and of the Third International, world revolution, accidentally coincided." It was equally quaint that the members of the Executive Committee were usually Russian citizens. Unless the Soviet government overtly divorced itself from the Comintern nobody would believe that the government and the Comintern did not work hand in glove. Chicherin made no reply to this unvarnished presentation of the facts.

Brockdorff-Rantzau impressed upon Chicherin that the continuation of Comintern activities in Germany could easily lead to a discontinuation of cooperation. Should the friends of the Soviet Union become alienated, the crusade of the Entente, with German participation, could materialize.

This sally resulted in Chicherin's informing of Brockdorff-Rantzau four days later that he would discuss ways and means to control Comintern activities in Germany with Krestinsky. The Count, in an effort to aid Chicherin, asked the Wilhelmstrasse to place pressures on the Russian chargé d'affaires, and inform him in definite language that a break of diplomatic relations was entirely possible unless the Soviet government formally divorced itself from the Executive Committee of the Comintern.[70]

Zinoviev, addressing the Congress of Metalworkers in Petrograd declared that "the Russian proletariat did not support the German proletariat with arms because such aid was not only unsuitable but would be detrimental." Besides, while the German soil had been prepared the German workers lacked "fighting experience."[71] The retreat of the Comintern Executive, initiated in November, continued. Obviously it was no longer suited to the purposes of the Russian leaders to beat a dead horse. The German proletariat and the leadership of the KPD were flayed as scapegoats for the monumental miscalculation the group around Zinoviev had made. In time the failure of the German revolution was to devour those who had attempted to pull the strings of what had been marionettes and not much more.

Brockdorff-Rantzau kept up diplomatic pressure to gain an open declaration by the Soviet government that the Comintern would be controlled. The Ambassador gave a formal dinner to which Litvinov, Krestinsky, Krassin, Sabanin, and the Director of the Soviet State Bank, Scheinmann, were invited. Neither Litvinov nor Krestinsky used the opportunity presented by the informal talk after dinner to make a statement to Brockdorff-Rantzau. The Ambassador was quite disappointed.

On December 10, Brockdorff-Rantzau had an extremely pointed discussion with Chicherin. During the exchange, which lasted from midnight until 1:30 A.M., the two went over the whole matter of Comintern interference in Germany in detail once again. Chicherin invited the Ambassador to bring some specially designated members of the Embassy to lunch later in the day. After lunch a long discussion took place between Brockdorff-Rantzau, Chicherin, and Radek, with all the members of the *Kollegium* of the Foreign Commissariat, as well as Krestinsky, present. From the German Embassy, Counselor of Embassy Radowitz, Counselor of Legation Graap, Hilger, and Attaché Hencke were in attendance. Brockdorff-Rantzau demanded a declaration by the Soviet government that it had no sympathy with the policies of the Third International. Certainly the open attempt to prepare a revolution in Germany was not at all conducive to the continuation of normal diplomatic relations. The KPD was not able to rule Germany and would only deliver it to the "beastly French [*Bestien von Franzosen*]."

Radek interjected that the KPD still had to show whether it could govern; the bourgeois government certainly had shown itself incapable. There was absolutely no reason for a formal declaration since there was quite definitely no proof that official aid had been given by the Soviet government. The policies of the Comintern and those of the Soviet government had to be considered separately. The Comintern would not let the government tell it what to do. To this Brockdorff-Rantzau retorted that it was not a question of the government giving instructions to the Comintern. All he wanted was a government declaration that it removed itself from the policies of the Comintern.

Chicherin at this point got into the exchange with his remarks of December 3 about Leopold, Brussels, and the Second International. Brockdorff-Rantzau handled the charge with the same counterarguments he had used before. He reminded Chicherin that in May of 1923 the English government had been assured that the Soviet government did not identify itself with the Third International. Now he had been informed that one of the leaders of the KPD, Ruth Fischer, had written to Zinoviev that Radek had been in Berlin during October. Radek called the letters forgeries based on a ninety-page report in the hands of the Berlin police. Brockdorff-Rantzau said that he did not accept the forgeries but had been instructed to protest against interference in Germany. Furthermore, it was certainly straining German-Russian relations to the utmost when Petrov, a former French officer, was made the military attaché in the Soviet Embassy in Berlin. That fact had made his involvement in the arms procurement especially painful. Radek pointed out that Petrov's involvement had never been proven. In fact, on November 7, during the celebration of the Revolution at the Embassy, General Hasse had stated openly that it had been a "dastardly act [*Schweinerei*]" to cast suspicions on Petrov. The latter, although his background was known to them, had the confidence of the Ministry of Defense. Major Niedermayer had paid Petrov a very cordial visit, when the latter lay ill, while the case was still pending. Petrov's recall had not been due to any proofs but because he was *persona non grata.* Chicherin now broke into the exchange with the remark that the Ambassador did not know the history of the Hohenzollern who used foreigners and dealt with the enemies of the Reich. Brockdorff-Rantzau replied acidly that the fact that Germany had profited from its history could be seen in the cooperation with the "revolutionary Soviet government." After all, Germany and Russia depended on each other. Radek, most probably for reasons other than the Ambassador's, agreed.

Brockdorff-Rantzau declared with the greatest, most deliberate emphasis that now was the time to "wipe the slate clean or there would be absolutely no purpose whatsoever in continuing cooperation." The talk with Radek had been a step in the right direction because he could only continue at his post "when he had influence in Berlin and was trusted in Moscow." Radek expressed his conviction that the Soviet government could work splendidly even with a reactionary German government. General von Seeckt had put it correctly by declaring that one had to cut the throats of the German Communists but could cooperate with the Soviet government.

The discussion ended with Chicherin's remark that he shared Radek's view that the Comintern and the Soviet government were separate entities. This declaration could be used officially. Brockdorff-Rantzau felt that the exchange had been worth-while because Chicherin, by bringing Radek into it, drew a line of demarcation between the government and the Comintern. Furthermore, the energetic action was a good lesson to those who held the reins of power in Russia.

In order to press the lesson home Brockdorff-Rantzau requested that Litvinov arrange an appointment with Trotsky. During the evening of December 14, the Ambassador had an hour-long, very serious and very frank talk with the Commissar for War, during which he repeated the points made during the confrontation with Radek. The Count inquired of Trotsky whether the rumors about an immediate *de jure* recognition of France had any justification. Trotsky replied that there was not even a particle of truth in these allegations, that in fact, the opposite was closer to reality. He told Brockdorff-Rantzau in the greatest secrecy that all orders placed in France would be turned over to Germany and that the Soviet press would launch a new campaign against the French. After the Ambassador took his leave inquiry at the Narkomindel revealed that Trotsky had informed Litvinov about the content of the talk and the Deputy Commissar stated that he agreed with the substance of the remarks made by Trotsky.[72]

The Soviet government decided that it could not afford to continue the strained relations. The statement demanded by Brockdorff-Rantzau was not a heavy price to pay for his continued labors in the Russian wasteland. The Wilhelmstrasse would be able to point to the declaration in defense of its Eastern policy and the support of Maltzan would be assured. Thus on January 9, 1924, Chicherin handed a note to Brockdorff-Rantzau in which the Soviet government pledged that it would take the most stringent measures against the Comintern agents and against any interference in Germany's domestic affairs by members of its embassy in Berlin. Brockdorff-Rantzau considered the note a weapon which could be used to force the Russian government to disavow the Comintern completely.[73] The Ambassador thought he saw a beginning of the disavowal in the severe reprimands administered to Radek during the Thirteenth Party Congress for his support of the "right wing" of the KPD and for disregarding the orders of the party's Central Committee. A scant three months later Brockdorff-Rantzau had to admit that it "could not be claimed as an absolute truth that the Soviet government could not get its way with the Comintern and the Russian party, but neither could the opposite view be substantiated. The truth lay somewhere in the middle." Any government which wanted to maintain relations with the Soviet Union was forced to recognize the duality of Russian politics, especially the extensive influence the party exerted on all policies pursued by the government.[74]

But even this knowledge did not affect Brockdorff-Rantzau's conviction that Germany's future depended on avoiding the mistakes which had made Russia an enemy in 1914. He did not minimize the negative, detrimental, and gravely disturbing effect which the Comintern's policies had on German-Russian relations. On the positive side a number of important political and economic gains had been achieved during 1923. While these were only beginnings they should not be jeopardized by orienting German policy toward the West. Nothing could be gained from such a change of course.

The Russian government would still insist that the Comintern was independent; the flow of agents and money from Moscow to Germany would not cease. If the recent Comintern attempts at revolution in Germany would lead to a break, the Ambassador's moderating influence over the Russians would be removed. The Communist regime would continue to rule the USSR because the Russian people had been used to brutal rulers for centuries, and the only alternative to Red rule was White terror. Brockdorff-Rantzau was convinced that the relationship with Russia gave Germany the power to bargain in international affairs. An open break would only benefit the Reich's enemies because it would drive Russia into the waiting arms of France. Brockdorff-Rantzau, always the realist, believed that

> anyone who in everyday life talks about gratitude and honestly believes in it, belongs in the pulpit, and he who counts on gratitude in politics belongs in an insane asylum. Something else is the instinctive feeling of belonging together and the community of interest of two peoples and the memory for their leaders which recognized this in good time.[75]

As a *Realpolitiker* Brockdorff-Rantzau was willing to deal with the Russians despite repeated and flagrant attempts by Moscow to overthrow the legally established government of Germany. He was obsessed with the idea that Germany's regeneration depended on her close relationship with Russia. Brockdorff-Rantzau's belief that he had the ability to exert considerable control over the Moscow dictators was shared by Maltzan.[76]

The Soviet Union had used Germany's diplomatic recognition as a *point d'appui* and her territory as a *place d'armes* for revolution. Russia's isolation was coming to an end. Great Britain's Labor government recognized the USSR on February 1, 1924, and Mussolini's Fascists followed suit six days later. During the October Days of 1923 the Soviet Union, in need of Germany's economic assistance, had thought that a successful Communist revolution in Germany would bring that country's resources at one blow to the proletarian state. In 1923, the military collaboration, considered necessary to the development of a modern armed force, was a trump in the hands of the Soviet leaders. There was no real guarantee that they would not reveal its existence, a possibility much dreaded by Brockdorff-Rantzau, Maltzan, and Stresemann. Twist or turn as they might the two countries were, for better or for worse, tied to each other. It all came pretty close to Brockdorff-

Rantzau's community of fate. Thus, throughout this crisis of democracy in the Weimar Republic Moscow was caught between the need for German economic aid and military cooperation and a desire to bring Germany into the Communist camp.

Germany in its turn, its economy in disarray, unemployment increasing, unrest of revolutionary proportions, occupation of its major industrial area, and suffering from runaway inflation, could ill afford to lose the Russian market.

Inquiry into the economic relations with the USSR by the Wilhelmstrasse revealed that there had been a steady and significant increase in the purchases made by the Russians in Germany. In 1920 the total purchases had amounted to 6.5 million gold rubles, in 1921 the amount had risen by an additional 5 million, while in 1922 the purchases had amounted to 30.25 million gold rubles. During the first nine months of 1923, propaganda and active preparation of revolution notwithstanding, the Russians had already placed orders for 24.5 million gold rubles. During the month of the German October 197 orders had been placed directly from Moscow amounting to 10 million gold rubles and an additional 797 orders coming to a total of 7.5 million gold rubles had been parceled out by the Soviet Trade Delegation in Berlin.[77]

If Germany could ill afford to lose Russian markets she could even less afford to do without Russian friendship, tainted and dangerous though it was, because it gave the Wilhelmstrasse operational freedom and the possibility of balancing the West against the East by adroit and subtle hints about the consequences which a complete alignment of Germany with the Bolsheviks held for the West. Given the prevailing *cordon sanitaire* mentality of France, coupled with a fear of German resurgence—possibly *à la* 1814, worse like 1870, or still more catastrophic like the blows of 1914–1918—of a Bolshevik army on the Rhine, and the preoccupation of the British in areas outside Europe, the Germans were in a rather good bargaining position. Maltzan, Brockdorff-Rantzau, and the other "Easterners" at the Foreign Office were unwilling to sacrifice the maneuverability they had achieved.

The good relations with Moscow which Brockdorff-Rantzau and Maltzan pursued with such consistent devotion were exposed to a most excruciating strain by an incident which started on May 3, 1924 in Berlin and which brought German-Russian relations to the breaking point before it was finally resolved almost three months later.

III

The Bozenhardt Incident

Early in the morning of May 3, 1924, the officers Grüner and Kässer of the Würtemburg Criminal Police arrived at the Anhalter Railroad Station in Berlin. In their custody was a German Communist, Johannes Bozenhardt. They were supposed to deliver Bozenhardt to Stargard, a town about twenty-three miles southeast of Stettin. The connecting train at the Stettiner Railroad Station had departed by the time the officers and their prisoner reached the station. According to Grüner and Kässer's subsequent testimony they asked their prisoner, who was well acquainted with Berlin, whether he knew of a place where they could get some good breakfast. Bozenhardt led them to the headquarters of the Soviet Trade Delegation in the Lindenstrasse, pretending that it was a restaurant. The trio entered the building about 10:15 A.M. Bozenhardt yelled out that he was a Communist under arrest for treason. He bolted and the detectives were stopped from pursuing the escapee by employees of the Trade Delegation who took them into the "Director's room" and locked them in. Only after they had written down their names were they allowed to leave the building. The officers went to the Berlin police headquarters to ask for aid. In the meantime Bozenhardt was spirited out a side door by another German employee who hid him in his apartment. Both were arrested by the Berlin Political Police on May 16.[1]

The lackadaisical attitude of the two officers is difficult to understand in view of the background of their prisoner and his alleged crime. Bozenhardt, a railroad engineer, became the chairman of the KPD in Parchim in 1921 and was elected Town Councilman. He lost that position in July of 1923. Without a job during those bad days he turned to Wilhelm Pieck, member of the Prussian Diet, who was the "manager" of the Berlin headquarters of the KPD, to ask him for support in getting a job on the railroads in Russia. Pieck advised against such a step and got him instead a position with the Soviet

87

Trade Delegation in Berlin. Bozenhardt left his family in Parchim and moved to Berlin at a salary of "five to six hundred gold marks" a month, a fabulous sum in July of 1923, the more so since the salary was paid to him in U.S. dollars. In October or early November of 1923 Bozenhardt was ordered by Pieck to give up the job in the Trade Delegation and organize the railroaders along the Bavarian border so that they could be used to stop rightist invasion from Bavaria. By the middle of December Bozenhardt had a quarrel with one of the clandestine Russian directors of his activities and demanded to be returned to his job with the Trade Delegation. He was re-employed on January 15, 1924. The Reichstag was dissolved on March 13 and a new election set for May 4. Four weeks before that date Bozenhardt was granted a paid furlough so that he could participate in the KPD campaign for Reichstag seats. He was arrested in Würtemberg during the night of May 1 on a charge of attempted high treason and violation of the law against the possession of explosives. The latter charge stemmed from his alleged possession of dynamite-filled coal and *Briketts* during his activities in 1923. The coal was to be placed among the fuel for locomotives. Bozenhardt was therefore no ordinary criminal simply taken through Berlin from one station to another; he was under arrest for attempted high treason.[2]

About two hours after Grüner and Kässer had made their report to the Berlin police about Bozenhardt's escape, the Chief of the Berlin Political Police, Regierungsdirektor Weiss, ordered a full-fledged assault by about two hundred policemen on the Soviet Trade Mission. After the large building was surrounded, seventy-five officers and men of the Political Police entered the premises and started a very thorough search.

The Soviet Embassy telephoned the German Foreign Office at 1:25 P.M. informing them that the Trade Mission was being searched by the police. Half an hour later Ambassador Krestinsky was received by Foreign Minister Stresemann. On Krestinsky's insistence Stresemann telephoned the Prussian Ministry of the Interior to request a cessation of the search and the immediate withdrawal of the police. Stresemann also told the Ambassador that the building was not extraterritorial. Krestinsky left the Wilhelmstrasse after a fifty-minute session with the Foreign Minister.

It was, of course, absolutely correct that the building occupied by the Trade Delegation was not extraterritorial. The agreement of May 6, 1921, had provided diplomatic immunity only for the chairman and seven members of the Delegation. Article 2 expressly stated, however, that house searches could take place only if extraordinary circumstances warranted them, and only after the Foreign Office had been informed in advance. The Wilhelmstrasse had so informed the Prussian Ministry of the Interior on August 8, 1923, and the Reichs Ministry of the Interior on February 16, 1924, on their respective inquiries.[3]

Ten minutes after Krestinsky had left the Wilhelmstrasse the Embassy called again to tell the Foreign Office that the search was being continued. Thereupon the Wilhelmstrasse contacted the Prussian Ministry of the Interior for the second time requesting that the police be withdrawn. Consul Druffel was sent by the Wilhelmstrasse to the Trade Delegation. It was not until 4:15 P.M. that the Consul and the Counsellor of the Russian Embassy determined that the search had ceased. Druffel found that several desks had been broken into and the Russians complained that the extraterritoriality of some employees had been violated.

The Prussian Ministry of the Interior informed the Wilhelmstrasse that violations of German interests through employees of the Delegation, who had aided Bozenhardt to escape, had necessitated the investigation. At 4:00 P.M., the Russian Embassy tried to reach Stresemann by telephone, but since the Minister was out they were asked to call back at 5:00 P.M. They did not do so; instead they sent a very strongly worded communiqué to the Wolffs Telegraph Bureau (WTB) for publication in the German press.

On May 3 the Soviet Embassy made no further attempts to lodge an official complaint or to discuss the case with the Foreign Office. Because of the complaint by the Prussian Ministry of the Interior a *Verbalnote* was sent to the Soviet Embassy on May 3. The note stated that the deposition made by the two Würtemberg policemen, which was appended, made it clear that the actions by employees of the Trade Delegation constituted a severe breach of German laws. A German prisoner had been aided in his escape and two officers had been illegally detained. This behavior led the police to surround the building and search the premises for the escapee. Five employees who had participated in the action against the officers were arrested; in addition two more were taken into custody during the search because they resisted and abused the police official conducting the search. One member of the Trade Delegation had been removed from the building on suspicion of holding a forged diplomatic passport. The Foreign Office underlined the fact that the Trade Delegation building did not have diplomatic immunity, and that the matter was now in the hands of the German law enforcement agencies.[4]

The German *Verbalnote* was published in the morning papers, on May 4, a Sunday. The Wilhelmstrasse also protested against attacks made by the Russians in the semiofficial communiqué transmitted by them to the Wolffs Telegraph Bureau for publication. In it the Embassy had charged that the Germans were the first to publicize the incident in the *Acht Uhr Abendblatt*. The German Foreign Office took exception to this charge, pointing out that it was a blatant subterfuge since it was plainly evident that the account was a journalist's work and had no possible official standing.

Ambassador Krestinsky ordered the Trade Delegation closed. On May 4 he sent two notes to Stresemann. In the first he insisted that the Trade Delegation was extraterritorial according to the sense of the May 21 agreement, and registered specific complaints about the police raid. Krestinsky made it clear that the extraterritoriality of members had been violated; he objected to the slowness with which the Delegation building had been vacated, and protested against the search of desks, as well as against the maltreatment and arrest of employees. Krestinsky demanded the immediate release of all those arrested.

The second Russian note, in reply to the *Verbalnote* of May 3, was cast in very strong language. Krestinsky expressed the view that the report of the Würtemberg detectives was not believable. Why, asked Krestinsky, had they not taken Bozenhardt to the nearest police station? How had they gotten into the Lindenstrasse on their way from the Anhalter to the Stettiner Bahnhof, and finally how could they, even for a moment, have mistaken the clearly marked Trade Delegation for a place where they could get something to eat? The note also contained thinly disguised hints that the incident had been provoked to harass the USSR by elements hostile to it.

The German reply to this note was forwarded on May 5, 1924. It defended the Würtemberg officials and rejected the hints about their motives. It reiterated willingness to clarify the divergence between the Russian account and the police report. The note again rejected the assertion that the Trade Delegation building was extraterritorial.

In Moscow Foreign Commissar Chicherin told Brockdorff-Rantzau that the raid was evidence of a complete change of Germany's policy toward Russia, and that it really constituted a change of alignment.[5] To emphasize the seriousness of the affair the whole Soviet government met in conference. Newspapers reported on May 5 that Krestinsky had been called home for an oral report. The Soviet Embassy made no attempts to discuss the incident. Hauschild therefore requested a talk with Bratman-Brodovsky, the chargé d'affaires, on May 6. On the excuse that Bratman-Brodovsky was too busy, the discussion did not take place.

During a conference of representatives of the Wilhelmstrasse with members of the Prussian Ministry of the Interior, it was officially admitted that "encroachments against extraterritorial persons had in fact taken place." Therefore, the German Embassy in Moscow was informed on May 7 that the Foreign Office was assuming responsibility for acts committed in violation of extraterritoriality. It offered to submit the incident to a mixed arbitration commission for settlement. Stresemann, in a personal telegram, assured Brockdorff-Rantzau that the Russian allegation that the raid indicated a change of policy was not true. He could underline this by telling Chicherin that the pamphlets containing propaganda designed to subvert members of the Reichswehr and the police would not be released to the German press. The Russians could show their own good will by accepting the arbitration proposal.

Maltzan sent a detailed account about the origins of the incident to Brockdorff-Rantzau. In his account Maltzan carefully placed blame on both the German police and the Russians. The Russians were quite concerned about the pamphlets in the hands of the German Foreign Office. They had even threatened to reveal the secret military collaboration if any of the material was published. Maltzan intimated to Brockdorff-Rantzau that the pamphlets would be kept on ice for use in future contingencies. Krestinsky had made an international incident out of the search. Maltzan maintained that the police action was unfortunate not because of the search of the "nonextraterritorial Trade Delegation" but because neither the Prussian Ministry of the Interior nor the Foreign Office was informed beforehand. It was also unfortunate that the police continued the search despite a request by the Wilhelmstrasse to stop the action.

Maltzan assured Brockdorff-Rantzau that he would try to convince Stresemann to make a qualified explanation to Bratman-Brodovsky as the Ambassador had advised on May 5. Maltzan thought the arbitration commission one possible way to resolve the case. However, he did not like having a "family quarrel turned over to a foreign committee. [He] preferred to have such marital discords settled in private."[6]

Brockdorff-Rantzau took the whole incident as a personal insult. He did not quite believe that the search had taken place without consultation of the Foreign Office and the "top political leadership." He wrote to his brother Ernst that the raid was and remains a colossal political mess [*Schweinerei*] and a *vulgar* lack of consideration for me. I can not become any plainer than I have been. But where this perfidy will end is not in the least discernible. . . .[7]

Once again the Count was convinced that he had the only right solution to the problem. He wanted the Wilhelmstrasse to be reasonable and resolve the incident as quickly as possible. Brockdorff-Rantzau considered the new rulers of Russia as *parvenu* and therefore extremely touchy about honor and dignity.

Brockdorff-Rantzau was sure that the "*Schwabenstreich*" (tomfoolery) would have the most unpleasant repercussions. The Russians, certain that this meant a new orientation of German foreign policy, would themselves look for a new alignment. Chicherin was extremely nervous because he seemed to think that the incident would cost him his "neck." His resignation would be a severe blow for German relations with Russia. The Count considered the "tomfoolery in the Lindenstrasse" unforgivable and an affront to the Russians unless a change of policy toward Russia was definitely contemplated. Since this was not the case, as Stresemann had made clear, it would be best to invite Krestinsky to the Wilhelmstrasse, depite his irritating behavior. After all, the Russians were the injured party and nothing would be gained by losing direct contact with Krestinsky who was an important member of the Communist Party. Brockdorff-Rantzau agreed that the arbitration commission was one possible way to forestall a break in relations.

Brockdorff-Rantzau's advice could not be followed. The Soviet Ambassador had departed on May 7. His return to Moscow had been announced in a most provocative style making it very difficult for the Wilhelmstrasse to follow a conciliatory course.[8] Before leaving, Krestinsky had closed the branches of the Trade Delegation in Hamburg and Leipzig and postponed the opening of another in Königsberg. The Soviet government also canceled plans to exhibit at the Leipzig and Cologne fairs. The situation had reached a point where only a speedy resolution of the incident would prevent a further deterioration in relations.

On May 10, Stresemann received Bratman-Brodovsky and reiterated his willingness to settle the incident and face the consequences if it could be proven that the rights of Russian diplomats had been violated. On the following day Brockdorff-Rantzau, according to instructions, proposed to Litvinov a mixed arbitration commission for the settlement of the incident. The Deputy Commissar rejected this proposal. He agreed that the final decision on the extraterritoriality of the entire Trade Delegation building could remain outside the discussion of the incident. However, should no immediate "expression of regret about the police action" be forthcoming, the Soviet government would be forced to present demands.

Two days later the Foreign Office transmitted a note to the Russian chargé d'affaires in Berlin expressing regrets about any violation of extraterritoriality. The note made the point that the police action had been prompted by the escape of a German traitor into the Trade Delegation. The Wilhelmstrasse again expressed its willingness to accept the consequences if German guilt was proven, but expected Russian reciprocity in similar cases. The Russians were advised that the propaganda of the Comintern could influence German employees of the Delegation and thus arouse the suspicions of the police.

The situation continued to deteriorate. On May 11 the Russians hinted that Bozenhardt was a police *agent provocateur*, and that the provocation was the idea of the German Ministry of the Interior. In response the German press published the fact that Bozenhardt was originally arrested as a traitor. The situation was further aggravated by mass demonstrations of workers in Russia, one taking place near the embassy in Moscow on May 11. The milling crowds were held in check by regular and mounted police.[9] Obviously, there was no intention of having the building attacked.

Stresemann, in a personal telegram to Brockdorff-Rantzau, again pointed out that the continued excessive attacks in the Russian press did not help matters. He requested that the Ambassador warn the Soviet government about continuing the agitation. The Russians had to be made to understand that the influence of the Foreign Office over other parts of the government and other interested circles had its obvious limits. The Wilhelmstrasse could not indefinitely remove the ill feeling occasioned by the Comintern and Zinoviev. The pro-Russian policy would be continued but the Ambassador should inform the Soviet government of the difficulties which were made for such a policy by their campaign of vilification. He should emphasize that Stresemann hoped the incident would only be a test of good relations and that it would not much longer interfere in the "basic and great questions of fruitful German-Russian cooperation."[10]

On May 14, Regierungsdirektor Weiss was relieved of all duties until the Bozenhardt incident was completely cleared up. Brockdorff-Rantzau was notified of this step by the Foreign Office. On the day Weiss was furloughed, Brockdorff-Rantzau telegraphed that a new Russian note was being sent. It would include demands for an immediate official apology, for the punishment of the guilty without delay and in a manner satisfactory to the Soviet government, compensation for the damages caused, and the acknowledgment by Germany that the whole Trade Delegation was, according to the agreement of May 6, 1921, an extraterritorial part of the Berlin Embassy. Moscow further demanded a guarantee against future violations of the Trade Delegation headquarters. The five-page note, signed by Chicherin and dated May 12, had been handed by Litvinov to Brockdorff-Rantzau with the oral statement that it contained the minimum of Russian demands. Litvinov had behaved "in an urbane manner," quite differently from the usual form adopted by Moscow in serious incidents. Despite this, Brockdorff-Rantzau complained, as instructed, about "the complete cessation of economic activities, stoppage of all negotiations, the withdrawal of accepted contracts, an extremely vociferous propaganda campaign, and demonstrations and street processions of a provocative nature." To the latter charge Litvinov replied that these demonstrations were spontaneous. Brockdorff-Rantzau countered that he was well aware of the manner in which these "spontaneous demonstrations" developed. To the Wilhelmstrasse he reported that Litvinov was at least partially correct; even "bourgeois" circles in Moscow were upset about the insult to Russian dignity.

Maltzan informed the Ambassador that the demand for complete extraterritoriality could not be granted. However, until the final status of the Delegation was determined in a subsequent commercial agreement, the Wilhelmstrasse was willing to agree to a *modus vivendi* under which the safety of the rooms, archives and the work of extraterritorial persons would be guaranteed.

Brockdorff-Rantzau replied that an immediate formal apology about the incident would have removed the chief weapon from the hands of the Russians and would have made it possible to "settle the matter in *camera caritatis.*" Now it had become a matter of prestige for both sides. According to Brockdorff-Rantzau the incident was now entirely in the hands of the Russian Communist Party. He advocated that Germany, in the interest of continued good relations with Russia, acquiesce to their demands. Otherwise, he warned, chauvinistic elements might get the upper hand and force a break of relations in order to bring about a Russo-French *rapprochement*.[11]

Brockdorff-Rantzau once again was willing to play the Russian tune first because the Russians had been insulted, and second because of his pathological fear that the Soviets would drop Germany and make common course with France. This meant, the Count was certain, that the old two-front squeeze could be applied and Germany would have little hope of regaining her prewar status. The Count, secure in his infinite egocentrism, refused to admit that Germany could regain her world position with the aid of the West as easily as with the help of Moscow. Brockdorff-Rantzau was committed to the regeneration of Germany with Russian aid, and was beset by a deep hatred of the French because of the humiliation they had inflicted on his honor at Versailles. It was for this reason, and because of his belief in the essential soundness of Bismarck's policies, that Brockdorff-Rantzau was willing to forgive the Bolshevik regime many things.

Brockdorff-Rantzau's apprehensions about a Franco-Russian *rapprochement* were enhanced by the uncertainty of leadership in the Kremlin since Lenin's death on January 21. Brockdorff-Rantzau had hoped that a rumor about Chicherin's being considered for Lenin's job as Chairman of the Council of People's Commissars would prove true.[12] Instead Alexis I. Rykov was chosen. In the Kremlin, power seemed to be in the hands of Zinoviev, Kamenev, and Stalin, all of whom Brockdorff-Rantzau considered chauvinists. As the Bozenhardt incident began to strain German-Russian relations severely, one can imagine how often the Ambassador must have wished that the power of his amiable, charming, gentlemanly friend had been enhanced.

On May 20 a new German note was sent to Brockdorff-Rantzau. The Russians were informed that a *Verbalnote* sent to their Embassy by the Wilhelmstrasse on March 21, 1924, had made it clear beyond any doubt that the Trade Delegation building did not enjoy extraterritoriality. The note further stated that Stresemann had made an apology on May 12, and the police officer in charge of the search had been relieved of duty. No mention was made of an apology for the search as such. The Russian demand for diplomatic immunity for the whole Trade Delegation building was again rejected.

Although the letter containing the German note arrived in Moscow on May 21, delivery to the German Embassy did not take place until two days later. Shortly after its arrival the note was delivered to Chicherin's personal secretary because Chicherin and Litvinov were attending the opening session of the Thirteenth Congress of the Russian Communist Party.[13]

The Wilhelmstrasse was subjected to increasing attacks from the German press and rightists in the Reichstag for its apparent softness and unwillingness to deal vigorously with the Communist regime of Russia. The May elections had given the Nationalists (Deutschnationale Volkspartei) and the so-called "Landliste" 106 seats, and thus made them the strongest faction in the Reichstag. The Nationalists demanded inclusion in the new Cabinet and proposed one of their leading Reichstag deputies, former Grand Admiral Alfred von Tirpitz. There was talk that Tirpitz' son-in-law should replace Maltzan at the Foreign Office. The Undersecretary used this political situation in an attempt to force the Russians to settle the Bozenhardt incident on the basis of the German note. Maltzan instructed Brockdorff-Rantzau to explain to the Russians that a cabinet with Tirpitz as a member would not be likely to restore good relations with Moscow. The Undersecretary in addition asked the Ambassador to remonstrate with Chicherin about the continuing disgusting propaganda against the Wilhelmstrasse. On May 21 a leading article in *Izvestia* had spread the tale that Weiss continued to direct the foreign policy of Germany and that Bozenhardt was a tool of the police. When Bozenhardt had found out that his beloved Soviet government had accused him of being a police spy he had been so shaken that he tried to commit suicide in his cell.[14]

Brockdorff-Rantzau shared Maltzan's trepidation. He had used similar arguments for more than two weeks at the Narkomindel. He had also exerted personal pressure on Krestinsky, who was still in Moscow. The Soviet Ambassador declared categorically that the question of extraterritoriality could not be divorced from the complex of questions growing out of the incident. Without it, any agreement was absolutely out of the question. He did not change his position even after Brockdorff-Rantzau insisted that the concessions made in the note were the limit to which Germany was willing to go, and had threatened the possibility of a break of diplomatic relations. Krestinsky appeared completely unmoved by Brockdorff-Rantzau's intimation that the Russians would lose all their friends in Germany if they did not settle the incident.

The Count had used such strong language in order to force Krestinsky to use his influence in the party in support of Chicherin. The Commissar for Foreign Affairs had not contacted Brockdorff-Rantzau, a situation which the Count ascribed partly to Chicherin's fear of the party. The Ambassador was under the impression that the Russians were going to use the "incident which was provoked in an unheard of manner" to blackmail Germany into granting full extraterritoriality for the Trade Delegation since the Italians had just done so, and in order to achieve the same end in London.[15]

The Bozenhardt incident showed Brockdorff-Rantzau that his independence from the Foreign Minister was not as definite as he had demanded it to be. For the first time he took advantage of his privilege to address President Ebert directly. Brockdorff-Rantzau assured the President that the most recent "clumsy incident," the ramifications of which could not yet be estimated, placed before him a serious decision, because the conditions under which he had assumed his post had ceased to exist. His continuation in Moscow would depend on additional authorizations which only the President of the Reich could grant. This was necessary because his policy, based on the *Promemoria* of August 15, 1922, had been threatened, if not completely destroyed. Despite the fact that he was independent of the foreign minister, he was vitally concerned in the kind of man who would fill the post at any given time. He asked for a private audience with Ebert as soon as the present strained conditions ceased and allowed his return to Berlin.[16]

On May 25, *Pravda* reported a speech made by Zinoviev to a session of the Thirteenth Congress. Brockdorff-Rantzau was absolutely convinced that Zinoviev was determined to destroy the German-Soviet relationship. In his speech Zinoviev stated that neither efforts by the German capitalists to prolong the incident despite its detrimental effect on them nor attempts by the Social Democrats to precipitate a break had made the affair more than a passing episode. The German government would soon capitulate because it would realize that the Soviet Union had no intention of retreating from her demands.

Stresemann instructed Brockdorff-Rantzau to tell the Russians that their attempt to connect other political questions with the incident made a settlement more difficult, although one could understand that this attitude was prompted by domestic problems, the Anglo-Russian negotiations, and the desire to create a better atmosphere for a Russo-French *rapprochement*. Maltzan asked Brockdorff-Rantzau to consider the political burden which the relationship with Moscow had imposed on the German government. Details about Bozenhardt—for instance that he had been Communist City Councilor—had come to public attention. This had been quite correctly interpreted as proof that prominent Communists were being indirectly supported by the Soviet government. No one could deny the determined "moral and material support" which the KPD received from Moscow. The recent Reichstag elections had increased Communist strength from four to sixty-two, and this development spoke volumes. Despite the relationship between the KPD and Moscow, the Wilhelmstrasse was willing to consider the question whether the "diplomatic advantage was sufficiently valuable and assured" to risk the domestic consequences which were a concomitant to relations with Russia. Until now, in agreement with Brockdorff-Rantzau, preference had been given to diplomatic relations. The decisive factor had been the heralded Franco-Russian negotiations. The Foreign Office wanted amiable relations between Berlin and Moscow so that it could keep informed about developments. Because of this, no use had been made of the incriminating material discovered during the police raid. Only Russian insistence on complete extraterritoriality for the Trade Delegation made the incident a "prestige question." The Wilhelmstrasse was willing to help the Narkomindel to find a way out of the dead-end street into which it had maneuvered itself, but not by yielding to all Russian demands. Brockdorff-Rantzau could propose a settlement on the basis of a protocol, but only if he thought that a settlement could thereby be effected.

There was general agreement in the Wilhelmstrasse that a protocol was the best solution of the problem created by the incident. Presentation of the protocol, at the right moment, would re-establish Brockdorff-Rantzau's independence of action, divorced from the notes. It would also present a means by which Russian willingness to settle could be gauged. If they rejected the protocol any possibility for a resolution of the conflict would be made highly unlikely.[17]

Just when the protocol was given its final touches in the Wilhelmstrasse, Krassin made a long and aggressive speech before the party Congress. He emphasized that Zinoviev had not given all the relevant details about the incident of May 3. The peaceful and conciliatory attitude of the Soviet government had not found any echo in Germany. The Soviet government demanded now "an apology for the insult suffered, punishment of those guilty, and confirmation that the Trade Delegation was untouchable as acknowledged by the agreement of May 6." Unless these demands were met, the Soviet Union would have to do without a trade delegation and maintain only a minimum of economic contacts. The incident was not just an episode, but a serious conflict which could drag on for many months.

Immediately after Krassin's speech became available Brockdorff-Rantzau demanded an audience at the Foreign Commissariat. He was received by Litvinov at 10:00 P.M. on May 27. The Ambassador made the sharpest possible protest against the speech, characterizing it as a deliberate provocation. He demanded to be told whether Krassin's speech was to be construed as a reply to the German note of May 20. He threatened to leave Moscow and demanded to be informed when and if an official reply to the German note would be made. Litvinov explained that Krassin's speech had been made to forestall stronger discussions of the incident by the Congress. The Russian government considered the note "completely insufficient." Litvinov told the Ambassador that the situation was most critical, jeopardizing the labor of the past years. A reply to the German note would be forthcoming within the next three days, because the importance of the reply required its consideration by all members of the government.

Brockdorff-Rantzau requested permission to leave Moscow. Stresemann did not think that the situation already required the application of this "most extreme and dangerous means." After additional information from Brockdorff-Rantzau, Stresemann telegraphed that he was considering letting the agreement of May 6, 1921, which had a three-month time limit, lapse unless the Soviet government would show a change of attitude in the reply to the German note announced for May 30.

The Wilhelmstrasse also took a public stand on Krassin's speech in a newspaper dispatch in which it advised the "disciples of the dogma" that the Trade Delegation building was extraterritorial to read the relevant article in the 1921 agreement. Hope was expressed that the Russian government would at least indicate its rejection of the kind of behavior by its employees which brought injury to German interests. Krassin, when he referred to German losses in trade, overlooked the fact that Germany's share in Russian imports amounted to 41.3 percent in 1923, but that was only 1.9 percent of Germany's total exports. The same disproportion held true for exports. In that case 32 percent of all Russian exports went to Germany, but, again, this was only 2.2 percent of Germany's imports. The Wilhelmstrasse had no intention of fighting with Mr. Krassin over the question whether it was Germany or Russia which suffered economically because of the Bozenhardt incident and its consequences.[18]

Maltzan was becoming much cooler toward the Russian relationship, and observed this attitude in others. He wrote to Brockdorff-Rantzau,

> . . . you have received an abundant amount of information regarding the incident. The mood of all circles, even that of the interested industrial circles, is turning more and more against the Russians. This is, of course, directly related to the unbelievable behavior of the Bolsheviks in the Reichstag, whose concert was observed by Brodovsky from the diplomatic box with at least a well-wishing smile.

Maltzan again referred to the possibility of a right-wing cabinet and the detrimental effect that would surely have on relations with Russia. Even such a well-known Russophile as Felix Deutsch (the chairman of the A.E.G., Germany's General Electric Company), was beginning to doubt the advisability of cooperating with the Soviet Union, especially since Zinoviev and Dzerzhinsky seemed to be gaining the upper hand and a drift to less favorable attitudes toward capitalists was becoming apparent.[19]

At this juncture, Hilger invited Radek for a private chat; despite the fact that Radek had taken the major blame for the fiasco of the German October, he promised to use his still considerable influence in the Kremlin to effect a settlement, if Brockdorff-Rantzau would withdraw his threat to leave Moscow. At 1:00 A.M. on May 30 the Ambassador went to Hilger's place, and the three continued their discussion for another four hours. Brockdorff-Rantzau complained that contacts with the Foreign Commissariat, except for sporadic meetings with Litvinov, had ceased. He hinted broadly that Krassin's speech made a break of relations very likely but expressed the hope that the reply to the German note would not extinguish the last glimmer of hope. Radek assured his German listeners that the note was conciliatory in tone. He promised to inform Trotsky, Stalin, and Zinoviev about the discussion and see to it that Chicherin would be instructed to receive the Ambassador. Brockdorff-Rantzau reported to the Foreign Office that the new Russian note had been composed in the Politburo.

During the night of the thirtieth, Brockdorff-Rantzau had an hourlong conversation with Chicherin, during which he made it quite clear that the German government was willing to resolve the conflict. Chicherin, for his part, insisted that Bozenhardt was a *provocateur* who had thrown a suitcase full of incriminating material into the room which was the first to be entered by the police.

On June 1, Chicherin personally delivered the Russian reply to the German note of May 20. All the old charges were repeated in an effort to show that the German point of view was unacceptable. The escape of Bozenhardt had all the earmarks of a provocation, the German notes had expressed regrets for acts against members of the Delegation who held immunity, but never had any satisfaction been given to the government of the USSR, which had been gravely insulted. Weiss should be fired, not just suspended from his job. The Trade Delegation had enjoyed *de facto* extraterritoriality until May 3, and the government of the USSR categorically demanded that this status be recognized to prevent a repetition of the transgression committed on that date. Unless these demands were met, preliminary discussions about a comprehensive commercial treaty could not proceed.[20]

The note and the remarks Chicherin made at the time he transmitted it convinced Brockdorff-Rantzau that the Russians were still quite intransigent but unwilling to force an acceptance of their demands at the risk of a break in diplomatic relations. The Ambassador decided to tell the Foreign Commissar that the Russian note made a settlement unlikely. If this proved insufficient he intended to leave Moscow in order to make a personal report in Berlin. Permission for this procedure was granted.[21]

Brockdorff-Rantzau had no interest in the discontinuation of friendly relations with Russia because Germany needed the "fiction of strong political, possibly even military, support by the Soviet Union." As long as Germany's enemies feared an alliance between Germany and Russia, the attempts by the West to force Germany into actions contrary to her interests could be rejected. Improvement in the material conditions of the Bolshevik regime would reduce the threat of Communist infection; therefore, continued aid in Russia's economic recovery benefited Germany. An end of Bolshevik control was extremely unlikely. The chauvinists, who wanted an end of Germany-Russian cooperation, were using the incident in an attempt to achieve their nefarious ends. Chicherin, the creator of the spirit of Rappallo, felt betrayed; his position in the party had never been strong, and the incident had further reduced what influence he had been able to bring to bear against the anti-German policies of the party. Krassin had been rewarded for his inflammatory speech by election to the Central Committee of the party, while Radek, who had attempted to mediate, had been left out in the cold. Litvinov, although objective, tended toward Anglophilism, and Trotsky had been exceptionally reserved since May 3. Bukharin and Rykov also kept in the background, but the most influential men in the party, Stalin, Zinoviev, and Kamenev, had little liking for Germany. In the final analysis, *Realpolitik* had to determine relations with the Bolsheviks who ruled Russia and not antipathy for their system.[22]

Since Brockdorff-Rantzau had not proposed a protocol, the Foreign Office used the presence of Victor Kopp in Berlin for a number of informal meetings at the Wilhelmstrasse and at Maltzan's home. Then on June 5, Gaus, Hauschild, and Schlesinger met with Kopp at the Foreign Office in an effort to get him to accept a protocol for a settlement of the incident. The Germans stated again that the Trade Delegation as a whole was not extraterritorial beyond the exceptions granted in the agreement of May 6, 1921. They admitted that the agreement, as well as international law, had been violated in regard to the members of the Delegation who were covered by extraterritoriality. The actions of the police had been arbitrary and injudicious because the Wilhelmstrasse had not been informed as it should have been under Article 2 of the 1921 agreement.

The Soviet government, for its part, was asked to state that Bozenhardt's escape had been aided by an employee of the Trade Delegation and that he had been hidden by the same employee; that the manner in which the escape took place indicated incorrect behavior of other employees. Because of this the Russians would again instruct all the employees of the Trade Delegation that they should not "in any way whatsoever participate in the domestic political struggle in Germany and see to it that this prohibition was not violated." Finally the various retaliatory measures each side had employed should be ended. The German Foreign Office refused to go beyond the concessions made in this protocol.

Kopp told Schlesinger on the following day that it was acceptable to him. Litvinov, who had been kept current on the talks with Kopp, apparently agreed. The draft of the protocol was forwarded to Brockdorff-Rantzau to be used as the basis for a negotiated settlement. Once again, as Schlesinger flatteringly emphasized, the fate of future relations with Russia was in the Ambassador's able hands.

But before the Ambassador received the protocol, he warned Maltzan that the Russians were not bluffing and were determined to get their demands accepted. He pointed out that anyone who knew the Soviet government had to be aware of the fact that once it had determined on a course of action it would pursue its ends without regard to the consequences, because of its confidence in the country's resources and the limits to which its people could be pushed. Furthermore, the Count warned, the Russians still had the letter General Hasse had written to Rosengolts. This alone placed Germany "in a very delicate position and left her wide open to the worst kind of blackmail if it comes to an open break."[23]

During 1924 the military collaboration of the two countries had been further expanded. In January an agreement had been negotiated over the strenuous objections of Brockdorff-Rantzau. Another venture of the Reichswehr in Russia, the production of all-metal airplanes by Junkers at Fili, had run into financial difficulties early in 1924, and the firm had been negotiating with the Sondergruppe R (Special Group R) of the Ministry of Defense for additional funds. The Special Group R(ussia) dealt with all aspects of the collaboration between the German army and the Red army. The Junkers negotiations dragged on into the spring of 1924.

The relationship between the Reichswehr and the Junkers firm had been established two years before by a contract signed on March 15, 1922 between Special Group R and Junkers. The airplane manufacturer bound himself to produce metal planes in Russia in return for the sum of 140 million paper marks (approximately one million gold marks). Eight months later, on November 26, 1922, a concession contract had been concluded between the RSFSR and the Junkers firm which called for the construction of airplanes and motors at the Russo-Balt Works in Fili and, if possible, for seaplanes at the Russo-Balt

Works in Petrograd. Junkers bound itself to build or complete the necessary buildings and maintain them during the concession period, which was to run for thirty years. During that period the firm was to produce 300 planes and the necessary motors and reserve motors annually. Serial fabrication was to start not later than October, 1923. The Red air force was to receive 20 percent of the yearly production. The Soviet government had provided a house in Moscow at 7 Nikolskaya for the Russian branch of Junkers. The director in charge in January, 1924, was Lieutenant Colonel (ret.) Friedrich Wilhelm Schubert, who had negotiated the concession as a representative of the Special Group R. He was assisted by Director Erich Pfeiffer, who was authorized to deal with the Moscow State Bank.

On March 31, 1924, the Junkers Zentrale für Russland had sent a twelve-page letter to the Main Concessions Committee, in which it listed the reasons for the delays in fulfilling the contract. The major difficulty had been due to the impossibility of purchasing aluminum from a supplier in Germany, who had been unable to make deliveries because of the Ruhr occupation. The two Russian plants which produced aluminum had refused to supply Junkers. This had prevented the start of production, although the facilities were ready to turn out twenty-five planes a month. Russian orders had not been placed, creating grave financial problems for the firm. Living quarters for Junkers' employees had been made available only after recourse had been taken to the courts to evict the tenants who occupied the quarters. This had delayed the transfer of specialists from Germany. The railroad spur into Fili had not been put into operating condition; Russian designers, despite promises to the contrary, had copied Junkers' patents. Obstacles had been placed in the way of fulfilling Junkers' concession, handled by the firm's Department for Air Service (Ableilung für Luftverkehr), to develop an air service from Sweden via Russia to Persia. Despite the difficulties, a line had been opened between Moscow and Tiflis. Russian cooperation and orders would be necessary for Junkers to fulfill its contracts.

On April 26, the Junkers branch in Moscow could report to its home office that a large order had been tentatively placed, waiting confirmation, for Junkers 21's to be built as a two-man fighter with a speed of 230–240 km. (*ca.* 143–150 mph) and an operating ceiling of 7,000 meters, capable of three-and-one-half hour's flight time. The airplane was to be equipped with a motor manufactured by the Bavarian Motor Works (BMW). An additional order called for the production of a cargo plane with a capacity of 800–1,100 kg. (*ca.* 1,764–2,204 lb.) and a speed of 180 km. (*ca.* 108 mph). The order came too late to stop the decision to close the factories at Fili because of lack of operating capital. Director Gotthard Sachsenberg (who had earned the *Pour le mérite* as a navy flyer during the war), had told Maltzan and Hauschild on April 27 that the Ministry of Defense had rejected a request for an additional grant of twenty million gold marks. Junkers had therefore advised its representative to shut down the Russian facilities and inform the thousand employees of the fact on April 27. The Moscow representative would talk with Brockdorff-Rantzau before he would make the announcement. Maltzan expressed his genuine surprise about the Junkers involvement with the Ministry of Defense and told Sachsenberg that he would try to get the Ambassador's advice and hoped that the undertaking could be saved.[24]

Brockdorff-Rantzau succeeded in preventing the closing of the Fili plant through an agreement with the Junkers representatives in Moscow to keep the factory running until the differences with the Special Group R had been clarified. Brockdorff-Rantzau became quite agitated when he found out about the relationship between Junkers and the Reichswehr, of which he had been unaware. Maltzan obtained confirmation of this additional evasion of the Treaty of Versailles directly from General Hasse. The two Junkers representatives in Moscow told Brockdorff-Rantzau that the parent firm in Germany was placed in financial jeopardy because of its involvement in the Russian venture of the Reichswehr. The orders promised by the latter for 1923–1924 had not been made. In anticipation of the orders, Junkers had taken five million gold marks worth of short-term loans which were due. Unless the Special Group R made this sum available, the proposed manufacture of airplanes in Russia would have to be abandoned. Brockdorff-Rantzau pleaded with the Wilhelmstrasse to see to it that the money needed by Junkers be made available by the Reichswehr or by the government. Otherwise the rest of the military collaboration would certainly be jeopardized. Maltzan agreed and made it unequivocally clear to General Hasse, who was directly responsible for the Special Group R, that abandoning Junkers was politically inexpedient. On May 5, the Special Group R agreed to make another four million gold marks available as a loan, in addition to four million already advanced in November, 1923, if Junkers could borrow an additional twelve million from other sources. Maltzan advised Brockdorff-Rantzau to impress upon the Russians, when he discussed the Bozenhardt affair, that the new agreement was an additional sign of German good will and sincerity.[25]

Directors Patze and Spaleck, the Junkers representatives in Moscow, traveled to Berlin to discuss the financial situation with the representatives of the Special Group R, Major Fischer and Captain Vogt, who left for the Soviet Union on May 7. Captain Vogt headed the Section for Air Armaments in the Weapons Office. The two officers were able to come to a satisfactory agreement, despite a somewhat cool reception by their Red counterparts, and departed on May 19. At the end of May, Colonel (ret.) von der Lieth-Thomsen, who had been Chief of Staff of the German air force during the war and who had participated in the original negotiations which had established Junkers in Russia, arrived in Moscow to take over the direction of Zentrale Moskau (Z. Mo.) under the cover name von Litz. Directly responsible to the Chief of the Reichswehr, Lieth-Thomsen led the Z. Mo. until 1928.[26]

This was where the situation stood when Brockdorff-Rantzau met with Commissar of War Trotsky on June 9. On the Ambassador's inquiry, Trotsky assured him that the Bozenhardt incident did not have the slightest influence on the mutually profitable military collaboration. The Count recounted a number of incidents during recent weeks in which snubs had been administered to Germans which could indicate that changes in the military relationship were contemplated. Trotsky refuted such a view. Brockdorff-Rantzau pointed out that the Russians were partly responsible for the strained financial situation in which the Junkers concern found itself because expected orders for planes had not been made. Colonel Thomsen had been in Moscow for over a week without seeing Rosengolts. Furthermore, six or seven out of ten of Germany's best pilots had been rejected for employment in the Soviet Union. He had also been shocked by the information that foreigners had inspected the German-run Tula arms factories about two weeks previously.

Trotsky assured him that he would investigate, but that the last report was "undoubtedly false." Brockdorff-Rantzau turned to the Bozenhardt affair and complained to Trotsky about Krassin's speech and Krestinsky's uncooperative attitude. Trotsky tried to overcome Brockdorff-Rantzau's objections by saying that Krassin really was a Germanophile and had only made the remarks to calm aroused public opinion in Russia, but he himself really did not know much about these diplomatic matters. The Ambassador now brought up Trotsky's assurances of December, 1923, at which time Trotsky had told him that France was the enemy of Germany as well as of Russia. Had his point of view changed since then? Trotsky emphasized that it had not. The old Tsarist debts stood in the way of really good relations with France and England.

When Brockdorff-Rantzau took his leave he asked Trotsky to use his influence to restore the old German-Russian relationship. Trotsky agreed, and the Count impressed upon him that cooperation would make it easier to continnue working with the Soviet government. The Russian note of May 31 amounted almost to an ultimatum, and the discontinuation of all economic contacts had done great harm. Brockdorff-Rantzau suggested that the incident be settled by a protocol. If this was acceptable a statement should be issued that both countries wanted to return to friendly cooperation in the spirit of the Rapallo. Trotsky promised to support the Ambassador.

Brockdorff-Rantzau was again favorably impressed by Trotsky, but wondered about his influence because he was being pushed into the background by such "sympathetic comrades" as Zinoviev and Stalin.[27]

When eight days passed without any definite developments, Brockdorff-Rantzau requested visas for himself and two aides. Kopp, who had returned from Berlin, received Hilger at his home during the evening of June 18. Hilger told him that Brockdorff-Rantzau thought a break unavoidable, since the proposed protocol had not brought any change in the Russian attitude. Kopp assured Hilger that Chicherin did not want a break. The Commissar received Brockdorff-Rantzau in the presence of Kopp during the night of June 19 and went out of his way to be pleasant, reiterating that he did not want a break in relations. Russian demands had already been modified. Germany would have to declare its regrets about the action taken by the police and grant extraterritoriality for the Trade Delegation. Brockdorff-Rantzau did not comment, but told Chicherin that he would discuss the details with Kopp.[28]

Brockdorff-Rantzau's hope that his threatened departure would lead to a settlement was disappointed, because the incident continued to disrupt all relations except military collaborations. Chicherin remained distant and sorely vexed, and thus no confidential information regarding Russo-French or Russo-British relations could be obtained from him. Even Hilger, who had many Russian friends, complained that his sources of information had dried up.

Adding to the strain was the Moscow heat, from which the Count began to suffer rather badly. His temper took a turn for the worse. Privately he blamed partly the Russians for delaying a settlement, partly the Wilhelmstrasse. As far as he was concerned, "the Russians behaved like pigs; but we are in the embarrassing situation where we have to try to get along with them, without running after them." Nothing had been discovered during the "frivolously staged" raid which would have proven that the delegation supported the revolutionary efforts of the KPD. Good relations with Russia had been undermined for nothing.[29]

Maltzan, who had been convalescing from an illness, returned to the Wilhelmstrasse on July 2 and immediately telegraphed to Brockdorff-Rantzau the contents of Stresemann's notes on two talks the Foreign Minister had had with Litvinov on July 1 and 2. It had been a painful surprise to hear that Chicherin had so modified the Kopp protocol that, de facto, the whole delegation would be extraterritorial if the demands were accepted. Such a concession was absolutely out of the question, for the Minister of the Interior as well as for the Cabinet. Both France and England had made inquiries at the Foreign Office about the contemplated modus vivendi and had been assured that no grant of complete extraterritoriality would be made. Litvinov had agreed with Stresemann that their talks were in no way meant to be final. Brockdorff-Rantzau was to complete the negotiations in Moscow. Stresemann had emphasized to Litvinov that, if the Soviets refused to come to an agreement, the German ambassador would be recalled from Moscow. Maltzan wrote that he had no intention of having the "very tender thread with Russia" broken, even for a short time. Brockdorff-Rantzau tried to extricate himself from resolving the incident because he had grave doubts about Moscow's willingness to come to an agreement. He asked Stresemann to settle the incident with Litvinov, who had more influence in the party than did Chicherin.[30]

Stresemann agreed that a settlement should be achieved, but not on the basis of Chicherin's latest formula, which would make seveneighths or four-fifths of the Trade Delegation extraterritorial. The Foreign Minister would agree to immunity for two-sevenths of the Lindenstrasse, which had over a hundred rooms, or a ratio of two to five. If a smaller house could be agreed upon, it might be possible to grant it complete immunity. In any event, extraterritorial status would apply only to the headquarters building and not to any other dwellings owned by the Trade Mission. After a discussion with Chicherin, Brockdorff-Rantzau telegraphed to Stresemann that if it were not possible to meet the Russian demands for domestic political reasons, then any "understanding was impossible."

Brockdorff-Rantzau, who tended to be pessimistic in favor of the Russians, had some reason to be quite concerned. On July 6, an official of the OGPU had appeared at the house in which Hilger lived and which belonged to the Embassy. The official had ostensibly come to seal the apartment of a German who had been deported. Hilger strenuously objected and told the OGPU man that the house was extraterritorial. The official finally left. Brockdorff-Rantzau sent a written complaint to

Chicherin, who informed him on July 11 that the official responsible had been arrested and had then been summarily fired from his position. Knowing the Russian methods, this could mean willingness to be conciliatory or intention to create an incident in Moscow to get a *quid pro quo.*

Brockdorff-Rantzau did not think that an additional hundred extraterritorial rooms would increase the danger of Communist infection. After all, the Soviet government had made concessions on the main point. If the Ministry of the Interior continued to oppose a settlement, the final responsibility would be theirs if a break occurred. Stresemann succeeded in getting agreement from the Cabinet for a settlement of extraterritoriality on the basis of a three to five ratio; that is, 27.5 percent of the Trade Delegation would be immune. This concession had been wrung from those opposed to the Communists after great exertion. He expected that this would be accepted by the Russians and would result in a settlement within a week. When Chicherin, during a two-hour confrontation on the evening of July 14 in the presence of Krestinsky, Kopp, and Hilger, insisted on 60 percent extraterritoriality (a ratio of three to two), Brockdorff-Rantzau rejected the demand by referring to the extreme difficulties Stresemann had had to overcome to achieve the three to five ration. Chicherin promised a final reply within two days, after consultation with the entire Soviet government.[31]

On July 19, Brockdorff-Rantzau sent Hencke to Berlin as his personal emissary to make an oral report to Stresemann and transmit the notes of the two-hours' discussion held on July 14. Hencke also carried a revision of the protocol worked out during the night from July 17 to 18 between Brockdorff-Rantzau and Chicherin in the presence of Krestinsky, Kopp, and Hilger.

In addition to the protocol, the German Ambassador had agreed to support the wish of the Soviet government vis-à-vis his own government for a written declaration at the time of signature of the protocol, which would state that the guilty officials had been punished. The Ambassador had further agreed that he would try to get cooperation from his government in case minor changes in the division of the building of the Trade Delegation should be desired by the Soviet government. The Soviet negotiators had made it clear that a trial of those of the employees of the Trade Delegation who had been involved in the incident of May 3 would create a politically undesirable situation, and that the Soviet government definitely counted on the fact that no trial would take place.[32]

On arrival in Berlin Hencke delivered a personal letter by Brockdorff-Rantzau to Maltzan. The Ambassador asked the Undersecretary to consider the protocol in the framework of the whole German-Russian relationship. The Count assured Maltzan that it was no pleasure to negotiate with the Russian gentlemen. For them the most important thing now was that the charges against their employees be dropped. Krestinsky had made the most trouble; he insisted that he would not return to Berlin except for the purpose of putting the finishing touches on the protocol. Should this protocol prove unacceptable, Brockdorff-Rantzau wanted to leave Moscow immediately. However, the Count could see one bright light in all this darkness: military relations were prospering. In fact, a letter by Chicherin to him showed that this relationship represented the greatest political success of the last three years.[33]

At this moment when a settlement seemed in sight the Prussian Ministry of the Interior served notice that it intended to restore Regierungsdirektor Weiss to his post. Cabinet members wanted restriction placed on the Russians in Berlin who continued overtly to support the KPD, in flagrant disregard for the problems such behavior created for the resolution of the Bozenhardt conflict. Despite these last-minute stumbling blocks the incident was about to be settled. Stresemann informed Brockdorff-Rantzau that he had been very pleased to hear about the cooperative attitude of Trotsky and Chicherin in matters of military collaboration. The Ambassador could proceed to put the final changes into the protocol in discussions with Chicherin.[34]

The Foreign Commissar was recovering from another of his numerous ailments, but received Brockdorff-Rantzau at midnight on July 25. The Commissar had to make a report on foreign affairs to the Presidium of the Executive Committee of the Soviet Union on Monday, July 28, in the afternoon. Rather "nervously, but in a friendly manner," Chicherin inquired whether the German government could come to a decision on the protocol by noon of the twenty-eighth. He warned that "the Soviet government had reached the absolute limit of the possible" in the matter of the protocol. During the night of July 27, Brockdorff-Rantzau, with Stresemann's authorization now in hand, had another three-hours-long discussion with Chicherin. The latter insisted that no agreement could be reached unless all the guilty police officers were punished. Brockdorff-Rantzau rejected this because Stresemann had written that the most which could be achieved was the disciplining of Weiss as the official alone responsible. This was especially so since the Russians insisted on the release of the employees who had been arrested and the prohibiting of any trial for them. Chicherin now modified his demand to the point of asking that at least those officials who had violated the diplomatic immunity of specific members of the Trade

Delegation be punished. Brockdorff-Rantzau again rejected this modification with Stresemann's arguments. At this point, Chicherin withdrew with Krestinsky and Kopp. Considerable time elapsed before the trio returned. Chicherin withdrew his demand, and Brockdorff-Rantzau initialed the draft protocol. Since Krestinsky was going to remain in Moscow for at least another week, the chargé d'affaires in Berlin, Bratman-Brodovsky, would sign the protocol.[35]

In a letter to Maltzan, the Count wrote that he "hoped that 'the Russian worry' which occupied both of us equally has now been settled for the immediate future." He advised Maltzan to phrase the press communiqué on the settlement in such a way that its official origin could not be detected. Nothing should be done to upset the Russians now.[36] The incident was settled on July 29, when Stresemann and Bratman-Brodovsky signed the protocol.

The protocol announced that the exchange of notes had been completed. The German government declared its regrets over the consequences of the "arbitrary act" of the police. Regierungsdirektor Weiss had been "relieved of his former duties." Others responsible for offenses against extraterritorial persons would also be punished. The German government had already expressed its regrets for the offenses committed against immunity. Compensation was offered for the damages caused.

The Soviet government affirmed that it would forbid all those employed by the Trade Delegation from interfering "in any form whatsoever" in the internal affairs of Germany. This prohibition would be strictly enforced. German citizens employed by the Trade Mission would, of course, be permitted to exercise their rights in Germany as long as they did so as private persons and not as employees of the Soviet Trade Mission. Three parts of the headquarters building of the Mission was declared extraterritorial, and members of the Mission could not be arrested in the remaining two parts, nor could the latter be searched without the previous knowledge of the Wilhelmstrasse.[37]

With the liquidation of the Bozenhardt incident, Brockdorff-Rantzau left Moscow on August 4 to start a well-earned three-months' furlough. Krestinsky had already returned to his post in Berlin. The resolution of the conflict had been achieved once the Russians modified their demands regarding complete extraterritoriality for the Trade Delegation and had promised to keep closer control over their employees. All repressive measures had been removed; trade had been resumed; political relations with Russia, important to the whole conduct of Germany's foreign relations, had been completely restored. Maltzan instructed the German representatives abroad to make it crystal-clear, during their discussions of the protocol with their host foreign offices, that Bolshevik propaganda and Communist agitation would be rejected by all means required. Any attempt by the Communists to try another *Putsch* would be "suppressed with the greatest severity."

On August 12, the German Constitution Day, Chicherin and Kopp, Stange, Director of the Western Department, Florinsky and Lorenz of the same department, as well as Rothstein, the Narkomindel's press chief, made it a special point to congratulate members of the German Embassy and the chargé d'affaires, Radowitz, in front of the invited members of foreign missions accredited in Moscow.[38] It was obviously the desire of the Soviet government to show that no hard feelings were left from the recent strain.

Chicherin, in his report on foreign relations to the Central Executive Committee on October 18, 1924, referred to the incident in very conciliatory terms. He exonerated the German Foreign Office of any complicity, but expressed the view that "public opinion . . . concerning the Soviet-German conflict was unfortunately influenced by the desire for Western orientation and exaggerated hopes attached to the Dawes Plan."[39]

The Bozenhardt incident revealed a number of interesting aspects of the German-Russian "community of fate." It showed that the foreign policy aims of the Wilhelmstrasse were somewhat limited by the anti-Communist orientation of individual Cabinet members, especially the Minister of the Interior. The Prussian police and the Prussian Ministry of the Interior had their own ideas about the clandestine activities pursued by the agents of the USSR in Germany. Primarily concerned with domestic tranquility, these departments had served notice during 1924 that consideration of diplomacy could not indefinitely subordinate domestic peace. In the Wilhelmstrasse itself, concern over the continuing Comintern interference, the overt expressions of sympathy with the German Communists, and the covert support channeled to the KPD coffers increased during the Bozenhardt affair. The escape of Bozenhardt came at a time when the Foreign Office was uncertain about the men who were trying to fill Lenin's shoes, and at a time when far-reaching negotiations with the West were underway.

The Russians had used the involvement of the Germans in their negotiations with the West to charge that the Bozenhardt escape had been engineered by those in Germany who favored a unilateral alignment with the West. That charge held a partial truth. Obviously the escape of Bozenhardt had presented the excuse for which the Berlin police organs had been waiting. The aid extended to a fellow Communist employee was construed as a present danger, and action was taken after a brief two hours of deliberation by the police and the other departments charged with maintaining public order. The only problem left is the ease with which the policemen in charge of Bozenhardt were lured to the Lindenstrasse. It appears conceivable that they had been instructed to give their prisoner a chance to get away so that he would lead the Berlin police to bigger game. He obliged when he treated the Würtembergers like naive provincials. The information about them is quite insufficient to allow a decision on whether they were naive or whether they and Bozenhardt were part of a larger plan.

Brockdorff-Rantzau was of the opinion throughout the incident that it was a convincing demonstration of the difficulties made for professional diplomats by fools in policemen's uniforms. He was a supporter of independence in the conduct of foreign affairs unhampered by domestic considerations and amateurs from outside the diplomatic corps. Brockdorff-Rantzau shared the Russian concern about a realignment of Germany's foreign policy, a concern accentuated by the acceptance of the Dawes Plan by the German government on April 16, by an odd coincidence the second anniversary of Rapallo. Based on the experts' evaluation of German ability to pay, the plan was designed to resolve the problems created by the reparation payments imposed upon Germany. A loan of 800 million gold marks was to be used to stimulate and expand the German economic potential in order to supply Germany with her own needs and leave a surplus for export. Some of the German Social Democrats considered the Dawes Plan a sign that the war had been liquidated and that the "international capitalists" had been victorious. In any event, the dangers of a German *rapprochement* with the West were not underestimated in Moscow. The Bozenhardt incident was settled so that relatively normal relations could be resumed and measures taken to bind Germany closer to Russia.

IV

Alliance with the East or Alignment with the West?

The Russian decision to settle the Bozenhardt incident was at least partly due to developments indicating that Germany was actively working toward a *rapprochement* with the West. There was widespread public interest in the conference to implement the Dawes proposals, which met in London on July 16, 1924.[1] The Dawes Plan had been accepted by Germany on April 16, the second, but unheralded, anniversary of Rapallo. *Pravda* wrote that the plan meant "peace among the capitalists and war against the working class."[2] Quite obviously, a relaxation of tensions among the capitalists was the last thing desired by the party. *Pravda* correctly expressed the concern of the Kremlin that the Dawes Plan would move Germany into the Western orbit.

The Russian fear was not completely idle. The British Prime Minister, Ramsay MacDonald, in a letter received by the German Foreign Office on August 29, inquired of Chancellor Marx whether Germany intended

> to have any observer at Geneva in September? The next piece of work that I should like to accomplish is to get Germany into the League of Nations, and if we could arrange how that is to be done, I should be particularly happy.[3]

The opportunity for which Maltzan and Brockdorff-Rantzau had waited had arrived. England was coming to Germany. Now conditions could be made for both the West and the East.

Maltzan had already prepared the ground for the exploitation of Russian concern. On July 30, he had written a private letter to Victor Kopp indicating that Germany was interested in "an exchange of views about matters of the greatest political importance [*Dingen der grossen Politik*]." Kopp had replied on August 22 that Chicherin was sick and Litvinov away on furlough. This had increased his own work load,

113

leaving little time to deal adequately with Maltzan's letter. However, Krestinsky had "extensive instructions" and the exchange of views should begin in talks between the Ambassador and the Undersecretary.[4]

In response to MacDonald's letter, the Wilhelmstrasse instructed its London Embassy to inform the Prime Minister that Count Harry Kessler would be in Geneva as an unofficial observer. In Geneva, Kessler discussed the conditions under which Germany would agree to enter the League of Nations. Germany demanded assurances that she would receive a permanent seat on the Council and that she would not be required to make any humiliating declarations about good behavior. Germany also asked for the evacuation of the Ruhr, participation in the mandatory system of the League, and exemption from the provisions of Article 16 of the Covenant.[5]

The German government had very sound reasons for insisting on exemption from the provisions of Article 16, which bound all members of the League to participate in sanctions against an aggressor, contribute armed forces if requested, and allow passage through their territory. Germany defended her demand by pointing out that she was disarmed and therefore could not aid the League militarily. Her geographical position did not allow her to antagonize her well-armed neighbors. This was to remain the basic argument. It was a clever way of making demands, which had a double edge. If Germany had to comply with Article 16, she would have to be permitted to rearm. This was opposed, particularly by France, but also by other states. Therefore, if Germany was to be in the League and thus become part of the Western group of powers, she would have to be granted exemption from compliance with Article 16. Exemption would allow Germany to thwart any action by the League detrimental to Russian interests. This would provide a means to calm Russian fears and maintain close contacts. Berlin did not intend to jettison Russian good will as long as Poland, that bête noire of postwar Germany, still held Reich territory. Immediate economic considerations strongly favored friendly relations with Russia. As a bargaining factor, the possibility of an alliance with Russia could be used by Germany to extract concessions from the West.

Just after the Dawes Plan had been submitted to the Reparations Commission, Brockdorff-Rantzau, who considered the proposed schedule of payments "shameless," had proposed that Germany enter immediately into an exchange of intimate views with the Soviet government. The Ambassador was certain that this was also the desire of Moscow. Chicherin had intimated that Rakovsky would denounce the "infamous treaty" of Versailles during the Anglo-Soviet Conference in London. Rakovsky was chairman of the Russian delegation to the Anglo-Soviet Conference, which was to discuss the still outstanding problems between Great Britain, which had extended *de jure* recognition on February 1, 1924, and the USSR. After the Conference opened, Rakovsky repeatedly attacked the Treaty of Versailles.[6]

Despite the cooperative behavior of the Russians, Brockdorff-Rantzau began to fear that Germany's pre-eminent position in Russia, and therefore his own ability to help in the shaping of Germany's foreign policy, was being jeopardized. After the Bozenhardt incident had been settled, Brockdorff-Rantzau spent his furlough at various German vacation spots. He carefully watched the approaches to the League of Nations. He considered even the dispatch of an observer an acute threat to the "community of fate," and thus to his own policies. On September 21, he arrived in Berlin "without any intention of offering unrequested advice," but determined to tell Ebert, Stresemann, and Chancellor Marx about the destructive impact that entry into the League of Nations would have on German-Russian relations.

In Moscow, the chargé d'affaires, Radowitz, had an extended discussion with Litvinov on September 13, during which the Deputy Commissar actively supported Kopp's attitude on the exchange of views. Litvinov requested that general information of German "policies in relation to the London Pact" be transmitted to the Narkomindel. He was obviously concerned about a reorientation of Germany's Russian policy. Maltzan instructed the chargé d'affaires to inform Litvinov that the London Agreement had not changed Germany's policy.[7]

On September 23, the *Berliner Tageblatt* published the content of a memorandum sent by the Foreign Office to the major powers, in which it stated that

> the German government believes now that, especially after the proceedings and result of the London (Dawes) Conference, the basis exists for fruitful cooperation in the League of Nations.[8]

On the same day, Moscow took an official position on the possible entry of Germany into the League of Nations. Radowitz telegraphed an *aide-memoire*, handed to him by Litvinov, in two uncoded telegrams because he thought "every hour saved important." The memorandum ran as follows:

> No formal reservation can change the fact that the Covenant of the League of Nations constitutes an international guarantee, a system which eternalizes the existing frontiers, especially those of

the Treaty of Versailles. This includes the present border of Silesia as well as borders which touch us more closely. The League of Nations is an association for the victors, a mutual insurance agreement of those who have gained something. The *beati possidentes* form in this way a common defense organization. Self-defense of victorious imperialism is not pacifism. In Rakovsky's declaration in London the system of the victors was confronted by its antithesis, a rational system of national self-determination and borders based on ethnographic principles and plebiscites. By its entry into the League of Nations, Germany joins a definite coalition; Germany thereby becomes a satellite, renounces its independent policy by subjecting its policies to those of the coalition. Germany's policy thereby comes into collision with the policy of Rapallo. Contrary to her own wishes, by the force of events, Germany thus might be drawn into combinations and actions which will lead her into conflicts with us. Germany thereby will sacrifice all those factors which are elements of international strength. Germany herself will decline to a mere pawn in the power politics of the Entente.[9]

Radowitz' second telegram arrived in the Wilhelmstrasse at 8:00 P.M. Two hours and ten minutes later, Stresemann wired that approaches to the League did not mean a change of German policy in relation to Russia. No immediate request for membership was contemplated, because Germany's demands would lead to long and difficult negotiations.

The assurances given by the German Foreign Office did not satisfy the Russians. During the morning of September 26, Bratman-Brodovsky visited Stresemann and told him that the Soviet government considered the move in the direction of the League as "the inauguration of a new policy which it observed with concern." On October 1, the Russian chargé d'affaires inquired about the memorandum that Germany had sent to the Powers. Stresemann told him about the content and gave him a copy "for confidential information." The Foreign Minister strongly protested against the publication of a private letter by Chicherin to Professor Ludwig Stein of the Mittwochgesellschaft, in which the Commissar expressed Soviet objections to Germany's joining the League of Nations in terms almost identical to those in the memorandum transmitted on September 23. Bratman-Brodovsky promised to forward Stresemann's objections to Chicherin.[10]

Rumors reached the Foreign Office that a *rapprochement* between Russia and Poland was being pursued. On October 15, the Wilhelmstrasse inquired of Radowitz in Moscow and Rauscher in Warsaw about the possibility of a meeting between the Polish Foreign Minister, Skrzyński, and Chicherin. The German representative in Warsaw thought it unlikely that such a meeting would take place before basic disagreements had been resolved. Litvinov told Radowitz that no talks were contemplated. In any event, Germany would first be consulted because of Maltzan's request to discuss matters of political importance.

On October 18, Litvinov transmitted a formal statement to the German government regarding Soviet policy vis-à-vis the League of Nations. The Soviet government was

> willing to enter into an accord with the German government by which either of the two countries bound itself not to become a member of the League of Nations without the agreement of the other.

Litvinov also stated that the Soviet Union had not bound itself in any way regarding the League. French *de jure* diplomatic recognition was almost certain, but no discussion about Russian membership in the League had taken place.[11] France did extend *de jure* recognition ten days later.

Litvinov's obvious criticism of German contemplations regarding League membership was cleverly put. The Wilhelmstrasse was already aroused about the unsubstantiated, but possible, approach of Moscow to Warsaw. The direct coupling of French recognition and the Soviet government's continued freedom of action in regard to the League was a deliberate attempt to give the Germans an acute attack of Bismarck syndrome. During the height of the Bozenhardt incident, the major reasons why diplomatic relations could not be broken off were based on the argument that direct contact with Moscow had to be maintained to determine the extent of Franco-Russian agreements.

On October 20, *Izvestia* published a report on foreign relations which Chicherin had made to the Central Executive Committee two days earlier. Chicherin had pointed out that Soviet relations with Germany had been marred by the Bozenhardt raid, which the police had made without the knowledge of the German Foreign Office. One could, however, conclude that

> public opinion . . . concerning the Soviet-German conflict was unfortunately influenced by the desire for Western orientation and the exaggerated hopes attached to the Dawes Plan.

Chicherin then repeated, almost verbatim, the content of the Russian *aide-mémoire* of September 23. He again warned that

Germany's entry into the League of Nations means the surrender of her independent policies and subjection to those of the Entente. Germany could be drawn into anti-Russian combinations.[12]

Stresemann, despite the Russian *rapprochement* with France, had no intention of being forced into precipitate actions by Soviet diplomatic proposals or to be disturbed by warnings in the press. He instructed Radowitz to inform Litvinov that membership in the League would be determined on the basis of Germany's best interest. However, the conditions attached to accepting membership, which were well known to the Soviet government, were designed to prevent a deterioration, or even a disturbance, of German-Russian relations. Germany placed the greatest value on an extension and deepening of relations with Moscow. Stresemann now made Maltzan's private proposal to Kopp official. He offered

> to enter into a confidential exchange of views about the further development of the question regarding membership by both countries in the League of Nations.[13]

Litvinov received the German reply on October 24 and told Radowitz that he was looking forward to Brockdorff-Rantzau's return with "really great expectations." The Deputy Commissar had no desire to fall into Stresemann's trap.

In the meantime, Zinoviev tried to raise the specter of a Communist revolution in Germany. On October 23, *Pravda* published a commemoration of the abortive rising of the German Communists in Hamburg. Zinoviev called that disaster the "brightest spot in the workers' movement in Europe in 1923, and perhaps in the last few years. . . ." He urged Communists the world over to use "Hamburg" as their battle cry.

> The proletarian revolution in Germany is drawing ever nearer, in spite of all the Daweses, Eberts, and Noskes. [Gustav Noske had destroyed the Spartacist rising in Berlin during December/ January, 1918/19.] The decisive major battles, the battles which decide the fate of a country for decades, have not yet taken place in Germany. These struggles, however, will come before very long.[14]

One day later, Zinoviev's sentiments were printed as a letter in the organ of the KPD, *Rote Fahne.*

On the twenty-eighth, the *Rote Fahne* published a manifesto of the

Executive Committee of the Comintern, signed by Zinoviev and Manuilsky among others, specifically aimed at the German proletarians, calling on them "to fight the class enemy," and ending with "Long Live the German Revolution." Once again, all the strings available to the Kremlin were being pulled to keep Germany isolated and dependent on Russia.

Stresemann expressed his consternation to Krestinsky on October 29. The Foreign Minister reminded the Ambassador of the detrimental effect for Russia that the letter of Zinoviev had had on the outcome of the British elections, which had resulted in a cabinet unfriendly to the USSR. The Soviet Ambassador gave a new twist to the old myth that the Comintern was independent of the USSR by describing Zinoviev as a member of the Central Executive Committee of the Congress of Soviets, which had 400 members and could best be compared to the Reichstag. Therefore, any remarks by him were to be regarded like those of a Reichstag deputy. Only the People's Commissars were members of the Soviet government. Stresemann refused to accept this version and insisted that the Soviet government be informed and reply to his complaints.[15]

Brockdorff-Rantzau, who returned to Moscow early in November, expressed his great concern over the Comintern articles to Chicherin during their first encounter on November 4. Most of their discussion dealt with the League of Nations. The Ambassador also transmitted Stresemann's assurances that entering the League of Nations was in no way a danger to the friendship initiated at Rapallo. Germany would accept membership only after she had been guaranteed exemption from Article 16.

Chicherin expressed his pleasure about Stresemann's view on Article 16 and remarked that no concrete reply had been made to the Russian "suggestion" of October 18. Brockdorff-Rantzau replied that a common procedure was no longer possible. If the demands made by Germany were accepted, she had to become a member.

Chicherin remarked that he placed a great value on an exchange of views in case the German demands were rejected. The Foreign Commissar, on the spur of the moment, or so it appeared to Brockdorff-Rantzau, asked that B. W. von Bülow, the director of the Wilhelmstrasse's division for League matters, be sent to Moscow for a few days to explain Germany's position.

Brockdorff-Rantzau asked his home office to send Bülow to Moscow. The Count inquired of Maltzan whether the demands regarding Article 16 were real "*conditions* for [her] entry into the League of

Nations [or] constituted only desiderata." He expressed the hope that Berlin would insist that its demands be accepted before joining the League.[16]

The Zinoviev appeal created a number of difficulties for the Wilhelmstrasse just at the time when attempts were being made to convince the Russians that friendship with them was really part of German foreign policy. At the festivities held at the Russian Embassy to commemorate the November Revolution, no official from either the Reich or the Prussian government put in an appearance because of the Zinoviev letter published in October. Leading members of the German Foreign Office attended in force. Stresemann did his best to make his hosts feel that the Foreign Office was willing to maintain correct relations despite insults by the Chairman of the Comintern.

Stresemann's approach was imitated by the Russians, who utilized for an ostentatious display of cordiality the arrival, on November 12, of the German delegation to the negotiations for a comprehensive commercial treaty between Germany and the USSR, headed by Theodor von Körner. A tea party in their honor was given by the Foreign Commissariat, at which Chicherin, Litvinov, Krassin, other leading members of the Collegium of the Narkomindel, and members of the Supreme Economic Council, as well as members of the press, participated. Two days later, at a solemn session held in the great conference hall of the Foreign Commissariat, the negotiations were declared open by Krassin. On the sixteenth, a lavish supper was given at Brockdorff-Rantzau's residence.

On November 17, negotiations started, and the Russian representative, Ganetzky, and Chicherin told Brockdorff-Rantzau that they hoped for positive results.[17] This mutual show of friendship only masked the Russian concern about the German drift toward the West. Chicherin used an article by Wilson Harris in the London *Daily News* of November 17 to bring this home to Brockdorff-Rantzau. He quoted part of the article to the Ambassador:

> There are unquestionably two policies—perhaps three—being pursued persistently, of which the country would do well to take account. One is the Russian policy of systematic cultivation of Germany. The other is the German policy, more doubtful and less resolute, of systematic cultivation of Russia.

If Russo-German relations appeared in that light to a "competent observer," Chicherin inquired, was there not room for thought?[18]

There was room for thought, the more so since the men in the Kremlin continued to insult the German government in the most derogatory manner possible. On November 27, the *Rote Fahne* carried an election appeal by Stalin which was intended to inspire the KPD to greater effort in the Reichstag elections to be held on December 7. Stalin compared the elections to ballots cast in prison (*Zuchthauswahlen*) and referred to the German government as a "prison regime." Stalin, using his best polemical style, made it quite clear that there were other means than casting ballots to gain power. In his words, the "German proletariat is not going to speak its last word in the elections. . . ."[19]

This latest piece of Communist insolence annoyed Maltzan considerably and led Stresemann to instruct Brockdorff-Rantzau to inform the Soviet government of German consternation. Although Stalin had signed in the name of the Central Committee of the Russian Communist Party, the fact was that he was a member of the "Presidium" of the USSR and, as such, a government official of greater importance than Zinoviev.[20]

Brockdorff-Rantzau's request for the dispatch of Bülow to Moscow was not welcome at the Wilhelmstrasse. Stresemann used a Brockdorff-Rantzau technique and got President Ebert's opinion. The President did not think it wise to send Bülow because

> the Ambassador has been informed about our position on the League in detail, and more than information cannot be involved in the talks in Moscow.[21]

Beyond this, Ebert was concerned that in the event the German request was rejected and Germany refused to reconsider its application, that decision would be blamed on some sinister deal between Chicherin and Bülow. Brockdorff-Rantzau repeated his well-worn warning that "a successful Eastern policy would become impossible" the moment Germany joined the League, and she would thereby be delivered helplessly to Western mercy. This situation could be avoided by accepting Chicherin's request for an exchange of "intimate views." Maltzan, also hiding behind the President, informed Brockdorff-Rantzau that Ebert was adamantly opposed to any trip by Bülow to Moscow. The Ambassador reluctantly accepted the fact that Bülow would not come, but hinted darkly that it had already been politically disadvantageous.[22]

The Russians decided to propose more specific items for German consideration. On December 4, Victor Kopp told Brockdorff-Rantzau that his government placed the greatest value on the continued exchange of views. Up to now, there had been only general assurances by Germany that she wanted to keep the road to the East open, while Russia had been quite definite about her desire for more intimate, confidential relations with Germany. One of the most important problems confronting both was Poland. It was of the utmost importance that an understanding on this matter be achieved. It was essential for the Russians to know whether Germany would continue her demands against Poland. The Poles only recently had made some inquiries in Moscow regarding Galicia and other areas bordering on Russia. Kopp did not think that these Polish wishes should be fulfilled and was sure that Chicherin felt the same way. If Germany kept to her demands regarding Silesia and the Corridor, "mutual pressure could be placed on Poland." It was obvious that an exchange of views was necessary, especially if Germany intended to continue an independent foreign policy.

Brockdorff-Rantzau replied that Germany would never relinquish her demands on Poland, but to try and change the status quo by force "would be madness." However, should the Polish question become the object of talks with Jean Herbette, the newly-appointed French Ambassador, whose arrival in Moscow was expected by the middle of December, he felt authorized to state that "if the Russian government should guarantee the western border of Poland, such a step would be considered as an unfriendly act by [Germany]." Kopp wanted to know how Russia should react if Germany, by entering the League of Nations, guaranteed the *eastern* border of Poland. The Ambassador replied that Kopp was well aware of his opinion on the League. Should Germany enter the world organization and

> thereby, according to the statutes of the League of Nations, acknowledge her own borders, which had been drawn by the *Diktat* of Versailles, she could not demand more of Russia than for herself.

Kopp seemed satisfied with this statement, but emphasized that entry into the League would be interpreted as constituting a new orientation and a turning away from Russia. Brockdorff-Rantzau again declared that he opposed entry into the League, "but, after all, the shirt was closer than the jacket." If Russian sabotage of his program did not cease, it might be possible that Germany, because of widespread demands for joining the League, would have no choice in the matter. Unless he was able to report some positive results to Berlin, his own influence would wane. The Ambassador asked Kopp to tell him what his government had done recently to show that it was interested in good relations.

Chicherin's press remarks on the League had sounded like threats and had a detrimental effect in Germany. Rykov, Chairman of the

Council of People's Commissars, had referred to Germany as a colony because she had accepted the Dawes Plan. During the Ruhr affair, the Communists had made the greatest difficulties, especially in Germany. Now Herr Stalin, immediately before the general elections, had published an appeal in the *Rote Fahne* in which he dared to call the German government a "prison regime" and make barely disguised threats of revolution. Finally, what was one to make of Rykov's announcement that the Soviet government was not responsible for the excesses of Communist parties abroad?

Kopp, obviously embarrassed, replied that he did not agree with Chicherin's remarks, and that Rykov's statement on the Dawes Plan had been a "political slip." He did not say anything about Stalin's appeal. At the conclusion of their talk, Kopp again repeated his earlier request that the Ambassador try to bring about a more intimate exchange of political views between their governments.

Brockdorff-Rantzau urged the Wilhelmstrasse to permit him to follow up Kopp's offer with concrete German proposals. The Count was convinced that the Russian offer should be taken up before Herbette arrived in Moscow, or dire consequences would certainly result, especially in regard to Poland.[23]

Maltzan authorized Brockdorff-Rantzau on December 13 to enter into a confidential exchange of views with the Soviet government on questions relating to Poland. The Count could admit that it was theoretically correct that Germany, after becoming a member of the League, would have to respect the territorial integrity of Poland. But this did not mean that Germany could never do anything about her frontiers with Poland. Germany had protested before and after the Treaty of Versailles was accepted that her frontiers with Poland violated Wilson's ethnographic principle. Brockdorff-Rantzau might mention that the major trouble in Eastern Europe stemmed from disregarding this ethnographic principle. Maltzan left it to the Ambassador's discretion to decide

whether he should already hint that the solution of the Polish question, for Germany and Russia, lay in pushing Poland back to her ethnographic borders. . . .[24]

These instructions were to be Maltzan's last in his capacity as Undersecretary. He had accepted an appointment as Ambassador to Washington. Brockdorff-Rantzau's primary concern was the effect that this would have on his own policies. He was convinced that Maltzan's transfer meant a much colder climate for his work in Berlin. The Count considered Carl von Schubert, who was to be Maltzan's replacement, singularly unfit for the job because his sympathies were with the West and he supported Stresemann's fulfillment policy.[25]

The Russians, like Brockdorff-Rantzau, considered the replacement of Maltzan by Schubert as proof that the emphasis of German foreign policy had definitely shifted to the West. The German Foreign Office tried to calm Russian apprehensions by publishing a communiqué on December 19, in which it stated that Schubert would pursue policies identical to those which Maltzan had followed; both men were interested in furthering the welfare of Germany and in continued good relations with the East and the West.[26] Needless to say, this communiqué did little to alter Russian opinion or to convince Brockdorff-Rantzau that his evaluation of Maltzan's transfer was not correct. Maltzan, closely associated with an Eastern policy, had to go so that the road to the West would be easier to travel for Stresemann. Russian concern could now be utilized for altering the Rapallo relationship without destroying its basic advantages. Schubert's well-known proclivity for the West, especially England, and his close relations with D'Abernon, the British Ambassador to Germany, gave the Russians nightmares about a continent united against them. This fear turned the tables on them: Germany regained its independence from Russia and at the same time from the West. That was Stresemann's great contribution to Germany's recovery to Great Power status. Brockdorff-Rantzau did not believe that Stresemann had no intention of cutting the wire to Moscow. He therefore attempted to deepen the relationship with Moscow before it was too late.

On December 20, Brockdorff-Rantzau informed Chicherin of Maltzan's telegram authorizing him to enter into a confidential exchange of views regarding the Polish question. The Commissar received that disclosure with great interest, but not without some sign of nervousness. He declared, in the course of the two-hour-long discussion, that the Soviet government had proposed a "continuing exchange of views regarding *general* political questions, and now [the Ambassador] told him that the German government would like it if Germany and Russia kept in confidential and continuous touch regarding *Polish* matters." Brockdorff-Rantzau pointed out that the telegram was a direct reply to questions discussed with Kopp, who had placed particular emphasis on Poland in connection with German League membership.

At this point, Chicherin proceeded to details. Germany, he said, promised neutrality vis-à-vis Russia but asked for her active support in regard to Poland's western frontier. When Chicherin insisted on this point, Brockdorff-Rantzau decided to intimate that the "solution of the Polish question, for Germany as well as for Russia, lay in the pushing back of Poland to her ethnographic frontiers." Chicherin welcomed this proposal for action and described it as being of special importance. The Commissar seemed to be quite agitated about Articles 10, 11, and 17 of the League Covenant. Article 17, he declared, could be used to force Germany to participate in sanctions. Brockdorff-Rantzau told Chicherin that the information he had transmitted constituted the beginning of a confidential exchange of views and that his concern would be transmitted to the Reich government. Chicherin replied that he too would consult his own superiors.

Chicherin and Brockdorff-Rantzau continued their talk during the night of December 25. Chicherin disclosed that his consultation with the leading men in the Soviet government had revealed that all of them appreciated the German frankness in regard to Poland. Before discussing Poland, he intended to lay the basis for "an exchange of views about concrete, general political questions." Chicherin repeatedly emphasized that the proposals he was about to voice constituted in no sense an ultimatum. Even if the German government should reject the Soviet suggestions, their friendly relationship would continue, but in "the *Polish question* no common treatment, in the sense proposed by Berlin, would be possible."

When Brockdorff-Rantzau interjected that the proposal to act against Poland had come from Kopp, Chicherin refused to endorse his subordinate. Kopp was not empowered to make such far-reaching proposals; only he and Litvinov could do that. Any settlement of the Polish question would have to be preceded by an agreement in which

> the German and the Russian governments bind themselves to enter into no political or economic alliance or understandings with third parties which are directed against the other.

When the Ambassador pointed out that this formulation went rather far and wanted to know whether this included entry into the League, Chicherin said that this was the second proposal which had to be accepted before a common attempt to solve the Polish question could be considered.

> Germany and the Soviet Union bind themselves to coordinate their activities, in the course of future developments, on the question about entering the League of Nations or the dispatch of an observer.

Chicherin added that the most ideal solution would be for Germany and Russia to enter together, or to send an observer together. Should the German government object to these propositions, the Soviet government would look forward to German suggestions.

Brockdorff-Rantzau said that the first proposal really was not too clear and that he would therefore like to add following "both governments bind themselves" the words "not to attack each other. . . ." Chicherin objected to the reference to "nonagression." The Ambassador pointed out that there had been rumors in 1923 that Russia had requested passage through Poland in the event of a Red revolution in Germany. Thereupon, Chicherin agreed without hesitation that the nonaggression phrase should be included in his neutrality clause. The Count suggested that "proposals of such political importance" would be more likely to be accepted if the Soviet government created a favorable atmosphere for cooperation. It could begin by doing something positive in the pending negotiations for the commercial treaty. Chicherin understood and asked that his proposals be treated as secret.[27]

In a letter to Stresemann, Brockdorff-Rantzau strongly advised the serious consideration of the Russian offer. Chicherin's ominous warning during their talk that a deal with the French could become possible if the Germans continued to move toward the West was, in the Count's opinion, not an empty threat. Chicherin's proposals augured well for the further development of Germany's relationship with Russia. The offer of a neutrality treaty was certainly an attempt to remove distrust between the two countries. Chicherin had made it quite clear that Russia would take a step, such as the solution of the Polish question, only if she first came to an understanding with Germany regarding all matters related to a common policy. The Foreign Commissar had said: "We do not do anything with Herbette if you do not do anything with Chamberlain." Brockdorff-Rantzau informed Stresemann that he had made it quite clear, and Chicherin understood, that such a promise would necessitate concessions to Germany. The Count then repeated what he had already said many times: direct contact with Moscow would not increase the danger of a Bolshevik infection, while contact with Germany might change Russia's brutal system. Under the given circumstances, Germany had no choice but to make common cause with the Soviet Union, unless it became obvious that Moscow used Germany only "as an experimental object for her plans of world revolution" and did not support her against the West. Then Germany would have to join the Western powers and any independent foreign policy would cease for a long time. Germany would not be able to do a thing but bide her time, grow strong, and remedy "the outrageous injustice committed against the German people, as far as time does not rectify it, on the basis of her own strength."[28]

Quite obviously, the Count was not opposed to using military power to overthrow the *Diktat*, but only as a last resort. But he was also trying to convince Stresemann that his policy of fulfillment would be aided by close cooperation, if not an alliance with Russia. On December 29, Schubert telegraphed that the Wilhelmstrasse could not understand why Chicherin had belittled Kopp's suggestion.

> The German government is naturally at any time ready for a continuing exchange of views on all general questions. The German government gladly followed Kopp's suggestion to begin an exchange of views with a concrete problem interesting both states equally.
>
> Your intimations of our intention to push Poland back to her ethnographic frontiers in cooperation with Russia agrees with the opinion here. They set a goal in general, the details of which, to be sure, need further discussion. The choice of means must naturally depend on the situation at the given time.

Chicherin's interpretations regarding the various articles of the League Covenant were "legally not quite applicable and bore witness to a lack of knowledge about the actual situation inside the League of Nations." Article 10, wrote Schubert, provided for the renunciation of aggressive war, which had no practical significance. Brockdorff-Rantzau should apprise Chicherin of the fact that Article 10 was quite controversial and that the English Dominions demanded its removal.

Germany, in its note to the League of Nations on December 12, had rejected participation in any forcible actions of the League. Therefore, "Articles 11 to 15, which guarantee peace, have become illusory in case of a widespread European conflict, especially as far as Russia is concerned."

Schubert summarized his reply to Chicherin by showing that

> Article 10 was of almost no consequence to Germany because of her special position, and therefore would not place any obligations on Germany to protect other members of the League, protection which has not even been organized. It will not be possible to apply the sanctions provided for in Article 16, designed to preserve peace, as long as Germany maintains its demand for neutrality, and she is absolutely determined to do so. That Germany would be forced to comply with Article 17 is so improbable that it does not even enter into the realm of practical discussion.[29]

On January 6, 1925, Brockdorff-Rantzau pressed Schubert for the immediate start of negotiations for a treaty on the basis of the Russian December proposals. In answer to this appeal, the Ambassador received a telegram two days later. Stresemann once again kept Brockdorff-Rantzau immobilized by acquainting Ebert with Brockdorff-Rantzau's report of December 20. The President, wrote Stresemann, had promised to discuss the Russian proposal in the near future. The Foreign Minister asked the Ambassador to inform Chicherin, if he thought it necessary, that another German Cabinet crisis made it imperative to keep any definite answer in abeyance until a new cabinet had been formed.

Two days later, Brockdorff-Rantzau transmitted the content of Stresemann's telegram to Chicherin. The Commissar expressed his dismay and regretted the fact that the foundation for closer relations was not going to be laid before Herbette arrived in Moscow. Chicherin explained that he did not intend to scare Germany with the possibility of a Russo-French *rapprochement*. England was trying to isolate the Soviet Union and was supported by France. Brockdorff-Rantzau agreed with the Commissar that England was attempting to separate Germany from Russia and asked Stresemann to take advantage of the opportunity created by this situation. He advised that the continuation of the talks with Chicherin was "absolutely necessary." If it was not done, a great opportunity would be missed.[30]

The Russians did everything to support Brockdorff-Rantzau. Radek, in *Pravda* for January 11, warned that "a disarmed country which cannot offer any resistance to imperialism armed to the teeth does not appear at negotiations as an equal partner" with the West. "This fact should revive the ideas of Rapallo, which were still alive in the USSR."

A week later, Radek wrote in *Izvestia* that the new German Cabinet formed on January 20 by Hans Luther was made up of representatives of heavy industry and landed property. The formation of such a cabinet showed that one year of economic recovery sufficed to restore the confidence of the old ruling classes. Stresemann, who continued as foreign minister, would continue to "tack in all directions." In Berlin, Ambassador Krestinsky requested an introduction to the new Chancellor, whom he did not consider quite as friendly to Russia as was Stresemann. The Foreign Minister promised to arrange an informal meeting and assured the Ambassador that Luther was "not unfriendly" toward the Soviet Union. With the new Cabinet installed, the reason given for delaying a reply to Chicherin's project disappeared. No action was taken by Stresemann, who wanted to keep Moscow in abeyance while he prepared the ground for better German relations with the West, especially with France.

Brockdorff-Rantzau was notified by Schubert on January 22 that the Wilhelmstrasse was considering proposing a security pact to the West. The Ambassador received two secret reports worked out in the Foreign Office. The contemplated approach to the West was in no way prejudicial to an extension of German-Russian relations as envisioned by Brockdorff-Rantzau, the Undersecretary wrote. A decision would soon be made on the reply to the Russian proposals. In the meantime, Germany could not relinquish her freedom to resolve questions arising from the Treaty of Versailles with France and England. In any event, it was primarily an attempt to defend Germany against French expansionism. It did not constitute a realignment of German policy vis-à-vis Russia.

A note had already been sent to London on January 20, in which Whitehall was informed of German willingness to consider a treaty of long duration, guaranteed by the United States, to assure France that Germany would not wage war against her.

On February 12, Schubert apprised Brockdorff-Rantzau of the fact that London and Paris had been secretly approached about the possibility of negotiating a Western security pact. Nothing was done about the Russian proposals. Eleven days later, Schubert apologized for his inactivity regarding the December proposals. Russia was a new field for him, and Maltzan's departure had left him "like a swimmer who for the first time finds himself in deep water without a lifesaver." Schubert thought that the knottiest problem facing him was the incorporation of the policy toward Russia into Germany's over-all foreign relations. He had "no intention of criticizing anyone," but the Russian policy had never been fully integrated. In any event, this had to be accomplished before decisions on details were made.[31]

Brockdorff-Rantzau replied that *he* knew the situation in Russia very well. Although he did not look at relations with the Soviet Union through rose-colored glasses, he wanted to make it perfectly clear that the only reason he had accepted the Moscow appointment was to knock the Treaty of Versailles into a cocked hat. The fulfillment of this aim necessitated at the very least the appearance that Berlin could fall back on Moscow for political support and economic advantages. "What I support is not a game at dangerous risks because of a desperate situation [*Vabanquespiel*], but a play in which we hold the trumps."[32]

The Russians became increasingly impatient about the continuing delay. The Kremlin had no intention of relinquishing its *places d'armes* in Western Europe, and decided on drastic action to turn Stresemann from his Western course. Since the December proposals had not succeeded in accomplishing that fact, Moscow decided to add to its original offer. Rykov told Brockdorff-Rantzau on February 21 that he wanted to see the Treaty of Rapallo expanded. The Soviet government had been offered a number of deals at the expense of Germany which his government was not necessarily willing to accept. Instead, the Soviet government wanted to develop closer relations with Germany. He "proposed an alliance [*Bündnisvertrag*]. The Soviet government was convinced that such an alliance would have a far-reaching, calming effect on the public."

Brockdorff-Rantzau was taken aback by this straightforward offer. He replied that a decision on a matter of such extensive consequences had to be made by his government. He was certain that Berlin would be willing to enter into close relations with the Soviet "*government*." However, he doubted whether any German government could get public support for a treaty with the Soviet Union as long as the conviction persisted that the "Russian government was identical with the Comintern." Rykov denied that the two were in fact the same. He agreed that the talks should be secret, but that Seeckt should be informed. In the Soviet Union, Rykov said, the General was considered one of the most ardent supporters of really cordial relations between Russia and Germany.

Brockdorff-Rantzau replied that he

> was very well aware of the outstanding role which the General played in German-Russian relations. I myself had taken over the post in Moscow to revise the *Diktat* of Versailles, but not as "Ambassador of Revenge." I wanted, if possible, to bring about the revision of the Treaty of Versailles in a peaceful way, but I did not have any illusions that Russia, as certain circles in Germany believed, would be ready to start "a war of liberation according to the example of the year 1813" for Germany.

He knew that the USSR was "guided exclusively by the idea of world revolution." The Count refrained from rejecting the offer in any harsher terms because he did not want to drive the Russians into the French camp.[33]

While Brockdorff-Rantzau officially played it safe, he had no such compulsion in private. On February 25, he sent his alter ego, Ernst Rantzau, to tell Schubert that a speedy answer should be made to the Russian proposal and to his own "great plan." Germany did not have to fear any indiscretion on the part of the Soviets, because they had enough material in "another area" to incriminate Germany. The situation in Russia was serious, and an immediate answer was absolutely necessary. Schubert refused to be panicked. He wrote to the Ambassador that German-Russian relations would not be sacrificed for membership in the League of Nations. On the twenty-fourth, Schubert had had one last talk with Maltzan, who was leaving for Washington the following day. Maltzan had cautioned Schubert against a secret treaty with the Russians because one could not be sure that they would adhere to it or that they would keep it confidential. He had advised his successor to continue negotiations with Chicherin with the greatest circumspection and all due delay. "The Russians," Maltzan had said, "come to us if we have the patience."[34] These sentiments ran completely counter to Brockdorff-Rantzau's policy. He was convinced that the opportunity at hand would never return.

On the last day of February, Brockdorff-Rantzau told Chicherin that Rykov had repeatedly touched on the possibility of a military alliance. Chicherin appeared to be genuinely startled and said only that Rykov must have been referring to the possibilities explored in December of 1923. However, at the end of the discussion Chicherin stated that if Rykov had spoken about "military agreements," those were not beyond the realm of the possible. After all, he told the Ambassador, "one should not forget that Russia needed Germany for her military reconstruction, and that Germany, in a manner of speaking, could use Russia as an arsenal." Brockdorff-Rantzau replied that he was well aware of this, but that he was somewhat concerned that the guns supplied to Russia might someday be used against Germany. Furthermore, it was utopian to assume that Russia would join Germany in a war of liberation à la 1812/13. The Ambassador also made another attempt to check the Comintern by an oblique threat that a successful conclusion of any treaty would depend on the removal of Zinoviev's interference. As long as Zinoviev, or Apfelbaum (he did not know what the fellow's real name was) had any influence (which he had heard was on the wane), a reasonable relationship in foreign affairs was hardly feasible. Chicherin avoided the Comintern issue, but assured the Count that Russo-German cooperation was by no means utopian, because Russia had her eyes on Asia and therefore a conflict with England, which would be supported by France, was quite likely.

Brockdorff-Rantzau wanted the Wilhelmstrasse to accept Chicherin's explanations. He concluded his report home with the observation that great changes were taking place in Russia and that "the Communist leadership, convinced of the uselessness of revolutionizing Germany, thinks of transferring its beneficial activity to the East." Despite this fact, he emphasized that he still "considered it dangerous in the highest degree to enter into an alliance with the Soviet government, especially in the military sphere." Privately, the Count continued to work for the acceptance of the Russian proposals. He was sure that nobody in Berlin would dare to "take the responsibility for the decision" to accept the Russian offer.[35]

The veil of secrecy with which the security proposals to the West had been surrounded had been partially lifted by the French Premier, Edouard Herriot, on February 27, after searching questions in the Chamber. On March 4, Chicherin informed the Central Executive Committee that the attitude of the Entente in regard to Germany's disarmament "compels Germany to maintain a policy of friendly relations with the Soviet Republic." It was only natural that Germany should like to get on an equal footing with the Entente. Despite this desire, German politicians would "always recognize the need of securing their rear in the East." No matter what vacillations occurred, the spirit of Rapallo would prevail.[36]

The discussion which followed the Herriot remarks in the German press made it necessary for the Wilhelmstrasse to insert a communiqué in the morning papers on March 5. On the following day, Stresemann instructed Brockdorff-Rantzau to inform the Soviet government that Germany had proposed a Western security pact to London and Paris. Stresemann repeated the arguments given by Schubert on February 12 and added that the press reports that Germany had renounced the use of military force to alter her geographic borders with Poland and Czechoslovakia were false.

Brockdorff-Rantzau transmitted this information to Litvinov on March 10. On the same day, Krestinsky, on Moscow's instructions, made inquiries at the Wilhelmstrasse. Stresemann told him briefly that the note to the powers contained only a statement of general willingness to guarantee the status quo in the West to avoid war with France. Arbitration treaties had been offered to resolve problems which could arise about Germany's eastern borders.

Krestinsky expressed his concern over the fact that no reply had as yet been received to the proposals of his government. Stresemann agreed with Krestinsky that the Russian suggestion did not conflict with the contemplated security agreements with the West. The death of President Ebert on February 28 had made it necessary to delay an answer to the Russian offer of an alliance. Stresemann promised to discuss the matter with the Chancellor, the President *pro tempore*, and with Brockdorff-Rantzau.[37]

It was quite obvious that Stresemann was not going to jeopardize his negotiations with the West. The Russians, afraid that Stresemann intended to abandon them, again played the Polish card. Schubert was invited to luncheon at the Soviet Embassy and introduced to a Mr. Michalski. This shadowy gentleman functioned as "scientific advisor" to the Soviet Embassy. He had been in close touch with Maltzan, who considered him one of the two most informed persons at the Embassy. Michalski, who was considered a friend of Stalin, continued his close relations with the Wilhelmstrasse until 1932.

Schubert and Michalski had an animated discussion about the security pact, during which Michalski informed Schubert that, in his opinion, Poland was about ready to come to an understanding with Russia. The English were disturbed by this possibility, because they wanted Poland as part of the anti-Soviet bloc. Schubert denied this on the ground that England wanted peace in Europe to enable her to devote herself to problems in her empire. Besides, England considered Poland "the major disturbance" of Europe's peace.

Michalski was not easily put off. He discussed the attitude of the United States Senator Borah, who, Michalski said, had spoken of the security pact as a new "Holy Alliance," which, Michalski insisted, would be directed against Russia. Schubert, whose historical sensibilities might have rebelled against the Borah-Michalski school of history, assured his companion that Germany only wanted to resolve the Rhineland question.[38]

In Moscow, the unofficial approaches continued. Rothstein, the Narkomindel's press chief, told Paul Scheffer, Moscow correspondent of the influential *Berliner Tageblatt,* who was considered to have Brockdorff-Rantzau's ear, that Russia and Poland were involved in discussing a general economic agreement but that nothing beyond this was contemplated. However, the Soviet government, "even before it made it possible for Poland to begin negotiations," had made "definite proposals to Germany which were designed to remove the unstable and quite insecure conditions which *now existed* between the two countries." That no reply to these proposals had been made was a matter of regret to the Soviet government. If Chicherin's proposals were accepted, Germany could continue an independent policy in Eastern Europe with Russian cooperation.

Scheffer, surprised over the revelation of Chicherin's offer although no details were given to him, reported the discussion to Herbert von Dirksen, who had taken over the Russian desk in February. Dirksen passed the information on to Schubert.

Litvinov expressed the opinion to Brockdorff-Rantzau that Germany would join the League without conditions because of Anglo-French pressure. The Havas News Agency had reported that the French and British governments had agreed that Germany had to apply for League membership and accept all provisions of the Covenant before negotiations on the West pact could commence.

Litvinov wondered whether a response to the December proposals could be expected within a short time. The Ambassador sent Hencke as a special messenger to Berlin to make an oral report, expressing Brockdorff-Rantzau's increasing apprehensions about the effect the conclusion of a Western security pact would have on German-Russian relations. Hencke also delivered the complete notes on the Ambassador's talk with Chicherin of February 28. Hencke informed Schubert on March 13 of his chief's advice to make at least a counterproposal regarding Poland and the League of Nations if nothing affirmative could be done about the December proposals. Brockdorff-Rantzau warned that even an arbitration treaty with Poland would lead to an agreement unfavorable for Germany between Moscow and Warsaw. Germany should not join the League of Nations but send an observer instead. Schubert was noncommittal and told Hencke that the Ambassador would receive "extensive instructions."[39]

On March 14, the Council of the League of Nations rejected Germany's application for membership until she accepted the Covenant without condition. This immediately created a tense situation with Moscow, where the charge that Germany would join now without conditions was endlessly repeated. Schubert assured Brockdorff-Rantzau that the "repercussions on German-Russian relations stood at the center of discussions" at the Foreign Office, but the political situation required that no rash decisions be made.[40]

The French Ambassador to Germany, Bruno F. P. J. de Margerie, informed Stresemann on March 16 that the French government intended to discuss the German proposals for a security pact with its allies. The Ambassador stated that Poland was afraid that Germany wanted to use the arbitration court to deal with the Polish borders. Stresemann asked de Margerie to tell him what Germany could do to quiet Polish fears, as a new guarantee of Germany's eastern borders was out of the question. The Ambassador shrugged his shoulders, remarking that Germany apparently assumed that peace in Europe could be assured by a solution of the problem created by her eastern frontiers.

Stresemann agreed wholeheartedly and emphasized that "a pauperized Russia" was more likely to go to war than one which had no serious demands. Why, asked Stresemann, solve these problems "in an ocean of blood." It would be much better to remove the mistakes which had been committed when the postwar borders were drawn.[41]

The playing of the Russian card was a deliberate move by Stresemann. There was great concern in Paris and London that Germany would react to the rejection of her demands by turning East. That was obvious from the note of the League's Council, which had not closed the door to membership but indicated that it looked forward to a new application with favor. Dr. Dufour-Feronce, Counselor of Embassy at the German Embassy in London, wrote to Schubert that the security pact was the best way to peace and the liberation of the Ruhr and the Rhineland. He strenuously warned against any kind of treaty, either open or secret, with Russia. Such a move would lose Germany the support of the United States and Great Britain.[42]

At the Wilhelmstrasse, all aspects of the situation were carefully evaluated. Obviously the time had come to deal with the Russian proposals. When Hencke returned to Moscow on March 22, Stresemann gave him a twenty-one-page memorandum for Brockdorff-Rantzau, in which the arguments already made in the telegram of March 6 were reviewed and in which the contemplated tactics in regard to the security pact and League membership were described.

Stresemann again pointed out that France's wish for security had to be fulfilled before she would evacuate the occupied Rhine zone. From the beginning it had been made absolutely clear that the *"conditio sine qua non"* for Germany's participation in any security arrangements would be her refusal to accept the existing borders in the East. Germany had offered and Poland had rejected, as expected, a procedure of settlement outside a court of arbitration.

The decision by the powers to have Germany join the League before any negotiations for a security pact were started had created great difficulties. If Russia was interested in deepening relations, she had to be interested in Germany's return to great power status. Stresemann, using Moscow's own favorite terminology, directed attention to the fact that the policy in the West was nothing more than

a defense against those tendencies of French imperialism which immediately threaten our existence. Should the Soviet government make the renunciation of this defense the basis for the maintenance of friendly relations with Germany, the only conclusion which could be drawn from such a position would be that she is not, in the final analysis, interested in fruitful political collaboration with us, but instead wants to bring our difficulties in the West to a climax, in the hope that such difficulties will make a consolidation of our domestic situation completely impossible and thus prepare the soil for a Communist revolution.

Stresemann again explained that membership in the League would be accepted only if Germany immediately received a permanent seat on the Council, which would make it possible to block any anti-Soviet move by using the veto. This condition should prove to Moscow that German membership in the world organization would benefit Russia tremendously. On the other hand, Stresemann admitted, should events occur which would make it possible to push Poland back to her ethnographic frontiers, "it was quite conceivable that an active intervention by Germany would at the very least be greatly hampered by her membership in the League." But even without membership, Germany was not yet strong enough to think of using armed force to regain her territories in the East, nor were Germany and Russia together strong enough to defeat the determined resistance of the Western powers. Therefore, it was quite correct, as Brockdorff-Rantzau had pointed out, that an "open or secret military alliance with the USSR" did not belong to "our political aims for the immediate future." However, Stresemann had no objection to entering into discussions regarding closer relations with Russia. The discussions should center on Germany's eventual entry into the League. If the Soviet government was willing to talk about the problems described in the memorandum, it would be possible to agree on the ways and means for the consideration of "a positive agreement concerning general political aims." Brockdorff-Rantzau should inform the Soviet government of the memorandum as discreetly as was possible.[43]

Stresemann's memorandum did nothing to allay Brockdorff-Rantzau's fears about the westward drift of German policy. He did not deliver Stresemann's proposal to the Foreign Commissariat because, in his opinion, it constituted a rejection of the Russian offer of December. He did not want any arrangement, with either the East or the West, which bound Germany by treaty. As long as the solution of the problems in the West was not connected directly to League membership, no burden was placed on the German-Russian relationship; in fact, it would make it possible to "resolve the Polish question in collaboration" with Russia. If Germany entered the League without insisting upon the granting of her demands, especially exemption from Article 16, then the relationship with Moscow would undergo a drastic change. Certainly the December proposals could no longer be considered unless Germany wanted to compromise herself. Russia feared isolation, and German membership in the League accentuated that fear.

Brockdorff-Rantzau reminded Stresemann that he had already tested Russian willingness to enter into discussions aimed at resolving concrete problems; they had responded much more favorably than could have been expected. Their proposals were of such importance that they had to be considered before any final disposition was made regarding relations with the West. Brockdorff-Rantzau pointed to the Damocles' sword which hung over Germany's head: military collaboration. He warned that the Soviet Union might feel free to reveal the whole business and thereby compromise Germany completely if she decided to join the League.[44]

Stresemann's refusal to come to terms with the Russians, coupled with the loss of his strongest support in Berlin, through Maltzan's departure and Ebert's death, had already prompted Brockdorff-Rantzau to ask Walter Simons, who had been appointed President *ad interim* on March 12, for assistance.

Simons wrote to Chancellor Luther on March 20, asking him to consult with Brockdorff-Rantzau before any change in policy was made. Simons voiced his personal concern about the interpretation placed on the German offer to the West by the Russians. He did not want Moscow to feel that Berlin offered Rapallo to the West as the *quid pro quo* for her admission to the League. Considering all the risks involved,

> even if the Chancellor and Foreign Minister have already agreed on the decision and are determined not to let the arguments of Count Brockdorff-Rantzau confuse them, I would still advise consulting him. No matter what success our Western policies may have, it always remains in our interest not to see the wire to Moscow cut. If Brockdorff-Rantzau comes to Berlin before the decision is made, the Russian rulers can believe, after his return, that we hold fast to our demands for exemption from Article 16 and the eastern border, or that we could renounce them without detriment to the interests of the Russians. If he remains in Moscow they will not believe him, because he himself will not believe it. One has to expect that he will give up the ambassadorship. It is even possible that he will be entered in the run-off [*Zweiten Wahlgang*] elections—he has the caliber—as a candidate for the presidency. His chances [for election] should not be too bad.[45]

Simons' intercession, despite the possibility implied in Brockdorff-Rantzau's chances for the presidency, proved barren. Luther and Stresemann did not recall the Ambassador for consultation. Brockdorff-Rantzau vented his anger in a letter to Simons, in which he threatened to resign. The indecent haste which Germany showed "would mean the voluntary acknowledgment of the *Diktat* of Versailles," and none of the crafty little excuses thought up to "decoy this fact" would convince him differently.[46]

On the day after Simons' letter to Luther, the Ambassador demanded of Schubert that negotiations with the East should run parallel
to those with the West. Brockdorff-Rantzau was convinced that he was
never informed in good time or asked for advice *before* decisions were
made."

Schubert officially informed Krestinsky on March 25 that German
application for League membership had been rejected. The Soviet Ambassador vented Moscow's resentment for not having been notified
until the last minute about negotiations with the West. Schubert
assured him that this had been done only because nothing in these
preliminary exchanges of views really interested the Russians. He had
been called in now because the Foreign Office wanted to discuss
Poland, in addition to matters concerning the League of Nations.[47]

In Moscow, Brockdorff-Rantzau still had not transmitted the instructions sent to him by Stresemann on March 22. The Foreign Minister, after again presenting his arguments, instructed the Count on April
1 to acquaint either Chicherin or Litvinov with the thoughts presented
in the memorandum. Stresemann explained that he did not want to be
confronted by a choice between the East and the West. Apparently the
Ambassador favored the East. Germany's immediate concern was the
solution of her problems in the West, and if this could be done only by
entering the League of Nations, that step had to be considered. He was
sure that Moscow did not want to present an "either-or" proposal.
Stresemann urgently requested that Brockdorff-Rantzau present the
German point of view with due emphasis. The Ambassador, still reluctant, carried out the order and presented the German explanations
orally to Litvinov on April 7, after having acquainted him with the
general tenor of the memorandum five days earlier. The Deputy Commissar asked that the note be transmitted in writing. Krestinsky would
present the Russian reply in the same fashion.[48] Chicherin, who was
again incapacitated with another attack of diabetes, received Brockdorff-Rantzau on April 8 to discuss the Stresemann memorandum.
After this discussion the Ambassador left Moscow on his regular spring
furlough, determined to argue his case personally in Berlin, where he
arrived on April 13.

Two days after his arrival in Berlin, the Count insisted to Schubert
that "a treaty designed to confirm and elaborate Rapallo" should be
worked out right away.[49] While the Count spoke with Schubert,
Stresemann had a long discussion with the Soviet Ambassador. The
Foreign Minister assured Krestinsky that "Germany maintained her
freedom of action with regard to the eastern frontier," and that she was
anxious not to endanger her relations with Russia and would not let
herself "be forced onto the side of Poland against Russia." But Moscow

had to understand that Germany could not base her policy "solely on an alignment with Russia."[50]

Brockdorff-Rantzau wasted no time. On April 16, he reported directly to Chancellor Luther. He told Luther that the Russians were adamantly opposed to the guarantee pacts with the West.[51]

On April 25, two days before Krestinsky's departure for Moscow, Schubert gave him a written, condensed version of Brockdorff-Rantzau's oral presentation to Litvinov and, in addition, a strictly confidential memorandum on Germany's position regarding Article 16. Krestinsky now proposed that Germany and the USSR conclude a guarantee pact along the same lines as the one with the West. Schubert rejected this on the basis that concurrent negotiations would be difficult. Germany would not join the League in the immediate future and would consult Russia before answering the expected note of the Western powers. Schubert also told Krestinsky that nothing further could be done on the Russian proposals of December until after the German presidential elections. The memorandum on Article 16 was based on the opinions of Gaus and Bülow. The arguments presented in the Gaus-Bülow memorandum were to remain basic in the negotiations with Moscow.

On the basis of their evaluation, Gaus and Bülow concluded that Germany, as a League member, would be obligated to act against Russia (a) in case of a Russo-Polish conflict after Russia had been requested, by unanimous vote of the Council, to submit the case to arbitration, (b) if Russia took warlike measures against Poland after rejecting or accepting the Council demand, or (c) if Russia was declared an aggressor. However, Germany, as a member of the Council, could prevent anti-Russian measures. Germany would not be able to prevent a vote of the Council in a clear case of aggression, but Germany could act if the matter were in doubt. Finally, military participation was up to each member, and the same was true of permitting the passage of troops through a member's territory. A marginal note in the memorandum added:

> Theoretically, Germany can make any action by the League impossible. If it comes to League action, Germany need not participate in military actions, including allowing the passage of troops, and can formulate an economic blockade according to her own interests. Germany maintains a free hand against Poland if the three suppositions, which is quite conceivable, occur.[52]

After Krestinsky had read the memorandum, he went to see Stresemann to tell him that Germany apparently had decided to join the

League of Nations without insisting that her conditions be accepted. The material he had been given by Schubert was obviously designed to convince his country that there was nothing to be concerned about. Stresemann assured the Ambassador again that nothing at all had changed in Germany's policy vis-à-vis the League. He could not understand how a strictly legal, unpolitical judgment of Article 16 could give the impression Krestinsky described. It was a sign of the deep confidence in which he held the Soviet government that a memorandum prepared for circulation in the Foreign Office had been given to him.

Krestinsky expressed his bafflement at Schubert's suggestion that entry in the League should be the basis for talks between Germany and the USSR. If Germany continued to insist that she be exempted from Article 16, what was there to discuss? Stresemann replied that the talks about Germany's possible entry into the world body were to be a starting point. He told Krestinsky that the Russo-Czech trade treaty had an introduction "which one could consider, in a certain sense, a treaty of neutrality."⁵³ The talks which he envisaged should try to develop a formula which would let Germany enter the League and continue its good relations with the USSR.

Secretary of Embassy Jacubovich, who attended as interpreter, agreed with Stresemann's view on the preamble. Krestinsky apparently did not know about the Russo-Czech treaty. In Moscow, Scheffer discovered that the Russians were not at all impressed with the approach proposed to them in Berlin. They expressed the hope that Brockdorff-Rantzau would offer something more concrete on his return.⁵⁴

On April 26, Paul von Hindenburg was elected President. The election did not lead to the commencing of negotiations for an alliance on the basis of the Russian proposal. The absence of Brockdorff-Rantzau from Moscow and of Krestinsky from Berlin provided a new excuse for the Wilhelmstrasse to continue its delaying tactics.

Brockdorff-Rantzau utilized his stay in Berlin, as usual, to get support for his policies. On the day of Hindenburg's arrival in Berlin, May 11, which was made a triumphal entry by the nationalistic parties and many others in sympathy with what the old *Generalfeldmarschall* symbolized, Brockdorff-Rantzau gave a luncheon "with political overtones."⁵⁵

Nor was Chicherin inactive. He addressed the Third Congress of Soviets on May 14 and pointed out that once Germany entered the League, her old friendly relationship with Russia could scarcely continue in the same degree as formerly. He pointed out that the negotiations for the commercial treaty, which were proceeding in Moscow, might become "a weighty factor in the settlement of international political relations."

Schubert called in Jacubovich, who was chargé d'affaires, and expressed the hope that Chicherin's speech was not meant to be an answer to the proposal made by Stresemann. Jacubovich thought that Krestinsky would bring an answer from Chicherin.[56]

Stresemann instructed Hey, chargé d'affaires in Moscow, to make immediate representations at the Narkomindel. Germany had not, as Chicherin had also asserted, proposed the guarantee pact on English prompting. No discussion of the speech had been made in the Reichstag by the German government; instead, it had insisted in public on the continuation of the Rapallo policy. This stand had been supported by a majority in the Reichstag. It was regrettable that Chicherin did not use the same kind of restraint in his public utterances. His speech gave the impression that he wanted to prejudice the outcome of the confidential talks which had just been initiated. The German government hoped that the speech was not meant to be a reply to the memoranda taken along by Krestinsky. The German government would wait for the Ambassador's return to make a final evaluation of the speech. In the meantime, the Soviet government might consider a reply, by way of her Ambassador, to the following points:

1. No matter how the Western pact negotiations would develop, the Treaty of Rapallo would remain the basis of German-Russian relations. The Soviet government should cease its recrimination and trust Germany. Without a certain amount of confidence, relations between the two countries were "unthinkable."

2. The assertion that Germany proposed the pact on English insistence was not designed to be well received in Germany.

3. Chicherin's speech could lead to the conclusion that the guarantee pact would make a continuation of the existing relationship impossible.

4. The German government would like to be informed about the intent of Chicherin's speech.

Hey was to follow the prepared text and not to enter into any debate. He delivered the memorandum to Chicherin on May 28. The Foreign Commissar said he would consult with the whole Collegium of the Narkomindel before replying. In the meantime, a few points could be clarified:

1. Since many other statesmen had discussed the proposed pact, why should he alone remain silent?

2. The European situation had become quite muddled since the proposals for the Western pact; there existed nothing like the Triple or Dual Alliances of old.

3. Russia did not doubt the sincerity of Germany, but did not think that her good intentions could be brought to fruition.

4. England wanted to isolate Russia and to this purpose separate Germany from her.

5. Joining the League would bind Germany to one order only. Chicherin would cease insisting that a balance of power could not be achieved in this manner when an "East pact was concluded at the same time as the West pact."[57]

On June 2, Krestinsky delivered Chicherin's reply to the Stresemann proposals and the memorandum on Article 16 to Schubert. The Russian reply answered each point made by the Germans. Chicherin concluded with a reminder that the December proposals had not yet been discussed and indicated that German entry into the League might force Russia to look for other arrangements. This was a clear threat at a Russo-French or, possibly, a Russo-Polish alignment. The final paragraph of the reply stated the Russian case bluntly:

> It appears, therefore, clear beyond any doubt that entry into the League of Nations, which was proposed by Germany, will make it difficult, if not impossible, to maintain and further strengthen the foundation for friendly political and economic relations laid in Rapallo.[58]

The Russian reply was shown to Brockdorff-Rantzau. On June 8, he transmitted a memorandum to Stresemann in which he expressed the hope that he would be able to convince the leading men in Moscow to change their point of view. This task would be made easier if he could deliver some concrete evidence that German membership in the League, after her conditions had been accepted by the powers, would not be detrimental to relations with Russia. Oral assurances simply were not sufficient to convince Moscow. Since the December proposals had not been acted upon, the possibility of a written commitment had now to be considered.[59]

Brockdorff-Rantzau's continued presence in Berlin and his opposition to any procedure which would allow a *rapprochement* with France created a difficult situation for Stresemann and Schubert. They attempted in various subtle ways to get Brockdorff-Rantzau to return to his post, but the Count was determined to exert all the influence at his command to get Stresemann to make positive counterproposals to the Russian attempts to create a closer bond between the two nations.

Krestinsky told Stresemann on June 10 that he was sorry that no reply to the Russian proposals had as yet been made. The Foreign Minister emphasized that negotiations between Germany and Russia were in progress. However, he simply did not care to conclude a secret treaty with Russia as long as negotiations with the West had not brought results. Stresemann repeated that he was not following an anti-Russian policy—that had been Germany's misfortune once before—but he wanted to be able to answer in the negative any questions that the Western powers might ask about the existence of a treaty with Russia. Brockdorff-Rantzau, who was "known in Germany as the special representative of the Eastern orientation," had been allowed to prolong his stay in Berlin so that he could participate in all discussions concerning Russia. If Stresemann had wanted to abandon the Soviet Union, he would not have kept the Ambassador in Berlin.

Krestinsky countered that he had heard that it was Brockdorff-Rantzau who had insisted on staying. Then, as if to test the possibility of a break between Stresemann and the Ambassador, Krestinsky asked whether the Foreign Minister would attend a dinner in honor of Brockdorff-Rantzau at the Soviet Embassy on June 16. Stresemann promptly agreed and declared that it would be his pleasure.[60]

On the day after his meeting with Krestinsky, Stresemann had a two-and-a-half-hour talk with Brockdorff-Rantzau, during which they discussed the situation in the terms that the Minister had already used with Krestinsky. Neither Krestinsky nor Brockdorff-Rantzau had been able to sway Stresemann, and the Soviets now sent Litvinov and Radek, the latter with a diplomatic passport in the name of Römer, to Berlin to try their skill; both of them played the Franco-Polish card for all it was worth. Radek had a tête-à-tête with Schubert, and Litvinov with Stresemann, on June 13. Both repeated the same general line that Moscow had followed since September. Litvinov was "greatly disturbed by the state of Russo-German relations." He said that he was particularly concerned that Germany might become part of the anti-Soviet camp. He warned that a *rapprochement* with Poland and France could easily occur. Stresemann repeated what he had said before. Entry into the League would not alter the German-Russian relationship; it would, in fact, be a boon to the Soviet Union if Germany sat on the Council. The Western guarantee pact was an attempt to relieve French pressure in the West, and Germany wanted to continue its exchange of views with Russia. Stresemann did not enter into a discussion when Litvinov complained that Germany had treated the Russian offer of a neutrality agreement in a very dilatory fashion. Neither did Stresemann react forcefully when Litvinov told him that the way in which Körner treated the economic negotiations made a rather strange impression. Körner obviously believed that the German government wanted to delay the conclusion of a commercial treaty until it had concluded the Western pact.[61]

Stresemann, who assumed that the Russians were bluffing when they talked about pursuing a *rapprochement* with France, did not completely discount the possibility of a Russian guarantee of the Polish boundaries. He decided to make a formal offer to include a preamble to the German-Russian commercial treaty to avoid having to accept the kind of neutrality treaty which the Russians wanted. The preamble was to be kept strictly confidential and was to be signed only at a time suitable for Germany. The final form of the preamble had been worked out by Gaus and was based on extensive consultation among Stresemann, Schubert, Wallroth, Dirksen, and Brockdorff-Rantzau, who had not accepted the *modus procendi* until June 19. The preamble read:

> Both governments are fully aware that the welfare of the German and of the Russian people demands a friendly agreement on questions which affect both countries mutually. They are therefore decided to continue to tend to their relation with each other on the basis and in the spirit of RAPALLO and to remain in constant, friendly contact regarding all political as well as economic questions, with a view to working for the general peace of Europe, and to avoiding all tendencies which could endanger this peace.

At the time the preamble would be signed, the German government would declare orally that it would consider League membership only if this would be the only way to revise the Treaty of Versailles. If Germany was not given formal exemption from Article 16, the government would make a public statement that would leave no doubt that it would interpret Article 16 on the basis of its own position. Germany "would not only refuse to participate in any action of the League of Nations against Russia," but would veto any such action. Should Russia decide to join the League, it would inform Germany in advance. As a member of the world body, it would behave toward Germany as she promised to act in reference to Russia.[62]

Stresemann discussed the preamble with Brockdorff-Rantzau on June 21 and convinced him to return to Moscow, where his "strong personal" influence was absolutely necessary in the present situation. Brockdorff-Rantzau agreed, but asked that Dirksen be sent along to expound the proposal to Chicherin.

The Foreign Minister inquired why the Count continued to insist that the preamble was worthless. Brockdorff-Rantzau replied that he did not underestimate its importance, but was sure that the Russians would consider the preamble as *quid pro quo* for German membership in the League, not as a response for the kind of treaty they had proposed. Under these circumstances, it might be wise to select an opportune time for the presentation of the preamble. Stresemann agreed and left the decision up to Brockdorff-Rantzau. On June 25, the Cabinet agreed to the preamble and procedure to be followed in the negotiations.[63]

After the Cabinet's approval, Brockdorff-Rantzau and Dirksen left for Moscow. Dirksen was convinced that he had been sent along to urge the acceptance of the preamble, because the Ambassador "did not react to such subtleties."[64] It was not a matter of subtleties that persuaded the Count to accept Dirksen's company. It was a deliberate attempt to dissociate himself from a diplomatic procedure which he considered a mistake. Brockdorff-Rantzau had spent a whole year attempting to strengthen Germany's relations with Russia before any *rapprochement* with the West took positive form. He remained unconvinced that Germany's status could be improved by Stresemann's policies, a conviction which was solidified when Maltzan was replaced by Schubert. Nothing which had occurred since then had changed the Ambassador's mind that only with strong Russian support could Germany hope to get maximum concessions from England and France.

The Russians, however, had decided to create another major incident, which led Brockdorff-Rantzau to doubt whether anyone could count on their cooperation. On the day before his departure from Berlin, the Soviet government had opened a trial which once again strained German-Soviet relations to the breaking point because Hilger was involved in the charges brought against the accused.

V

One Step East—One Step West

On June 24, 1925, the public trial of three young men opened before the Special Board of the Supreme Court of the USSR. All three of them had been students at the University of Berlin; two were Germans, Karl Kindermann and Theodor Wolscht, and the third an Estonian by the name of Max von Ditmar. They were charged with conspiracy to assassinate Stalin and Trotsky, who had been removed from his position as Commissar for War in January. The "Student Trial," as it was soon dubbed by the press, became a major incident, because Hilger was accused of having aided and abetted the two German students in their nefarious, terroristic designs.

Hilger had met the students on the Riga-Moscow train on October 13, 1924. They told him that they represented a German machinery manufacturer who had financed their trip to Central Asia. When Hilger cautioned them against pursuing their plan, the two young men reacted with "a frivolous devil-may-care attitude and with puerile stubbornness. . . ." Out of concern for their safety, Hilger asked them to visit him at the Embassy as soon as they arrived in Moscow. He gave them his calling card, on which he had written his address and telephone number.

After their arrival in Moscow, Kindermann and Wolscht were given lodging by the Commissariat for Education. Ditmar, whom Kindermann had met in Berlin in July, arrived in Moscow three days after his two traveling companions. He was a member of the German Communist Party and had been extremely helpful in procuring the necessary papers by introducing the two German students to members of the Soviet Embassy in Berlin, including Secretary of Embassy Jacubovich. The latter had advised them to join the KPD to remove difficulties in their travels in Russia. Kindermann succeeded in getting his membership card, but Wolscht was not as successful; he declared himself, however, to be in sympathy with communism. This satisfied Jacubo-

146

vich, who saw to it that the students received letters of recommendation for Lunarcharsky, Commissar of Education, Madame Krupskaya, Lenin's widow, and others.

With the cooperation received at the Embassy, there remained only the problem of finances. Dr. Theodor Wolff, Editor-in-chief of the *Berliner Tageblatt,* gave them about $500 as an advance on articles about Siberian student life.

> Various German firms, who found out about the pending journey, gave [them] commissions and supported the trip in the hope that [the students] would send them information about economic possibilities in Siberia.[1]

In Moscow, the two naive Germans continued in their rather foolish way. They agreed to forward all their mail via the courier service of the Comintern, accepted beds in the Home for Emigré Communists, where they could be easily watched, and continued to trust their friend and guide Ditmar.

During the night of October 26 the three students were arrested on "suspicion of political and economic espionage." The German Embassy found out about the arrests through the U.S. Student Aid on October 28 and immediately requested information from the Narkomindel. More than two weeks later, the Commissariat replied that it could not do anything because political espionage was involved.

During January, 1925, Wallroth directed a number of inquiries to Brockdorff-Rantzau, and the Ambassador went to Chicherin, as well as to other men in the Foreign Commissariat. His questions led to the revelation that the students were members of Orgesch, also known as Organization Consul, whose members carried out acts of terrorism. In June, 1922, three members of Organization Consul had murdered Rathenau. On January 24, Chicherin told Brockdorff-Rantzau that Krestinsky had discussed the case of a Russian citizen, Arkady Maslov, who was incarcerated in Germany, with Stresemann. Maslov had already been jailed for several months, and the Soviet government had not been given any reasons for his imprisonment. Brockdorff-Rantzau knew nothing about the man or his case. Wallroth enlightened the Ambassador three days later. Maslov had been arrested for entering Germany, although aware that he would be arrested because he was suspected of having participated in the "high treason activities of the district organization of the KPD, of which he was a member."

On January 30, 1925, Brockdorff-Rantzau sent a personal letter to Chicherin, enclosing copies of correspondence with the Rector of the University of Berlin which proved that Kindermann and Wolscht were bona fide students. In a light-hearted tone, he pointed out to the Commissar that the two young heroes were no danger to any country but their own. The thing to do was to return them to their parents for a "good strapping."

The Ambassador's advice to the Wilhelmstrasse was not as unconcerned. He wanted measures taken to let the German press know about the "actually existing criminal machinations and the real wire-pullers before the cudgel was taken up for obviously misled, immature boys." The press should wait with its discussion until the results of the investigation, which had already uncovered some "rather peculiar material," were published. The German press was informed about the situation by the Foreign Office.[2]

As February progressed, the effort to effect the release of the two students continued. Brockdorff-Rantzau more or less accepted the Russian charge that the two students had planned the assassination of Stalin and Trotsky, and even of himself. He was angry with everyone in the Wilhelmstrasse for not having told him that the two "louts" were connected with Communists and Fascists (Völkischen). The Count was sure that only his splendid, personal relationship with Chicherin would prevent a major incident.[3] Despite the personal relationship with Chicherin, however, the two students were not released.

The OGPU refused to let anyone from the Embassy visit the students, but allowed Litvinov to see them and convince himself of their well-being. On February 6, Kindermann wrote a detailed confession, which Brockdorff-Rantzau was allowed to peruse in Litvinov's office. The student had admitted that he belonged to the Organization Consul and that Wolscht was a former naval officer who was wanted by the Entente Powers for having sunk a hospital ship. Wolscht had been involved in terroristic acts in Germany, had been arrested and freed from jail by Orgesch. Kindermann also admitted that he had worked in a Berlin detective agency.

After his confession, Kindermann had written a letter to President Kalinin asking for a pardon. Brockdorff-Rantzau thought it possible that the confession had been extracted by force or that Kindermann, as a member of the KPD, was cooperating with the Russian Communists. Wolscht and Ditmar had not confessed to anything, as far as the Ambassador knew.

Investigation by the Wilhelmstrasse revealed some curious discrepancies in Kindermann's confessions, consisting of facts he could not possibly have known and indicating that the OGPU had mixed up Wolscht and Ditmar. There existed a Lieutenant (j.g.) John Claus Boldt and another Lieutenant (j.g.) Ludwig W. F. Ditmar, who on July 16, 1921, had been convicted of sinking a hospital ship during the war and who had been removed from jail by a right-wing organization. Kindermann had, however, worked for a detective agency. The Russians presented an unconvincing answer: Kindermann knew Wolscht as Boldt in the right-wing organization, and Ditmar had confessed, corroborating his friend's statements. Shortly thereafter, Wolscht also confessed to the charges against him.

The Wickingbund, a right-wing organization, which had absorbed Orgesch, stated categorically, upon inquiry by the Wilhelmstrasse, that the three students had never belonged to the organization; that the assertion was quite improbable because Kindermann was a Jew and thus not eligible for membership.[4]

At the time of the students' arrest in October, 1924, the German Embassy had been unaware that a trial was being prepared in Germany against sixteen Communists who had been involved in the violence of the German October Revolution.[5] This so-called "German Cheka Trial" opened in Leipzig on February 10, 1925, before the State Court for the Protection of the Republic, Judge Neidner presiding. The trial, the first against Communists who had been arrested on various charges for acts committed during October, 1923, and after, was attended by great crowds of spectators and covered by the world press. Very quickly it was established that the defendant Hellmuth, also known as Hermann and Gorew, was really a Russian OGPU General named Peter A. Skoblevsky, who had resided in the Soviet Embassy in Berlin. He had been sent to Germany to organize within the KPD a secret force, patterned after the Cheka. Their primary task was to assassinate prominent Germans, including General von Seeckt. They killed only one man, a Communist barber by the name of Rauch, whom they suspected of being a stool pigeon. They had failed twice "by a hair's breadth" to kill Seeckt.[6] The chief witness for the prosecution, one Felix Neumann, implicated all leading German Communists, including the party's Reichstag deputies. Neumann testified that he had actively planned revolution and murder on Moscow orders. On the second day of the trial, Neumann stated that he had received $35,000 from the Soviet Embassy in Berlin on a draft by Wilhelm Pieck (KPD Reichstag Deputy). According to Neumann, the Embassy had expended about $200,000 for the purchase of arms and explosives for the KPD. Skoblevsky denied that he had organized a Cheka or that he had any Russian connections.[7]

In Moscow, Chicherin told Brockdorff-Rantzau that the proceedings in Leipzig could easily have a very detrimental effect on German-Russian diplomatic relations. The Ambassador requested that Schubert do everything possible to prevent a situation by which the trial could be interpreted as deliberately directed against the USSR. If necessary, Walter Simons, President of the Supreme Court, who knew the Count's attitude toward Russia well, might be informed of Chicherin's remark.

Schubert replied that everything possible had been done to keep the Soviet Embassy out of the trial. However, this was a splendid opportunity for Moscow to show once and for all that the accusations against the Soviet Embassy in Berlin were without basis in fact. The efforts of the Wilhelmstrasse did not prevail against the needs of domestic politics. The public continued to be admitted to all sessions, and the Embassy received its share of condemnatory evidence.[8]

On February 23, the *Reichskommissar* for Public Safety transmitted an interesting piece of confidential information to the Wilhelmstrasse. According to a source close to the OGPU, Skoblevsky was to be taken from jail. If bribes did not accomplish this feat, attempts would be made to exchange Germans incarcerated in the USSR, including Kindermann and Wolscht, for Skoblevsky. On March 3, the *Reichskommissar* had another tidbit from his well-informed source: the arrest of Kindermann and Wolscht had been prepared by the Foreign Department of the OGPU and its representatives in Berlin. In Moscow, preparations were under way to compromise Counselor of Embassy Hey.

Brockdorff-Rantzau took precautions against an involvement of Hey, and continued to press for contact with the students. He was sure that the case "had become a trial of strength between the Foreign Commissariat and the GPU/Cheka." The latter had the upper hand thus far, and the Council of People's Commissars had refused permission for anyone from the Embassy to visit the two "rascals." Brockdorff-Rantzau had threatened Litvinov with leaving Moscow unless the matter were speedily resolved. The Ambassador again asked that Simons, who was then still acting President of the Reich, should use his influence to prevent too deep an involvement of the Soviet Embassy in the Cheka Trial.

Stresemann advised Brockdorff-Rantzau that he and his staff were doing all they could to keep the Russians in good spirits. The *Vorwärts* on March 25 attacked the Foreign Minister for not doing enough to get the students released and for having voiced strong objections to the *Ministerpräsident* (President of the Council of Ministers) of Prussia for installing Weiss, of Bozenhardt fame, as Deputy Police President of Berlin. This was evidence, the *Vorwärts* had written, that the Wilhelmstrasse kowtowed to Moscow. Stresemann asked the Ambassador to use this in conversations to show how wrong the Russians were in alleging that Germany was turning away from them.[9]

On April 22, the Leipzig court handed down its verdict. Three of the defendants, including Skoblevsky and Neumann, were sentenced to death for murder. The thirteen other defendants received prison sentences ranging from six months to fifteen years. In its summation, the court declared that the accusation, that the government of the USSR had planned the overthrow of the German Republic, had been substantiated. According to the verdict, the Berlin Soviet Embassy had been used as a meeting place by German and Russian comrades to plot revolution and terroristic activities. The Russian government refrained from official moves at this time in an effort not to upset its plans to turn Stresemann from taking the path to the West. Litvinov did tell Hey, who had taken over the Embassy during Brockdorff-Rantzau's absence, on April 30 that he hoped that the death sentence of Skoblevsky would not be carried out. The latter had lost his Russian citizenship but had reapplied for it before the trial. If Skoblevsky were executed, there would never be a chance to negotiate. Hey was not quite sure what Litvinov meant, but reported home that it was probably an indication that Moscow wanted to do some exchanging later on.[10] With Brockdorff-Rantzau absent and the OGPU still preparing the case against Kindermann and Wolscht, little was done in Moscow or Berlin. Repeated representations by the Moscow Embassy resulted in permission for chargé d'affaires Hey to visit the students on June 20.

When Hey talked with the two students, they had no serious complaints about their health. However, a "certain nervousness and a strong psychological depression due to long incarceration was obvious." The OGPU officials had told them that the Embassy had no interest in their case and had avoided getting in touch with them. Wolscht had been on hunger strikes twice and Kindermann seven times. Once he had to be fed "artificially" to bring him back to normal functioning.

Since the Court had rejected the admission of German defense attorneys, the Embassy procured the services of two well-known Moscow criminal lawyers, Sommerfeld and Muraviev. Both of them accepted, but then gave up defending the accused for "personal reasons." The Court appointed two lawyers by the names of Koriakin and Duchovskoi. The latter was to defend Kindermann, who had decided to carry on his own defense but retained the "rather deaf old man who could not understand a word of German as 'advisor on judicial questions.'"[11]

On the twenty-sixth, Ditmar took the stand, declaring, among other things, that it had been decided in Berlin to forward reports and other materials through the German Embassy in Moscow. When he arrived in Moscow he discovered that the liaison man was Counselor of Legation Hilger. In earlier testimony, Ditmar had involved Dr. George Michaelis by charging that the former Imperial Chancellor was in charge of the Organization Consul in Berlin. Dr. Michaelis denied the charge under oath in Berlin.

During the afternoon session, Kindermann related his treatment during his investigatory incarceration and said he would prove that the investigating judge had committed a "serious crime" against him. Attorney General N. V. Krylenko lectured him on the fact that false accusations were punishable. As in previous sessions, Kindermann and Wolscht defended themselves awkwardly, both insisting on their innocence and the artificial creation of the case against them.

Hey felt that Kindermann especially "showed a childish, almost pathological misunderstanding of the situation." Ditmar's speech was "undoubtedly strongly inspired." He obviously intended to save his life by betraying his comrades. Another OGPU witness, Baumann, was really a stool pigeon who was put in the cells of both Kindermann and Wolscht.[12]

After the students' trial had been underway five days, Stresemann informed Brockdorff-Rantzau that it could easily endanger the whole complex German-Russian relationship. Echoing a fear expressed by the Ambassador, Stresemann wrote that it was obvious to everyone that the trial had been staged to provide a "companion piece to the Leipzig Cheka Trial." The involvement of Hilger was an attempt to neutralize the way in which the Soviet Embassy had been compromised. In addition, the Russians wanted to have hostages for the eventual exchange of Skoblevsky and Maslov.

The Foreign Minister expressed his dismay over the fact that the Soviets started the trial at a time when they were deeply involved in far-reaching political and economic negotiations with Germany. He told Brockdorff-Rantzau that this new conflict could prove absolutely disastrous to continued friendly relations with the Soviet Union. The Wilhelmstrasse had seen to it that the involvement of the Russian Embassy in the Skoblevsky case was kept from the public as much as possible. But if Moscow continued to involve the German Embassy in the students' trial, the Foreign Office's circumspection would have to be discarded. If this happened, another Bozenhardt incident could easily result. Stresemann instructed Brockdorff-Rantzau not to discuss the preamble until he had discovered whether the Russians had decided that the German negotiations with the West had given them such a tactical advantage that they could proceed with the trial and the involvement of the Embassy and Hilger without political disadvantages to themselves. The Ambassador was to use "absolutely plain language" in the sense of the telegram. Stresemann intended to be equally plain with chargé d'affaires Jacubovich in Berlin. Brockdorff-Rantzau was to emphasize to Chicherin that Stresemann was "beginning to be confused about the intentions of the Russian government."[13]

Brockdorff-Rantzau, too, considered the trial an almost impossible burden on relations between Germany and Russia. He had given Chicherin to understand, during their first meeting on the evening of his arrival, June 28, that the "scandalous" manner in which Hilger had been involved was the best way for the USSR to lose German friendship and wind up in splendid isolation. He had left no doubt in Chicherin's mind about the grotesque impression the mimicry of the Cheka Trial made. Chicherin appeared quite obviously disconcerted, especially after Brockdorff-Rantzau told him to his face that the trial was without a doubt another instance which showed the "helplessness of the Foreign Commissariat vis-à-vis the Secret Police." Brockdorff-Rantzau was certain that Chicherin knew full well what consequences the action of the OGPU, designed to get hostages to exchange for Skoblevsky and Maslov, could have.

The German students continued to do badly as the trial continued. The Ambassador had attended the evening session on June 29. He had met there Dr. Heinrich Freund, who had been retained by the parents of the two students and who had stayed on in Moscow although he had not been allowed to act in the defense of Kindermann and Wolscht. Judging from the remarks that Freund made to Brockdorff-Rantzau, the Soviet court might have done the young men a favor. The lawyer told the Ambassador that the boys deserved "little sympathy." In a memorandum sent to Berlin, Freund wrote that Kindermann compromised Germans in foreign countries because it had been proven that he had "forged documents" and chased after "utopian phantasies which invited the damnation of absurdity" on his head.[14]

The trial was drawing to its close, but Hilger had not been called to testify or defend himself. Wallroth wanted the Embassy to counteract the impression that Hilger had not appeared because the German government had something to hide. Besides, testimony about "the childlike and simple-minded behavior" of the accused, which Hilger had formed on meeting them, could affect the verdict. If Hilger could not testify, an explanation by him should be published in *Izvestia*.

Hilger was not called. The students were condemned to death

at 1:00 A.M. on July 3, after an all-night session. Neither the German government, the Embassy, Hilger, nor Michaelis was mentioned in the verdict. The Embassy took steps immediately to appeal for mercy in the name of the parents of the German students.

The verdict did, however, establish that the judges had satisfied themselves that the students had been sent to Russia to assassinate "Stalin, Zinoviev, Trotsky, and Dzerzhinsky." In addition to this they were to determine whether there existed any relationship between the Trade Mission, the Soviet Embassy in Berlin, and the KPD.[15] This was a clear-cut attempt to whitewash the Trade Mission in the Bozenhardt incident and get the Soviet Embassy out of the embarrassing involvement with the KPD. The device was simple. Fascist *provocateurs* had compromised the quite innocent organs of the USSR in Germany. The head of Germany's armed forces, Seeckt, had been marked for assassination, and Trotsky too had been placed on their list. Both men were known to favor close German-Russian collaboration. Kindermann and Wolscht thus became archcriminals of a stature equal to that of Skoblevsky. Nowhere in the verdict was there any explanation about the means which the young men were going to employ to assassinate four of Russia's leading men. Obviously poisoning them, as had been asserted, required access to the inaccessible leaders.

In Berlin, all newspapers, with the exception of the Communist press, protested the condemnation of the students and indicated that the death sentences were applied to make them into hostages for Skoblevsky. The latter, according to the newspapers, was convicted on sound evidence, while the students were found guilty on the basis of fantastic charges made by the OGPU *provocateur* Baumann and by Ditmar, who was clearly a pathological case.[16]

Brockdorff-Rantzau had no objection to the way in which the German press treated the trial. He wanted the Wilhelmstrasse to see to it that something about the Russian charges was mentioned. Kindermann had admitted forging documents, and both Kindermann and Wolscht had

> in general told every person they met what that person wanted to hear, until their childish talkativeness and mendacity had caught them in such a net of contradictions that even the most thorough observer found it impossible to separate truth from falsehood.[17]

After this had been mentioned, the press could point out that a miscarriage of justice had taken place. Brockdorff-Rantzau did not want to get involved in long discussions with the Russians about the one-sided reporting of the German press. Dr. Freund had no such problem. In the brief which he submitted to the Foreign Office he concluded that

the accused had become victims of the coincidence of unfortunate occurrences with their own inability. Dignified and intelligent behavior during the preliminary investigation and proper conduct of the defense might have succeeded in destroying the existing suspicious circumstances.[18]

Kindermann maintained later that he had been forced into confessing by OGPU methods applied in the Lubjanka prison. His book, published in 1931, does not remove the evidence of naivete and "childish talkativeness." In any event, the students were to move into the background while the German government attempted to have the Soviet government admit that neither Hilger nor the Embassy had been involved in the students' schemes.

Stresemann instructed Brockdorff-Rantzau to insist on an official and complete exoneration of Hilger and the Embassy, because the court had refused to let Hilger testify. The "continuation of the economic and political talks [should] be made dependent on the degree of cooperation by the Soviet government for the German request."[19]

The negotiations with the West were in a new stage after the French government had replied on June 16 to the German note of February 9. Paris rejected the German demand for exemption from Article 16 and insisted that Germany join the League without conditions. The French further proposed that discussions should commence on the legal framework for a Rhineland pact, for treaties of arbitration between Germany and the powers included in the pact, and "other powers."[20] The French note created considerable work in the Wilhelmstrasse, particularly in its Legal Department. There was no need to rush negotiations with the Russians on the proposed preamble, and thus the Hilger involvement, unfortunate as it was, provided a welcome new excuse for delaying actions. Dirksen had spent the entire trip from Berlin to Moscow trying to change the Ambassador's mind about the usefulness of the preamble to satisfy Russian demands and assuage their fears about losing German friendship. Dirksen had succeeded in removing a few of Brockdorff-Rantzau's doubts about the suitability of the preamble as a reply to Chicherin's proposals. Brockdorff-Rantzau had hinted at the new German formula during his first meeting with Chicherin on June 28, which Dirksen also attended. The latter was convinced that the Ambassador, now that he was actually before the hurdle, would clear it elegantly.[21]

Dirksen's effort to remove the major disagreements in the economic negotiations ran into even greater difficulties than his attempts to win over the Ambassador. Körner and Brockdorff-Rantzau had assumed over-all direction of the German delegation, with Dirksen in actual control, ably assisted by Schlesinger and Hilger.

It proved to be extremely difficult to get the Russian negotiators to make any concessions. Therefore, a breathing spell in the economic talks would provide time to plan a new strategy and develop fresh tactics.

Schlesinger, who was an old hand at bargaining with the Russians, had complained to Dirksen many times since the negotiations for an inclusive and extensive commercial treaty had opened in Moscow in November of 1924 that only "political necessity" made it possible to carry on. The negotiations had produced agreement on a large number of items, but the talks stalled over German insistence on direct contact with the buyers of their products, that is, a demand to bypass the Soviet government's monopoly control of foreign trade exercised abroad by the Trade Mission; the Germans wanted equal rights for Germans trading in Russia with the commercial organs of the state and the unrestricted application of the most-favored-nation clause of the Treaty of Rapallo.

The Russian negotiators had adamantly rejected these German propositions, but had pressed for concessions which the Körner delegation, backed by Berlin, refused to make. The Russians asked for a 200-million mark, two-year, low-interest credit, training opportunity for technicians in Germany, and incorporation of the Trade Mission into the Soviet Embassy in Berlin. Further, they wanted diplomatic immunity for all members of the Council of the Trade Mission, tax exemption, the right to open branches in other German cities, full extraterritoriality for the building of the Trade Mission in the Lindenstrasse, and the acceptance of the right of the mission to represent all economic aspects of the USSR. Schlesinger had been more or less convinced that even the minimum results expected by the Wilhelmstrasse could not be realized. With these conditions in mind, the Wilhelmstrasse had set June 15 as the final date for the completion of the negotiations in Moscow. Initially, the Russian negotiators had agreed to that date, but during the session of June 12, Ganetzky, the chief Russian negotiator, had told the German delegation that the sessions would have to result in a signing of the agreements already reached or end with a communiqué stating that no treaty would be concluded. He had rejected Körner's proposal to initial the parts agreed upon and leave disagreements for future talks. Körner in turn had refused to sign the agreements as they stood. During the ensuing discussion the Russians had offered to withdraw their demand for tax exemption if the building in the Lindenstrasse were given extraterritorial status and the immunity of the archives of the Trade Mission branch in Hamburg guaranteed.

The German delegates had insisted that the most-favored-nation principle be accepted, but the Russians had not entered into debate on this issue. The stalemate thus continued on the major disagreements.

On the day set for the termination of the negotiations for the summer, Körner had been told by Chicherin that there was no reason why the talks could not continue in the fall if agreement could not be reached before the pending session closed. To the Wilhelmstrasse the signing of a treaty without the resolution of the outstanding problems was impossible. Stresemann had gathered from remarks by Litvinov, which were corroborated by Chicherin, that the Russians were willing to initial each of the completed parts of the treaty without insisting on signing the whole. Ganetzky and Stomoniakov, Chief of the Trade Delegation in Berlin, had obviously tried to bluff Körner into accepting the treaty as it was. Stresemann had instructed Körner, who was eager to return home in order to take his wife on vacation, to remain in Moscow until Brockdorff-Rantzau returned to his post.

All the ministries involved in the economic negotiations had agreed with Stresemann that the treaty should not be accepted as it stood. Unfortunately, the Foreign Minister wrote to Körner, the problems in the economic sphere coincided with the political ill humor created among the Russians because of the negotiations with the West. It would, therefore, be unwise to continue the tough attitude and instead lead the negotiations into more quiet waters. Stresemann had not been able to get Cabinet approval of complete extraterritoriality for the building in the Lindenstrasse. Wallroth had been equally unsuccessful in obtaining support among German businessmen and financial circles for the loan requested by the Russians.

In Wallroth's words, Germany had been caught between an "economic Charybdis" and a "political Scylla." Somehow, a way out had to be found. A memorandum by Schlesinger proposed a number of ideas designed to move the negotiations out of Scylla's reach and away from the whirlpool. The talks had made it quite clear, wrote Schlesinger, that German businessmen would not be allowed to work freely in the Soviet Union; they would have to carry on through the system of concessions. Nevertheless, the increasing economic relations needed treaty regulation, if only to remove the greater part of business contacts from political disturbances. Furthermore, political relations could only benefit from the development of German business possibilities in Russia.

Neither political nor economic pressures would result in an acceptance of the German demands. Germany had material, Russia primarily tactical, interests. They wanted a treaty to show that economic relations between a capitalistic and a communistic system were possible. This, they hoped, would ease economic negotiations with other states and develop competition among the capitalist nations for a share of the Soviet Union's market. Moscow did not fear a discontinuation of the economic talks because it was convinced that neither Germany's political nor her economic interests would be served by such a move. Therefore, Germany was well-advised to make the most of the available chances for success.

Schlesinger proposed that the Russian main demand, extraterritorial status for the Lindenstrasse headquarters, be granted. Credits would be made available if German businessmen received a guarantee of 50 percent by the Reich government. It simply did not make sense to say that Germany was penniless. If the 100,000-man Reichswehr would be increased to 200,000, not a voice would be raised to argue that the money was not available. Once the problems regarding extraterritoriality and credits were resolved, Germany could reject limitations on its demand for most-favored-nation treatment.[22]

This was the situation when Brockdorff-Rantzau and Dirksen met with Chicherin and Krestinsky on July 1, two days before the end of the student trial, to discuss the German-Soviet relationship. Dirksen, after an introduction by the Ambassador, elaborated on the German motivation for a preamble to the commercial treaty. He left no doubt that Germany wanted to continue relations with the USSR in the spirit of Rapallo and had absolutely no desire to follow in "England's wake."

Chicherin insisted that Germany had not answered the question of what she would do should her demands about Article 16 be rejected. If Germany joined the League of Nations, accepting the Covenant unconditionally, it would be equivalent to withdrawal of her objections to Article 16. If, on the other hand, the Entente Powers did not make any objection, the maxim "qui tacet consentire videtur" could be applied.

The preamble, Chicherin said, was "weaker and not as clear" as the Russian December proposals. He had offered a neutrality declaration and a mutual obligation not to enter any economic or political combination which was directed against the other. The German preamble was simply a polite phrase. The desire to maintain peace and tranquility in Europe was praiseworthy and correct, but not a proposal for a treaty. Much more definite was the Russo-Czech treaty, which contained an open agreement on neutrality. Using the opening provided by Stresemann Chicherin underlined that Czechoslovakia belonged to the League. At the end of the talk, Chicherin asked his visitors not to consider his evaluation as final. He would discuss the German reply with the Collegium of the Narkomindel.

Brockdorff-Rantzau and Dirksen gathered from Chicherin's remarks that the Commissar was more concerned about German participation in economic sanctions than in her support of military actions.

On July 6, after the students had been condemned to death, Brockdorff-Rantzau saw Chicherin again. The Commissar began to read from notes. Brockdorff-Rantzau interrupted, to Chicherin's visible surprise, and said that he had come to discuss the commutation of the death sentences against Kindermann and Wolscht and the exoneration of Hilger. Unless something definite was done, the economic and political negotiations would be discontinued. Chicherin replied that the executions would be delayed but that the verdict remained in force. The demand for an exoneration of Hilger would meet grave difficulties from the Council of People's Commissars.

Brockdorff-Rantzau rejoined that Hilger could be exonerated by an Embassy explanation in *Izvestia* which the Narkomindel endorsed. Chicherin rejected this and Brockdorff-Rantzau apprised him that this was the minimum request. Stresemann, the Ambassador stated emphatically, was beginning to be confused about the intentions of the Russian government. Brockdorff-Rantzau assured Chicherin that he understood that the party accused him of not representing the interest of the proletariat. But it was really impossible to conduct foreign relations according to the party's principles. Chicherin did not respond, but tried to return to a discussion of the political proposals. Brockdorff-Rantzau refused to consider these proposals until the problems arising from the student trial were resolved.

Two days after the Ambassador's talk with Chicherin, the Director of the Narkomindel's Western Department, Boris Stein, came to report officially that the Soviet press had published an announcement that Kindermann and Wolscht would not be executed. However, Brockdorff-Rantzau's ultimatum had aggravated the already existing opposition to an exoneration in the Cabinet. The Count retorted that the mood of the Cabinet made no difference to him, the exoneration was an absolute necessity.

Two hours after Stein's departure, Chicherin called to ask Brockdorff-Rantzau to visit him at midnight. On the Count's arrival, Chicherin declared that the Soviet government requested that the German Ambassador report to Berlin "that it considered the step taken by the German government as an ultimatum, and that it could not possibly retreat before this ultimatum." The Soviet government wanted to resolve the difficulties connected with the students in a friendly manner, but in order for this to take place, the suspension of the political and economic talks had to be withdrawn.

Brockdorff-Rantzau immediately pointed out that his statement had not been an ultimatum, but the one Chicherin had just delivered most certainly fell into that category. He would be happy to report to Berlin that Moscow wanted to resolve the difficulties in a friendly manner.

Chicherin, who had made his government's position clear, emphasized that the withdrawal of the ultimatum was a matter of prestige. Brockdorff-Rantzau, undaunted, shot back that Moscow was strangely sensitive; after all, Germany had been affronted. It would simply not do for the Soviet government to act the "injured innocent." Economic and political negotiations could not continue, but he would report that the Soviet government wanted to resume the talks. On this basis, a satisfactory way out might be discovered.

Brockdorff-Rantzau's procedure was approved by Stresemann. At the same time the Foreign Minister expressed his concern that the Russians would demand political and economic concessions in return for the exoneration of Hilger. He asked the Ambassador to continue the economic negotiations, without making definite commitments, so that the Russian move could be checked.[23]

In Berlin, Jacubovich visited Stresemann on July 11 (Krestinsky was still in Moscow and did not return until the fifteenth) to inquire whether the German delegation in Moscow had received definite instructions for the completion of the economic negotiations. The Foreign Minister told him that the Russian demands had created difficulties the resolution of which would take some time. The discussion ended with Stresemann calling Jacubovich's attention to the "great burden" created by the Kindermann-Wolscht trial and verdict. The sooner this burden was removed, the sooner would German confidence be restored.

Secretary of Embassy Alexander Stange visited Ernst Rantzau, the Ambassador's brother, on the same day and casually mentioned the student trial. He asked Ernst Rantzau to influence his brother. Stange repeatedly stated, unofficially to be sure, that the exoneration of Hilger would take place; Brockdorff-Rantzau should not insist on an immediate resolution. Stange also tried to find out whether the Ambassador would leave Moscow.[24]

An interesting situation now existed. The Soviet government wanted to proceed with the economic talks and bring them to a conclusion while Germany was involved in the Western pact and League negotiations. Since Germany could not really afford to antagonize Moscow completely, the Russians apparently felt an opportunity existed to force the Russian demands. Furthermore, the Soviet Union held the exoneration as a second card to get concessions from Germany in the economic and political spheres. In addition Kindermann and Wolscht were kept on ice by the OGPU to be used in exchange for Skoblevsky.

Stresemann wanted Moscow to accept the German preamble because its publicatio, at the opportune moment, would show the Western powers that Germany retained her freedom of action. The preamble was to make it possible to get concessions from the West in regard to the evacuation of the Rhineland. On July 13, he asked the Reichschancellery to place new proposals for the economic negotiations, which included granting extraterritorial status for the Trade Mission building, on the agenda for the next Cabinet meeting.[25]

On July 14, Brockdorff-Rantzau informed Chicherin that Stresemann wanted to continue the economic negotiations. Chicherin expressed his surprise at the difference between the Ambassador's harsh stand and the Foreign Minister's position. Brockdorff-Rantzau sharply rejected the intimation of a discrepancy between his acts and those of Stresemann. Having made that point, the two agreed that Ganetzky should invite Dirksen and that the economic negotiations should resume immediately.

The Ambassador insisted that Hilger's exoneration should now take place. Chicherin thought that a satisfactory answer would be forthcoming in a few days.

Chicherin also dictated the Russian counterproposals to the German preamble directly to Brockdorff-Rantzau:

Both governments, imbued with the knowledge that the active interest of the peoples of Germany as well as those of the USSR requires the continuing friendly cooperation of both countries, are absolutely determined to further develop their mutual relations in the spirit of the Treaty of Rapallo and to strive toward permanent mutual friendly contact and agreement in all political and economic questions which affect one or the other of the treaty powers, based on the point of view of the necessity to maintain general peace.

Based on these suppositions, the German government and the Soviet government bind themselves not to commit direct attacks or an unfriendly act of any other kind against each other and to enter neither political nor economic blocs, treaties, understandings, nor combinations against the other treaty power.

Among such combinations have to be enumerated all kinds of unofficial as well as informal economic agreements, which have the purpose of making it difficult for the other treaty power to carry on trade, to obtain credits, to undertake financial operations, or to receive visas necessary for the business travels of the employees of her official establishments.

The German and the Soviet governments bind themselves further to coordinate their activities regarding entry into the League of Nations or the dispatch of an observer. The coordination of their activities presumes agreement between them previous to making decisions.

After he had dictated the Russian preamble, Chicherin told Brockdorff-Rantzau that the German proposal had been incorporated into the Russian counterproposals. The Ambassador agreed that this was true. The German preamble was designed for publication, not necessarily for a political agreement; the Russian version would have to be kept secret. Finally the German preamble was designed to make it possible for her to enter the League of Nations and still remain on friendly terms with Russia.

Chicherin retorted that he wanted to be quite frank. Russia felt

that the proposals from Berlin were vague allusions, and pretty phrases turned to the melody *"und wenn Europa Ruhe hat, dann hat Europa Ruh',"* but not concrete proposals. The Russian answer was a positive proposal, without its being *"mise en demeure."* Moscow wanted to know "whether the German government was ready to enter into firm commitments or not?"

Brockdorff-Rantzau interjected that he did not think that the international situation would permit the German government to bind itself in the manner suggested by Chicherin. The Commissar declared that it was the USSR which bound itself much more strongly because it was she who would be "bound not to do anything with France or Poland under any circumstances."

Brockdorff-Rantzau immediately rejected the mentioning of Poland in this context, because, he lectured Chicherin, Poland had provided the strongest "cement" to bind Germany and Russia together during the past centuries. The Commissar, for his part, pointed out that this had not been true of relations with France. The discussion concluded with

Chicherin expressing the hope that Germany would present counter-proposals.

In his report home, the Ambassador cautioned Stresemann against too brusque a rejection of the Russian preamble so that it would not strengthen the belief that Germany intended to disregard the December proposals.[26] The last sentence reflected Brockdorff-Rantzau's own evaluation of the German preamble. All his doubts had not been removed, although he was "elegantly taking the hurdle," just as Dirksen had expected. He still was convinced, as he had been during his stay in Berlin, "that the Russians were right on some points" and that "some of the fault lay with Germany."[27]

During the morning of July 15, Dirksen and Ganetzky met again to discuss the commercial treaty. The Germans had registered one major gain the day before when Ganetzky transmitted an article of the treaty which dealt with economic espionage. The article stated that citizens of the states party to the treaty had the right to collect the material necessary to judge the economic situation and pass it on to third persons. On July 15, Dirksen told Ganetzky that the German delegation would request complete extraterritoriality for the Lindenstrasse building. The demand for the incorporation of the Trade Mission into the Embassy and immunity for the Archives of the Hamburg branch of the Mission would be reported to Berlin. Dirksen did not think it would be approved. The debate on the most-favored-nation principle stalled over Ganetzky's demand that Germany give up equal status with Turkey. At the end of their discussion, both decided that the negotiations be suspended until something concrete was done about the still existing divergencies.

Krestinsky and Jacubovich followed up Ganetzky's lead during a discussion with Stresemann and Wallroth. The Soviet Ambassador declared that extraterritoriality for the Lindenstrasse building should no longer make any difficulties. Germany should not demand equality with Japan, China, and Turkey in the most-favored-nation clause and should grant the importation of fifty million *pud* of rye (900,000 tons) without tariffs, or at a very low rate.

Stresemann informed Krestinsky that the demand for extraterritoriality had met very determined resistance during the Cabinet session on July 15. In any event, approval was doubtful. The new exemptions in the most-favored-nation clause could not be accepted. He would try to convince the Cabinet during its evening session to approve new instructions for the negotiators in Moscow. As to the tariff exemption on rye, the request had to be rejected.

Stresemann turned to the exoneration of Hilger and the Embassy, expressing the hope that Krestinsky had brought a satisfactory declaration by his government. The Ambassador interrupted, saying that the Brockdorff-Rantzau ultimatum had created difficulties but that there was no reason why all pending questions could not be discussed. Stresemann countered by insisting that giving satisfaction for the involvement of Hilger was so obvious that it needed no negotiations. Krestinsky thought that the German Embassy in Moscow could publish a communiqué in the Soviet press explaining that Hilger was not involved in the crime of the students. Stresemann demanded that the Soviet government exonerate Hilger on the basis of the proposals submitted by the German Ambassador.

During the evening session of the Cabinet, Stresemann once again tried to get approval for new directions. No agreement was reached, and Stresemann requested that a decision, one way or the other, be reached by the following day. The Cabinet, after further objections, acquiesced in the continuation of economic negotiations to determine whether a compromise solution resolving the major disagreements could be found.[28]

On July 21, Brockdorff-Rantzau went to see Chicherin, since the promised answer on the Hilger involvement had not been forthcoming. To the Ambassador's surprise, Ganetzky was also present. The reason, Chicherin enlightened the Count, was that a remark made by Dirksen had given the impression that the German government wanted to break off the economic negotiations. Brockdorff-Rantzau made it quite clear that his government intended to conclude the commerical treaty, but that he wanted to discuss Hilger's exoneration. The Count proposed that the communiqué Krestinsky had offered to Stresemann be published by the Narkomindel. Chicherin refused to go beyond an Embassy notice in *Izvestia,* and that only if there was a decrease of tension in the economic negotiations. Brockdorff-Rantzau expressed his regrets about Chicherin's attitude and then informed him that the economic negotiations would be discontinued until Hilger was exonerated by the Soviet government.

Brockdorff-Rantzau used Chicherin's refusal to inform the Wilhelmstrasse that Moscow had apparently decided that Germany was about to join the West. The Count hoped that Chicherin, under the influence of their talk, might succeed in convincing the Russian government to be conciliatory. Brockdorff-Rantzau indicated that he did not really think that Chicherin would be successful. As so often before, the Count warned his home office that the Soviet Union was probably pursuing a *rapprochement* with France. That Chicherin was personally and honestly trying to find a satisfactory solution was beyond the shadow of a doubt, as was the fact that he resisted the attempts of the party and Comintern to interfere in foreign policy. Unfortunately, Chicherin had little influence "inside the almost all-powerful party, and it seemed almost completely unteachable in its present intransigence." Despite this Germany had no choice but to continue her cooperation with the Soviet Union. The Count emphasized once again that Germany's relations with Russia constituted the only means by which the Reich could escape complete dependence on the West. As far as he was concerned, it was not so much a question of whether Russia could be trusted to adhere to its treaty obligations, as the plain fact that Germany was not free in her choice of friends. Therefore, the utmost patience had to be exercised vis-à-vis Soviet provocations, as long as this was compatible with Germany's honor. Six days later Brockdorff-Rantzau thought that one way in which Russian concessions could be achieved would be to threaten his departure from Moscow.[29]

Both Stresemann and Chancellor Luther shared Brockdorff-Rantzau's view about the seriousness of the situation. Both were willing to do everything possible to avoid a break in relations. Despite the unconciliatory attitude of the Soviet government, Brockdorff-Rantzau was instructed to remain at his post. Stresemann wanted Brockdorff-Rantzau to weigh the possibility of a compromise in the matter of the proffered communiqué in *Izvestia*. A sentence could be included in the Embassy's communiqué that the Commissariat for Foreign Affairs had been officially informed of its contents and had made no objections to it. This procedure, Stresemann pointed out, would achieve the same purpose, "as if the Foreign Commissariat had made the declaration directly." Should this approach be successful, the economic negotiations could proceed, since the Cabinet had decided to send new instructions to the German delegation. Further steps regarding the Russian preamble could be taken after Brockdorff-Rantzau had accepted the proposed *modus procendi*.[30]

Brockdorff-Rantzau objected to the *modus* proposed by the Foreign Minister and forwarded a memorandum by Dirksen, who was returning to Berlin. In the memorandum, the Ambassador pointed out that relations with Russia had become difficult after the Ruhr occupation. From that moment forward, Moscow considered Germany less important economically and politically. The Bozenhardt incident disturbed relations deeply. The Western pact negotiations, the six-month waiting period for a reply to the December proposals, the student trial and the accompanying polemics in the German press, the guilty conscience regarding the developments which led to the Leipzig trial, and, finally, the realization that the economic agreement would not be concluded on the basis of the Russian demands—all of these circumstances had created a serious situation. The Ambassador assured Stresemann that the Russians were not particular about means as long as they achieved their ends. This fact had to be recognized before a way out of any critical confrontation could be found. Brockdorff-Rantzau agreed with Stresemann that the Soviets had chosen this specific moment to accuse Hilger because they wanted to provide themselves with objects of exchange for Skoblevsky and Stalin's friend, Maslov. Not the slightest apology had been made for the involvement of Hilger; on the contrary, the Soviet press continued to stir up strife. Chicherin had made it unequivocally clear that he would agree to an exoneration of Hilger only if broad concessions in the economic negotiations were made. Even if these were granted, all he would permit would be a purely German declaration in *Izvestia*.

Brockdorff-Rantzau explained that he would not follow Stresemann's instructions, because he did not think they would achieve the desired result. He then hinted broadly that he would rather resign than to see his program, designed to "revise the *Diktat* of Versailles," thwarted. He did not have the slightest intention of achieving the exoneration of Hilger on the basis of German concessions which he could not approve. Brockdorff-Rantzau explained that the new instructions sent to the economic delegation would be rejected by the Russians; in fact, they would further deepen the feeling that Germany intended to desert them. Moscow not only wanted the economic negotiations to end in a positive agreement, but was really interested in some definite German counterproposals to Chicherin's preamble of July 14. Brockdorff-Rantzau repeated his request for permission to leave Moscow for a furlough until Hilger was exonerated. Such a procedure would prevent a formal break of diplomatic relations and warn the Russians not to use brutal tactics. Brockdorff-Rantzau warned that at this precarious juncture, great care had to be taken to prevent the Soviet government from using blackmail of the most critical kind, *i.e.*, revealing the military collaboration.[31]

Stresemann's instructions to resolve the conflict over the exoneration had hurt the Count's vanity. His advice, tempered by thirty years of experience in the diplomatic service, had been neglected by a man he considered an amateur despite all evidence that he had become a seasoned diplomat. Brockdorff-Rantzau advised flexibility in foreign relations, a balancing of the West by the East, but a balance weighted on the Russian side. He demanded that Berlin accept his basic good will toward the West as a matter of fact, despite evidence to the contrary. On the other hand, the Count, because of his characteristic morbid suspicion, refused to accept the assurances that Stresemann's Western orientation was as much of a tactical maneuver as was his own advocacy of good relations with Russia, and that both policies were designed to return Germany to great power status.

Brockdorff-Rantzau was convinced that the Wilhelmstrasse was unwilling to be firm in the matter of Hilger's exoneration. He was sure that a retreat, at the cost of his personal honor and detrimental to Germany's interest, was being prepared.

On July 30, Chicherin invited Brockdorff-Rantzau to visit him at midnight. They talked until two in the morning about the exoneration of Hilger. Chicherin was eager to settle the matter before it lead to greater difficulties. The Ambassador agreed that a perilous phase had been entered. Unless Hilger and he were protected against provocative lies, he would leave Moscow. When Chicherin, who knew his friend, interjected that his departure would be catastrophic, the Count replied that it was up to the Soviet government to prevent such an event. He pointed out that he could not continue in Moscow unless he and the Embassy staff were given protection against such

> unheard of accusations. Who, I continued, guaranteed that the same calumny (I used a less parliamentary expression) as that leveled against Hilger would not be made against me?

Chicherin assured Brockdorff-Rantzau that such a thing could not happen, to which the Count retorted that after the latest events, absolutely nothing would surprise him. Besides, it would really be ironic if the Russians "would do the English and the French governments the favor of making my continuation here impossible." The absolutely crackbrained accusation against Hilger, the Count told Chicherin, made him begin to doubt that the Soviet government was really as smart as he thought it to be. They certainly could not believe that the two German boys "could, in this brutal manner, be prepared as hostages for Gorew-Skoblevsky and Maslov."

Chicherin, who had listened in silence, inquired whether it would be agreeable if he asked the Cabinet to approve publication of an Embassy explanation in *Izvestia* without a government declaration. Brockdorff-Rantzau rejected this and insisted that the Foreign Commissariat add a statement of its own to the Embassy communiqué exonerating Hilger. Chicherin protested, but agreed to discuss the Count's demand with his colleagues and promised a speedy reply.[32]

Brockdorff-Rantzau had decided not to propose Stresemann's compromise solution because he was determined to get acceptance of his own demand. On August 2, Chicherin tried again to get the Count to accept a compromise. The "Narkomindel would publish the declaration of the German Embassy and at the same time state that Counselor of Legation Hilger was not mentioned in the verdict." The Ambassador was not satisfied with this offer, although it fulfilled Stresemann's minimum demand, but he informed Chicherin on August 3 that he was willing to compromise on the communiqué. He requested that Chicherin, or someone else, meet with Dr. Martius (of the Legal Department of the Wilhelmstrasse, detached as legal advisor to the German economic mission in Moscow) for this purpose.

Reporting this step to his home office, Brockdorff-Rantzau added that the Soviet government acted as it did because of the trials involving Communists and the Embassy in Germany and not because of the German negotiations with the West.

> Fully aware of the dangers which lie in the visible darkening of our relations with Russia, I feel it is not consistent with the dignity and prestige of the Reich to give in to the Russian demands. Only a rejection in the form proposed by me can possibly lead to any success.

Capitulation would not be understood by the German people or have the slightest effect on the Russian government. As a matter of fact, "they would be strengthened in their conviction that they could do anything they pleased to us in the future." He, for one, would not participate in the conduct of German-Russian relations under such circumstances.[33]

Brockdorff-Rantzau was sure that Berlin opposed him and did not realize the seriousness of the situation. He demanded that Krestinsky be told emphatically and unequivocally by the Foreign Office that they also considered relations to be near the breaking point.

Stresemann informed the Ambassador that Chicherin's offer to publish the Embassy's declaration with a Narkomindel explanation that Hilger's name had not been mentioned in the verdict met the German minimum demands.

> Since the Soviet government, as is evident from Chicherin's behavior during the talk with you, is also looking for a way out, it seems it has in the meantime realized that further resistance only plays the game of the Western powers.

Stresemann pointed out that the disagreement now was only about nuances, not essentials. However, if a settlement unacceptable to Brockdorff-Rantzau was proposed he could inform the Soviet government that he would immediately leave on furlough. Stresemann would invite Krestinsky soon and make a declaration, according to Brockdorff-Rantzau's advice. Stresemann, using the Count's own techniques, had now placed squarely on Brockdorff-Rantzau's shoulders the responsibility for pushing German-Soviet relations to the breaking point.

The Ambassador, confronted with this fact, retreated part of the way by informing Stresemann that he intended to use the authorization to leave Moscow as a threat to achieve the desired statement. Chicherin and Martius had discussed the exoneration, but no result had been immediately achieved. The delay was proof, the Ambassador informed Stresemann, that "it is Chicherin and not the Soviet government who is looking for a way out." If the Reich government felt that the Commissar's offer was satisfactory, he would negotiate on that basis. He personally felt that it was not a matter "of relatively small formal nuances. . . ."[34]

After the dispatch of this message, Brockdorff-Rantzau's anger at having been bested by Stresemann slowly accumulated. On August 7, he shot off a telegram to Stresemann which sizzled with indignation. The Ambassador told his superior to read and to pay attention to the dispatches sent from Moscow. The Count found it difficult to understand how anyone could conclude, on the basis of his reports, that the Russian government had come to its senses. After thirty years in the diplomatic service, he expected that his advice was considered in any decision made regarding the Hilger exoneration. Stresemann should "kindly interest himself personally in the critical state" German-Russian relations had reached, and receive Krestinsky without further delay. The Count warned that a break with Russia could be avoided only if his approach to the Hilger exoneration was supported by the Foreign Office. If he received no support, he would resign.[35]

Less than an hour after forwarding his impertinent lecture and threat to resign, Brockdorff-Rantzau was personally informed by a representative of the Foreign Commissariat that the formula worked out between Martius and Chicherin had been accepted. With the Ambassador's agreement it could be published that same evening. The Ambassador accepted the offer. The communiqué was published in *Izvestia* for August 8, and it read:

From the People's Commissariat for Foreign Affairs:
The German Embassy has, with reference to its earlier explanations in the case of the trial against the German students, sent the following explanation, some time ago, to the Narkomindel:
(1) Counselor of Legation Hilger's meeting with the two stu-

dents on the Riga-Moscow train on October 13, 1924, had been entirely accidental. (2) The students had introduced themselves to Counselor of Legation Hilger after they had heard from fellow travelers that he was a member of the Embassy. They told him that they planned a scientific trip to Turkestan and Siberia. Counselor of Legation Hilger, who felt that their plans were poorly prepared and impossible to realize, invited them to come to the Embassy for advice. There was no conversation about meeting in a private apartment, and Hilger never advised them to destroy compromising documents. (3) After his arrival in Moscow on October 14, Counselor of Legation Hilger heard nothing from the students until the 26th, when Wolscht called to ask for a discussion. Counselor of Legation Hilger made an appointment for Wolscht to appear at the chancellery of the Embassy on October 28 at 11:00 A.M. Wolscht never appeared. On October 29 the Embassy learned that the students had been arrested during the night of October 26/27, 1924. (4) Counselor of Legation Hilger never laid eyes on Ditmar until the trial, nor had he ever met him previously.

Insofar as the Narkomindel published the declaration of the German Embassy, it points out that Counselor of Legation Hilger has not been mentioned in the verdict. On the basis of negotiations carried on in the meantime, both governments consider the matter as closed.[36]

Brockdorff-Rantzau immediately informed Stresemann that the publication of the notice negated his communication of the preceding day. He requested that the press be continent in its commentary on the exoneration. There should be no discussion about the "retreat of the Russian government." The extremist press should, if possible, be muzzled if it tried to describe the exoneration, "which in fact went beyond the demands of our government," as the "lamentable product of a weak German surrender" or some such remarks.[37]

Stresemann sent his congratulations for a job well done and then turned to his subordinate's lecture. The Foreign Minister refuted Brockdorff-Rantzau's accusation that no attention was paid to his reports, and that his advice was not heeded. In fact, both Krestinsky and Litvinov had been told that very morning, before news of the exoneration had been available, that Brockdorff-Rantzau's demands had to be met or the Ambassador would be recalled. Litvinov proposed an exoneration of the Soviet Embassy from the accusation leveled against it during the trials of German Communists. Stresemann had immediately rejected this and cut off further discussion of Litvinov's proposal with the statement that a note would be presented to the Soviet government on the Cheka Trial, and it could then take a stand on the involvement of the Soviet Embassy.

After Schubert, who had attended the talk, had been called out and had been informed of the exoneration, the talk had proceeded to the economic negotiations. Stresemann had rejected extraterritorial status for the archives of the Hamburg branch and expressed an "urgent wish for the speedy completion of the treaty." Stresemann had reiterated German's position on the security pacts, League membership, and Article 16. He replied to Litvinov's questions about the contemplated procedure regarding the Russian preamble that Chicherin had not really given the German formulation due credit. It was the maximum that could be offered, in view of Western attitudes. Chicherin's preamble went too far. Litvinov inquired whether Germany intended to wait until negotiations with the West were completed before proceeding with his own country. Stresemann replied that the negotiations could run concurrently. The delay had not been entirely Germany's fault; after all, much time had been lost by the students' trial, the refusal to exonerate Hilger, and the delays created in the economic negotiations by Russia's delegation.[38]

On August 10, Brockdorff-Rantzau telegraphed a conciliatory message expressing his appreciation for Stresemann's congratulations. He also explained why he had sent his complaint. The statement that the Russian government was looking for a way out had given him the feeling that his reports were misinterpreted because only Chicherin had been conciliatory and had tried to find a solution. This contrasting attitude had been a source of major concern because, the Count continued, he was not entirely convinced that his personal influence over the Foreign Commissar was sufficient to "strengthen the Minister and move the [Russian] Government to yield." The démarche had cut deeply into his principal of trust and personal influence, and because of that he insisted on support for his policy by Berlin. During the latest incident, the Russians had interpreted his unilateral procedure as "an unauthorized step which was opposed to the intentions of my government." Stresemann's assertion that the difference between the Russian offer and the German demands was only a matter of "small nuances," Brockdorff-Rantzau felt, was an interpretation which sharply differed from his own. The Count assured Stresemann that working in Moscow had become extremely difficult because of the various problems, but especially "since the Western pact negotiations have aroused the distrust of the Soviet government, which it has thus far been impossible to eradicate." Stresemann's frank talk with Krestinsky and Litvinov was a move in the right direction. Litvinov had far greater influence in the party, and thus directly on the government, than did Chicherin. It was to be hoped that he would attempt to get a relaxation of the tensions which had developed during the past six months.[39]

With the exoneration of Hilger, the economic and political negotiations could again proceed at an increased rate. The economic talks had not yet resolved the outstanding differences, although Brockdorff-Rantzau, Schlesinger, Chicherin, and Ganetzky had discussed these sore points for over four hours on August 3. Chicherin, contrary to his normal behavior, was unusually aggressive and irritated. He insisted that the Trade Delegation become an integral part of the Berlin Embassy and that the Hamburg archive be given immunity. Even after Brockdorff-Rantzau made it perfectly clear that insistence on these concessions could lead to the total collapse of the negotiations, Chicherin maintained adamantly that this was the *"conditio sine qua non."* Ganetzky supported Chicherin, of course, but told Schlesinger that he was willing to give up the demand for exemption from tariffs on rye exports to Germany, as well as the demand for credits.

On August 11, Stresemann agreed, with Cabinet approval, that the Trade Delegation could be incorporated into the Soviet Embassy if the treaty would fail without this concession. However, there was absolutely no way in which immunity for the archives of the Hamburg branch could be granted. The Wilhelmstrasse would approach the Senate of Hamburg for an agreement that the police would deal only through the Senate with the Trade Delegation branch.

The Foreign Minister also succeeded in getting Cabinet approval on August 25, in principle, to guarantee a 100 million mark credit which the Russians wanted to use for the purchase of German consumer goods. The Soviet government proposed to sell grain in Germany through a consortium of German dealers to repay the loan. The acceptance of this deal was another concrete expression of Germany's desire for friendly relations with the Soviet Union.

Despite these moves by the Wilhelmstrasse, the economic negotiations appeared again near collapse by the end of August. The Russians proved absolutely intransigent, refused even to countenance the inclusion of China and Turkey in the most-favored-nation clause, and insisted that the approach to the Hamburg Senate was completely insufficient. They did not even mention protection against arrests for economic espionage; finally, they tried to force acceptance of the treaty as it stood by declaring that the "limit of the possible" had now been reached. The German delegation agreed unanimously that Brockdorff-

Rantzau was to tell Chicherin on August 31 that the unyielding attitude of the Russians meant the collapse of the negotiations and that
the German delegation would leave Moscow during the week. The
door was to be left open for a resumption of talks in Berlin.[40]

The Wilhelmstrasse had no interest in the collapse of the economic
negotiations, because the preliminary discussions for the West pacts
were already underway. Gaus had gone to London to participate in the
discussions of the legal experts of the Foreign Offices of England,
France, Belgium, and Italy on the proposed treaties, and the meetings
to put the finishing touches on the work of the jurists were soon to take
place.[41]

The Soviet government had invited a representative group of
German scientists to attend the bicentennial celebration of the found-
ing of the Russian Academy of Sciences, and the professors had balked
at attending because of the trial and the verdict against the students
Kindermann and Wolscht. On August 11, *Krasnaya Gazeta* had published an article by Radek in which he had called the professors
Fascists, imperialists, despoilers of the people, and a number of other
choice epithets. Radek had concluded his vituperation with a masked
allusion to the economic and political difficulties. He wrote:

> The history of the German people will last longer than the politi-
> cal maneuvers of Stresemann and the credit hunger of Stinnes
> and Wolff. The friendship of the peoples of the USSR, which
> alone in the whole world protested against the Peace of Ver-
> sailles, can yet bring some advantages. As for you, *Herren* scien-
> tists, it is not smart to spit into the well from which one might yet
> have to drink.

Brockdorff-Rantzau thought that the exoneration was sufficient reason to attend the celebration and that not to send a delegation would
be a grave mistake, since, in his view, good relations between leading
scientists were a necessary part of the total relationship between Germany and the Soviet Union. Schubert tried to persuade the professors
to accept, but they refused to go. They finally agreed to accept the
invitation on the persuasive urgings of the Wilhelmstrasse which was
trying to please the Russians and avoid repercussions.

The bicentennial began on September 5, lasting for nine days, with
the German professors and rectors and Brockdorff-Rantzau in conspicuous attendance at the great celebration of Sunday, the sixth. During
the evening a banquet was given by Kalinin and Lunarcharsky, with
the German Ambassador occupying the seat of honor at Kalinin's right.
During dinner, Brockdorff-Rantzau made a short speech extending the

best wishes of the German government. He remarked that some who themselves had sown hatred maintained that hate had brought Germany and the Soviet Union together. Dreamers talked of love which led the two people together. While love was certainly "a strong bond, it was not strong enough to hold people together when their interests ceased to run parallel." What brought people together and held them together was neither hate nor love, but "intelligence and spirit."[42]

Brockdorff-Rantzau's speech was an indication, despite its generalities, that the economic negotiations were beginning to show some improvement. Brockdorff-Rantzau had actually threatened the departure of the delegation during an interview with Litvinov. The German press reported the unsatisfactory stand of the negotiations, and Dirksen had told Bratman-Brodovsky that the negotiations were about to be broken off. Influenced by the Foreign Office, representatives of the Deutsche Bank had told Tumanov, President of the Soviet State Bank, that the credit would be easier to negotiate if the economic negotiations improved.

On September 7, the Russian negotiators in Moscow indicated that concessions on the most-favored-nation clause could be discussed. Stange had told Dirksen that the crisis was due to an apparent misunderstanding.[43]

On September 19, Stresemann inquired of Brockdorff-Rantzau whether the economic treaty could be concluded, positively or negatively for Germany, by September 26. The forthcoming Foreign Ministers' Conference about the West pact would delay Cabinet discussion of the economic treaty until the middle of October. For diplomatic reasons, Stresemann did not want that much time to elapse and wanted to get an early signing of the treaty. If Brockdorff-Rantzau would use this argument with the Russian government, it would counteract Russian contentions that Germany wanted to delay signing the treaty until after the West pact had been safely brought home. Brockdorff-Rantzau agreed and the two delegations completed the final drafts. The seventy-page document left Moscow by special courier on September 24.[44]

After Hilger's exoneration, Stresemann had told Litvinov that the Russian preamble went too far. The Foreign Minister proposed on August 14 that Brockdorff-Rantzau communicate a number of observations to the Soviet government. In general, the Russian proposal gave the impression that Moscow had no understanding for Germany's position on world affairs. If Russia intended to compromise Germany with the West, then a further discussion of the preamble was of no value. Stresemann repeated that Germany was not going to be forced into an option for or against Russia. If it came to the latter, it was Moscow's own fault.

Brockdorff-Rantzau should discuss the following with Chicherin:

1. The last sentence in the Russian preamble prohibits German entry into the League without Russian permission. Germany cannot possibly accept this restraint.

2. The neutrality obligations were acceptable only if the League members unanimously exempted Germany from Article 16. This cannot be achieved. Therefore, neutrality must still make it possible for Germany to belong to the League.

3. The Russian proposal of neutrality compromised Germany, while her proposals achieve neutrality without such stringent terms.

4. The German preamble is the maximum concession Germany can make, in view of the fact that the preamble would be published, and because of the West pact negotiations.

5. The oral explanations are additions to the preamble and therefore bind future German governments as much as the preamble itself.

6. Article 17 becomes applicable after Article 16 has been activated. Germany will, however, make an oral commitment to quiet Russian concern.

Time was of the essence. Stresemann did not want to publish the preamble before the conclusion of the West pact negotiations. The best procedure would be inclusion in the economic treaty, which would still take a number of weeks before it was ready for signing.

Brockdorff-Rantzau did not think that the discussion of the Russian preamble would be of much value, since it went much further than the December proposals. He had already discussed point 1 with Chicherin. Stresemann's second point needed further explanations, and as to point 3 he did not think that he would be able to convince Chicherin that the German proposals included a political obligation to cooperate in a positive way. In the Ambassador's opinion, the Russian proposal was not intended to compromise Germany with the West, but was due to Russia's fear of isolation. As to point 6, Chicherin had continually emphasized the importance of Article 16 to Russia. Points 4 and 5 would be transmitted to the Foreign Commissar.

Brockdorff-Rantzau advised against delaying the signing of the economic treaty, once it proved acceptable. Instead, the treaty should be concluded without preamble, but an official statement should be made at the time of the signing, acknowledging that a preamble would be incorporated into the treaty and published as part of it. If Chicherin wanted to discuss the preamble, it would be done on the basis outlined above.

Stresemann agreed that the economic agreements should be signed without the preamble and that a statement should make it clear that it would be included later. For Brockdorff-Rantzau's information, Stresemann added that the German preamble *was* a reply to the December proposals. If the Russians accept it, "although *contre coeur*," it would keep them on Germany's side even after the latter entered the League.

On August 25, Brockdorff-Rantzau sought out Litvinov, who now directed European policy while Chicherin concentrated on the East. The Deputy Commissar did not think that the economic agreements should be delayed because of the preamble which was not acceptable in the German form, but he would report Brockdorff-Rantzau's explanation to the Cabinet so that discussions could continue.[45]

The political talks had now been separated from the economic negotiations, and the two could proceed at the same time. Delays in the first would not lead to difficulties in the second. Stresemann's tactic had worked. The West pact could be pursued, while Russia was given sufficient assurances to prevent her withdrawal from Germany at this critical juncture in Stresemann's attempt to wrest concessions from the West. The Russians decided to use the old technique of approaches to Poland and France to persuade Stresemann not to conclude any agreements with the West detrimental to Russia. Chicherin, who had told Brockdorff-Rantzau early in September that he intended to consult an Austrian specialist near Vienna, did not leave as planned because "running ulcers on his leg" kept him bedridden. His physicians thought that he would be able to travel by the middle of September.

On September 15, the *Vossische Zeitung* carried a report that Chicherin would arrive in Warsaw on September 20 for a two-day visit with the Polish Foreign Minister, Count Alexander Skrzyński. Chicherin would then proceed to Berlin.

Brockdorff-Rantzau replied to the Wilhelmstrasse's inquiry as to the accuracy of the report that Chicherin had intended to leave for Berlin via Riga, not Warsaw, on September 19 but had to delay his departure because of a worsening of his condition. It was possible that Chicherin would now choose the Warsaw route because it was shorter.

On September 24, Chicherin invited Brockdorff-Rantzau to visit him at 1:00 A.M. He then confirmed that he would leave the next day via Warsaw to consult a specialist in Berlin. He requested that Brockdorff-Rantzau arrange an audience with President Hindenburg. The Ambassador asked his home office to grant Chicherin's request in view of the "combinations which could be expected in Warsaw. . . ."

During the evening of September 25, Chicherin left Moscow by train. The Russians made it a rather "ostentatious ceremony" not quite in keeping with the announced reason for the trip of the Foreign Commissar to Germany. An honor company was drawn up opposite the salon car Chicherin was using, and almost the whole diplomatic corps was in attendance, as well as all the members of the Collegium of the Narkomindel, led by Litvinov. Chicherin looked exhausted, addressed a few words to the diplomatic corps and made it a point to thank Brockdorff-Rantzau "very cordially" for having come.

Bratman-Brodovsky approached Schubert during the morning of September 26 in the Reichstag to tell the Undersecretary that Chicherin's journey was entirely private and that his visit to Warsaw, promised some time past, had "no political significance." Schubert did not go into the accuracy of Brodovsky's statement, but did say that a meeting between Chicherin and Hindenburg, who was in the country, could conceivably be arranged. Bratman-Brodovsky expressed his pleasure, but asked that arrangements remain tentative, since Chicherin's physical state was such that he might not be able to make the visit.[46]

From Warsaw, the German Ambassador, Ulrich Rauscher, inquired of the Wilhelmstrasse whether Cabinet approval of the draft of the German-Soviet economic treaty could not be "leaked" to the press to have a counterweight to the planned reception of Chicherin, which, Rauscher had been informed, was to be made into a "big thing."

Brockdorff-Rantzau refused to admit that the trip to Warsaw was a deliberate attempt to put pressure on Germany. He reported to the Wilhelmstrasse that there was absolutely no proof that Chicherin had intentionally misled him about his health or the reasons for his trip. Rauscher, who met Chicherin in Warsaw, did not notice any signs of poor health; on the contrary, the Foreign Commissar seemed quite vigorous.

Brockdorff-Rantzau, in an urgent telegram, cautioned that a strong tendency existed within the Soviet government for a new orientation of Russia's policy vis-à-vis Germany. Since Chicherin, according to the Count, was absolutely loyal to the Rapallo friendship, the continuation of that relationship depended on the success of the Commissar's Berlin visit. Brockdorff-Rantzau was sure that Chicherin did not want to place everything on the "French-Polish card."

Chicherin, despite Brockdorff-Rantzau's fine words, played the Polish card for all it was worth during his stay in Warsaw. During a luncheon on September 28, Skrzyński characterized Chicherin's visit as a political act which the Poles understood. The Commissar, in turn, was sure that the outstanding reception accorded him was an indication of Poland's desire for continuing a policy of harmony. During a private discussion, Chicherin mentioned "a nonaggression pact," but Skrzyński refused to accept it unless the Baltic States and Rumania were also included.[47]

Brockdorff-Rantzau continued to be very much disturbed by the approach of the Locarno Conference. He was convinced that the Wilhelmstrasse deliberately withheld precise information about the proposed security pacts with the West from him. The Count tried to get inside information by asking Hencke, who was on furlough in Germany, to get details from Dirksen or any other high official in the Foreign Office. Hencke failed in his mission and advised the Ambassador to come to Berlin himself. Brockdorff-Rantzau decided to remain in Moscow because the situation required his presence, but sent an urgent note to Stresemann warning the Foreign Minister that German-Russian relations had entered the most precarious stage since he, the Count, had taken "personal responsibility for German-Russian policy." He recommended that Stresemann consider a special report he was sending with Martius, who was due to arrive in Berlin on the last day of September, "in the light of the conditions which were specifically confirmed to me before assuming the Moscow post and which were reconfirmed in July of this year . . ." by President von Hindenburg.[48]

Chicherin arrived in Berlin on September 30, and was met at the station only by Schubert and Krestinsky. At 10:30 in the evening, he was received by Stresemann, and their talk (attended by Krestinsky) lasted until 1:30 in the morning.

Stresemann wanted to know whether Article 40 of the proposed commercial treaty granted Germany most-favored-nation treatment. Chicherin and Krestinsky were sure that it did. The German Foreign Minister then outlined the difficulties caused by the Russian demand for complete extraterritoriality for their Trade Delegation. It had taken four Cabinet sessions to secure concession, and these had been granted only because he and the Chancellor insisted on it. The Cabinet's resistance had been due mainly to the perpetual and flagrant interference by Zinoviev and the Comintern in Germany's internal affairs. Stresemann voiced his regrets that these encroachments continued to disturb the good relations between Germany and Russia.

Chicherin was rather cool and insisted that he was on furlough; therefore, Litvinov should be consulted about these matters. Besides, the Soviet government could not be blamed for the actions of the Comintern just because its seat was in Moscow. If its headquarters were in London, Stresemann would have to blame England. Stresemann insisted that Zinoviev was not a private person, but Mayor of Leningrad, and it was certainly no coincidence that the Comintern was located in Moscow. Chicherin could rest assured that a speech by the Lord-Mayor of London, calling for revolution in Germany, would result in the strongest protests. It was certainly not in the spirit of the

Rapallo Treaty to raise havoc in Germany. He most certainly did not have to tell Chicherin what would happen should the *Bürgermeister* (mayor) of a major German city call for a counterrevolution in Russia. Stresemann added that he knew that the Commissar had no control over this agitation, and, he hoped, did not approve it.

The talk returned to the proposed commercial treaty, and Stresemann emphasized that the decision had been made to sign it before the negotiations for the West pacts were completed. This showed that Germany had no intention of turning away from Russia. As a matter of fact, he intended to publish this acceptance of the commercial treaty before he left for Locarno. Stresemann further pointed out that Germany's fight against Article 16 of the League Covenant should be positive proof that there was no truth in the endless polemic about a German-English alliance against Russia. He asked Chicherin to tell him the basis for these allegations.

Instead of replying, Chicherin launched into a detailed review of German-Russian relations since 1922. The Treaty of Rapallo, according to Chicherin, was primarily economic, but it had created "the spirit of Rapallo." He could not understand Germany's policy. In December of 1924, Brockdorff-Rantzau had proposed Russo-German cooperation in pushing Poland back to her ethnographic frontiers. The words "push back [*Zurückdrängen*]" could not be understood except as an appeal for military cooperation, in order to destroy Poland. He had taken this proposal by the German government to be so important that he had immediately called a session of the Russian Cabinet. Proposals had been forwarded to the German government during December which were designed to define Russo-German relations more precisely and to prepare a treaty of neutrality and nonaggression. Instead of an answer, the German government had sent out invitations in February, 1925, to the Western powers for discussion of a security pact. The Russian proposals, on the other hand, had been acknowledged by a formula good for a toast but not for a treaty. One could call them, with Goethe, "avowals of a beautiful soul." At the same time, Dirksen had declared in Moscow that Germany might enter the League unconditionally, and only after joining make a unilateral declaration about Article 16.

Stresemann, who was well informed about the Russian proposals of December, 1924, expressed his great surprise at the information by Chicherin that Germany had approached Russia about an alliance for the division of Poland. Stresemann interrupted the talks to call Undersecretary von Schubert, despite the fact that it was already well past midnight. Schubert denied that Germany had approached Russia about such an alliance. He told Stresemann that it had been Kopp who had broached the Polish question. Schubert thought it conceivable that Brockdorff-Rantzau had casually mentioned that Poland had a right to exist within her territorial boundaries. But an offer of an alliance had never been made. Stresemann then called Gaus, who deemed it impossible that Dirksen had ever made the remark about Article 16. After the telephone calls, Stresemann emphasized that he was "thunderstruck and surprised" about the People's Commissar's remarks. It had been Kopp who had approached Germany about an alliance.

Chicherin declared "very sharply" that Kopp did not have the authority to do so, nor could such an interpretation be placed on his remarks. Stresemann rejoined that Kopp was a member of the Commissariat for Foreign Affairs, and that the Wilhelmstrasse had only responded to his allusions. He had never heard that any steps had been taken against Kopp's "arbitrary" action. It was absolutely out of the question for Dirksen ever to have made the remark ascribed to him. Germany had no intention of joining the League unconditionally. The Foreign Office had been negotiating with Sir Eric Drummond (Secretary-General of the League) for the past eight months about Article 16. Stresemann also pointed out that Krestinsky was well aware that no other note had been sent to the League regarding that article. Germany would enter the League only if she received exemption from Article 16. Krestinsky confirmed that the declaration had been given to him and that this was the reason for the consternation at Dirksen's remark. Stresemann stopped further discussion at about this point until he could reach Dirksen and look at the records to determine what had taken place in Moscow. He then proceeded to discuss the Locarno Conference, emphasizing that "no guarantee of the Polish borders" would be made because Germany would "never voluntarily recognize the Polish frontiers."

Chicherin became more conciliatory and pointed out that despite problems, the old relationship between Russia and Germany continued. An example of this was the attendance of German and Russian officers at their respective maneuvers. German officers were the only foreigners allowed to witness Red army maneuvers. Stresemann replied that this was also true, as far as he knew, of Soviet officers at German military exercises. Chicherin could deduce from this how foolish all the talk about Germany's Western orientation was. The Foreign Minister also pointed out that France, not England, dominated the League of Nations. Russia could not seek a *rapprochement* with France and, at the same time, see in the League a world alliance directed against the USSR. Should Germany enter, which was not yet definite, she would defend her own interests and, at the same time, prevent the League from becoming an instrument for war against Russia. He was convinced that France would not repeat the mistake of Napoleon I. Furthermore, Germany had no interest in Russo-British antagonism in China or India, and would not become the "continental sword" for English use against Russia. Why did the Soviet Union consider herself threatened by Germany's entry into the League? Chicherin became uneasy at this direct question and said that it needed a separate discussion, into which he would be glad to enter. Since Krestinsky had fallen asleep, and because there was nothing else to be gotten out of Chicherin, Stresemann requested that they continue their talk the next afternoon.[49]

Despite the confidential nature of the Stresemann-Chicherin discussion, the press reported that the Russian had objected to Germany's unconditional entry into the League as detrimental to the spirit of Rapallo. The papers further stated that Stresemann had assured Chicherin that Germany would enter only "on condition that she be relieved of the obligations imposed by Article 16." Chicherin reportedly was willing to make far-reaching concessions to prevent Germany from joining a British-directed, anti-Soviet bloc.

Izvestia, according to *The New York Times,* had warned that the Western pacts made Germany a *place d'armes* for an attack on the Soviet Union. Poland could easily provide the spark which could ignite the anti-Russian conflagration. But all this collapsed if the Poles and Russians were friends.[50]

During the Cabinet session of October 1, Stresemann informed the assembled ministers that only two points regarding economic relations with the Soviet Union had not been resolved. These were extraterritoriality for the Lindenstrasse building and the auditing of the Trade Delegation's books. The Minister of Finance agreed that the books of the Trade Mission would not be checked to determine the taxes due, if the Russians would agree to paying the taxes levied by the Reichsministry of Finance. Stresemann then told the Cabinet that the Russians had withdrawn their demand for immunity for the archives of the Hamburg branch. After a few remarks by some of the ministers, Chancellor Luther declared that the commercial treaty had been unanimously accepted.

On October 2, the German Cabinet announced, as Stresemann had promised, that agreement "in principle" had been reached to sign the German-Russian commercial treaty, as soon as agreement on a few outstanding points had been reached. A small German delegation would go to Moscow to resolve the differences. The beneficial effect of this announcement became clear during the day. Chicherin gave an interview to the *Berliner Tageblatt* in which he stated that it was British policy to encircle the USSR and separate her from Germany by "forcing an anti-Soviet policy" on her after conclusion of the West pact. England, aided by France, could offer benefits at Poland's expense; thus, "you have the policy of the carrot and the whip." However, the commercial treaty "about to be concluded between the USSR and Germany . . . [is] proof of Germany's desire not to be diverted from the Rapallo policy."[51]

With the atmosphere thus purified, Stresemann continued his conversation with Chicherin and Krestinsky on October 2. He told the Russians that his perusal of the records had shown that Kopp had, indeed, made the offer of an alliance and also said that one of the "most important questions appeared to him the Polish one, and here an understanding with us was urgently wished for." Kopp had also indicated that Chicherin agreed, and the Commissar had not repudiated Kopp in his talk with Brockdorff-Rantzau.

Chicherin did not deny this but repeated the sentence from Maltzan's telegram that Brockdorff-Rantzau had read to him, namely "that one of the many causes of the disturbances in eastern Europe was the nonobservation of the ethnographic principle in determining the Polish frontier." Stresemann said that this was nothing but a description of Germany's attitude toward Poland, and not an offer of a military alliance, as Chicherin had seemed to think when he repeatedly pointed to the words "push back" during that first talk. Brockdorff-Rantzau had told Kopp immediately that the use of force by Germany would be madness.

Chicherin now declared that the Ambassador had hesitated after reading the sentence, then had read another one which was definitely about "forcing Poland back to her ethnographic frontiers." Stresemann admitted that the telegram contained this sentence, but not as the "heart of our statements." The Ambassador's report showed that the talk had been about Articles 10, 11, and 17 of the League Covenant. The sentence in question had been an "intimation." According to Brockdorff-Rantzau's report at the time, "Chicherin greeted the intimation with great enthusiasm." Because the Commissar said nothing, Stresemann felt that the origin of the proposal for a miliatary alliance had been proven.

Stresemann next read the wording of the document Dirksen had transmitted to Chicherin during his stay in Moscow in July:

Should a *formal* exemption from the obligations of Article 16 prove unattainable, Germany will make its point of view unam-

biguously clear to the world and will act according to this point
of view as a League member.

Stresemann explained that Germany always had made a distinction
between *de jure* exemption, which had to be approved by a majority of
the League members, and *de facto* exemption, which would consist in
an "unambiguous" interpretation and would in fact leave it up to Germany to decide what to do in case of League implementation of the
article. This had been so thoroughly aired that he had been positive
that Chicherin understood the difference. In any event, an inquiry at
the Wilhelmstrasse would have produced an immediate clarification.

Stresemann discussed the German stand on Article 16 further, and
Chicherin accepted the German interpretation with satisfaction. Stresemann declared that the proposed German preamble for the commercial
treaty, to remain "in constant friendly touch in order to strive for
mutual understanding, with the intention of working for the general
peace of Europe and refraining from designs which might possibly
threaten this peace," could hardly be characterized as fit for a "toast" or
as the "avowals of a beautiful soul." If one added Germany's position
on Article 16 to it, one had a far-reaching obligation by Germany
which eliminated her participation in a war against Russia better than
the phrase proposed by Moscow.

Chicherin insisted that the Russian formulation was the better one
and returned to it again and again. Certainly Schubert's assertion that
news of such a treaty would be equal to an earthquake was a bit far-
fetched. Stresemann defended Schubert by saying that he had probably thought of the repercussions caused by the Treaty of Rapallo.
What should be avoided was the suspicion that some great military
preparations were behind the proposed preamble. Such a belief among
the Western powers could cause a lot of trouble for Germany. Stresemann reiterated that he had refused to sign a secret treaty because he
wanted to be able to answer any question at Locarno about such a
treaty in the negative. The Cabinet had not yet made a final decision
on the wording of the preamble, and the Russians could still propose
changes. In the meantime, Stresemann offered to discuss Chicherin's
objections to the preamble with Chancellor Luther and also with the
Cabinet.

When Chicherin prepared to leave, Stresemann pressed him again
for an explanation of why Russia feared an Anglo-German alignment.
Chicherin replied only that he did not expect an immediate military
collision with England. He was bothered by English attempts at a
financial boycott. He had heard an English bank had asked a large
German bank not to grant credits to Russia. Stresemann assured him

that no German bank would let the English tell it how to conduct its business. Exemption from Article 16 also included nonparticipation in economic boycotts.[52]

Chicherin had failed in his last-minute mission. Even the threatened Russo-Polish *rapprochement* had not had the desired result. Stresemann, by keeping Chicherin at bay, could go to Locarno in a stronger bargaining position because of having avoided the Russian attempts to turn him from the path to the West. The Foreign Minister played the Russian card to advantage once he arrived in Locarno. During a press conference, he informed the assembled representatives of the world press that he was quite upset about Russian demands to "force the German Government into initialing a Russo-German commercial treaty with a spectacular preamble, which was to reaffirm the Treaty of Rapallo."[53]

These remarks were strictly for Western consumption. The German government had no intention of antagonizing the Russians. Chicherin was cordially received by President Hindenburg on October 6. On the same day, a short-term commercial credit of 75 million reichsmark (later raised to 100 million) was granted by a number of German banks, including the Deutsche Bank, which had made the offer first on September 18. The credit agreement provided that the State Bank of the USSR draw two drafts each in one-half the amount of the loan, payable in U.S. currency in New York on January 29 and February 28, 1926. The interest rate was set at 8½ percent per annum.[54]

In Moscow, Commissar for Finance Sokolnikov, announcing the loan in *Izvestia*, called it of the greatest importance because it was the "first breach in the credit blockade directed against the USSR."

On October 12, Brockdorff-Rantzau, Körner, Litvinov, and Ganetzky signed the Commercial Treaty in Moscow, without the preamble, because Moscow insisted on secrecy and continued to object to the German wording. The treaty consisted of seven parts in addition to general provisions. These were

I. Agreement concerning conditions of residence and business and legal protection;
II. Economic Agreement;
III. Railway Agreement;
IV. Agreement concerning navigation;
V. Fiscal Agreement;
VI. Agreement concerning commercial courts of arbitration;
VII. Agreement concerning the legal protection of industrial property.

On the same day, there were also signed an "Agreement Regarding Reciprocal Legal Assistance in Civil Matters," and a "Consular Treaty, with Annex and Final Protocol." Agreements I through V had a two-year, VI and VII four-year time limit. Unless denounced six months in advance the respective time limits were automatically extended for "successive periods of six months until such time as they are denounced, six months' notice being given."[55]

On the day that the Commercial Treaty was signed, Chicherin still tried to worry the Germans "with the spectre of a Russo-Polish-French agreement . . ." by paying an ostentatious visit to the French Embassy in Berlin. In a lead article, *Pravda* warned that the decisive hour had arrived for Germany's statesmen, upon whom it depended whether Germany would voluntarily "place its foot in the trap set by the Entente at Locarno."[56] But it was all for naught. Four days later, on October 16, Stresemann joined the representatives of Belgium, Czechoslovakia, France, Great Britain, and Italy in initialing a number of documents which collectively made up the Locarno Pact and which heralded a new era of peace and tranquility for Europe. Under the provision of the Rhineland Pact, the boundaries established by the Treaty of Versailles were recognized by Germany, France, and Belgium, and guaranteed by Great Britain and Italy. Germany also signed treaties of arbitration with Belgium, France, Czechoslovakia, and Poland, respectively.[57] The refusal of the Germans to accept the finality of their borders with Poland and Czechoslovakia was somewhat offset by treaties of mutual assistance, in the case of an unprovoked German attack, between these two countries and France.

During a friendly talk with British and French Foreign Ministers Chamberlain and Briand on the steamer *Fleur d'Orange*, which was plying the calm waters of Lake Maggiore on October 10, Stresemann had succeeded in getting agreement for Germany's demand for exemption from Article 16 of the League Covenant. England, France, Belgium, and Italy, in a collective note to Germany, accepted as a fact Germany's disarmed condition. The new interpretation left it entirely to Germany's discretion whether to participate in military or economic sanctions against any other state, after she joined the League of Nations.

During the Cabinet session on the Locarno Pact, which took place nine days later, with Hindenburg presiding, Stresemann explained that the main struggle during the ministerial talks had been over French guarantees for Eastern Europe and Germany's position vis-à-vis the League of Nations. The idea of an Eastern security pact was dropped, and the arbitration treaties written on the basis of German usage, that is, "arbitration applied to all legal questions but not to political questions." Therefore, the arbitration treaties with Poland and Czechoslovakia did not mean that Germany recognized the existing boundaries with these two states. Under the new procedure, France would come to the aid of Poland only if the latter were attacked and a declaration of aggression made by the League. This, Stresemann declared, invalidated the existing Franco-Polish Treaty.[58]

Stresemann had entered into the West pact negotiations because he wanted to calm French fears of a resurgent Germany and in order to remove France's opposition to the evacuation of the occupied German territories. At the same time, Stresemann had maintained Germany's freedom of action in the East. In a speech at Karlsruhe, the Foreign Minister emphasized these thoughts and insisted that Germany attached the greatest possible importance to the continuation of the old relationship with Russia.[59] Moscow had tried to prevent the realization of the Locarno Pact by offering a common procedure against Poland. Neither the Bolsheviks nor the Germans were alone or together capable in 1925 of re-establishing the prewar border. Stresemann knew this and so did any competent, intelligent diplomat, including Brockdorff-Rantzau and Chicherin. That is why the Russians offered an alliance which included a common procedure against Poland at some convenient time.

Stresemann, despite Brockdorff-Rantzau's eloquent defense of the Russian case, his pessimistic threats that Moscow would make an agreement with France and thus leave Germany at the mercy of her enemies, refused to negotiate a secret agreement of any kind as long as the good will of Great Britain and France was needed to restore Germany to great power status. On the other hand, abandoning the Rapallo arrangement would not have been wise, because that would have removed Germany's ability to gain Western concessions on the basis of her alignment with the USSR. Stresemann was determined to balance between the East and the West and therefore did not cut the wire to Moscow. As evidence of his desire to maintain good relations with the Soviet Union, Germany insisted upon and received exemption from Article 16 of the League Covenant before she even made application for membership. On the eve of his departure for Locarno, Stresemann had been able to deliver to Chicherin Cabinet approval of the Commercial Treaty, despite the fact that the German negotiators had failed to break the foreign trade monopoly. In addition to this Russian success, Moscow achieved complete extraterritoriality for the building of the Trade Delegation, which was attached to the Soviet Embassy in Berlin.

The Russians had not succeeded in having their preamble accepted. In view of the fact that their proposition amounted to a treaty of neutrality and nonaggression, and insistence on Moscow's permission before Germany could enter the League of Nations, and a prohibition of German participation in any kind of economic agreement which the Soviet government thought adverse to its own interests, it is not surprising that Stresemann rejected it. The stringent provisions make one suspect that the Kremlin did not really think that Germany would accept the preamble. The tactic involved was to keep Germany in negotiations until the time was more propitious for Russian gains. Efforts continued to persuade the Wilhelmstrasse to conclude an agreement which would give the USSR a treaty as close to Russian design as was possible under the changed circumstances.

VI

The Treaty of Berlin

After the Locarno Pact became reality, the Russians continued their efforts for a neutrality and nonaggression treaty. Stresemann, who had avoided the conclusion of such a treaty by proposing the preamble to the Commercial Treaty, was not willing to go beyond the general agreement of neutrality incorporated in his proposals. The question of German membership in the League of Nations and the evacuation of the Rhineland zone were the next two problems Stresemann intended to resolve. He did not break off negotiations with the Russians, but neither did he rush precipitately into a treaty which could create difficulties for his Western policies.

Russian pressure began to be exerted almost immediately after Stresemann's return to Berlin. Krestinsky and Bratman-Brodovsky visited Stresemann on October 29 to inquire whether he now had the time to talk about an "understanding with Russia." Stresemann evaded a direct answer with the remark that the political situation was still unstable. He wanted to await Brockdorff-Rantzau's arrival to discuss the question with him. Krestinsky replied that Chicherin would attend the celebration of the anniversary of the revolution at the Embassy, and that would provide the opportunity for the exchange of a few words.

On the day of Krestinsky's call on the Foreign Minister, *Izvestia* announced that the Soviet ambassadors to Paris and London would exchange appointments. Krassin would go to London and Rakovsky to Paris. This, Brockdorff-Rantzau was convinced, was "payment for Locarno," because Rakovsky was a confirmed Francophile.

Brockdorff-Rantzau arrived in Berlin on November 4 and requested an interview with Hindenburg before reporting to the Foreign Office. The first intimation the Wilhelmstrasse had that the Count was up to something came when the President's office asked that all recent telegrams of the Count's be sent to them for Hindenburg's perusal. Hindenburg also asked Brockdorff-Rantzau for a memorandum incorporat-

188

ing his ideas about Germany and her relations to the League. On November 7, the Count sent the requested memorandum to Hindenburg and a copy of it to Stresemann, but did not indicate to whom the original had been sent. Brockdorff-Rantzau attacked the Foreign Minister's policies sharply. He informed the President that entry into the League would constitute a voluntary acknowledgment of Versailles, which was not justified by the gains made at Locarno. He warned, as he had done so many times before, that membership in the world organization would almost certainly end Russian support of Germany. This would absolutely destroy any flexibility that still remained in Germany's foreign policy. The Russians saw in Locarno alone an option for the West. If Germany now entered the League, Moscow would look for an alignment with France. Any talk that Germany, as a member of the League of Nations, could make things easier for the Soviet Union was false and "unscrupulous." The Reich could not expose itself to the accusation that it treated the Covenant like a scrap of paper. By such action, it would "gamble its existence for the second and final time."[1]

On November 14, Brockdorff-Rantzau went over the same ground with Wallroth. Just before the conclusion of their discussion, the Count hinted quite strongly that the "spirit of Rapallo" could be revived by the conclusion of a "military-political nonaggression pact" with Russia. In addition, he advocated a formal agreement that Germany would not let the League force her into participating in political or economic acts directed against the Soviet Union. When Wallroth voiced his doubts that this would satisfy the Russians, Brockdorff-Rantzau declared, "Just leave it to me, I will take care of it."[2]

In the face of Brockdorff-Rantzau's continued opposition, it is hard to understand why Stresemann did not take some drastic measures against his uncooperative subordinate. Most certainly, the times demanded a more flexible attitude than Brockdorff-Rantzau exhibited. The Foreign Minister's relations with Brockdorff-Rantzau, already severely strained by the difficulties over the Hilger exoneration, received a further shock when Hindenburg referred to Brockdorff-Rantzau's memorandum about Germany and the League during a Cabinet session on November 17. The President insisted that measures be taken to assure German freedom of action under Article 16. He pointed out that he had reason to believe that the Russians were convinced that the West could force Germany into anti-Soviet actions. Stresemann tactfully assured the President that Krestinsky had indicated, on the day before, that Moscow wanted to enter into talks about expanding relations with Germany. This showed that they did not really believe that the situation had changed. Furthermore, the Russians liked to bluff. Hindenburg seemed unconvinced and emphasized that he did not want German-Russian relations to change.[3]

The gains Stresemann had made at Locarno were subjected to another threat when news of a super-secret meeting between Chicherin and General von Seeckt on November 19 was leaked to the press. Newspapers reported two days later that the General approved of the treaties and of Germany's eventual entry in the League. He had also allegedly assured Chicherin that the German army would not participate in Western actions against Russia. As could be expected, the leak precipitated a rash of rumors that Chicherin had offered a formal military alliance to Seeckt. The French continued to print statements about the military alliance until the end of December.[4] It is quite conceivable that Chicherin actually made Seeckt such an offer. The clandestine collaboration between the German and Red armies was an additional reason for Chicherin to approach Seeckt about a secret alliance. If Seeckt could be won over for such an alliance, his influence could suffice to get Cabinet approval for the Russian preamble.

The source of the leak about the meeting between Chicherin and Seeckt became a matter of speculation. One newspaper alleged that it had been Brockdorff-Rantzau who wanted to sabotage a *rapprochement* with the West. The Foreign Office issued a *dementi* in which it did not deny the meeting, but suggested that it was a courtesy call. It rejected the rumor that Brockdorff-Rantzau was being investigated for the possibility of having caused the leak. It also denied that poor relations existed between the Ambassador and the Foreign Office.[5] This was not entirely true. Brockdorff-Rantzau was determined to halt further progress on the road to Geneva. For that purpose he had taken advantage of his permission of direct access to the President to present his objections.

The Russians had the same idea. On November 21, 1925, Krestinsky, Bratman-Brodovsky, Schubert, and Stresemann had a long discussion. Bratman-Brodovsky read a new draft preamble which, he emphasized, fitted the changed situation. The first three paragraphs repeated, except for stylistic changes, the wording dictated by Chicherin to Brockdorff-Rantzau on July 18. The last paragraph of the July version was deleted, and instead two new paragraphs had been added. These read:

4) In the case one of the contracting parties becomes involved in a war with a third group of powers, the governments bind themselves to maintain a friendly neutrality.

5) In case the entry of Germany into the League of Nations, as contemplated at Locarno, takes place, the German government binds itself, as a member of the League of Nations and of the Council of the League of Nations, to take all measures at her command against the possible application of military and economic sanctions against the USSR.

During the ensuing discussion, Stresemann inquired of Krestinsky whether the proposal was to become a treaty and, if so, was it to be published? Krestinsky replied that his government did not care whether it became an open or a secret agreement, except for the last paragraph. The proposal was based on the fact that his government was not assured by the declaration of the powers on Article 16. Nothing stood in Germany's way to give Russia assurances. Stresemann told the Ambassador that the new proposal would have to be evaluated by the Legal Department because it was in everyone's best interest to create a document which was not open to attacks.

The Foreign Office immediately set to work to find a way to soften the Russian draft treaty and to devise a formula which could be published. On November 28 Schubert, Wallroth, Dirksen, and Gaus met with Chancellor Luther. Schubert pointed out that the Russian draft was a stronger recasting of the July preamble. He advised that it should be rejected, as should be the Russian intimation that the preamble should follow the example set by the Russo-Czech treaty of 1922. It was, however, of the utmost importance that a position be taken before the Chancellor departed for the signature of the Locarno Pact. This would make it possible to counteract a charge by Moscow that Germany sought English advice. After weighing a number of possible replies, Dirksen voiced the opinion that the Russians ought to be offered some agreement; otherwise, Locarno was only "half successful." In order to find a solution, Luther agreed that Schubert should tell Krestinsky that a definite reply could not be given because Stresemann was ill and not available.[6]

At 7:30 that evening, Schubert, as instructed, told Krestinsky and Bratman-Brodovsky that their proposal still needed additional study. It went beyond that of July, and even then Brockdorff-Rantzau had told Chicherin of his doubts about the acceptability of some of the points. Krestinsky confided that the new phrasing of the neutrality clause was a response to Stresemann's repeated reference to the Russo-Czech treaty, which contained such a clause (a marginal comment, in Stresemann's handwriting, read, "Impertinence!"). Certainly Germany did not intend to lag behind Czechoslovakia. Germany's international position had been strengthened by Locarno, and she now could offer more to the Soviet Union.

Schubert insisted that Germany was willing to go to the limit of the possible, but the arrangement had to be "clear and unequivocal." The talks could be resumed after Stresemann returned from London where the Locarno Pact was to be ratified.

Krestinsky remarked, with a smile, that he hoped that by that time Germany would have "increased courage." He hoped that the agreement could be signed before he left for Moscow on December 10. It appeared to Schubert that Krestinsky himself really did not believe that this would happen.[7]

The Reichstag accepted the West pacts (300 against 174) and voted (275 to 183) for entering the League of Nations. On November 28, President Hindenberg signed the law for accepting the Locarno Pact. Stresemann, accompanied by Chancellor Luther, left for London where the exchange of the instruments of ratification took place on December 1.

On the very day that Hindenburg had signed the Locarno acceptance, Brockdorff-Rantzau forwarded his resignation. He gave as his major reason the "expectations under which I took over the post of Ambassador to Moscow no longer exist." Brockdorff-Rantzau emphasized that an "unconditional entry into the League of Nations closes off—of that I am sure—the road to the East, which I worked to open up. The now completed step can only lead to complete subjugation or to a policy of disaster; I reject the one as well as the other."

Hindenburg received the Count in private audience and persuaded him to withdraw his resignation. Brockdorff-Rantzau, before agreeing, insisted that the President inform Stresemann that he had requested the Count's memorandum. Hindenburg wrote the promised letter to Stresemann and emphasized that Brockdorff-Rantzau would continue to enjoy immediate access.[8] The Count remained in Berlin to use his influence in order to get acceptance of the Russian treaty proposal. He remained in close touch with the Soviet Embassy and with the Wilhelmstrasse.

On December 11, Krestinsky and Bratman-Brodovsky returned to the Wilhelmstrasse and held a lengthy discussion with Stresemann and Schubert. The Foreign Minister apologized that Chancellor Luther could not be in attendance because of previous commitments.

Stresemann opened the talks by taking issue with two leading articles, one in *Pravda*, the other in *Izvestia*, both published on November

27. The articles had attacked his speech in the Reichstag delivered during the debate about the Locarno Pact and amounted to "malicious falsehoods." The assertion that an English memorandum existed which proved that Germany would become part of the anti-Soviet camp was completely untrue. Even more serious was the charge that Germany would not remain neutral in the event that Russia was declared an aggressor. Stresemann read directly from his Reichstag speech to show how wrong the newspaper accusations were. What he had said was that in the event of a vote on aggression, Germany would be obliged to cast her own. But this did not mean she had to "participate militarily, allow passage, and join in economic sanctions."

Krestinsky pointed out that even the acknowledgment that the Soviet Union was an aggressor would encourage other states. Stresemann agreed that Germany's vote could have some moral value. The important thing was that Germany remained free to decide whether to participate in actions against the USSR.

Stresemann asked the Ambassador to use his good offices in Moscow to see to it that President Hindenburg would not again be attacked as he had been in the *Pravda* article (in which Radek had accused the President and Stresemann of having been "imperialistic agitators" and for good measure held Hindenburg responsible for the "perfidious policy" followed at Brest-Litovsk). Krestinsky agreed to remonstrate at home.

The next topic concerned the political negotiations. Krestinsky informed Stresemann that Moscow had instructed him that the treaty could be "open," but if Germany wished it could be kept secret. Stresemann immediately interjected that he had always opposed secrecy. Both then agreed that the treaty should be an open one.

The discussion turned to the Russo-Czech treaty of June 5, 1922, which Krestinsky said was still in force. Stresemann explained that it had never been registered with the League of Nations. Krestinsky shrugged this off as being of little consequence. Besides, he was of the opinion that the Russo-German treaty should be concluded quickly before Germany became a member of the League.

Stresemann, who was playing for time, continued to place great emphasis on the nonregistration of the Russo-Czech treaty, which, he told Krestinsky, did mean that it was not "legally binding." The Ambassador stated that League members might hold it illegal, but not the Soviet Union and Czechoslovakia. Besides, the Russo-German treaty was independent of any other. Stresemann agreed, and said that he had been trying to determine how the League looked upon such a treaty. There was no sense in beginning membership with a conflict. Krestinsky said that Germany could be useful to Russia by providing a precedent.

Stresemann turned to the Russian proposal and informed Krestinsky that it went far beyond Chicherin's proposals, which had already been rejected. Paragraph 5 could not possibly be included in a treaty. Germany's position on Article 16 of the Covenant had been made absolutely clear and had been supported by the Locarno powers, as well as by Poland and Czechoslovakia. The Russians could be notified of this solemn declaration, but it could not be incorporated into a treaty; it could, however, be part of the exchange of notes. Krestinsky thought this a possible procedure.

When Stresemann inquired, Krestinsky told him that he had received the impression, during his talk with the Chancellor on December 8, that Luther opposed "an obligation of neutrality." The Chancellor apparently wanted to avoid the mentioning of war. Stresemann agreed that paragraph 4 should be a declaration of peaceful intentions without mentioning the possibility of war.

Krestinsky emphasized that the Soviet Union had to consider its encirclement. When Germany's relations with the West had been strained, "a case of war" between her and Russia had been "as good as impossible." Better relations with the West and entry into the League had "changed the situation quite considerably for Russia, and she therefore needed a security treaty with Germany."

Stresemann characterized such a treaty as impossible because Russia had the means to pursue war, while Germany did not. If Germany concluded a treaty such as Krestinsky had proposed, it would appear as if Germany, committed to disarmament, was really toying with the idea of war. Maybe a formula could be found by which both powers would propose "to do everything for the general peace and avoid warlike involvements between Germany and Russia." In any event, nothing definite could be done, since Gaus was on furlough. Chicherin had called the German preamble good for a toast. He wanted to point out that "toasts often had had a greater political significance than treaties."

Stresemann emphasized that Germany was quite willing to work out a formulation which expressed the willingness of Germany and Russia to avoid war against each other and to work for peace. Discussion ensued, at the end of which Stresemann declared that paragraph 4 should be positive and state the desire to maintain peace. Krestinsky said that he was going back to Moscow and would like to take along something positive. Could he say that Germany agreed in principle to a neutrality formula? Of course, he added immediately, the German preamble was insufficient. Stresemann avoided an affirmative reply and sought refuge in another excuse. The Locarno Pact had taken a long time. It would not be wise to rush into a German-Russian treaty. Krestinsky agreed, but pointed out that negotiations between his country and Germany had been in progress for a year. Stresemann again emphasized that he wanted a treaty, but that it would be best to wait for the formation of a new Cabinet.[9] (The crisis which began with the Cabinet's resignation on December 5 was not resolved until the formation of the second Luther ministry on January 14, 1926).

Chicherin, who had been in Paris for extended talks with Briand, arrived in Berlin during the evening of December 18. He was received by Dirksen and "other gentlemen of the Russian department" of the Wilhelmstrasse. He accepted an invitation for luncheon with Stresemann on December 21.

According to confidential information, Chicherin's talks with Briand had been without positive results. The French Prime Minister allegedly had made the resumption of the "old, good relations" dependent on the settlement of the Tsarist debt due France. Chicherin had objected to this. The same confidential source had revealed that Chicherin had been extremely disturbed by his failure to thwart Germany's participation in the Locarno Pact and her expected entry into the League. The Foreign Commissar had proposed a *rapprochement* on the basis of extensive French credits. He had even intimated that the USSR would renounce Rapallo. These approaches had been rejected by the French, who advised Chicherin that they based their hope for peace and security on Locarno and the League. If Russia was so much concerned about maintaining peace, she should join the League of Nations. Chicherin finally offered to pay nine to ten billion paper francs, without acknowledging the debt. Payment could begin within ten years.[10]

On December 19, Chicherin and Schubert discussed the Russo-French negotiations, which, the Foreign Commissar said, would be started by Rakovsky in January. There would be three committees to deal with a review of old treaties, finance, debt, and credit, and general political questions. He expressed concern that England would use Locarno to drive a wedge between Germany and Russia. This was the major reason why a neutrality agreement between their two countries was important. He emphasized that such an agreement should be completed before the Russo-French negotiations started in January. Schubert, who felt that this was a clear indication that Chicherin thought an opportunity could be lost, told him that the Foreign Office was hard at work on new proposals. During the evening, after a dinner at Brockdorff-Rantzau's, Schubert proposed to Chicherin, with the Ambassador's concurrence, that one way to come to an agreement would be to have Gaus and Sabanin, both outstanding jurists, discuss the matter. Chicherin was noncommittal.

Chicherin and Stresemann discussed Article 16 and related problems on December 22, 1925. Stresemann assured the Commissar that Russia need not concern herself with the effect of that article at all; Germany would not participate in any kind of sanctions against the USSR. The collective note by the powers had definitely settled the matter. Chicherin, according to Stresemann, gave the impression of a man released from the nightmare of a continent united against Russia. Chicherin then asked whether a neutrality treaty could not now be signed. Stresemann pointed out that the Russian formulation of one of the proposed clauses gave the impression that Germany had warlike intentions against Russia. What was really important was for both countries to state unequivocally that they were interested in preserving the peace. Chicherin interjected that he was less concerned about stressing Russian neutrality than he was about Germany's stressing hers. Stresemann passed over the remark and read an article prepared by Gaus to Chicherin, who indicated no opposition to it.[11]

After Chicherin had left, the French chargé d'affaires, Laboulaye, came to transmit information about the Foreign Commissar's visit to Paris. He inquired about the talks Chicherin was holding in Berlin. Stresemann told the chargé d'affaires that the Russian government "wanted to enter into negotiations with the Reich government which were aimed at the renunciation of war, force, and invasion." The proposal was similar to the one contained in the Russo-Czech treaty concluded some years earlier.[12]

Stresemann and his advisors now decided to avoid a treaty by offering the Russians a protocol incorporating a number of the Russian ideas, but avoiding the binding obligation of a treaty. On December 24, a discussion of the second half of a protocol worked out by Gaus took place in the Reichschancellery. Present were Luther, Undersecretary Kempner, and Ministerialdirecktor Herman Pünder of the Chancellery, Stresemann, Schubert, and Gaus. The Chancellor agreed with the new draft, which incorporated a number of changes suggested by him. Stresemann underlined the need for a "speedy transmission of the protocol with a private letter to Chicherin. In this way, the démarche would be considered a natural follow-up to the talk.

Luther insisted that the other members of the Cabinet (Gessler, Brauns, Stingl) be asked for their opinion. Stresemann accepted the delay on the condition that the result be in the Wilhelmstrasse no later than December 28, to allow transmission to Chicherin on that day.

Stresemann got Gessler's agreement after the meeting, and President Hindenburg approved the protocol and the manner of its delivery. The approval by the two other ministers, who were away from Berlin, was not received until December 24 at 4:45 P.M. Schubert invited Bratman-Brodovsky and gave him the protocol with Stresemann's covering letter, asking him to treat both with the greatest circumspection. He requested immediate transmission to Chicherin and gave the chargé d'affaires a brief resumé of the way in which the protocol had been developed. Bratman-Brodovsky promised to send the documents to Moscow by the next courier, who would leave within two days.

The chargé d'affaires wanted to know whether the Foreign Office had discussed the neutrality agreement. Schubert replied that no further discussion had taken place, but the German position that the pact proposed by Chicherin was not "compatible with the Covenant of the League" had not changed. He was of the opinion, Schubert pointed out, that the protocol proposed by Stresemann was suitable to put German-Russian relations on a "strong and clear basis." [13]

In his covering letter, Stresemann referred to Chicherin's remark that it would be a good idea to put the thoughts expressed during the talk into a protocol. This was an excellent idea, wrote Stresemann, because it had the advantage of flexibility not possible in a treaty formulation. Because of the resignation of the Cabinet, it was not possible to transmit an "official form" of the protocol. Since Chicherin had expressed hope for speed, Stresemann was now sending him, for his private information, a draft of the kind of protocol he personally envisaged. He hoped that agreement could be reached quickly on the fact that the protocol included all that could be done for the moment and that it presented a definitive clarification of all the many questions which had occupied both governments for such a long period of time.

The protocol stated:

1. The Treaty of Rapallo remains the basis for German-Russian relations, which liquidated the war not by a dictated peace but on the foundation of mutual equality and on the basis of the most-favored-nation principle.

2. A concrete agreement for continued cooperation has been found desirable by both countries.

3. Therefore, both governments are determined to keep in friendly touch regarding all mutual political and economic questions in order to achieve agreement. This, they are convinced, will contribute to the general peace.

4. In this spirit, the two governments agreed on the basic question deriving from Germany's imminent entry into the League.

Should a movement take shape which is contrary to the basic idea of peace and directed against Russia, a situation Germany does not feel will develop, then Germany would not participate and would try to counteract it.

5. This basic position cannot be limited by the obligation Germany assumed under Articles 16 and 17 on sanctions. Such sanctions would apply only if Russia were to attack a third party. This will not happen, since Russia has no such intentions. Hence, sanctions are not applicable. Besides, German participation depends on her agreement, and the extent of her obligations has been clarified by the note of the powers on Article 16 and Chancellor Luther's declaration (held in a similar vein) in the Reichstag on November 27, 1925.

6. Germany's participation in a conflict against Russia is theoretical at best. The same is true of Russia's involvement against Germany, should the latter attack a third party. Both countries can rest in the knowledge that no "warlike" situation will involve them.

7. Neither Germany nor Russia would participate in economic or financial boycotts directed against the other.

8. Both powers agree to enter into negotiations for an arbitration agreement which will provide for arbitration procedure on questions of law and for other questions and procedures aiming at a settlement.[14]

During his regular visit on January 6, 1926, Bratman-Brodovsky expressed his personal opinion that the protocol was "very vague"; he had expected a "rigid treaty." No reply had as yet been received from Moscow, but a perusal of Chicherin's notes had shown that the Foreign Commissar had proposed a protocol in addition to a treaty, not in place of one. Schubert said Stresemann understood it differently. After all, what could a treaty contain, since Germany thought the neutrality treaty proposed by Chicherin contrary to the League Covenant?

Ten days later, the chargé d'affaires returned and delivered Chicherin's reply, dated January 11, 1926, without any additional declaration. Wrote Chicherin:

> In the same nonobligatory and unofficial manner in which you have had the kindness to send to me the draft of a German-Soviet protocol, do I take the liberty to inform you quite candidly of my point of view.

Having set the tone with this introductory sentence, Chicherin proceeded to take issue with the various paragraphs of the protocol. It was a mistake that he had intended to make the agreement in the form of a protocol; it was to be a supplement. In no way was it to sacrifice the "much more valuable form of a regular treaty." The Soviet government continued to look toward a "precise agreement based on real obligations." The draft contained "arguments and conclusions." Even as an addition to a treaty, it had to become more precise.

Point 1 delineated the historical development inaccurately. It would suffice to state that Rapallo placed relations on the "basis of mutuality and equality" and provided a base for continuing cooperation and enduring friendship. Peace was a necessity, but to qualify it on the basis of the League was "entirely foreign" to Russia's way of thinking. Points 5 and 6 had the character of arguments, not of obligations. Point seven dealt with hostile combinations on the basis of friendship without the slightest reference to combinations, blocs, or a specific treaty obligation. Chicherin expressed the hope, as Stresemann had, that a speedy agreement could be reached on the questions which were of "utmost importance" to the USSR. He concluded with the sentence, "My ideas regarding this subject are already well known to you."[15]

After the receipt of Chicherin's letter, the Wilhelmstrasse worked out a new protocol which incorporated the objections voiced by the Foreign Commissar. However, nothing really had changed. The Germans wanted to avoid a formal treaty with the Russians and give to the eventual agreements more of a declaratory than a constitutional character. Fundamentally, it was the old problem of balancing Locarno and League membership with some agreement with Russia. Otherwise, Russia might conceivably make some arrangement with France. Furthermore, almost all German political parties had insisted that Locarno should not destroy the relationship with Moscow, and German businessmen continued to be hypnotized by the possibilities for great profits in the Soviet Union.

Schubert asked the German ambassadors in Paris and London for their position on the new protocol. Both Hoesch and Sthamer opposed a neutrality treaty because it could easily lose Germany the good will created at Locarno.[16] The opinion of the ambassadors indicated the major reason why Schubert and Stresemann refused to conclude a neutrality treaty. The protocol, unacceptable to Moscow, was an attempt to maintain relations with the USSR on the basis of the spirit of Rapallo—that is, without a really binding treaty which could tip the precarious balance decisively to the East. Dirksen, who participated prominently in the framing of the protocol, insisted that something had to be done to clarify relations with Russia because, in his opinion, political relations between the two countries "were as good as dead." It was urgent that Russian intentions regarding relations with France be discovered, because a move in that direction held an element of danger for Germany. The new protocol at least showed that the Reich was willing to be cooperative in the political sphere.[17]

The desire of the Wilhelmstrasse to negotiate an agreement satisfactory to Germany was not shared by Brockdorff-Rantzau, who objected to the protocol even more than he had resisted the preamble. Stresemann finally decided to take action against his uncooperative subordinate. During a meeting on December 14 the Foreign Minister left no doubt that he considered the Ambassador's tactics out of place. Stresemann refused to accept Brockdorff-Rantzau's lame excuse that Hindenburg had asked him to express his opinion on German-Soviet relations directly. Brockdorff-Rantzau left Stresemann with the remark that no great hopes should be placed on his future effectiveness in Russia. Stresemann wrote to Hindenburg that it was absolutely essential, for the smooth operation of the Foreign Office, that the Ambassador to Moscow forward his reports directly to the Wilhelmstrasse. In cases where the President received a direct report, a copy should be sent to the Wilhelmstrasse. Finally, Brockdorff-Rantzau's case was to be an absolute exception; even during the Empire, chiefs of mission did not have the right to report to the head of state. Otto Meissner, undersecretary in the President's office, acquainted the Count with the contents of Stresemann's letter. He told Brockdorff-Rantzau that the President would continue the privilege of direct access only if copies of all reports were sent to Stresemann. As a special, personal concession, Hindenburg would be glad to receive private letters from the Ambassador.

Stresemann's determined attitude had ended the privilege of direct access, which Brockdorff-Rantzau had used in any event, only two or three times. There still remained the refusal of Brockdorff-Rantzau to send evaluative reports about Russia's relations with other countries directly to the Director of the Eastern Division. This problem was solved when Schubert asked the Count to forward regular reports to the appropriate department. Under these circumstances, Brockdorff-Rantzau realized that it would be futile to send even private letters to Hindenburg. The Count had suffered two sharp defeats and decided, albeit reluctantly, to leave for Moscow on January 28.

On the day before his departure the Ambassador took his official leave of Schubert. They agreed that Gaus should discuss the new protocol with his Soviet Embassy counterpart, but that the negotiations be transferred to Moscow as rapidly as possible. Nothing definite would be done until after the problems resulting from the arrest of German consular agents in the Caucasus had been resolved. Schubert optimistically expected that case to be settled within a week after Brockdorff-Rantzau's return to his post.[18]

Brockdorff-Rantzau arrived in Moscow on the last day of January. The Ambassador lost no time in telling Chicherin that his return had been delayed by the serious consequences of the arrest, by Soviet authorities, of the German consular agents in Baku, Poti, and Batum, on December 13, 1925. The Count made it clear that only an immediate settlement of the incident would prevent his return to Berlin. Such action would appear like a break of relations. Chicherin promised to speak to Litvinov and see to it that the incident was settled.

At the time of the arrests, Litvinov had insisted that the consular agents were in fact private persons (which was correct), appointed by the German Consul in Tiflis whose right to do so was not acknowledged by the USSR. The only reason why the Soviet government had never challenged this usurpation of its powers had been its regard for the friendly relations that existed with Germany. The consular agents could have continued at their posts if they had not become involved in military espionage. Two weeks before Brockdorff-Rantzau's return to Moscow, Litvinov had warned Hey not to be too vigorous in the defense of the consular agents, because they could not have spied without the connivance of the German government.

The Wilhelmstrasse had not challenged the arrests of the agents, but had taken the position that the confiscated archives and the official mail were covered by the extraterritoriality of the Tiflis Consulate. Berlin, therefore, demanded the return of these materials, an apology for the confiscations, and punishment of the Soviet officials responsible for the break of international law. The Russians had not taken any action on the German complaint, but instead had added insult to injury. The Tiflis Consulate had given an officially sealed package to a German employee of the Siemens Werke who was going to Moscow. Upon arrival there, he found that his trunk had been removed from the baggage car in the Tiflis station. The trunk finally arrived on January 15, broken, and the package tampered with. The package had been rewrapped and closed with forged stamps. The original contents were missing; in their stead were found a German Bible, three envelopes stuffed with Tartar newspapers, and a hook. Hey immediately made the strongest representations to Chicherin and termed the inclusion of the Bible a "mockery of the German Reich's representation by official Soviet organs."

Stresemann instructed Hey on January 20 to express the consternation of the German government about the new incident and to warn that it constituted a serious threat to the friendly relations which "should have found a visible expression in the ratification of the extensive treaties concluded on October 12, 1925." The German government placed the "greatest value on an immediate and unequivocal satisfaction for this new incident." Stresemann added, for Hey's personal information, that ratification of the Commercial Treaty would be delayed until the situation looked satisfactory.

Litvinov told Hey to complain to the railroad administration, not to make a lost trunk the basis of a diplomatic protest. He advised the Embassy "to avoid such attempts, which were in no way conducive to the solution of conflicts and the maintenance of correct relations." He also complained about the prolonged absence of Brockdorff-Rantzau from Moscow.

The Wilhelmstrasse published a note on the trunk incident in the German newspapers, in which it was stated that the Russians would give satisfaction. The Soviet Embassy had been informed of the note's content before its release.

This firmness worked. Stein, attired in a dark suit, came to the German Embassy in Moscow on January 29 and made oral apologies for the package incident. He also handed over a note by Litvinov which placed the blame on an overzealous, but minor, OGPU official in the Caucasus who had been dismissed and would be punished. The Caucasian government had given orders to prevent a recurrence. This closed the incident over the package, but not over the violations which had taken place at the time of the arrest of the consular agents.

Brockdorff-Rantzau went to Litvinov on February 2, the day after his complaint to Chicherin, to demand that the Deputy Commissar take some positive action in the case of the consular agents. Litvinov was adamant, insisting that the Foreign Commissariat had done all it could. The Count threatened that the ratification of the Commercial Treaty would be delayed and that he would return to Berlin. Only then did Litvinov promise a note for February 3, which would say something like "the Foreign Commissariat, without entering into the principles involved, expresses its regrets." The Ambassador asked Berlin to accept this offer, because there was some evidence that the agents had been involved in military espionage.

The note which Litvinov forwarded to the Embassy fell short of Brockdorff-Rantzau's expectations. He requested permission from the Wilhelmstrasse for his departure from Moscow. Berlin did not recall the Ambassador, and the case dragged on into April before Brockdorff-Rantzau on definite instructions from Schubert agreed to settle the case accepting the Foreign Commissariat's official regrets for the violations committed against the archives and the Tiflis Consulate's mail.[19]

Two days before Litvinov's offer to express regrets, on February 1, Schubert told Krestinsky that Gaus stood ready to discuss the protocol with the Embassy. Schubert again emphasized that the protocol was the best possible solution, because a neutrality treaty along the lines of the Russo-Turkish treaty was impossible.

The Russo-Turkish Treaty of Friendship and Neutrality, signed by Chicherin in Paris on December 17, 1925, provided for neutrality in case of military action by "one or several other powers," non-aggression, nonparticipation in alliances or agreements directed against the other. It was valid for three years. In a protocol, both parties agreed not to participate in "financial or economic agreements" directed against the other.[20]

During a talk with Brockdorff-Rantzau also on February 1, Chicherin said

> He did not operate with empty threats—that was entirely foreign to him—but a favorable decision in this question [the neutrality treaty] would, in the face of the imminent negotiations in Paris, be of the greatest value to him in making a decision regarding the formulation of future German-Russian relations.[21]

Russian pressure for the conclusion of a guarantee pact, already strong, increased after Germany applied for League membership on February 10. Before the exchange of ratifications for the Commercial Treaty on February 11, Krestinsky asked Schubert when negotiations about the political agreement would be resumed. Krestinsky again declared that the German protocol was absolutely unacceptable, because it did not bind Germany sufficiently. Schubert thought that the talks could resume after the new Cabinet (installed on January 19) had become sufficiently acquainted with the matter. On February 19, after a luncheon, Krestinsky asked Stresemann when the negotiations, which had not been mentioned for over four weeks, would start. The Foreign Minister replied that a definite formulation had been agreed upon and that negotiations could possibly start during the second half of the following week.[22] Stresemann had decided that nothing but a regular neutrality treaty would satisfy the Russians. Therefore, a way had to be found to present a draft which would neither bind Germany to a secret treaty nor tie her to an open treaty which would jeopardize Germany's relations with the West.

The promised discussion took place on February 25; present were Schubert, Gaus, Dirksen, Krestinsky, and Jacubovich. Schubert told the Soviet Ambassador that Germany had accepted Chicherin's preference and was willing to conclude a treaty accompanied by a protocol. The draft he was about to read constituted the absolute limit of what

Germany could concede. Krestinsky objected that Article 3, which stated that the contracting parties would not participate in coalitions among third powers formed in peacetime for the purpose of pursuing an economic or financial boycott, did not guarantee German neutrality under all possible circumstances. Gaus explained that it was impossible for Germany to bind herself formally. Point 3 of the protocol made it clear that Germany would remain neutral unless the USSR were declared the aggressor against a third state. It had to be phrased in this manner because Germany simply could not declare that she would never look on Russia as an aggressor. However, Article 1, paragraph 2, contained the strongest arrangement for an entente that he knew of in any treaty. An unrestricted statement of neutrality was impossible for a member of the League. Krestinsky agreed finally that the draft treaty was a perfect rendering of the protocol and said he would inform his government.

Stresemann sent the draft of the treaty and of the protocols to Brockdorff-Rantzau on February 26 and instructed him to inform Chicherin that with this offer the limit of the possible had been reached. The treaty could not be concluded until the League had handed down its final decision on the German application for membership. Since publication would follow the signing, Germany's case in Geneva could conceivably be prejudiced, because the conclusion of the treaty would make it appear as if Germany looked on her entry into the League as an accomplished fact.[23]

Brockdorff-Rantzau had remained adamantly insistent that a strong treaty was the only thing which would prevent the replacement of Germany by France in Russia. He was still convinced that Locarno had been the first step designed by England to place Germany exclusively in the Western camp. He remained confirmed in this view despite assurances by the Wilhelmstrasse to the contrary. Not even the announcement, on March 1, that Russia had been offered a loan of 300 million reichsmark, 35 percent of which was guaranteed against default by the German government and 25 percent by the states, for the purchase of industrial goods in Germany, really convinced him that the Wilhelmstrasse had no intention whatsoever of cutting the wire to Moscow. The Count continued to complain that membership in the League would spell the doom of his policy. As so often before, Hencke went on furlough and reported to the Count's alter ego, Ernst Rantzau, in Berlin.[24] The information Hencke divulged to Count Rantzau reached the ears of those whom the Ambassador intended to influence.

Chicherin, who had already played the French card, pulled the Polish one out of his sleeve on March 2. He told Brockdorff-Rantzau, during a dinner the Ambassador gave for Admiral Behncke, that Russia would have to come to some agreement with Poland on that country's eastern border, as regulated by the Treaty of Riga. This was necessary so that England could not use Poland as a "ram." However, no guarantee of Poland's western border was contemplated.

Wallroth and Dirksen telegraphed to Brockdorff-Rantzau that the discussion of Poland's border would emasculate the planned German-Russian treaty. Hencke had visited Dirksen and disclosed that his chief had some qualifications about concluding the treaty protocol because it might prejudice the situation with the West. Dirksen assured the Ambassador that he could rest easy on that particular problem.

Chicherin continued his pressure for the conclusion of the treaty by telling Brockdorff-Rantzau that the Polish demands had been rejected absolutely and definitely and that no counterproposals had been made. The pending Russo-Polish economic negotiations would also be delayed. Krestinsky had already received the changes the Narkomindel wanted made in the German draft of the treaty. Brockdorff-Rantzau advised the Wilhelmstrasse to tell Krestinsky that the proposed treaty was based on the definite assumption that Russia give up any idea about guaranteeing Poland's border.

Krestinsky had mentioned on March 5 that he had received new instructions. He had expressed his hope that the treaty could be signed during the week. This was rejected by the Wilhelmstrasse until a final, authentic text had been agreed upon. In addition, a decision could not be made because the German delegation, headed by Stresemann, was leaving that very night to attend the special session of the League called to discuss Germany's application for membership.[25]

On March 13, Chicherin "made a formal declaration that he would never accept a guarantee" of Poland's western border. Brockdorff-Rantzau expressed his conviction that the German-Russian treaty under consideration would lose all value if any guarantees were given to Warsaw. There was no objection to Russia's desire to create peaceful conditions along her borders, but

> Moscow should not forget that the well-known December negotiations of the year 1924 had been conducted on the basis of a common German-Russian interest in pushing Poland back to her ethnographic borders.

Chicherin admitted that a short-term nonagression pact with Poland had been considered but again emphasized that no guarantee of Poland's eastern border had been contemplated.

He stated that the Russo-Polish nonaggression negotiations could be considered a failure and the economic talks would also be delayed. If Poland agreed to negotiate without the Baltic States, then a formula for a nonaggression pact would have to be found which would in no way disturb the friendly relationship with Germany. However, everything would depend on the successful completion of the pending negotiations between Berlin and Moscow.[26]

On March 17 the League of Nations rejected Germany's application for membership and postponed reconsideration of Germany's admission until the regular fall session in September. The most serious stumbling block had been the insistence by Portugal, Spain, and Brazil on a permanent seat on the Council.

On March 25, Krestinsky transmitted the changes Moscow wanted to be made in the German treaty draft and informed Stresemann that his government was ready to accept the reworked draft. Krestinsky proposed that the treaty be signed within a fortnight so that the Central Executive Committee, which would then be in session, could immediately be asked for ratification. Stresemann did not react to the date.

On the following day, Brockdorff-Rantzau reported that Poland's eastern border was being discussed between the Narkomindel and the Quai d'Orsay. Paris was placing pressure on the Soviet government to conclude such a pact. Since Chicherin had only been categoric in his rejection of a Russian guarantee of Poland's border, the speedy conclusion of the German-Soviet treaty was of some importance.[27]

The Wilhelmstrasse, which had so long delayed signing the treaty, stood ready to complete it. On March 30, Schubert, Gaus, Dirksen, Krestinsky, and Jacubovich met to put the finishing touches to the agreement, which had been redrafted to incorporate some of the changes Russia had insisted upon. The German draft consisted of four articles and two notes, to be exchanged at the time of signing.

Article 1

The Treaty of Rapallo remains the basis for the relations between Germany and the USSR.

The German government and the government of the USSR shall remain in friendly contact with each other in order to bring about an understanding about all political and economic questions which mutually affect their two countries.

Article 2

Should a third power, or should several third powers, without being provoked, attack one of the contracting parties, the other contracting party shall observe neutrality for the complete duration of the conflict

Article 3

Should a coalition be formed among third powers for the purpose of placing one of the contracting parties under an economic
or financial boycott because of a conflict of the kind mentioned in
Article 2, or at a time when neither of the contracting parties is
involved in warlike complications, then the other contracting
party will not adhere to such a coalition.

Article 4

This treaty shall be ratified, and the ratification shall be exchanged in _____.

The treaty shall enter into force with the exchange of ratifications and be valid for a period of five years. Both contracting
parties shall confer in good time before the expiration of this
period regarding the further aspects of their relation.

German Note

Mr. Ambassador:

With reference to the negotiations regarding the treaty signed
today between the German government and the government of
the Union of Soviet Socialist Republics, I have the honor to state
the following in the name of the German government:

1. Both governments, during the negotiations for this treaty as
well as its signing, proceeded from the concept held by them
that the principle enunciated in Article 1, paragraph 2, regarding
agreement on all political and economic questions which mutually affect them will materially contribute to the preservation of
the general peace. In any event, both governments will be guided
by the point of view of the necessity of the preservation of the
general peace in all their negotiations.

2. In this sense, both governments have also thoroughly discussed the basic questions which are connected with Germany's
entry into the League of Nations. The German government is
concerned that the membership of Germany in the League of
Nations cannot constitute an obstacle to the friendly development
of the relations between Germany and the Union of Soviet Socialist Republics. In accordance with its fundamental idea, the
League of Nations is dedicated to use all its power to resolve all
international confrontations on a peaceful and just basis. The
German government is determined to use all its power to cooperate in the realization of this idea. Should, however—a possibility the German government does not expect—tendencies develop within the framework of the League of Nations which, in
contradiction to this principal idea of peace, are directed against

the Union of Soviet Socialist Republics, then Germany would counteract such tendencies with all due emphasis.

3. The German government proceeds from the point of view that this fundamental attitude of German policy vis-à-vis the Union of Soviet Socialist Republics cannot be prejudiced through the loyal observation of the obligations incumbent on Germany after her entry into the League of Nations under Articles 16 and 17 of the Covenant of the League of Nations concerning the application of sanctions. According to these Articles, the consideration of sanctions against the Union of Soviet Socialist Republics, aside from other considerations, can only be taken under advisement if the Union of Soviet Socialist Republics should start an aggressive war against a third power. In this connection, it must be borne in mind that the question as to whether the Union of Soviet Socialist Republics is the attacker in an armed conflict with a third state can be decided with a binding effect on Germany only with her own consent, and that thus an accusation brought by other powers against the USSR, if considered an unfounded accusation by Germany, would not force Germany to participate in any kind of measures started on the basis of Article 16. In regard to the question whether and to what extent Germany would be capable in an actual case of participating in the application of sanctions, the German government refers at this opportunity to the note of December 1, 1925, regarding the interpretation of Article 16, which was given to the German delegation at the signing of the Locarno Pacts.

4. In order to create a solid basis for the smooth settlement of all questions which might arise between them, both governments think it necessary to start immediate negotiations regarding the conclusion of a general agreement for the peaceful solution of conflicts which might arise between the two parties, whereby the possibilities of applying arbitration and mediation procedures shall especially be considered.

The Russian note was a verbatim replica of the German note except that it contained only three points, point 3 being omitted and point 2 reading:

In regard to the basic questions which are concerned with the entry of Germany into the League of Nations, the government of the USSR takes cognizance of the explanations contained in paragraphs 2 and 3 of your note.

Before the start of the discussion, Schubert insisted that Krestinsky take a stand on "two important political points": a Russian guarantee of Poland's eastern border which did not agree with the aims of the German-Russian treaty and Germany's demand for a definite guarantee that neither now nor later would agreements on the borders be reached with Poland. Schubert added, in order to forestall Russian use of the argument, that arbitration treaties between Germany and Poland were only an "appendage" to the treaties of Locarno. This fact was understood everywhere, expecially by Poland, which was placed in a very uncomfortable position.

Neither Krestinsky nor Jacubovich seemed convinced, but they made no objection. Krestinsky repeated Chicherin's assurances to Brockdorff-Rantzau and added his own very definite personal opinion that no agreements about borders would be concluded between his government and that of Poland. Germany should not be concerned if Moscow gave the appearance of negotiating with Poland in earnest. Schubert declared himself satisfied, but asked that the Soviet Ambassador keep him informed about a possible East Locarno. Should such treaties be concluded, not only Russia but Germany too should participate. Krestinsky assured the Undersecretary that he would be glad to keep him informed. The discussion now turned to the treaty.

Krestinsky again asked for the signing of the documents by April 10 because of the session of the Central Executive Committee. Moscow was willing to accept the treaty as it stood, in order to eliminate delays, although the developments in Geneva placed an "unlimited" treaty of neutrality once again into the realm of the possible.

Gaus interjected that this was not possible. However, Germany would agree to turn the protocol into an exchange of notes. The discussion continued on the various changes Moscow wanted made. Krestinsky was particularly adamant that the phrase "without being provoked" in Article 2 be stricken. Gaus was willing to rearrange the wording, but unwilling to remove the phrase itself. Krestinsky also wanted a definite statement that neither Germany nor Russia would take economic measures detrimental to each other in wartime, not just in peacetime. Gaus proposed a new wording for Article 3 which he thought would remove Russian concern.

Krestinsky agreed to forward the new draft to Moscow, which would make an immediate decision. Schubert now made it clear that the treaty could not possibly be signed by the tenth because Stresemann would be on his Easter vacation and would not return to Berlin until April 20. Besides, haste was not wise; German public opinion and political parties would have to be prepared, and the Cabinet also had to discuss the wording. Krestinsky seemed to accept the new delay.[28]

Brockdorff-Rantzau was informed of the discussion and Krestinsky's assurances. He was instructed to have a final and definitive talk with Chicherin on Russo-Polish relations. The Ambassador was also asked to persuade Chicherin to accept the German formulation of the treaty.[29]

On March 31, Schubert discussed the German-Russian treaty with Lord D'Abernon. Schubert told of the Russian attempts to get a treaty before Locarno, in February, 1925. In order to keep Germany out of the League, she had been offered "a treaty which differed little from an alliance." In addition, Moscow had had the "presumption" to propose that Germany join the League only with Russia. Germany had rejected this, to Moscow's great disappointment. When negotiations for the Locarno Pact became known, it had almost led to a break of relations. When Locarno became a fact and therefore German membership in the League a necessity, the Russians had "overwhelmed Germany with new proposals." They wanted an unlimited treaty of neutrality which would cover all "possible cases of war." Again Germany had rejected the Russian proposal. Germany had made it clear to Russia that she would not start on an anti-Soviet course and that she had made this amply obvious to the West. D'Abernon here interjected that this was indeed the case.

Schubert continued, stating that after the return from Locarno, it had been possible to prove to Moscow "on the basis of the *lettre du bateau*" that they need not worry about Article 16. Nevertheless, Moscow continued to press for an unrestricted treaty of neutrality, especially after German membership was refused at Geneva. Again Russian overtures had been rejected, despite Germany's less favorable international position. Undaunted, Krestinsky appeared at the Wilhelmstrasse on the day before, but this time it appeared that Moscow would accept the German formula. Their willingness was apparently prompted by the Polish-Rumanian treaty (of March 26, 1926), which thwarted Russia's plans vis-à-vis Poland.

Schubert gave the British Ambassador a summary of what he called "a rather small agreement of a few paragraphs and an exchange of short notes." Of course, the Russians would not really be satisfied, but, in view of the Polish-Rumanian treaty, would accept "a little rather than nothing." Then, as if it were an impromptu afterthought, Schubert alluded to the consequences of a renewed denial of League membership in the fall. Such a contingency, in his personal opinion, would prompt the Soviet Union to ask Germany to make common cause, or at least sign an unlimited treaty of neutrality with her.

D'Abernon had listened very attentively, fully aware of the import of Schubert's revelations; he had taken notes and repeatedly asked questions. He agreed that Germany's hand was somewhat forced, but pointed out that the treaty would have far-reaching consequences.

Schubert assured him that the treaty was vague but useful to stop Russian games with Poland at Germany's expense. After negotiations which had lasted "for years," it was the least that could be offered. The Wilhelmstrasse had considered waiting until after the fall meeting of the League had again considered Germany's application for membership, but had convinced itself that this could lead to a break with Russia, which Germany simply did not want to risk.

D'Abernon directed attention to the possibility that some would say that the treaty was a result of Germany's failure at Geneva. Schubert readily agreed but pointed out that Germany had stood ready to join; the rejection was not her fault. At the conclusion of their illuminating talk, D'Abernon asked Schubert's permission to inform Sir Austen Chamberlain. Schubert agreed, but asked to keep it confidential. He was considering instructing Ambassador Hoesch to inform Briand.[30]

During the afternoon of April 1, D'Abernon telephoned Schubert to tell him that he had informed Chamberlain by telegraph after leaving the Wilhelmstrasse. Schubert now sent a courier with a copy of the treaty and a covering letter to Hoesch, in which he informed the Ambassador that the signature would take place between April 20 and 25, after Stresemann's return from his Easter vacation. There was a chance that the signature, coming so soon after admission to the League had been denied, would be interpreted as a reaction. This was not true at all, nor was it meant to be an "epoch-making or sensational political occurrence." Schubert instructed Hoesch to inform Briand or Berthelot (the chief political officer at the Quai d'Orsay) "personally and in the strictest confidence" in the manner in which Schubert had informed D'Abernon. The notes on that discussion were sent along to Hoesch.

Another courier went to Ambassador Sthamer in London with a copy of the material sent to Hoesch and the instructions not to take any steps unless inquiries were made by the Foreign Office. In that case, Sthamer was advised to reply on the basis of the information sent to Hoesch. Sthamer was asked to telegraph if he thought it wise to inform the English press before the treaty was published.

During the morning of April 3, D'Abernon counseled Schubert to prepare Western opinion well for the German-Soviet treaty. He advised the Undersecretary to make it clear that "Germany was called upon to tame Russia. The road from the West to Russia, one should say, went through the Brandenburg Gate."

Sthamer telegraphed on the third that it would be best to hold information for the press until it was time to publish the treaty. One could not count on a favorable reception, because the agreement would strengthen German-Russian ties and thus thwart England's attempt, exemplified by Locarno, to weaken them.

At 7:30 P.M., exactly four hours after Sthamer's telegram had been received at the Wilhelmstrasse, Hoesch's telegram arrived bringing the news that he had spoken with Briand on the evening of the second before the special courier arrived, and, since the Prime Minister was too busy on April 3, Berthelot had been informed before noon. Berthelot had received the *démarche* with a serious face. He had asked whether Article 2 would prevent Germany from participating in League actions against Russia. Hoesch denied this possibility and pointed to the word "unprovoked." Berthelot said only that under no circumstances should this be deleted, because otherwise Germany's position vis-à-vis the League would become untenable.

Schubert telegraphed a lengthy exposition of the treaty to Hoesch, asserting that Germany could participate in League actions. Articles 16 and 17 of the Covenant became operative only if Russia became the aggressor. But Moscow, despite this, demanded an unrestricted treaty of alliance. Germany did not collapse under the pressure applied, because an unrestricted treaty would, indeed, have conflicted with the obligations imposed by the League Covenant. This was the very important difference between the proposed German-Soviet treaty and the Russo-Turkish treaty, in which neutrality was not qualified but applied equally to offensive and defensive war.

Schubert also had an hour-and-a-half discussion with the French Ambassador de Margerie on April 6 and another with D'Abernon lasting an hour. The French Ambassador compared the treaty to Bismarck's Reinsurance Treaty. D'Abernon insisted that the information he had been given differed from that transmitted to Paris. Schubert denied this. D'Abernon insisted that the treaty was almost an "alliance."

Schubert's worst fears seemed to have materialized. He had been very concerned that the charge of a second Rapallo would be leveled against Germany and that the reaction would go beyond the one which had been activated by the 1922 treaty.[31]

After Rapallo, the Wilhelmstrasse had done nothing to counteract rumors that the treaty had deeper implication than appeared in the published text. The opposite was true now; Germany simply did not want to lose Western good will. Stresemann had succeeded in delaying the conclusion of an agreement with the Russians until it suited his purpose. It was not part of his policy to antagonize the West, which alone could made the kind of concessions in which the Foreign Minister was interested.

On April 8, the Belgian Foreign Minister, van der Velde, when approached by the German representative, told the latter that he had already been informed by Paris. Schubert now instructed the German Ambassador in Rome to communicate with Mussolini's representative in a general way, but only if discretion were assured and no press campaign would be waged. The information had become necessary because the French had informed London and Brussels, and it was possible that they had also divulged the treaty to Rome.

All German representatives in the European capitals, except those in Luxembourg, Lisbon, Tiruna, Danzig, and Memel, were sent a copy of the treaty by courier and given instructions on the language to use after the treaty was published. The events since Locarno were recapitulated for their general knowledge, and they were also told, without any details, that Russia had made proposals in December, 1924, which would have amounted to a "far-reaching political connection of Germany to Russia." Instead, the present agreement had been negotiated. After publication, if the government and diplomatic corps should ask for details, it should be explained that the treaty was an addition to, not a change of, Locarno, and had no connection with the rejection of Germany's application for League membership. In fact, Germany's loyalty to the West was such that the content of the treaty was based on German membership in the League, although this was not even assured. The treaty was not a second Rapallo, because that had been a unilateral action with Russia without a corresponding "compensation" in the West. The agreement was designed to assure Russia that Germany's entry into the League would not lead to her participation in anti-Soviet actions. Finally, the German representatives were advised not to present the treaty either as a "close political connection" or to characterize it as "a contentless and empty formula." Instead, they were to keep their replies between these two extremes, according to the personalities of the inquirers.[32]

During the morning of April 9, D'Abernon came to the Wilhelmstrasse to deliver an *aide-mémoire* by Chamberlain. The Foreign Secretary expressed his appreciation to Stresemann for the transmission of the "substance" of the forthcoming pact. He expressed the assumption that it would be "in harmony with the Covenant" and especially Articles 16 and 17. He did not object to referring to the "letter of the

Locarno powers" on Article 16, "but must warn Herr Stresemann of commenting on or interpreting its terms. Herr Stresemann must not forget that the German claim to be "neutral" was categorically declined as being inconsistent with the Covenant." All members of the League are bound to act against aggression. The note of the powers merely established the fact that the contribution of each state "must be conformable with its circumstances."

D'Abernon emphasized that the Foreign Secretary was most concerned about a lax interpretation of Article 16. Schubert again assured the Ambassador that this was nothing to be worried about. The Undersecretary also expressed his view that a leak of information might have occurred to the London *Times*. The article could have the most unpleasant and dire consequences for Berlin. D'Abernon agreed but made no other comment. The *Times* had reported on April 8 that Chicherin had demanded an unequivocal acknowledgment of Rapallo and agreement that Germany would "under no circumstances participate in actions directed against Russia."

In the evening, D'Abernon returned to show and discuss a telegram in which he told Chamberlain that the German Foreign Office was "very satisfied" with the *aide-mémoire*. He declared too that he was now convinced that the pact was completely within the framework of Locarno. Since D'Abernon was leaving on a ten-day furlough, Schubert asked that he tell Chamberlain that the German declaration to Russia on the Locarno note did not constitute a commentary.[33]

Schubert telegraphed the *aide-mémoire* to the German ambassadors in London, Paris, Rome, and Brussels on the evening of the ninth, with the comment that "England evaluated our intentions vis-à-vis Russia more understandingly than was the case in Paris." The next morning, a telegram by Hoesch arrived apprising Schubert that Briand had been "very understanding and judicious." He had been concerned after Berthelot's report, but admitted that Germany had, indeed, "considered Locarno as well as the League Covenant." He would do his best to remove the difficulties which were sure to arise. He urgently requested that the signature and publication be delayed until May or at least until the end of April so that he could first secure Senate acceptance of the Locarno treaties. Briand also mentioned that it had been unavoidable that the other powers were consulted.[34]

On April 11, a journalist from the *Times* appeared at the London Embassy to get details on the pending treaty. He knew that something was in the wind, but received no confirmation of his suspicions. Sthamer deduced that the *Times* was willing to bring an objective account of the German point of view.

Indications that no real objection would come from the powers were further supported by the attitude of the United States State Department, which received the news about the contemplated treaty "without a sign of astonishment or surprise, as well as quite understandingly."[35]

Thirteen days after he had received the proposed treaty, Krestinsky brought Moscow's answer. The Kremlin still insisted that "without being provoked" in Article 2 had to be removed. Schubert informed the Cabinet during its afternoon session and received unanimous support for his insistence that unlimited neutrality could not be granted. He informed Brockdorff-Rantzau, who passed the rejection to Litvinov, who was in charge of the Narkomindel since Chicherin was again sick.[36]

On April 13, the Russian-born anti-Bolshevik publicist, Poliakov (Augur), paid a visit to Dufour-Feronce. He wanted confirmation about the rumored German-Russian treaty. Dufour-Feronce assured him that nothing contrary to the League or Locarno was included. He also put his mind to rest about secret clauses. On the following day, the London *Times* reported that it had been informed by "an excellent source" that Germany and Russia were about to conclude a pact which would adapt Rapallo to the terms of the Treaty of Locarno. It could be labeled a "reinsurance treaty." It was stated, wrote the *Times*, that nothing contrary to the "spirit or letter" of Locarno was included. The article was followed by a report from the *Times* Berlin correspondence that Germany continued its old policy in regard to the West but kept the path to the East open.

The *Temps*, commenting on the treaty revealed by the *Times*, said that it was

a veritable counterpart to the Locarno agreements constituting a new fact of the greatest importance for the whole of European affairs.

Sthamer was instructed to tell Chamberlain that the sensational and false report in the *Times* that the contemplated German-Soviet treaty was a reinsurance treaty had placed Germany in an awkward position. She was now forced to conclude the treaty as soon as possible, and thus could not delay signing to give Briand a chance to push the Locarno Pact through the Senate.[37]

The *Times*'s indiscretion was extremely timely for the Wilhelmstrasse. It made it impossible to do Briand the favor of delaying the signature of the treaty and made it equally imperative that Moscow accept Article 2 as it stood because delay might make conclusion difficult if not impossible. Brockdorff-Rantzau was appraised of the leak of the *Times*, and, after Krestinsky had been informed, as well as the English chargé d'affaires, representatives of the German press were received by Luther in the library of the Reichschancellery. Schubert asked that the information he was about to give be kept confidential. The pending treaty was due to Russian concern about Locarno, but contained nothing contrary to its terms. He could, regrettably, give no details except to stress that the treaty contained no secret appendages. Chancellor Luther asked that nothing be printed about an alliance, because that would alienate the Anglo-Saxon world. On the other hand, Luther told the journalists, their articles should not sound as if the agreement were of a secondary nature. They could point out that Germany did not intend to make a "choice between East and West."[38]

While Berlin made the most of the *Times* report, Brockdorff-Rantzau tried to convince Litvinov that "without being provoked" had to remain in Article 2 or the whole treaty would be wrecked. He stressed that Germany retained the right to decide whether Russia was an aggressor in any given case. But Brockdorff-Rantzau himself was still convinced, as he had been in Berlin, that great difficulties could be expected from the West in regard to the exemption of Germany from Article 16.[39]

The British and French Foreign Offices continued to use their influence to calm the press in their countries. There was less of a stormy reaction in England than in France, and in that country it took quite a bit of persuading before public opinion was reassured. In fact, it was not until June, 1926, that Stresemann, after extensive talks with de Margerie, succeeded in convincing the Quai d'Orsay that Germany had no intention of ignoring her obligations under the Locarno Pact and the League Covenant. Briand made a statement to that effect in the French Assembly on June 4.[40]

The Polish and Czech governments were even harder to convince that the proposed treaty was only an appendage to Locarno. The Polish press explained that Locarno had given Germany a free hand in the East, and she now wanted to be sure that she could count on Russian aid. On the other hand, the United States showed little interest in the German-Russian agreement. An Associated Press report expressed the American attitude perfectly when it stated that Germany's admission to the League in September would be enough of a preventive against any possible danger from the pact with Russia.[41]

On April 17, Litvinov complained to Brockdorff-Rantzau that Germany had informed the Western powers prematurely. He also told the

Ambassador that the Soviet Cabinet insisted that "without being provoked" be deleted from Article 2. Three days later, Krestinsky repeated the same demand to Stresemann, asserting that if the words remained, one could think Germany agreed with those who claimed that Russia had imperialistic aims, and that Berlin thought it possible that Russia would start a war "without provocation." Doubts could arise about aggression, and Germany might turn to the World Court in The Hague, which was anti-Soviet, for a decision. Finally, should the Social Democratic Party gain power in Germany, it would interpret Article 2 in a sense unfavorable to Russia.

The Ambassador's explanations were followed by a long discussion, during which Stresemann, Gaus, Schubert, and Krestinsky brought forward the arguments which had all been used before. The session ended with Stresemann's announcement that the Cabinet would again be approached, but that he did not think that a change would be allowed. Krestinsky replied that the Soviet Cabinet would reveal itself to be equally adamant in its insistence that the words be deleted.[42]

On April 21, Stresemann telegraphed Brockdorff-Rantzau that he had proposed a new wording to Krestinsky, since it was certain that the Cabinet would reject the Russian demand. Anticipating objections, Stresemann pointed out that there was not really much difference in the new wording, but it did remove "without being provoked." Brockdorff-Rantzau was to make it clear to Moscow that this was the time for a final decision. The change proposed by Stresemann read:

> Should one of the contracting parties, despite its peaceful behavior, be attacked by a third power or several third powers, then the other contracting party shall observe neutrality for the complete duration of the conflict.

At 5:00 P.M. on April 22, Brockdorff-Rantzau's reply was in the Wilhelmstrasse. Litvinov had agreed to the new wording, and had informed Krestinsky. The Deputy Commissar requested signature early Saturday, April 24. The reason given by Litvinov sounded rather strange: he wanted to avoid an interpellation in the Central Executive Committee.

Schubert replied that Krestinsky had been informed that the signing could take place Saturday at 1:00 P.M. The announcement of the signature of the treaty would be made during the morning of the twenty-fifth, while the text of the treaty and the notes would be published on April 27 in both capitals.[43] During the morning of April 24, the Cabinet agreed that the signature should take place at the time appointed by the Wilhelmstrasse.

Stresemann and Krestinsky signed the treaty and exchanged the notes. The Foreign Minister sent a congratulatory telegram to Brockdorff-Rantzau for his "substantial part" in the conclusion of the treaty. To Chicherin the Foreign Minister wired that the treaty, the basis of which had been discussed between them during the preceding year, would serve to promote "friendly and peaceful" cooperation between their two peoples and promote world peace. Chicherin, equally noncommittal, replied with similar diplomatic platitudes, expressing his great delight that their discussions had led to this "positive and highly gratifying result."[44]

Litvinov told the Central Executive Committee that the treaty was a "supplement rather than an elaboration of the Rapallo Treaty, and it fully corresponds to the friendly relations that have been established between the Union and Germany." A further indication of friendship was the support by the German government for the 300 million credit. Litvinov's announcement was greeted by prolonged applause.

The fact that the treaty was unanimously accepted by the Foreign Affairs Committee of the Reichstag prompted D'Abernon to comment that "the Germans are unwilling to separate themselves from Russia. The gods themselves would fight against this without avail."[45]

Brockdorff-Rantzau considered the treaty a "great political success" which had made him the center of envy in Moscow's diplomatic corps. He had received a number of congratulatory telegrams, among them Stresemann's which had pleased him very much. Two days later, on April 26, the Count was sure that Stresemann was trying to take all the credit himself. Brockdorff-Rantzau, concerned that his historical role was being challenged, wanted a direct congratulatory message from President Hindenburg. The Count asked his brother Ernst Rantzau to see to it that Hindenburg's telegram included an acknowledgment of the outstanding role Brockdorff-Rantzau had played in bringing the treaty to its successful conclusion.

When Hindenburg's confirmation of the Count's historical part apparently was not forthcoming, Brockdorff-Rantzau wrote a "private letter" to the President. In it the Count traced the history of the treaty back to the Russian proposals of December, 1924, emphasizing that it had been due primarily to his labors that the treaty was concluded. He assured the President that it had been extremely difficult work because German relations with the Soviet Union were always more like those resulting from "a shotgun wedding [Zwangsehe]" than those based on a love-match." This letter finally brought the acknowledgment by Hindenburg on July 14 that the conclusion of the treaty was due primarily to the Count's untiring labors. Brockdorff-Rantzau replied with a telegram he had already drafted late in May. He thanked Hindenburg for the kind words, which were a matter of "historical satisfaction" to him.[46]

It is difficult to understand why Brockdorff-Rantzau, who had fought desperately to get a "reinsurance treaty," was so extraordinarily proud of the Treaty of Berlin, which contained little of any real importance. He flattered himself with the belief that it had been concluded only because of his insistence. In fact, Stresemann had consented to concluding the treaty only after the West had shown some reluctance about admitting Germany to the League of Nations. The Foreign Minister had no intention of turning from his Western course, despite Russian threats to align themselves with Poland or France. Stresemann had successfully kept Chicherin at bay while the Locarno Pact was concluded and entry into the League contemplated. He had accomplished this without pushing the USSR into the arms of France, and without making the concessions demanded by Moscow. Germany, despite the rejection of her application for admission to the League of Nations in March, had not withdrawn her application. Stresemann had taken a small step East, while he was preparing to take a major stride West.

Given the public attitude in Germany toward the Soviet Union and its agents, either of the KPD or of the Comintern brand, Stresemann had skilfully avoided domestic pitfalls, as well as the traps set by Brockdorff-Rantzau and the Russians. The Ambassador's attitude was conditioned by an excessive fear that history would repeat itself. He still looked upon the relationship with Russia as a "community of fate" and was extremely concerned that England or France, or both, would isolate disarmed Germany, forcing her to accept Western dictation. Brockdorff-Rantzau simply did not believe that Stresemann, by diplomatic skill alone, would be able to restore Germany to her place in the sun.

However, the Ambassador's energies were soon absorbed in resolving a number of problems created by the Soviet government and its organs, during which he found renewed evidence that the "community of fate" was not a "love-match." During the final stages of the negotiations for the Treaty of Berlin the Soviet Union's newspapers had been relatively quiet in regard to Germany. In return little adverse criticism directed against Russia had appeared in the German press. With the publication of the treaty the temporary quiet was broken by demands in publications for the release of numerous German citizens imprisoned in the USSR.

VII

The Reorganization of Military Collaboration

In late April, 1926, German newspapers published a series of articles about the refusal of the Russian government to release forty-four German citizens incarcerated or awaiting trial in the USSR. These articles aroused public opinion to the point where the Foreign Office found it necessary to approach Moscow about the release and consequent deportation of these Germans. Among those still in prison were Kindermann, Wolscht, and the consular agents arrested in the Caucasus. Brockdorff-Rantzau thought that he might be able to achieve the release of the latter, but seriously doubted that he could do much for the others unless Berlin agreed to release a number of Russians imprisoned in Germany. Litvinov had proposed to wipe clean the slate and exchange all political prisoners held by both countries.

On May 10, Krestinsky officially transmitted Litvinov's proposal to Stresemann. The Russians were particularly interested in exchanging Skoblevsky, who was still in a German prison for the part he had played in the abortive "October Revolution" in 1923, and Maslov. Stresemann told Krestinsky that it would be most difficult to get a pardon for Skoblevsky. The Foreign Minister informed Brockdorff-Rantzau on May 22 that an inquiry at the Ministry of Justice had revealed no objection to Skoblevsky's release on judicial grounds. The Ministry had pointed out that the German cases in the USSR fell into a different category from those of the Russians imprisoned in Germany. The Ministry had warned that the release of the Russians could easily establish a precedent and lead to a continuation of the "hostage system" instituted by the Soviet government. Stresemann informed Brockdorff-Rantzau that the release of Skoblevsky could be justified to the latter's cohorts and the German public only if Moscow granted pardons to at least fourteen Germans, including the consular agents arrested in the Caucasus, the two students, and the Junkers' engineer Scholl.[1]

220

Brockdorff-Rantzau felt that it would be possible to come to an early agreement about the exchange. He thought it best to arrange a complete "political amnesty by both sides." The Ambassador was eager to settle the matter as quickly as possible because he wanted to attend the exchange of ratifications of the Treaty of Berlin in the German capital. Aside from this, he suffered from various maladies for which he wanted to consult specialists in Germany.

The Russians spoiled Brockdorff-Rantzau's plan by demanding the release of a certain Ozol, who had been convicted by the Prussian State Court in Königsberg, in addition to Skoblevsky and Maslov. This new demand necessitated negotiations between the Wilhelmstrasse and the Prussian Ministry of Justice and made further delays a certainty. This, as well as the objections of the Reich Ministry of Justice, made it necessary to place the exchange before the entire Cabinet. Brockdorff-Rantzau, eager to leave Moscow, intended to back the Foreign Office by telling the Russians "categorically that we will not countenance further bargaining, chaffering, and haggling." He intended to press for the release of the two students and the consular agents so that he could leave Moscow for his furlough.[2]

Despite the Ambassador's displeasure about the addition of Ozol, the Narkomindel requested that a certain Georg Lossin and his wife be substituted for Maslov, who was about to complete his term. This meant further negotiations with the Prussian Ministry of Justice for the Wilhelmstrasse, because Lossin too had been convicted by a Prussian court.

The new demand by the Soviets also delayed the Count's departure. Brockdorff-Rantzau's nerves, frayed by heat and sickness, began to give out. The "cow-trading" and almost daily addition of another "bastard [Schweinehund]" disgusted him thoroughly with the Russians. He decided that no matter what happened, he would take ship at Helsinki on July 7.

Despite his personal anger, Brockdorff-Rantzau was careful not to make the ratification of the Treaty of Berlin dependent on the release of the Germans held in the Soviet Union. He was certain that such action would only stir up further trouble with the Russians. Berlin agreed, and, on June 29, Stresemann and Krestinsky exchanged the instruments of ratification.

After ratifications had been exchanged, the Russians became more conciliatory. They informed Brockdorff-Rantzau that they would be satisfied if the German government declared, at the time of Skoblevsky's and Ozol's deportation, that the Lossins would follow within eight days. The Soviet government would release the Germans thirty-six hours after the German agreement was received. At its July 3 session, the German Cabinet deferred any decision on the release of the Russians until the arrival of Brockdorff-Rantzau in Berlin.[3]

In the Count's opinion, this decision created a dangerous new situation which threatened to destroy the good feeling created by the ratification of the Treaty of Berlin. Since both Stresemann and Schubert had presented the Count's point of view to the Cabinet, Brockdorff-Rantzau saw no need to do so personally. He informed the Foreign Office that he would delay his departure for the fourth time, despite the advice of his physicians to the contrary. However, Brockdorff-Rantzau warned, it was probable that Moscow would immediately start a trial against the consular agents and, worst of all, against the Junkers' engineer, Scholl. There was no question in the Count's mind that this would "compromise our policies vis-à-vis the Western powers irretrievably and make our entry into the League of Nations definitely impossible." Therefore, he would inform the Russians only in a general way that difficulties had arisen that had to be removed. Because of the seriousness of the situation, he would send Hencke to Berlin with an extensive private letter and additional oral reports, which should make it unnecessary for him to come personally to Berlin. Brockdorff-Rantzau warned that Scholl's trial would reveal Germany's military collaboration with Russia and destroy all hopes of entering the League. Refusal to deport Skoblevsky would prompt the "Soviet government to proceed with its accustomed ruthless brutality." He added that in the past he had repeatedly stressed the fact that Germany was "in the hands of political blackmailers."[4]

Scholl was employed by the Junkers firm at its Fili plant near Moscow. The engineer had been accused of bribing Russian officials. Once again, the possiblity that the clandestine military collaboration with the Soviet Union would be revealed forced the hand of the Germans. Ironically, the major opposition to the release of Skoblevsky came from the Minister of Defense, Gessler. He did not think that his department would be the most deeply compromised, or that Scholl's trial could have serious effects on Germany's newly established relations with the West. Because of Gessler's opposition, the Cabinet decided to postpone final consideration of Skoblevsky's release until the Ministry of Defense and the Foreign Office had discussed the matter.

Brockdorff-Rantzau was thoroughly upset by this evidence of military disregard for the political consequences of its collaboration with the Red army. He advised the Wilhelmstrasse to remind Gessler that it had been due only to hard diplomatic work that past indiscretions by the military had not resulted in political disaster. The Minister should be reminded of General Hasse's letter to Rosengolts, Hagen's briefcase, and the Petrov case. If this were not sufficient, Gessler could also be told that it had only been because of Brockdorff-Rantzau's insistence that the military relations were "the strongest political bond between us and the Soviet government" that President Ebert had agreed to permit the continuation of what he had considered to be "frivolous recklessness." In addition, Gessler should be told that only Brockdorff-Rantzau's intercession had convinced the Reichsbank, in July, 1923, of the necessity to grant the large sum required for the continuation of the military collaboration. These arguments should suffice to bring Gessler to heel.

During the conference between Schubert and Gessler on July 14, the latter agreed that his ministry could be compromised if the military collaboration became known to the German public. Gessler expressed the opinion that it would be wise to reduce the military collaboration, but refused to agree to Skoblevsky's release. He threatened to resign if the Cabinet decided to support a pardon. Since Gessler insisted that Skoblevsky's testimony was needed in forthcoming trials against German Communists, the Foreign Office decided to advise the Russians that Skoblevsky would not be released until he had testified.

Despite the fact that the Russians had assembled all Germans at Leningrad, Gessler remained absolutely adamant in his refusal to support Skoblevsky's release. He proposed to Chancellor Marx on July 19 that Skoblevsky be deported only if Scholl and the consular agents were condemned to death. During the Cabinet session that evening, Gessler presented his point of view and then left the meeting to start a previously arranged vacation.[5] After Gessler's departure from the meeting, Schubert told the assembled ministers that the situation created by the delay in the exchange of the prisoners was due entirely to "the most delicate and secret matters." If Scholl, who had admitted that he had bribed Russian officials, was placed on trial, the result would most certainly be an international scandal. The Russian Communist Party would use the occasion to place the German bourgeoisie in the pillory.

The first thing to be revealed would be the Junkers-Defense Ministry relations with the Red air force. This consisted, as was probably known, in the construction of war planes for Germany and the training of pilots, particularly at the flying school at Lipetsk, "where German flying-students are instructed in bombing and machine gun handling." Any leak of these matters would soon involve the whole German military collaboration with Russia and show that a number of clauses of the Treaty of Versailles had been violated. Violations included the manufacture of ammunition for the German army. These munitions were not all delivered to Germany, but a certain amount was stored in Russia for the use of the Germany army. Furthermore, the Reichswehr had constructed a poison gas factory at Ivoshenko and conducted a school for tank warfare at Kazan. To this school German officers were sent who had been detached from active service. In addition, Germany and the USSR exchanged army and navy missions. Schubert placed the extent of the military collaboration in perspective by revealing that during the "time of inflation, 75 million gold marks were used for these purposes."

Schubert emphasized that the disclosure of these clandestine relations would convince the world that Germany played a double game and that she had a military alliance with the USSR. The seriousness of the whole business was highlighted by the fact that Junkers, because of its problems with the Ministry of Defense, had given all the material connected with its Russian venture to the press and members of the Reichstag. The Foreign Affairs Committee would soon discuss the case. All this could be kept confidential in Germany. But, since there was no control over events in Russia, Schubert advised the Cabinet to eliminate military collaboration as quickly as possible, without insulting the Russians, in order to avoid a recurrence of as equally impossible a situation as the present one. After a long and bitter debate, the Cabinet decided to recommend Skoblevsky for a presidential pardon, if Gessler agreed.[6]

Brockdorff-Rantzau was pleased with the way Schubert had handled the Cabinet session but appalled by Gessler's attitude. The Ambassador expressed his surprise to Schubert that "a Defense Minister believes that *he* can take the consequences of foreign policy upon himself." To his knowledge, the Foreign Minister, the Chancellor, and the President, next to the Ambassador to Moscow, had to bear the responsibility if grave mistakes had been made. Brockdorff-Rantzau found it interesting that Gessler had finally admitted that his department could be compromised. The Count considered stupid Gessler's proposal to release Skoblevsky only if the Germans were condemned to death. Brockdorff-Rantzau thought the emphasis in this matter had been misplaced. It was not just Skoblevsky's exchange which should be considered. He did not intend to minimize the shortcomings of the Russians in this case, but it would look well if the Treaty of Berlin were underlined by making "*tabula rasa*" as far as all political problems still outstanding between Germany and Russia were concerned. Skoblevsky had to be released; otherwise the cases of the consular agents and the "less sympathetic" students could not be resolved in the foreseeable future. Gessler's threat to resign sounded like blackmail.

It might sound good to the gallery, to declare proudly that one does not want to deal with extortioners, but such a declaration is contradictory *after* one has delivered oneself into the hands of blackmailers.[7]

Three weeks after Brockdorff-Rantzau's forceful letter, the Cabinet decided to request a presidential pardon for Skoblevsky. Two days later, on August 14 a communiqué was given to the press by the Wilhelmstrasse, which stated that Skoblevsky's release was a certainty. Brockdorff-Rantzau had already arrived in Berlin, and the completion of the routine details in Moscow were left to the chargé d'affaires, Hey. Ten days after the first communiqué, the Germans announced that Skoblevsky, Lossin, and Ozol would be released "in the spirit of the treaty of April 24, 1926." The Russians, in a similarly worded note, announced the release of the Germans. A number of delays held up the exchange of the last prisoners, Skoblevsky, Kindermann, and Wolscht, until the end of October.

Three months before the exchange was settled, Litvinov had told Schubert that he considered the matter closed.[8] Another crisis in German-Russian relations had passed. As so often before, the military collaboration had been the Damoclean sword which forced the hand of the Germans; they could ill afford any revelations while their admission to the League of Nations was still undecided.

Germany was admitted to the League of Nations on September 8, 1926. Two days later, the French Foreign Minister, Briand, lauded Germany in a very enthusiastic speech at the ceremonies for her admission to the League. He followed this by a long talk with Stresemann on September 17, with whom he had gone to Thoiry to escape the journalists. There the two statesmen talked about the possibility of settling the problems which existed between their two countries. Foremost in Stresemann's mind was the evacuation of the Rhineland and, on Briand's, France's poor economic situation. Briand proposed that a part of the reparation due France be realized from a sale of German Reichsbahn obligations. In return, Stresemann asked for a binding commitment that the Rhineland be evacuated by September 30. The settlement involved highly technical financial manipulations beyond the competency of either man. They prudently decided to leave the details to the experts.[9]

Germany's entry into the League and the Thoiry talks prompted

Brockdorff-Rantzau to ask Schlesinger to evaluate the new situation. Schlesinger complied and wrote that it meant, as far as he was concerned, that Germany was now aligned with the West. The policy of balance, which had found its overt expression in the Treaty of Berlin and Locarno, had ended with Thoiry. Since the Russians were as aware of this as anyone else, it would be wise to show them by some definite act that Germany was not deserting them completely. There were no concrete possibilities in the political area which permitted a step East; but it was possible to do so in the economic field. This was so because the precarious situation of the Soviet Union forced her to consider the question: "who gives me credits, and not who has given me credits." Despite the fact that loans did not generate gratitude, Germany was forced, if she wanted to maintain a hold on Russia, to give her further aid. Since the risks attending investments in Russia were great, a consortium, made up of various countries under German leadership, could be formed to aid Russian reconstruction.

> Our political position must then be strengthened, because the Soviet government depends politically on Germany and cannot renounce her because she is the state through whose mediation the basis for the security of her existence is procured.
>
> In the fulfillment of this proposition lies the security of our position in the Soviet Union.[10]

Brockdorff-Rantzau returned to Moscow on November 22. During their first talk, Chicherin complained that he had not been told about Thoiry in time. Brockdorff-Rantzau rejected this. The Foreign Commissar indicated that he thought Germany would now make a deal with Poland. He told the Ambassador that Russia "naturally approves when Germany extends her geographic borders which were drawn by force through the *Diktat* of Versailles; we only wish that this would not be done at Russia's expense." Brockdorff-Rantzau rejoined that only an economic understanding with Poland was possible. He also rejected the allegation that Seeckt's retirement on October 8, and his replacement by General Wilhelm Heye, was due to a deal made at Thoiry. Chicherin was only trying to irritate the Count, because one of General Heye's first visitors had been Krestinsky. The General assured him that no change in the Reichswehr collaboration with Russia was contemplated. Brockdorff-Rantzau asked Chicherin to discuss any future rumors openly to prevent a misunderstanding. He impressed upon the Commissar that he did not intend "to take over the ridiculous role of continuously reporting Russian complaints, which in the end dissolved into nothing or ended in good feelings."[11]

The Count was clearly becoming less enthusiastic about the relationship with Russia. His most recent experience with the double-dealing, double-talking Communists had sorely upset his equilibrium. Brockdorff-Rantzau knew that Russia had been the first foreign government to be informed about the Thoiry talks, because he had received an advance copy of the material Schubert discussed with Krestinsky on September 27 and with Bratman-Brodovsky on September 30. During that talk, Schubert had categorically denied that the English had proposed a solution of the Polish Corridor question at Lithuania's expense. He had admitted to Krestinsky that Lithuania had proposed a nonagression pact but Germany had refused, because she had no intention of concluding such a pact in the East. Germany's "main goal had to be the liberation of the Rhineland and the regaining of full sovereignty over our whole territory."[12]

While the Russians were somewhat reassured that no anti-Soviet deals had been made at Thoiry, they were not so sure about a possible *rapprochement* between Germany and Poland. Chicherin, who was on another of his health jaunts to Frankfurt, arrived in Berlin, where he had two long discussions with Stresemann and Schubert on December 2 and 3. Their talks ranged over the whole complex of German-Russian political relations, but centered on a possible German-Polish deal over the Corridor. Stresemann reiterated that no deals had been discussed with anyone. He conceded that he had told a journalist that the best solution of the question would be to grant Poland guaranteed access to the sea for the return of the Corridor. However, German policy was designed to bring about a return of the Rhineland. No government in Poland would be able to do anything about the Corridor.

Chicherin stressed that he was concerned about Poland's swallowing Lithuania. Russia wanted to prevent Poland from becoming a great power. Brockdorff-Rantzau had informed him that Germany would not like to see the removal of Russian pressure from Poland's eastern frontier. The Ambassador favored a continued and simultaneous pressure from East and West. Chicherin told Stresemann that there was no danger of an understanding between Russia and Poland as long as the latter acted as the protector of the Baltic States. During the discussion on December 3, the Russians broached the idea of a new loan. Stresemann told Chicherin that such an event should be left until the 300 million reichsmark credit had been completely used, and until after a new adjustment of the Dawes Plan. He did not want to jeopardize Anglo-American loans by giving the impression that Germany was rich enough to do without them.[13]

While the second discussion was still in progress, the *Manchester*

Guardian published an article by its Berlin correspondent about Russian involvement

> in the illegal activities of the German monarchists and counter-revolutionaries. The Communists . . . are afraid lest the facts be made public. I am in a position to assert that these facts are of very grave character. The only consoling feature in what might otherwise have become an international incident is that the German Government is genuinely determined to put an end to schemes and intrigues in which Germany stands to lose a great deal.[14]

The article then revealed that Junkers had been pressured by the Reichswehr into building military planes in Russia, that two chemical factories had been producing poison gas for the German and Russian military for at least five years, and that German officers visited Russia regularly. In addition, there had been deliveries of munitions from Russia to the German army. The correspondent was relatively certain that Seeckt, who was on the best of terms with high officers of the Red army, knew about the collaboration. However, Gessler probably did not, while Stresemann was not known to be a Russophile. In any event, the German government could not be held responsible, and a thorough investigation would soon end the whole matter. On December 6, the *Manchester Guardian* gave more details on the Junkers involvement, which were taken from an eighty-page typed memorandum which Junkers had circulated among Reichstag members during the summer in an effort to get support for the firm's demands for payments it claimed were due from the Ministry of Defense. Junkers blamed its poor financial condition on the contract made with the Ministry early in 1922.

The memorandum was a desperate move by Junkers to recover its financial equilibrium. Attempts to force the Reichswehr's Special Group R to grant additional funds had failed. During autumn 1925, Junkers had demanded that the matter be settled by a court of arbitration (*Schiedsgericht*). The Defense Ministry had refused to go to court, but had granted an extra seventeen million reichsmarks in October. As security for the new grant, Junkers had had to turn over 80 percent of his stocks to the German government, which had appointed a supervisor to the firm's board of directors. Professor Junkers had been even more upset than he had been before. In December, 1925, the Ministry of Defense had asked the President of the Reichsgericht, Simons, to investigate the matter. The Ministry wanted Simons to ascertain whether the Junkers firm had fulfilled its obligations under the original contract and whether it had used all the funds for the purposes for which the firm had received them. The Ministry also wanted Simons to determine whether it was "morally obligated to Junkers."[15]

Simons had reported the results of his investigation to Stresemann on April 23, 1926, the day before the Treaty of Berlin was signed. In his evaluation, the Judge agreed that Junkers was near bankruptcy primarily because of his involvement in the Russian venture. Because of this, the Cabinet should see to it that further financial assistance was given to Junkers. If the firm collapsed, details of the military collaboration could easily become public and have the widest political repercussions. The Ministry of Defense had agreed that Junkers' financial condition was quite hopeless; in fact, the seventeen million reichsmarks granted in October of 1925 had already been spent. Publicity would be detrimental to Germany, but the Ministry would delay any steps in the matter until Simons' report had been received.[16]

The attitude of the Ministry of Defense was shared by the Director for Aviation in the Reich's Ministry for Transport, Brandenburg, who had earned the *Pour le mérite* as the commander of a bomber squadron during the war. He had been placed in the Ministry for Transport through Seeckt's influence. Brandenburg conducted his department in close cooperation with the leading air force officers in the Ministry of Defense. He saw to it that funds were channeled into civilian aviation, again permitted for Germany although within strict limits, so that the maximum military benefits could be derived. He was one of the key figures in the overt and covert reconstruction of German military aviation. It is small wonder that Brandenburg was convinced that Junkers' financial condition was due to mismanagement and attempts to expand the firm into a world concern, and not to the Russian venture. On May 3, representatives of the ministries concerned in the Junkers matter had met to discuss the fate of the firm. It was discovered that another grant of 13 million reichsmarks would be necessary in 1926 to allow the concern to continue its operations. All those present at the meeting agreed that a gradual curtailment of production should take place. During this period, 4 million reichsmarks owed to Junkers by Russia and 1.38 million due from Turkey should be collected. Major Fischer, for the Ministry of Defense, insisted that fifteen large planes (*Grossflugzeuge*) already paid for by Russia be delivered to that country. He also advised that the Junkers factory at Fili be transferred to the Soviet government, but that it should be staffed by German experts. The Russians would not be too unhappy about the situation, because they felt that Junkers had overcharged them and also that the firm had bribed Red officers. At subsequent meetings, it had been decided to send the former Reich Finance Minister, von Schlieben, to Moscow to negotiate the planned transfer of the Fili plant. Schlieben accepted the mission and arrived in Moscow on June 10.[17]

In the meantime, Junkers had decided to inform the German press that the firm's financial difficulties were due to contracts made with the Reich exchequer (*Fiskus*). This little bit of political blackmail had infuriated General von Seeckt. He had recommended to Chancellor Luther to let Junkers use the regular courts to settle his demands. The Ministry of Defense saw no danger in this procedure, because the German public already knew that Junkers was involved with the government. A regular trial could make a definite decision on the point of law involved and could be held *in camera*. The last would prevent the revelation of anything secret.[18]

The only definite thing in the Junkers situation was that those involved completely disagreed on the reasons for the firm's bankruptcy. Simons was sure that the starting point of the financial troubles was the "Russian adventure" in which Prof. Junkers was involved by the Ministry of Defense, especially through promises made by Major (ret.) von Niedermayer. Simons also doubted that it had been legal for the Reich to take 80 percent of the firm's stock in exchange for the seventeen million reichsmarks grant made in October, 1925. These arguments, as well as political considerations, had prompted the Cabinet to decide that a new credit should be given, if the Reichstag agreed, but that production be curtailed. Schlieben had returned from Moscow, where he had spent about ten days, and reported that the Russians were willing to enter into discussions about the changes in the concession to Junkers. They had agreed to extend the delivery dates for the big planes, whose price had been reduced. They had also urged a quiet settlement of the Scholl affair.[19] It was at this juncture that someone at Junkers decided to lobby for the additional funds, and thus the memorandum had been sent to members of the Reichstag.

The revelations of the *Manchester Guardian* were publicized by the Socialist press. On December 5, a Sunday, the *Vorwärts* reprinted the *Manchester Guardian* article under the heading "Soviet Shells for Reichswehr Artillery." The official paper of the SPD used the opportunity to point out that Soviet Russia armed the counter-revolution and then incited "German workers against machine guns loaded with Russian ammunition." The new revelations about Reichswehr intrigues would become part of negotiations already underway between the SPD Reichstag deputies and the Government regarding military excesses. The English press did not follow up the *Manchester Guardian* article, but since the *Vorwärts* article held the possibility of creating a problem with the USSR, the leaders of the SPD were urged by the Reich Chancellery to stop further attacks in their party press. The rest of the German press was informed by the Wilhelmstrasse that pursuit of the topic would jeopardize Germany's position at the meeting of Foreign Ministers then in progress at Geneva.[20]

Stresemann telegraphed from Geneva during the evening of December 5 that he expected with some certainty that the other foreign ministers would ask him about the *Manchester Guardian* article. It would be impossible to say that the report had no basis in fact or that he knew nothing about the matter. That was especially so because the *Vorwärts* was already on the newsstands. He would say first of all, and with all due emphasis, that no secret deals had been made with the Soviet government. The matters reported by the *Manchester Guardian* had to do with German participation in Russian industrial development. Unfortunately, this was "used by certain departments of the Reichswehr to provide themselves with the opportunity to alter the lack of ammunition and other defensive material for certain critical situations" during the first years after the end of the war. This was primarily done because of their concern about the fate of East Prussia. One really had to sympathize with the military, because there had been quite definite signs that Poland wanted to annex that part of Germany. To this were added the fears evoked by the Ruhr occupation in 1923. But even during "that catastrophic time," the attempts of the military had not been very extensive.

> As soon as the authoritative departments of the Reich government had found out about the facts, they immediately saw the peril in the situation. All that was necessary to reduce this relation of one department with Russia was immediately ordered; a complete break in a short time had been impossible in practice, especially since this would have been taken by the Soviet government as an unnecessary affront. We, therefore, had consciously arranged our attitude in such a way that all these matters would disappear gradually. This had already been carried out to the widest extent, so that no actual military or political importance of any kind could be attributed to the whole matter.[21]

Chicherin and Krestinsky met with Chancellor Marx on December 6 to discuss the extension of the due date for the 300 million credit and the granting of a new loan. Krestinsky brought the conversation to the *Manchester Guardian* article and the reprint in the Sunday (December 5) issue of *Vorwärts*. Both Russians indicated that this was very embarrassing to the Soviet Union. Chicherin wanted to know how much there was to the allegation that the Entente had definite knowledge of the "military agreements between Germany and Russia." The Chancellor was not sure how much, if anything, had been discovered by the International Military Control Commission. He was definitely sure that the German government had never informed the Entente. The government intended to issue a communiqué on this very day which would pass over the *Vorwärts* article in as harmless-appearing a fashion as possible.[22]

Chicherin was not the only one concerned about the repercussions of the *Manchester Guardian* article on the future of the Reichswehr-Red army collaboration. General Heye inquired at the Wilhelmstrasse whether it was all right for him to receive Chicherin. The General was worried that a change of policy had been decided upon in regard to the clandestine relationship with Moscow. The Foreign Office informed him that no change had been made in "the agreement between Stresemann and [himself] regarding direct negotiations with Russian departments." The General could go ahead and meet Chicherin, but in as covert a manner as was possible. Heye and Chicherin met on December 8 to discuss Heye's attitude on matters of military cooperation.[23]

The communiqué that Chancellor Marx had mentioned was based on Stresemann's recommendation and stressed that "no secret military agreements of any kind had been made." The material contained in the *Manchester Guardian* article had been familiar to political circles because of the polemic Junkers had distributed and also from earlier articles which had appeared in the French press during June about German munitions ships caught in the ice of the Bay of Finland. This news concerned a number of ships owned by Derutra (German-Russian Trade Company) which had been caught in the ice of the Bay of Finland. The French articles had given the Wilhelmstrasse quite a few bad moments. According to the reports, the ships, consigned to Russian ports, were loaded with war materiel from Germany. Protests from the English and French governments necessitated a series of high-level discussions during which the German Foreign Office proved that the freight did not include anything that Germany was prohibited from manufacturing by the Treaty of Versailles. The incident was settled by the middle of August, 1926.[24]

The situation was well in hand by December 16. The German press made no further mention of the *Manchester Guardian* article, except for the SPD, which tried to use it as a lever to remove Gessler. Fortunately, according to the Ministry of Defense, the SPD leadership knew definitely only about the Junkers venture, the gas factory, and the munitions transports from Leningrad to Stettin which had taken place during the summer of 1926. The party had presented these three points for clarification by Christmas. The Ministry of Defense planned to inform them that the Junkers involvement would soon be liquidated. The gas manufacture had failed, and Moscow demanded eight million reichsmarks, but would settle for five. The Ministry hoped that the Socialists would support a financial grant by the Reichstag to pay the Russians. After the Russians had been paid, the Ministry of Defense would also be rid of this involvement. The munitions shipment was to be explained as having been part of the materiel the Reichswehr had needed after the Ruhr invasion and was prevented from manufacturing by the International Military Control Commission in disregard of the Treaty of Versailles.

During the second half of August, Major Fischer had told Dirksen about the munitions shipments. Dirksen had requested that they be delayed because any leak would "amount to a catastrophe" and would jeopardize Germany's entry into the League. Once again the Foreign Office had given in to the military, when Fischer assured Dirksen that a delay was impossible and that the Ministry of Defense would take all responsibility.[25]

The SPD leadership did not wait for an answer to their questions. On December 16, Scheidemann made a long speech in the Reichstag. He denounced Russia for aiding the militarists. He revealed that munitions shipments had been made to Stettin and that several hundred war planes had been manufactured by Junkers in Russia. During his speech, there were shouts of "Traitor, blackguard, that's treason . . ." —and the extreme right walked out. Scheidemann demanded a vote of confidence, and Chancellor Marx's Cabinet was defeated by a crushing majority. The Foreign Office, the military, and the Moscow Embassy were upset about the Socialists' disregard for a relationship which had been created for the benefit of the whole nation. Conservatives and solid citizens chided the SPD for discussing military matters which were really beyond public discussion.[26]

Now that part of the military collaboration had become public knowledge, the Russians placed it in the context of their own reconstruction. *Pravda* could see no difference between foreigners' selling consumer goods and Germans' selling materials for Russia's defense. Radek admitted in *Izvestia* that Junkers had helped to strengthen Russia's defenses against foreign imperialists. This public bravado only imperfectly hid Moscow's concern. On the day after Scheidemann's speech, Krestinsky asked Schubert whether the revelations of the *Manchester Guardian* had caused any repercussions at Geneva. Schubert was pleased to tell him that not even an allusion to the matter had been made. The Undersecretary further informed the Soviet Ambassador that the Foreign Office would disregard Scheidemann's speech unless the French press took it up. In that event, an interview with the Chancellor, designed to quiet French fears, would be published in the German press. Krestinsky appeared obviously relieved, especially after he was given assurances that he would be consulted about any statement to the press.[27] The Wilhelmstrasse had good reasons to be pleased with the way the evasions of the Treaty of Versailles had been received by the European powers. On December 12, the final protocol abolishing the International Military Control Commission, effective January 31, 1927, had been signed. Any problems about Germany's rearmament were now placed under the supervision of the League of Nations, in which Germany held a permanent seat on the Security Council.

The campaign to minimize and annihilate the *Manchester Guardian* article had worked very well. The Washington, D.C., *Evening Star* best expressed the attitude of the foreign press. The whole matter was

> advanced by the Socialists . . . to precipitate the crisis culminating in the resignation of the Chancellor. Thus the alleged secret relations between Germany and Russia need cause no serious alarm in the world on the score of a determined purpose to precipitate another general conflict.[28]

The Foreign Office saw no need for the continuation of the Junkers effort in Russia. Discretion was no longer necessary, because of the publicity the Fili venture had received. On the basis of a Cabinet decision on December 18, Junkers was presented with an ultimatum. The firm would receive preferential stock worth 7 million reichsmarks; the German government would renounce all claims to the loans and advances totaling 26,450,000 reichsmarks and all interest on this amount. Junkers would have to forego further claims, pay 1 million reichsmarks, and turn over equipment worth 2.7 million reichsmarks and fifteen great planes (*Grossflugzeuge*). Needless to say, Junkers accepted.[29]

Only the SPD refused to let the military collaboration rest, and on January 9, 1927, *Die Welt am Montag* published an article by the Reichstag member Künstler (SPD) about an interview he had held with two German workers who had been employed in the Stolzenberg gas factory in Russia.[30]

Major Fischer told the Foreign Office that these continued attacks should be stopped, if necessary by force. The Ministry of Defense even thought of starting proceedings of high treason against the two workers who had given Künstler the information. The Ministry was less concerned about German and foreign public opinion—"because they cared little for these details"—than it was about the possibility that the Soviets might decide to discontinue the existing collaboration.

Fischer was told that the Foreign Office was making every effort to stop the press campaign. But the Soviet and German Communist papers were partly to blame, because they baited the SPD. Brockdorff-Rantzau was trying to stop the Soviets, and Fischer could aid the effort by speaking to the Russian military attaché. After all, the German press really controlled itself, except for such "sensationalist" papers as *Die Welt am Montag*.[31]

However, the Wilhelmstrasse decided that the time was opportune for the reorganization of the existing military collaboration. At a meeting on January 24, Brigadier General Wetzell, now Chief of the General Staff, Major Fischer, Schubert, and Dirksen discussed the situation. Schubert insisted that all the cards had to be put on the table. It was no longer possible for the Foreign Office to know as little as possible about military cooperation with Russia. From now on, they wanted to be informed of even the smallest details. Wetzell assured Schubert that their conference was to serve that very purpose. According to the General, there still existed the pilot training school at Lipetsk. It was financed by German funds, but every officer who attended it left the active service for the duration of the course. There was also a purely scientific experimental station for gases at Saratov, at which German experts acted as advisors, and an experimental station for tanks at Kazan. Finally, there was the exchange of General Staff officers and participation at each other's maneuvers. The last two were legal, Wetzell pointed out, while the other three did not exactly fall within the provisions of the Treaty of Versailles. The continued collaboration was absolutely essential because there was no opportunity in Germany to provide training in the use of war planes and tanks. These two weapons would play decisive parts in any future war. It was absolutely essential for the Reichswehr to have at least an acquaintance with them.

Schubert replied that he did not like the idea of dependence on Russian discretion. He emphasized that he was no judge of the military value of planes and tanks, but wondered whether "the military advantages outweighed the political risk which was involved in the continuation of the two schools."

Wetzell assured Schubert that the Russians had a keen interest in the two institutions, and their discretion had always been beyond reproach. If all military relations were discontinued, Moscow would turn to the West for military aid. In that event, political as well as economic advantages would also be lost to Germany. The independent organization set up to supervise the military collaboration, such as GEFU and its replacement, Wirtschaftskontor (WIKO) had been liquidated. The military collaboration which remained, Wetzell emphasized, was vital for Germany. Schubert made no commitment. He stated that he would have to consult Stresemann to decide whether the German negotiations for the evacuation of the Rhineland and the restitution of full sovereignty could bear the risks involved in the continuation of military collaboration.

In December, 1925, when the decision was made to replace GEFU by a new organization because it had aroused the suspicions of the French and the British, the Wilhelmstrasse had insisted on a continuation of the military collaboration because it feared that the Russians would turn to France for military aircraft. This would have meant the loss of information about "a most important military weapon" to Germany.

During a discussion with General Heye, Stresemann agreed to the continuation of the two training schools, but stipulated that "no officers on active service could be sent in any form to attend the courses" during 1927. The incident was now absolutely finished. There was no danger that Russo-German military collaboration would be discussed in the Reichstag.[32]

The German army withdrew from the Junkers negotiations with Moscow and left it to Brockdorff-Rantzau to satisfy Russian demands on the firm. The Soviets accepted the discontinuation of the Stolzenberg contract for the production of poison gas in Russia. Colonel von der Lieth-Thomsen, the representative of the Ministry of Defense in Moscow, started the negotiations for the liquidation of the undertaking at the end of January, 1927.[33]

A few days later, the wisdom of continuing the schools was challenged by the defection of a Red pilot. The *Kurjer Warszawski* published an interview with a Commander Klim, in which he talked in great detail about Lipetsk, the length of the course, the German officers who attended in mufti and under aliases, and the kinds of planes used. On February 14, the Paris Embassy forwarded the French translation of the interview, which had been distributed by the French news agency, Havas. Wallroth sent it to Dirksen with the marginal comment: "Best would be a declaration by Klim that the Polish press made up these remarks."

The Russians as well as the Reichswehr wanted to keep the escape of Klim as quiet as possible. Bratman-Brodovsky urged Schubert, on February 18, to prevent Gessler from discussing the case in the Reichstag's Foreign Affairs Committee, or admitting any of the continuing military collaboration. When Schubert said that the details discussed by Scheidemann could not easily be denied, Bratman-Brodovsky aggressively told him that the Soviet Union would think twice in the future before trusting Germans with military secrets.[34]

In Moscow, during the evening of the same day, Litvinov, in a state of great excitement, asked Brockdorff-Rantzau whether it was true that Germany was going to make a public admission of the military collaboration. "He begged . . . the Ambassador to inform [his] government that he [Litvinov] was extremely concerned." The Count warned the Wilhelmstrasse that any admission would definitely give the coup de grâce to German-Russian relations. Because of the importance of the situation, he wanted the Chancellor, and if necessary the President, to be informed of the dangers if the collaboration received further publicity. Brockdorff-Rantzau wanted the military collaboration to continue because he still considered it of the greatest importance to German-Russian relations. He invited Lunev, who was the Soviet Union's military attaché at its Berlin Embassy and who was in Moscow at the time, to lunch and impressed this fact upon him.

Schubert informed Brockdorff-Rantzau that the government had no intention of publicizing the matter. However, it could not be completely denied before the Foreign Affairs Committee of the Reichstag. If a leak occurred, it would come from Communist members, and then only the Soviet Embassy would find out about it. The Ambassador telegraphed that it would be "highly desirable if the explanation on the part of the government could be avoided." An official admission, even to the smallest number of people would have an adverse effect in Moscow.

Despite Brockdorff-Rantzau's warning, Gessler spoke to the Foreign Affairs Committee on February 23. He admitted that clandestine relations had existed during 1922–1923. The Minister of Defense appealed to the patriotic sense of the Committee by pointing out that this had been necessary for the defense of Germany. The Entente had not even allowed the production of the permitted quota of ammunition. Because of this chicanery, the German war and aviation industry looked for places to work and escape destruction. Dornier went to Italy, Fokker to Holland, and Junkers to Russia. The Reich government subsidized these efforts because the situation demanded it. After the emergency passed, no further grants were made, and the original funds had been completely used. Gessler assured the members of the Committee that

238 COMMUNITY OF FATE

"establishments or agreements contrary to the Treaty of Versailles no longer exist." He requested that his remarks be kept absolutely secret in loyalty to the USSR. Schubert saw Bratman-Brodovsky right after the session and acquainted him with the Defense Minister's statement. He asked the Russian chargé d'affaires to see to it that further Communist propaganda cease.[35]

At this juncture, it would have been possible to eliminate the whole clandestine relationship with Russia, despite military necessity. During the very final stages of the negotiations for the Treaty of Berlin, the Soviet Deputy Commissar for War, I. S. Unshlikt, had come to Berlin to negotiate an extensive financial grant. Generals Seeckt and Wetzell had agreed to this in exchange for training facilities in the USSR. During a meeting with Unshlikt on March 30, 1926, Stresemann and Chancellor Luther had refused to become involved in any new deals. After the *Manchester Guardian* revelations, Stresemann had not demanded a termination of the remaining collaboration; he had only insisted that great caution be used.

On February 26, a special meeting called by Chancellor Marx took place in the Chancellery with all ministers, their undersecretaries, General Heye, Admiral Zenker, the new Chief of the Navy High Command, and the press secretary present. A draft protocol drawn up by Dirksen and Fischer was to be the basis of a discussion about the German-Soviet military collaboration. But the Russian involvement did not come up. Schubert made a date with Heye to discuss the protocol at a later date.[36]

Heye informed the gathered ministers on the twenty-sixth that secret preparations in the East had been transferred from the voluntary defense organizations (*Wehrverbände*) to the Reichswehr. Most of the illegal weapons were now under army control. They amounted to about 350,000 rifles, 12,000 light and heavy machine guns, 400 mine throwers, 600 light and 75 heavy guns, and ammunition sufficient for one day of battle. The amount of ammunition would increase with stepped-up German production. In addition, there were secret depots of moving stock (*Fahrzeuge*) and stores of clothing. All of this was insufficient, and the Cabinet had to make a decision about rearming. Germany had neither heavy artillery, pilots, tanks, nor gas weapons. If the Cabinet agreed to end this condition, then laws would have to be applied to prevent the kind of treason "which has been possible up to now."

The chief of the navy agreed with Heye's presentation. The navy, too, lacked critical equipment, such as planes and submarines. Fortunately for future contingencies, the navy had an excellent arrangement with the Spanish government which allowed German naval officers to observe and study new developments in Spain's submarine fleet. The Reich Ministry for Traffic (Verkehrsministerium) had made money available for the development of big seaplanes by the civilian Lufthansa. Schubert voiced his concern about these preparations, pointing out that foreign states had a very effective espionage system. A discovery of the clandestine military preparations could have the most serious consequences for Germany's newly developed good relations with the West. The ministers heeded Schubert's concern and did not take immediate action on the request which had been made by the military leaders.[37]

On May 18, at a meeting in the Wilhelmstrasse at which Stresemann, Gessler, Heye, Colonel Werner von Blomberg, Schubert, and Gerhard Köpke, Director of Department II (western, southern, and southeastern Europe), were present, General Heye presented the protocol originally prepared for the Cabinet meeting of February 26. All those present agreed that it should not be formally signed, but referred to as "notes of a talk by the above-mentioned gentlemen."

The protocol described the status of the military collaboration with the Red army. The war industries which had been developed in Russia on the basis of agreements made in 1922 and 1923, that is, Junkers, Bersol (poison gas), and the manufacture of ammunitions, had been liquidated or were in the process of liquidation; no members of the Reichswehr would participate in the flying and tank courses or the poison gas experiment during the summer. The question of such participation would be reopened in the fall. The continuing participation at each other's maneuvers and travel for training purposes could continue, since this was not illegal. However, in each case the Ministry of Defense would consult with the Foreign Ministry. The close cooperation between Brockdorff-Rantzau and the representative of the Ministry of Defense in Moscow, von der Lieth-Thomsen, was to continue.

Heye announced that Litvinov had requested the Reichswehr to procure the agreement of the German Foreign Office for the conversion of the tank training school at Kazan into a legal company with limited liability. Stresemann had no objection to the establishment of the school, but he wanted to talk to Brockdorff-Rantzau, who was in Berlin, to see whether the Ambassador would agree to make an affirmative statement in Moscow.

General Heye then told the group that the Reichswehr intended to carry out experiments at Orenburg to discover effective means of protection against gas attacks. Stresemann voiced his concern that the Russians could one day become enemies, and, in any event, they were receiving too much information for the *quid pro quos* they offered. It would be in the interest of Germany if the experiments were carried on in secret at the Reichswehr troop training area at Grafenwörth. Brockdorff-Rantzau would be instructed to inform the Russians that financial difficulties prevented the pursuit of the experiments in the USSR. Stresemann agreed to Heye's request that the German and Russian officers should be allowed to attend each other's maneuvers in uniform. When the General inquired whether officers could again go to Russia for language study, Stresemann also agreed.[38]

Brockdorff-Rantzau insisted that the military inform the Russians about the decision to conduct the gas experiments in Germany. He made an official statement, endorsing the Kazan "experimental station," to Chicherin on August 15 only after a number of sessions with Schubert and Deputy Commissar for War Unshlikt, who had again come to Berlin in July. Unshlikt tried to get an immediate increase in German military collaboration, which Heye reluctantly refused, claiming financial difficulties. Because of the Scheidemann speech, the Commissariat of War had been ordered to clear all military relations with the Reichswehr through the Narkomindel and insisted that the German Foreign Office become equally involved.[39]

The Wilhelmstrasse became completely involved in the military collaboration and was informed about the activities of the Reichswehr in Russia in detail. The legalization of the military collaboration converted the Zentrale Moskau into the even more innocuous sounding "Home for German Employees" under the direction of Major (ret.) von Niedermayer. Upon the insistence of the Reichswehr, the Foreign Office agreed that the gas experiments could be carried on in Russia at Volsk (Tomka); the flying school at Lipetsk, also converted into a legal experimental station, received a yearly complement of about forty trainees. Red army officers were regularly detached to the Reichswehr and received training in the General Staff college. Contact between high-ranking officers of each army increased and continued on the friendliest personal basis, even during periods of difficulties on the diplomatic level.[40]

The *Manchester Guardian* revelations and the subsequent publicity had served to remove the deadwood, the unprofitable relationship with Junkers, the almost defunct Stolzenberg gas factory, and the munitions shipments, which had been of some consequence during 1923, when German factories could not supply anticipated needs. The Wilhelmstrasse had succeeded in achieving efficient cooperation with the Bendlerstrasse, and the clandestine relationship could continue, better organized. Both ministries could congratulate themselves on the way in which the matter had been resolved.

The Russians had not used the opportunity to blackmail Germany into some major political concession, as Brockdorff-Rantzau and Schubert had feared. Neither had the Western powers, attempting to revise Versailles and aid Germany in every possible way to regain her status as a Great Power, taken the revelations too seriously. Because people wanted to believe that the Weimar Republic had made the leading Germans democratic and peace-loving Europeans, the revelations of the drastic evasions of the Treaty of Versailles were relegated to the same dust-heap where rumors about such a military resurgence had been pushed ever since Rapallo. German prestige emerged unscathed. The most essential part of the military collaboration, in view of future developments, continued unabated. The existence of the schools for the training of experts in tank and air warfare was discounted as part of the rumors circulated by those who wished Germany ill. For instance, when the wife of a German colonel told the spouse of the *Manchester Guardian* correspondent in Berlin that the colonel had been in charge of a flying school in Russia since 1923, and went into the most intimate details about the school, it was not used by the correspondent.[41] On June 29, an interpellation in the House of Commons regarding "the import by Germany from Soviet Russia of poison gas bombs" was directed to the Secretary of State for Foreign Affairs (Locker-Lampson). He informed the House, "I am given to understand that the import into Germany, in contravention of Article 170 of the Treaty of Versailles, of arms and ammunition from Russia, had now ceased and all transactions in connection with such imports have been liquidated." If infractions of the Treaty of Versailles would be discovered in the future, the Council of the League of Nations would be notified. In any event, "these transactions took place between subordinate departments of each of the Governments. These were not official transactions between Governments. The German Government has made it quite clear that they disapproved of these transactions and they have stopped them."[42]

There was no intent on the part of the British government to antagonize the German government at a time when an extremely tense situation between Great Britain and the USSR existed, created by the hostile anti-British propaganda issuing from the USSR. Great Britain, desirous of creating a strong front against Moscow, had no intention of pushing Germany into the waiting arms of the Soviet Union. Stresemann's policy continued to bear fruit: Germany could balance between the East and the West, deriving political, economic, and military benefits from this position.

VIII

The End of an Era

While the German Foreign Office was still occupied with streamlining German-Russian military collaboration, another problem arose, which developed from the increasing deterioration of Moscow's relations with London. Comintern propaganda against England had reached such a pitch that Austen Chamberlain, in a note on February 23, 1927, threatened the possibility of a break in diplomatic relations. Even before the English note to Russia, the Wilhelmstrasse had attempted to prevent a worsening of the situation. Brockdorff-Rantzau had been instructed to sound out Litvinov on the possibility of German aid in bringing about a conciliation. Litvinov had not been too interested, but the Russians had asked Germany to issue a *dementi* declaring that the British had never asked them to join in any actions against the Soviet Union.[1]

Brockdorff-Rantzau supported the Russian demand. He advised Berlin to make it unequivocally clear to the British that Germany would fulfill its obligations under the Treaty of Berlin. He was convinced that the Soviet government wanted to avoid an open break. The Ambasssador saw no reason why the Reich had to make a choice between the protagonists. However, any declaration against Russia would mean the end of all support in the East. The Bolsheviks were not actively preparing for world revolution, because the Soviet Union needed peace. The final aim had not been abandoned, but the means to reach it had been changed. The government wanted to consolidate internally. In evaluating the reasons for the propaganda against England, Brockdorff-Rantzau drew attention to the fact that Soviet foreign policy was not made by the Narkomindel.

Three factors determine Russian domestic and foreign policy: these are, as is well known, the Comintern, the party, and the Foreign Commissariat. The most important is the party. The decisions of the Foreign Commissariat depend on it.[2]

242

Despite Brockdorff-Rantzau's support for the Russian demand for a German *démarche,* the Foreign Office had no intention of taking the side of Moscow openly. Even before Brockdorff-Rantzau's advice, Chamberlain had been informed of Germany's position should it come to an open Anglo-Russian conflict. Dirksen felt that it was most important to prevent the latter, because German neutrality would become academic the moment that warlike measures were taken by either side.[3]

Since Germany could ill afford to support the Russians openly, the Wilhelmstrasse continued to offer its good offices for mediation. Moscow showed little interest, but demanded absolute certainty that Germany was not going to support the British. When, on March 7, the French journal *Excelsior* published an interview with Schubert, the Russians immediately seized upon it to renew their pressure for a *dementi.* The Undersecretary was cited as having said that Germany would not prevent armies from passing across her territory to aid Poland or Czechoslovakia.[4]

Schubert had indeed given the interview on March 6, but had been misquoted. In order to rectify the mistakes, a *dementi* was issued through the French news agency Havas on March 10. Berlin hoped that this would put the matter to rest. The Russians refused to let the opportunity pass. *Izvestia* referred to the article under the headline: "Undersecretary Schubert Reveals the Secret Background of Locarno." According to *Izvestia,* the interview proved that an anti-Soviet deal had in fact been made in 1925.

Before the foreign press corps at Geneva, Stresemann characterized *Izvestia*'s allegation that England had offered Danzig, parts of Upper Silesia, and the Corridor in return for a German break with Russia as "wild inventions and stinking lies [*erstunken und erlogen*]." He expressed his surprise that the official organ of the Soviet government dared to place such nonsense before its readers. Germany was deeply interested in Russia's economic development and her good relations with other countries. Certainly the world's economy would not easily recover if 150 million people remained at a low standard of living and thus presented no market.

Izvestia could not understand why its factual reporting should be called "wild inventions," especially since no official denials of Schubert's interview had yet been made. *Pravda* wrote that Schubert could not have chosen a less suitable time for his confessions. Russia now had "irrefutable proof" that Germany had been drawn into the English camp at Locarno, at which time she "had to undertake obligations which were now harmful."

The Wilhelmstrasse instructed Brockdorff-Rantzau to inform the Soviet government that Schubert had never made the statement about transit. The Ambassador was to request a cessation of the Russian press campaign. Brockdorff-Rantzau followed his instructions and demanded of Litvinov that no further lies be attributed to Schubert. The Deputy Commisssar informed the Ambassador that he was less concerned about Schubert's remarks than about knowing whether "Germany actually declared its willingness at Locarno to let French troops pass through if necessary."

Krestinsky confronted Stresemann with the *Excelsior* interview on March 16 and asked for an official explanation. Stresemann blew up and energetically told him that he "would not stand for Mr. Litvinov expressing doubts about the German Foreign Minister's veracity [*Wahrheitsliebe*]." Litvinov had been given every detail regarding passage during the negotiations for the Treaty of Berlin. No new official explanation would be made; the attitude of Litvinov might make further diplomatic talks impossible.

Stresemann also sent a telegram to Brockdorff-Rantzau, the tone of which was set by the first sentence: "The obligations which we assumed at Locarno are very well known to your Excellency as well as to the Soviet government." The telegram continued that the *Excelsior* article had received little circulation in Germany and none in France. Therefore, no reason for a *dementi* existed. He had already told Krestinsky off, and Brockdorff-Rantzau should kindly do the same with Litvinov.

The Ambassador, who considered the telegram an impertinence on the Minister's part, replied that he was well aware of the obligations assumed at Locarno. He was equally sure that he had expressed his doubts about the interpretation the Western powers would make of Article 16 in an emergency. In any event, the invented interview had deeply disturbed the entire Soviet government. Litvinov had not intended to cast doubts on the German Foreign Minister's veracity. The Deputy Commissar had asked whether the Soviet government could publish a communiqué stating that it had been informed by Berlin that the Schubert interview was not true and that no agreements regarding troop transit existed.

Instead of accepting the Russian request, the Foreign Office took two steps to end the matter. Wolffs Telegraph Bureau (WTB) published a notice that the remarks attributed to Schubert in the *Excelsior* interview were pure fiction, that Germany would never participate in any combination against the USSR. The news agency Tass transmitted the WTB notice to the Russian press. Stresemann re-emphasized the statements made in the WTB communiqué during his budget speech to the Reichstag on March 22. Schubert instructed Brockdorff-Rantzau to show Stresemann's speech to Litvinov and express the hope that this would suffice to prove Germany's loyalty.

After Stresemann's speech, the Foreign Office considered the matter closed. It interpreted Krestinsky's silence about the *Excelsior* interview, during a visit to Schubert on March 26, as proof that the Russians were satisfied with the way in which the case had been resolved. However, the Russians continued to castigate the German government in *Izvestia*. On March 26, the newspaper hinted rather strongly that Stresemann could not issue a direct denial about troop transit because there was some truth in the allegation that such an agreement existed.

Brockdorff-Rantzau reported home that he had strenuously objected to this continuing press campaign. Litvinov had indicated that this would be stopped if he were allowed to insert a notice that no rights of passage had been granted by Germany. The Ambassador informed the Foreign Office that he had rejected this demand. However, Litvinov was under party pressure and intended no blackmail.

Once again Brockdorff-Rantzau was on the Russian side. He suspected that a deal had been made at Locarno. This suspicion was strengthened by the fact that the right of France to march through Germany had not been denied by the Wilhelmstrasse. The Count refused to accept the assurances that Schubert had never made the remarks attributed to him. Here the Count's dislike of Schubert, aggravated during his latest stay in Berlin, took the upper hand. Brockdorff-Rantzau apparently saw in the *Excelsior* interview a chance to embarrass Schubert, to get even with him for the insult he imagined the Undersecretary had administered to him.

Stresemann wrote personally to Brockdorff-Rantzau, on April 6, that he did not find Litvinov's attitude any more understandable because of party pressure. All Litvinov had to do was to publish the budget speech. Krestinsky had never presented any Russian proposals. If Litvinov insisted on issuing a statement, he could do so, provided that it included the definite statement that Schubert never gave the interview attributed to him by the *Excelsior*.

Brockdorff-Rantzau transmitted Stresemann's tentative agreement for a Russian press notice to Litvinov on April 9. The Ambassador pointed out, as he had been instructed to do, that the Russian demand might lead to further complications. Litvinov was not disturbed by the possibility of trouble. He told the Ambassador that Krestinsky would be taken to account for not having presented the Russian proposals to Stresemann.

The storm aroused by the *Excelsior* interview was finally calmed by Russian concessions. Krestinsky was instructed on April 12 to tell Stresemann that a new press notice was unnecessary. Rykov would allude to the matter in a forthcoming speech. Krestinsky was also to tell the Foreign Minister that he had been instructed to request a *dementi* on March 21, but had decided to refrain from making the request because Stresemann's budget speech seemed to make a Russian press notice unnecessary. Brockdorff-Rantzau privately continued to blame Schubert and Krestinsky for having caused the entire "political chagrin." Krestinsky justified his actions during a two-hour discussion, after which he left Brockdorff-Rantzau, their friendly relationship restored.

Rykov told the Fourth Congress of Soviets of the USSR on April 19 that it had assembled "in an extremely tense and alarming international atmosphere." Many of the recent events were similar to those which had "more than once occurred on the eve of armed conflict." However, relations with Germany had been most amiable during the past five years. In regard to recent rumors, Stresemann had made the most explicit official declaration to the Soviet government that Germany had not assumed any obligation to let foreign troops pass across her territory.[5]

Brockdorff-Rantzau decided that the situation was calm enough to leave Moscow for his regular furlough. He arrived in Berlin on May 13, and remained in Germany until August 7. On the day of his arrival, the London police forcibly entered the quarters of Arcos (All-Russian Cooperative Society) and the Russian Trade Delegation in the British capital. According to the German Ambassador to the Court of St. James, this action had been taken on the basis of a "decision by the most important Cabinet members" made the previous morning. Sthamer was sure that the English government had no delusion about the seriousness of this action. They thought that it was justified because they had suspected for several months that elements in English ministries were delivering secrets to the Russians. The raid by the Chinese on the Soviet Embassy in Peking on April 16 had turned up evidence which supported these suspicions.

Pravda announced that the Arcos raid was an English provocation which proved that the British were preparing for war against the Soviet Union. *Izvestia's* lead article followed the *Pravda* one, as did that of *Ekonomisheskaya Shisn*, which added that British attempts to isolate Russia were absurd and doomed to failure.[6]

The Germans found themselves in the enviable position of being courted by two suitors. The British, through Undersecretary Gregory, made it clear that they were interested in German support. Gregory told Counselor of Embassy Dieckhoff on May 25 that the English were "endeavoring to rid ourselves of one of the obstacles to peace, this Asiatic menace to Locarno. . . ."[7]

On May 26, the "House of Commons approved . . . with 375 to 111 votes [the] government decision regarding the break of relations with Soviet Russia." The German government, in response to a Soviet request, assumed the protection of Russian interests in England on May 27. The Wilhelmstrasse made it patently clear that this was done because of international usage and had no other "political significance."

The German diplomatic missions abroad were informed that the break was the result of a "policy long pursued by the diehards and their continually increasing influence in the English Cabinet." There seemed to be no likelihood that the break would lead to war. The German public and the press had taken the news calmly. The German government would maintain the strictest neutrality. In this crisis, Locarno and the Treaty of Berlin remained the cornerstones of German foreign policy. "We will be pulled neither into a compromising intimacy by Moscow nor into an anti-Soviet combination of any kind whatsoever."[8]

On the day after the break of diplomatic relations, the Wilhelmstrasse contacted Brockdorff-Rantzau by telephone at his estate in Schleswig. The Ambassador advised the caller that Germany should place less emphasis on neutrality, lest it give Poland the idea that she had a free hand in the East, and more emphasis on the Treaty of Berlin.[9]

The break of diplomatic relations by the English was utilized by Moscow to deepen the war scare, which was designed to divert the attention of the Russian people from the internal problems created by Stalin's program of industrialization. Dirksen, in evaluating the Russian propaganda, thought it conceivable that it was born out of the Russian fear that Britain would actually attack them. Germany's position in this East-West struggle was becoming ever more precarious, and Dirksen advised consultation with Paris and London.[10]

Litvinov told the German chargé d'affaires in Moscow that England's real aim was the launching of a great war against the Soviet Union. This could take years and might be changed by the next election. In the meantime, England would attempt to get others to enter her camp.

A few days later, Klementi Voroshilov, the Commissar for War, told a workers' rally that war with the imperialists was unavoidable. "We do not know the day war will break out but we must be prepared at any moment." Krestinsky informed Dirksen on June 2 that there were definite signs that Poland was preparing an attack on the USSR.[11]

Chicherin, who had been in Paris, discussed the Russo-British crisis with Stresemann on June 7 in Berlin. The German Foreign Minister had to inform his visitor that the Russian Ambassador to Warsaw, Peter Voikov, had been assassinated that very day. Chicherin received a telephone call and told Stresemann, with evident relief, that the assassin had been arrested and that Premier Pilsudski and the Polish Foreign Minister had expressed their official regrets at the Soviet Embassy.

The discussion returned to the conflict with England. Chicherin did not think that the English Conservatives would start a war. The real danger lay in Pilsudski's dream of uniting Byelorussia, the Ukraine, and Lithuania with Poland into a federated system. Pilsudski could provoke a border incident which would suffice to make Russia the aggressor. Thus the French would be forced to march, and the question of passage would confront Germany.

Stresemann wanted to know whether the Commissar's pessimism stemmed from his talks with Poincaré and Briand. Chicherin replied that both had assured him that no change in French relations with Russia was contemplated. He personally felt that Paris would use the situation to force Russia to pay the Tsarist debts.

Stresemann rejected the idea that Poland had aggressive intentions or that France would fight her battles. He reiterated that Germany would not participate in anti-Soviet actions. Once again, as so often before, Stresemann complained about Comintern propaganda against Germany. Chicherin agreed that his job was handicapped by the Comintern but that he could not do a thing about it. The Comintern was an independent organization. The official communiqué about the Stresemann-Chicherin talk stressed the fact that the severance of Russo-British relations only strenghened Germany's determination to remain absolutely neutral.[12]

Stresemann, who had gone to Geneva, discussed the Anglo-Russian break with Briand. The French Foreign Minister did not think that the USSR would pay the Tsarist debts. He considered the English action a bad mistake which was mitigated only by the madness of the mass executions and deportations sweeping Russia in the wake of the Voikov assassination. But France would not be driven into a war against the Soviet Union.[13]

At the June 15 session of the League of Nations, Stresemann was asked to use his influence with the Russians to prevent a disaster over Voikov's murder. The representatives expressed their disbelief in

Chicherin's assertion that Poland's attitude would lead to war. In the response to the League request, Stresemann instructed the Foreign Office that either Köpke or Brockdorff-Rantzau talk to Chicherin to prevent the Russo-Polish relations from deteriorating completely. Chicherin was to be told that a Soviet ultimatum to Poland would arouse world opinion against the USSR. Because of the continuing mass executions it was already extremely difficult for statesmen friendly to the Soviet Union to overcome public revulsion.

A week later Stresemann told the Reichstag that no change in German foreign policy was contemplated. It would continue to be based on Locarno, League membership, and the Treaty of Berlin. Germany's leitmotiv remained noninterference in the domestic affairs of other countries, and she expected that other states would not interfere in the domestic problems of Germany.[14]

The last remark was a direct hit at the Comintern, but *Izvestia* gleefully advised its readers that the speech had disappointed the "opponents of the Soviet Union inside and outside Germany" who had hoped that the Comintern would disturb good relations between the two countries.[15]

While the Germans were trying to follow a middle course in the Anglo-Russian conflict, they continued their efforts to bring about mediation. They urged the Russians to take advantage of the conciliatory attitude shown by the British, who continued trade and even publicized new orders received from the Soviet Union, by offering to discuss the settlement of the Tsarist debts and the cessation of anti-English propaganda.[16]

Brockdorff-Rantzau returned to Moscow early on August 7. His furlough had not been shortened, because the Foreign Office did not want to contribute to the already serious situation. Chicherin greeted him with a greater show of heartiness than ever before. During the course of several conversations with the Foreign Commissar, the Ambassador tried to sound Chicherin on the possibility of German mediation in the Anglo-Soviet conflict. The Commissar emphasized that he had no intention "of calling for the mediation of a third power."[17]

The Russians were not interested in mediation, because it was still domestically advantageous for them to keep the artificial war scare alive. Stalin, in *Izvestia* for July 28, had announced that English plans to provoke a war, including the assassination of Voikov, had thus far failed. Despite these setbacks, the threat of a new war continued.[18] In addition, Moscow pressed its campaign to force Germany into the Russian camp. *Pravda*, in a lead article on August 23, warned that the forthcoming League session would reveal where Germany stood.

Chicherin, in a letter to Brockdorff-Rantzau a week later, wrote that the possible admission of Finland to the Council of the League looked like an appeal for war against the USSR.

Brockdorff-Rantzau agreed that Finland's admission to the Council should be prevented because it possibly "could discharge the explosive material in the atmosphere." In his report home, the Ambassador reported that the danger of war was considered imminent "even among prudent members of the [Russian] government." A leading member of the Commissariat for Foreign Affairs had told him that war was a certainty in 1928. According to his informant, the war would be provoked by an English-inspired attack of Poland, aided by the Baltic States, on the USSR. Finland had already indicated her willingness to join if London would give her financial aid. A war was inevitable because otherwise the English policies were completely absurd. Only an attack on Russia would assure a Conservative victory in the next election. Germany would simply be overrun if she refused passage.[19]

Despite this alarmist telegram, Brockdorff-Rantzau received no direct information from Stresemann, who was still in Geneva. The Ambassador found the continued lack of information scandalous and attributable not only to "incompetence, but to intent." He resented being left out of the mainstream of German politics. He considered writing to President Hindenburg, but then thought better of it.[20]

Brockdorff-Rantzau was beginning to feel that German-Russian relations no longer held the political importance that he had given to them during the early years of his tenure in Moscow. The Russian economic system had not returned to capitalism, a hope which had been fostered by Lenin's New Economic Policy. The economic gains hoped for under the Commercial Treaty of October 12, 1925, and the 300 million marks credit had not materialized. In fact, German exports to Russia were falling off. From October, 1926, to July, 1927, exports of industrial goods, metals, and other raw materials had dropped by 30 million rubles. In addition, the Russians constantly complained that delivered merchandise was below standards, but refused inspection to ascertain the truth of these allegations. In consequence, the interest of German businessmen in Russia had declined.[21]

Brockdorff-Rantzau continued in Russia but expected no further brilliant successes. His embassy to the east had become another routine post. Stresemann's adherence to the fulfillment policy had won out, and Brockdorff-Rantzau's dreams of revenge for Versailles had not materialized. Despite the new atmosphere, the Russians made Brockdorff-Rantzau's fifth anniversary as Ambassador to the Soviet Union the occasion for a gala dinner. The political implications of the celebration were clear. Moscow used it to show the British that German-Russian relations were still strong. Chicherin lauded the great contributions Brockdorff-Rantzau had made to the "strengthening of the friendly relations between Germany and the USSR."

Brockdorff-Rantzau, in reply, expressed his gratitude for the honor being done to him. He remarked that his only credit was the fact that he saw an opportunity to work with the Soviet government five years earlier, and took it with confidence.

I came as a friend and remained a friend!

I know quite well that one should not carry on politics with the heart, but I believe that it cannot harm politics when the heart has its say. Our community of fate and our common interests have led me to this certainty; in it I administered my duties here.

We are all seekers!—that is the great community of fate of those who honestly strive for the truth. I am not as sceptical and resigned as the poet who said: "While Man's desires and aspirations stir, he cannot choose but err." On the contrary, I expect much of this striving.

I have never given unrequested advice, neither to the left nor to the right. But one thing I am convinced of: no one is infallible; to no one is given the monopoly of knowing the final truth. I mean, in the end everyone should have doubts in the battle of spirits and powers, may it be in politics or in the greatest problems and fateful questions of mankind. I work in this conviction.

I raise my glass and drink to the Soviet government and the fortune of all peoples, to the Union, the future success, and the continued cooperation of our countries.

Brockdorff-Rantzau considered his address "an ingenious rejection [*eine geistreiche Absage*] of bolshevism." The political coloration of the Soviet Union had never appealed to the Ambassador, and working with the persons who represented the new Russian state had always been based on *Realpolitik*, not liking. The relationship with Chicherin, on the other hand, had deepened through the years. After the celebration the Count sent his framed and inscribed photograph to Chicherin. He concluded the accompanying letter with a tribute to their personal friendship.

In cordial esteem and with the assurance, coming from innermost conviction, that I consider it as the fortune of my life that fate was kind enough to bring us so close together, not only as politi-

cians but also as *human beings,* I remain, highly esteemed Mr.
Chicherin (I *can* not be quite "official" today) your,
Brockdorff-Rantzau.[22]

On November 10, the good feeling created by the anniversary dinner was shattered. A German revolutionary, Max Hölz, who was incarcerated in a German prison for his guerilla activities in Saxony during 1923, was decorated with the Order of the Red Banner *in absentia.*
Voroshilov made a speech praising Hölz and gave the decoration to a
German Communist for transmission to Hölz. Brockdorff-Rantzau told
Chicherin that he regarded this action as an affront, not only to a
friendly government but also to himself personally. He threatened to
leave for Berlin unless satisfactory amends were made immediately.[23]

Stresemann agreed with the action taken by Brockdorff-Rantzau
and told Krestinsky on November 19 that he had succeeded only with
the greatest difficulty in preventing the case from becoming a *cause
célèbre.* How would Moscow react to a German decoration for Trotsky?
The Soviet Ambassador repeated what Chicherin had already told
Brockdorff-Rantzau: the Narkomindel had no foreknowledge of the
action of the Commissariat for War. Despite this, Stresemann demanded that an explanation be made by the Soviet government.

Despite the strong language he employed with Krestinsky, Stresemann did not think it wise to consider the decoration of Hölz as a
provocation. The Foreign Minister asked Brockdorff-Rantzau to remain
at his post because the German press had hardly mentioned the matter.
In fact, Cabinet members, as well as President Hindenburg, had not
known about Hölz's decoration until Stresemann had informed them
about it.

Brockdorff-Rantzau considered Stresemann's instruction a deliberate attempt to give the impression that he was trying to make an
incident out of an indiscretion. This view was supported by Chicherin's
remark that there seemed to be quite a discrepancy between Berlin
and its Ambassador. On November 25, Krestinsky was again told by
Stressmann that Berlin demanded an explanation and supported its
Ambassador's stand absolutely. President Hindenburg asked the Foreign Office to prevent the presentation of the Order to Hölz, which
they succeeded in doing after negotiations with the Ministry of Justice.
Despite these initial successes, it was not until December 23 that the
incident was settled by a Russian note to the German Foreign Office,
which stated that the Red army had acted without consulting the
Commissariat for Foreign Affairs. Hölz had received the Order for

services as a partisan against the French before the Treaty of Versailles had been signed.[24]

After this tempest, relations with Russia returned to routine matters. Foremost was the demand for more economic aid. Early in February, 1928, Scheinmann, of the Commissariat for Economic Affairs, had arrived in Berlin for discussions on the extension of the Commercial Treaty of October 12, 1925, which was to expire on April 1. He had requested a new credit of 600 million marks, to be paid in two installments of 300 million marks each; 30 to 40 percent would be used for the purchase of consumer goods in Germany. In addition, Scheinmann inquired about the possibility of floating loans in Germany and having the bonds admitted to the Berlin Stock Exchange. The German Foreign Office had advised the Russian that it would be best to wait with the new credits until after the May elections for the Reichstag. Furthermore, loans were out of the question until the Soviet Union settled the Tsarist debts due German citizens. Scheinmann at first threatened to look elsewhere, but then indicated that Moscow was willing to make concessions in the treaty negotiations. The Germans made everything dependent on a favorable outcome of these negotiations.[25]

Brockdorff-Rantzau continued to complain about being deliberately ignored by the Wilhelmstrasse. He decided to go to Berlin during March and have a personal talk with Hindenburg. He again contemplated resigning, but reconsidered when Chicherin pleaded with him not to leave. The Count was sure that his policy in Russia was being undermined from home, because the drift away from Russia and toward the West continued despite all his warnings about the dire consequences which would befall Germany if she disregarded the East. All of this forced him to

> ponder the question whether I can square working with Stresemann with my conscience. Under no circumstances do I wish to stay here only to be kicked out by him, as he has already intimated, at a time which seems suitable to *him*.[26]

Before Brockdorff-Rantzau could leave for Berlin, another incident prevented his departure. On March 7, 1928, the German Consulate in Kharkov informed the Embassy in Moscow that five German technicians, who had been installing turbines and mining machinery in the Donbas, had been arrested for industrial espionage, sabotage, and working as cohorts with the *émigré* owners of the mines. Chicherin told Brockdorff-Rantzau, during the evening of the same day, that a public trial including the Germans would be held in the near future. He implored the Ambassador to use his influence to prevent a break of relations.[27]

On March 10, Felix Deutsch, Chairman of the Board of the General Electric Company (A.E.G.), four of whose technicians had been arrested, telegraphed Brockdorff-Rantzau, using the facilities of the German Foreign Office, requesting that he inform the Soviet government that the A.E.G. would withdraw its entire operation in Russia unless its employees were immediately released. He termed absurd the charges leveled against them. The Ambassador read the telegram to Chicherin on the following day. He followed this with a rigorous protest to the deputy director of the Commissariat for Foreign Affairs in charge of the case. Director Bleimann, of the A.E.G., who was in Moscow, telegraphed to Deutsch that Brockdorff-Rantzau had the impression that the matter would be settled in an acceptable way.[28]

Two of the Germans, Goldstein and Wagner, were released ten days later. Three others, Max Maier, Ernst Otto, and Wilhelm Badstieber, remained in prison. The last was not an employee of the A.E.G. but of another German firm, Knapp, which supplied mining machinery to the Russians.

Upon his return to Berlin, Senior Engineer Goldstein reported to the Wilhelmstrasse on the background of the arrests. In his considered opinion, the catastrophic decline of production, as well as the numerous accidents and disturbances in the Donets Basin area, was due to the Soviet system and not to sabotage. Goldstein saw a basic mistake in the fact that control of production was left to inept party members and their cohorts. Their attitude, as well as the ever-present threat of arrest for the merest bagatelles, seriously curtailed the efficiency of the nonparty Russian specialists. These were perfectly aware that their presence was suffered only until they could be replaced. The workers, disinterested in their jobs and poorly supervised, accomplished only one-third to one-fourth of what was expected of German workers on similar jobs. This situation was aggravated by the thirty-hour week for labor in the mines and power plants, and seven to eight hours per day for other categories. Efficiency was further curtailed because the workers wasted days in negotiations about piecework rates.

The mines and power plants in the coal-mining area were in absolutely lamentable conditions. In many cases, the capacity of the turbines was far below that required to produce the energy needed to power the machinery. Equipment was utilized in the most haphazard way. As a consequence, it rusted or otherwise deteriorated in a short time. All work was pervaded by astonishing slovenliness. Goldstein cited an example he had observed at one mine. A rail spur was laid on frozen ground and the ties were not properly packed. In the spring the whole line buckled, leaving a "hill and dale" railroad of absolutely no use. During construction, some cable drums had lain in the way of the spur. Instead of removing them, the railroad gang had laid the rails around the obstructions.

Engineer Goldstein was convinced that the real reason for the arrests of the engineers and technicians was that the Bolshevik regime had boasted for years that it would pass not only Western Europe but also the United States within ten years. Instead of this brilliant accomplishment, there had occurred a catastrophic decline in industrial production, aggravated by a poor harvest and the failure of the forced loans placed on the peasants. It was obvious that the German and Russian specialists were to be used as scapegoats for Bolshevik failures.

Goldstein concluded his report with the exasperation of a man who had been duped, whose talents have been utilized, and who has then been discarded by a system he failed to understand.

> In appreciation for having given their total knowledge and ability to bring order into the ruined Soviet industry, the German engineers are threatened with jail on the basis of crazy charges of "counterrevolutionary" activity! Let this be a warning to every German engineer not to make his ability available to the Soviet government.[29]

Brockdorff-Rantzau agreed with Goldstein that the arrests were due to the breakdown of the ambitious industrialization program. He demanded that Berlin take a firm stand in order to effect the release of the imprisoned Germans and to bolster Chicherin against the OGPU. Therefore, the Count left no doubt in anybody's mind in Moscow that he would resign if the situation did not improve.[30]

The German Foreign Office found it difficult to understand why Moscow had chosen this time, when negotiations to extend the Commercial Treaty of October 12, 1925, were in full progress, to attack German industry.[31] On March 15, the Wilhelmstrasse acted to reinforce the Deutsch ultimatum and suspended these negotiations. Stresemann, addressing the Foreign Affairs Committee of the Reichstag, emphasized that the arrests violated Part I of the Commercial Treaty which detailed conditions of residence, commercial activities, and general legal protections. *Izvestia* published the statement on March 22, and Chicherin wrote to Brockdorff-Rantzau that it was "too bad the German public was being misinformed."

The A.E.G.'s Board of Directors had second thoughts about the Deutsch ultimatum by March 13, when Director Bücher told Wallroth that Brockdorff-Rantzau acted as if the arrests were the private concern of the A.E.G. Private industry had to insist that the Reich government protect its citizens abroad; all the A.E.G. could do was to support governmental actions.

Two days later, representatives of the A.E.G. reiterated this position during an interview with Stresemann. Upon the Foreign Minister's request, the Reichsverband der Deutschen Industrie (Association of German Manufacturers) passed a resolution on March 17 objecting to the Russian action. At the same time, a committee of the Reichsverband issued a report pointing out that a recall of all A.E.G. employees from Russia would constitute a breach of contract. The committee advised the members of the association to exercise the greatest caution in regard to new contracts with the Soviet Union and to give technicians a choice on whether they wanted to go to Russia. No firm should in any way influence the decisions of its employees, because this, too, could be interpreted as a breach of contractual obligations.

After the committee's report had been issued, the A.E.G. withdrew its representatives from the Soviet Trade Delegation and sent no new personnel to the Soviet Union. The A.E.G. informed the Wilhelmstrasse that it was willing to recall all of her employees from Russia who were not bound by contract. However, the firm insisted that the German government take the necessary precautions to prevent the Soviet authorities from refusing exit visas for the personnel to be recalled. It was now obvious that the A.E.G. was unwilling to stand behind Deutsch's ultimatum. The real reason was quite simple: the A.E.G. feared that it would lose its large investment in Russia. All future actions would have to be initiated by the German government.

A major political incident now developed. The arrest of the German technicians, which had shown signs of settlement with the release of two of those arrested, now became a matter of policy.

It was obvious that the Foreign Office could no longer count on more than token support from German industry. The refusal of the Soviet government to transmit the charges against the Germans or to permit communication with them further aggravated an already explosive situation. The refusal to transmit the charges clearly violated Article XI of Part I and the addendum to Article XI of the Commercial Treaty which read:

Each of the Contracting Parties undertakes to adopt the necessary measures to inform the consul of the other Party as soon as possible whenever a national of the country which he represents is arrested in his district.

The same procedure shall apply if a prisoner is transferred from one authority to another.

(Addendum to Article XI)

1. The consul shall be notified either by a communication from the person arrested or by the authorities themselves directly. Such communications shall be made within a period not exceeding seven times twenty-four hours, and in large towns, including capitals of districts, within a period of not exceeding three times twenty-four hours.

2. In cases of detentions of all kinds, requests made by consular representatives to visit nationals of their country under arrest, or to have them visited by their representatives, shall be granted without delay. The consular representative shall not be entitled to require officials of the courts or prisons to withdraw during this interview with the person under arrest.[32]

The Eastern Department now made a staff study of the effect the incident would have, and already had had, on the over-all German-Russian relationship. The department decided that despite the new affront, Germany's policy would continue along the lines laid down by the Treaties of Rapallo and Berlin. It hoped that the new incident would be quickly settled so that the economic negotiations could be resumed. The department experts were concerned about the adverse effect of the arrests on the attitude of the German business world, but since the economic recovery of Russia was absolutely essential to the economic development of Europe, everything had to be done to quiet the apprehensions of the industrial magnates.

The Foreign Office informed Brockdorff-Rantzau on March 22 of the A.E.G. decision to continue its construction projects in the Soviet Union. With the Deutsch ultimatum removed, and despite the Ambassador's vigorous diplomatic protests, the Soviet Union continued its refusal to release the three Germans or to permit access to them. Stresemann, on March 27, instructed Brockdorff-Rantzau to demand that the charges against the incarcerated men be officially transmitted. The Ambassador was to insist that the German Consul in Kharkov be permitted to visit the technicians. A refusal would be considered an act of "political unfriendliness." Secondly, Brockdorff-Rantzau was to lodge an emphatic protest against the unhygienic and despicable conditions in the jail, as described by Goldstein, and demand that German citizens, whose guilt had not yet been established, receive "humane treatment," according to the "procedures established among civilized peoples." Finally, the fact that two Germans had already been released showed that the "Soviet judicial authorities had proceeded with irresponsible frivolity." It appeared highly unlikely that the engineer Otto had given 200,000 rubles to the mysterious Köster for unlawful purposes.

For the Ambassador's personal information, Stresemann added that any move by the Russians to prevent the departure of the technicians whom the A.E.G. had tentatively offered to recall "should be forced with all means available, and even a political extension of the conflict was not to be feared."

Stresemann's instructions and additional information crossed a telegram by the Ambassador in which he reported that he had lodged a strong protest about the false arrests of Goldstein and Wagner and their "inhumane" treatment on the basis of a Foreign Office report brought by diplomatic courier. He had demanded that the "well-being and the accommodations" of the Germans still under arrest be taken care of. Furthermore, he had demanded that the prisoners be given permission to correspond with their families. He had told Chicherin that an embassy official would go to Rostov even if the Soviet government should refuse permission for a visit to the incarcerated men.

On March 29, twenty-two days after the arrests, the Narkomindel telephoned the German Embassy granting permission for the German Consul in Kharkov to visit the three technicians. At 11:00 P.M., Chicherin repeated this offer to Brockdorff-Rantzau, who refused to accept it. He pointedly told Chicherin that Rostov was within the area of the Moscow Embassy. He had already dispatched Secretary of Legation Schliep; it was absolutely impossible to change this decision. Chicherin objected, and the Ambassador threatened to go to Rostov himself to find out "*whether one would dare to refuse the German Ambassador access to his countrymen.*"[33] Chicherin pleaded with Brockdorff-Rantzau to accept the Russian permission. The Ambassador adamantly refused, even when the Commissar implored him to consider how difficult it had been to wrest the visitation from the "Talmudists." The Ambassador absolutely declined to change his decision; instead he transmitted Stresemann's *démarche* to the Commissar.

The German newspapers reported on April 1 an interview with Deutsch of the A.E.G. in which he expressed his belief that the incarceration of his employees on unfounded charges would lead to the downfall of the OGPU and thus to the improvement of commercial relations with the USSR.[34]

Izvestia characterized the German press reports about the innocence of the accused German technicians as "a primitive method of proof." The Soviet people simply could not agree that all of Deutsch's colleagues were as virtuous as he. Some of his subordinates would find it difficult to defend their innocence, "because all financial operations [*i.e.*, bribery] were carried on by an authorized agent of the firm and by banks close to it."

Despite *Izvestia's* innuendo, the Soviet government granted permission for Secretary of Legation Schliep to visit the prisoners on April 2. He saw them each separately for ten minutes in the presence of three OGPU officials. The Germans had been kept in single cells since March 15. Before that date they had been crowded together with the Russian prisoners. Maier had shared one small room with fifteen others. Schliep found the new accommodations to be satisfactory.

Maier complained about "red and yellow spots" on the upper part of his body. He also could not move his right arm. Maier emphasized that he had always enjoyed the very best of health. Otto seemed in the best of spirits, while Badstieber appeared "depressed and feeble." There were no emotional outbursts nor any requests for aid from the Embassy.

The firmness of the German government resulted in the appearance of Jacubovich at the Wilhelmstrasse. The Soviet emissary tried to convince Dirksen that the Soviet government had nothing but good will for Germany. The arrests of Dirksen's countrymen and the ill treatment of Goldstein and Wagner had been due to the ineptitude of the provincial authorities in the Ukraine. Jacubovich requested that the German Foreign Office publish a *dementi* about the assertion of the German Association of Manufacturers that Moscow had broken the treaty of October 12, 1925. Dirksen, who knew very well who had inspired the Association's statement, advised Jacubovich to get in touch with the Association itself.

On the day of Schliep's visit to the prisoners, the A.E.G.'s letter to the Foreign Office was received by Brockdorff-Rantzau. The Ambassador's reaction to this epistle was one of consternation and of caustic sarcasm, of which he was a past master, for the people who wantonly destroyed a powerful diplomatic *quid pro quo* because they feared material losses. The Ambassador informed Stresemann, with considerable exaggeration, that never in all his thirty-five years in the diplomatic service had he been confronted with so dastardly an action. He insisted that the A.E.G.'s directorate be put in its place. Deutsch had made his ultimatum spontaneously and Brockdorff-Rantzau had informed Chicherin accordingly. It was absolutely scandalous for the A.E.G. to assert that he had treated the arrests as the private affair of that noble concern. The Ambassador emphasized, rather irritably, that his representation of the Reich's interest needed no affirmation; it was an open book for all to read. He fulfilled his duty without regard for the favor or disfavor of powerful private companies "who yell for the Reich's assistance under the cover of patriotism in order to insure their own profits."

Brockdorff-Rantzau continued that, in disregard of the fact that the employees of the A.E.G. were charged with dangerous acts against the Soviet government, he had demanded their immediate release. The Deutsch ultimatum had been used as a lever to pry them loose. This had been done despite Chicherin's open warning that the German government should proceed cautiously in the case, because the burden of proof against the three Germans was overwhelming. The Russians were well aware of the A.E.G.'s contractual obligations and the fact that Herr Felix Deutsch's investment was protected up to 60 percent by Reich and State guarantees under the agreement regarding the 300 million credit. Deutsch's boast that he was one of the Soviet Union's staunchest friends was appreciated, as *Izvestia* articles had shown, as well as the fact that this friendship had resulted in very handsome profits. Deutsch's proposal that Brockdorff-Rantzau should confer with the accused Germans in order to ascertain their innocence was, at the very least, naive. That anyone could seriously expect the German Ambassador to hold a conference with persons accused of high treason was unbelievable. Brockdorff-Rantzau concluded his verbose telegram with the warning to Stresemann that he would not take the blame for the failures of the A.E.G., which tried to make a culprit out of him, so that it would be covered before its stockholders. He, personally, would defend himself against "cowardly attacks."

Stresemann, who knew from previous experience with the Ambassador the extent to which he would pursue a personal slight, assured Brockdorff-Rantzau of his absolute support. Stresemann disclosed that he too was quite upset about the "cowardice" of the A.E.G., especially since his remarks to the Foreign Affairs Committee of the Reichstag had been based on Deutsch's ultimatum. He had personally given the A.E.G. directorate a piece of his mind. However,

despite the attitude of the industrial circles, I hope that you agree with me that our common efforts will have the desired result, namely to safeguard our position vis-à-vis Russia, without letting our regular relations with her be disturbed for a long period.[35]

Stresemann's cooperative attitude prompted Brockdorff-Rantzau to write a long private letter to the Foreign Minister. He told his superior that his telegram had calmed his concern regarding the stability of their relationship, which had haunted him ever since the Hölz Affair. He had then felt a definite lack of confidence on Stresemann's part. This feeling was accentuated by the Foreign Minister's agreement to continue the direct secret cooperation between the Reichswehr and the Red army.

Brockdorff-Rantzau pointed out that this clandestine relationship again precluded the use of vigorous steps to settle the present incident. He still considered the military relationship

> one of the most important binding agents of our common policy, but he had always emphasized, last in July of the preceding year, that the final decision regarding foreign policy did not belong to [him] but to the main office.[36]

Brockdorff-Rantzau felt that the military relationship interfered constantly with the process of regular diplomatic relations. He wrote to his brother Ernst that the situation in Moscow was not complicated by the latest internationally-known "*Schweinerei*," but because of the consequences of the military agreements made in 1923.[37] Stresemann agreed that the military relationship should be curtailed. But he emphasized that the most recent agreements were "really not an extension," as Brockdorff-Rantzau apparently assumed, but "a retrenchment of the relations." In any event, the political situation made an immediate cessation impossible.[38]

It was quite true that the Shakhty affair was not the best time to discontinue the clandestine military collaboration. However, despite the ever-present danger that the Russians would reveal this collaboration, neither Stresemann nor the army had any intention of discontinuing the profitable relationship. The possession of training facilities for tank crews and combat pilots and the access to the Soviet defense and chemical industry was much too important to be scuttled. The German military experts had made it quite clear to the Wilhelmstrasse that even the threat of dire political repercussions was not sufficient to discontinue the training of experts in the arms which would be decisive in any modern conflict. The Soviet authorities had never revealed the pernicious relationship, but they always held this particular trump, and they could use it at any time to discredit the Weimar Republic.

On April 17, *Vetshernaia Moskva* printed an excerpt from a speech by Bukharin to the plenary session of the Central Committee and the Central Control Commission of the Communist Party. According to Bukharin, now a full member of the Politburo, the OGPU had uncovered an organization connected to foreign capital and capitalistic organizations. Through foreign engineers, "some of whom turned out to be members of fascist organizations, especially of the German Stahlhelm," contact had been maintained with foreign countries. There was even the possibility that the defense and chemical industries had also been affected. This bit of blackmail was a clear warning to Berlin that Moscow could, at any time, destroy the Reich's good relations with the West.

It was precisely this Damocles' sword which required a certain amount of discretion on the part of Germany in its dealings with the Soviet Union. During discussions with Litvinov, Stresemann and Schubert strenuously objected to the tactics employed in the Shakhty arrests. The Deputy Foreign Commissar assured both that Germany placed too much meaning on such episodes. Litvinov pointedly told the Undersecretary that the Soviet Union resented interference in its domestic affairs. If the Germans were found to be innocent, they would be released. Schubert interjected that "it was somewhat complicated for foreigners to act correctly in Russia." The proper way to deal with the matter would have been for the Soviet government to have given some indication of its suspicions. Then those suspected could have been reprimanded or removed from the USSR. The indecent haste of the arrests was, indeed, a piece of "lamentable foolishness." Litvinov pointed to the equally hasty discontinuation of the economic negotiations. Schubert retorted that this had been inevitable under the circumstances.

Stresemann told Litvinov that the German government was willing to resume the economic negotiations as soon as the conclusion of the trial brought a quieter atmosphere. He did, however, emphasize that the German business world had been quite discouraged about the unprofitable business relations with Russia. The arrests of the German technicians had further aggravated an already bad situation. Many businessmen believed that the conditions in the Donets area were symptomatic of the lagging recovery of Russian industry in general.

Litvinov hinted that Germany had suspended the negotiations on the extension of the Commercial Treaty because of pressure from England. Schubert termed this "simply laughable." *Izvestia* re-emphasized Litvinov's charge, adding that neither the Economic Ministry nor the Foreign Office had taken any measures to refute the "fairy tales" about the deterioration of German-Russian economic relations. Voroshilov told the Conference of Secretaries of Army Party Cells that the economic blockade of the capitalists would fail. Industrialization was progressing, and the Shakhty incident with Germany seemed close to settlement. Two weeks later, Stalin sweepingly described the Shakhty

plot as an example of renewed foreign intervention. Military intervention had failed in 1918–1920. Now the same end was to be accomplished through economic pressure, sparked by bourgeois technicians.

All this Communist rhetoric was an indication of Soviet attempts to
beguile the German government into resuming the negotiations for the
extension of the Commercial Treaty without any previous Soviet concessions. The three Germans remained among the fifty-three persons
being prepared for the public trial. Badstieber, Maier, and Otto were
transferred to Moscow on April 7 and incarcerated in the Butyrka jail.
Some material for their defense arrived from Germany two days later.
The Russian judicial authorities refused to admit German defense
lawyers but appointed Russian defenders for the three technicians.
Because of this, Brockdorff-Rantzau requested that an attorney, selected by the Foreign Office and not by the A.E.G., be sent to act as an
observer and as legal advisor to the Embassy. The Wilhelmstrasse sent
a well-qualified member of the legal profession who knew Russian law,
named Munte.

The start of the trial had been announced for the middle of April,
but on the eleventh of that month, Stein informed Brockdorff-Rantzau
that a delay was necessary. The preliminary examination of the
accused had produced an abundance of new evidence which had to be
sifted and analyzed. On April 17, Schliep visited the Germans at the
Butyrka jail. He was permitted to talk to each man separately in the
presence of an official from the Foreign Commissariat and four OGPU
men. Maier complained about the inadequacy of the prison fare and
requested that one pound of butter per week be sent to him from the
Embassy. Three Russian physicians had found that he suffered from a
heart condition, but he had not received any medical attention. He did
feel better, but still lacked writing and reading materials. He also
wanted his wife to be sent back to Germany from Kharkov, where she
still remained.

Badstieber felt fine and told Schliep that he was in no mood to
communicate with anybody. Otto, like the other two, complained that
the cells were insufficiently heated, forcing him to stay in bed all day
long. He agreed that the food was poor, but this condition was mitigated by the possibility of purchasing additional supplies at the jail
commissary. He, too, was in no mood to write to his family, but asked
that they be told that he was in good health. Schliep felt that the
physical and psychological condition of the prisoners had improved
since his last visit. He saw no reason to complain about the efforts of
the Moscow officials regarding accommodations and treatment.

On May 5, Schliep visited the German technicians again. This time, only one OGPU man was present, and the same procedure as before was followed. Schliep told the men that their Russian defense lawyers were Messrs. Domatovsky, Worms, and Ozep. He counseled them to read the indictment carefully when they received it and to discuss it with their defenders. Badstieber insisted that he had already requested that the court, in view of his difficult case, select a German-speaking lawyer for him. Maier repeatedly complained about "heart and nerve problems" and the fact that no doctor had visited him during the past week. He stuck to this even when the investigating judge insisted that he received three weekly visits from a physician. Otto and Badstieber had no complaints.

Brockdorff-Rantzau's request to see the prisoners had been denied. Chicherin told him that Attorney General V. N. Krylenko had not thought it wise to permit the visit because he feared that the Ambassador would give the accused information about the trial. The Ambassador retorted sharply that he would not smuggle any secret information to the prisoners. Following this exchange with the Foreign Commissar, the Ambassador received permission for a visit. The prisoners were brought in separately, and Brockdorff-Rantzau spoke to them in the presence of the investigating judge, two officials from the Narkomindel, and Hencke.

Maier again complained that his health was not taken care of and that he had been given only two letters from his wife, who was a prolific letter writer. Otto, who was brought in next, had no complaints. He still had not corresponded with his relatives.

Badstieber made a "rather peculiar impression" on Brockdorff-Rantzau. He immediately complained that the lawyer Ozep, who had been promised to him by the investigating judge, had not been assigned to him. The Ambassador told him that Ozep, who spoke no German, had been assigned to Otto, who had a perfect command of Russian. When Brockdorff-Rantzau told Badstieber that he could count on the protection of the German government, Badstieber said that all he wanted to be sure of was that he would be supported, should the trial result in a long sentence. The Ambassador assured him that he would. Before he left, Badstieber

> declared spontaneously that he wanted to impress the fact on [Brockdorff-Rantzau] that he had absolutely no complaints about anything in the jail. On the contrary, he was treated so well that he "could only praise everything!" He was willing to attest to this in writing.

Brockdorff-Rantzau found that the three men were generally in good health. Maier's was shaken, but not enough to arouse concern. Only Badstieber seemed to have cracked under the strain of the incarceration and the Soviet methods of interrogation. He gave the impression of a man who was psychologically broken.

On May 8, Brockdorff-Rantzau, accompanied by Hencke, went to the Foreign Commissariat to look at the indictment. In the main, it tried to show that the

> Director of the Eastern Department of the A.E.G., Bleimann, knew about the counterrevolutionary organization and its aims, and, so to speak, was the center of the movement.[39]

This accusation was based on the confession of a certain Bashkin, whose brother was an employee in the A.E.G.'s Berlin office. According to Bashkin, the firm paid a 3 percent commission on all orders, and this money was used for illegal purposes; in addition, the management of the A.E.G. maintained close relations with the former owners of the mines. The specific charge was that a conference had taken place in Bleimann's Berlin office in March of 1927 "during which the details about the procedure of the counterrevolutionary organization were discussed." The accusations against Otto, Maier, and Badstieber did not seem very substantial to Brockdorff-Rantzau.

The indictment only confirmed what Brockdorff-Rantzau had been able to find out about the alleged unlawful deeds of the three technicians. A few weeks earlier, the Ambassador had questioned an engineer of the A.E.G. and found that Otto had brought a package of clothing for Bashkin from his brother in Berlin. He had also brought a university certificate for a Russian engineer who had been among the first to be arrested. The chief engineer of the Knapp firm, Seebold, during a confidential talk with Brockdorff-Rantzau, had categorically rejected the accusation of counterrevolutionary activities by the accused Germans. The chief engineer admitted that other firms, not his own, had expended considerable sums on bribes to increase orders from the Soviet government.

Brockdorff-Rantzau tried to find further evidence, but failed. It appeared, therefore, that the technicians were involved in the trial because Otto had been charitable and Badstieber had allegedly transmitted bribes from his firm.

The German Foreign Office questioned the A.E.G. about the accusation of bribery. The firm's legal department refused to take a stand on this point because the charge of bribery had not been made against it. A week before Brockdorff-Rantzau had been shown the indictment, a "friendly source" had supplied the Wilhelmstrasse with a report of the Polish Consul in Kharkov to his Foreign Ministry. According to this report, bribes had been paid by the German firms to increase orders and to get defective and unneeded equipment passed by the Soviet inspectors. The Polish Consul had found out that there was not a shred of evidence to show that an organized counterrevolutionary organization existed in the Donbas.

Brockdorff-Rantzau received information from the Lithuanian Ambassador, Jurgis K. Baltruschaitis, whom he trusted implicitly, which indicated that sabotage had been carried on by a large Polish-financed organization near Shakhty. This organization had allegedly sabotaged the mines in a manner which was designed to render them almost useless to the Bolshevik regime but to make their restoration to full capacity possible after the regime had been overthrown. Baltruschaitis had also discovered why the trial had not yet started. New material involving the Polish Ambassador in Moscow had been uncovered. A natural son of the Ambassador's, Songe or Sounier by name, who had been a liaison officer between the OGPU and the Narkomindel, had apparently transmitted information to England via the Polish Embassy in Moscow. Songe had already been shot by the Secret Police.

Izvestia, Pravda, and *Ekonomisheskaia Shisn* published particulars about the indictment on May 8 and 9 which corroborated some of Baltruschaitis' information. The newspapers followed the official line that there had indeed been a large and closely-knit counterrevolutionary group in the Donbas which had proved to be much more dangerous than had at first been suspected. Not only did it have connections with the hard coal administration in Moscow, but also with other branches of industry and with the "organs and personalities of foreign powers which had nothing to do with the anthracite industry as such." The organization perpetrated sabotage and hoped to cooperate with the enemy when the threatened intervention of capitalist forces would occur. After 1923 these bourgeois specialists had lost hope that the Soviet regime would immediately collapse. They had then devoted themselves to disorganizing and destroying the effectiveness of the Donbas mining industry.

The German technician Badstieber had confessed that he bribed administrators on the orders of his superior, Seebold. The Knapp firm had paid 2,500 rubles to the chairman of the Receiving Commission so that he would accept the firm's substandard machinery. According to Badstieber, the delivery of this kind of machinery had a dual purpose: (1) its speedy deterioration made for new orders, and (2) it would thus bring about the destruction of the Soviet economy. Further evidence given by the accused "parasites" pointed directly to the A.E.G., which had added a tax to its bills. This extra money was given to the Berlin Bashkin, who, with the assistance of Director Bleimann, transmitted the funds to the counterrevolutionary organization in the Donbas.

The *Deutsche diplomatisch-politische Korrespondenz,* the official organ of the German Foreign Office, reprinted details of the indictment for German consumption. The editor commented that German individuals were placed on trial because they had transmitted a letter or participated in bribery. But such acts were most certainly no basis for the sensational, politically inspired accusation of counterrevolutionary activities. Moscow should carefully weigh the effect of such accusations on the future economic cooperation with great foreign firms. The article concluded with the conciliatory note that the trial had apparently been prepared in a correct fashion, and that one had to await developments to find out what had actually been discovered. *Izvestia* commented that the article in the "semi-official *Deutsche diplomatisch-politische Korrespondenz*" followed the same anti-Soviet line as did most of the German newspapers, which fished in murky waters and misinformed the public.

The Shakhty Trial, progenitor of the great show trials of the thirties, opened on May 18 at 10:00 A.M. in the Hall of Columns in the House of the Trade Unions in Moscow. The Chairman of the Supreme Court of the USSR, Andrei Y. Vishinsky, presided. Fifty-two pallid prisoners, the fifty-third having been left raving in his cell, were arraigned before five judges sitting behind red-draped tables in the white-walled hall. "Most conspicuous in a special box reserved for foreign diplomats was the tall figure of the German Ambassador . . . with his tired but unfathomable expression."[40]

Just before the trial had started, Brockdorff-Rantzau had received a further indication of how it had been prepared. Two of the accused Russians had demanded that their defense lawyers be changed. The Ambassador discovered that the lawyers had advised them to take back a number of false statements. They refused to withdraw their confessions because certain "concessions" had been made if they kept to them. At the opening day of the trial, Brockdorff-Rantzau was confronted by another technique. The indictment was not read, and Brockdorff-Rantzau had heard that the Foreign Commissariat had declared eight pages secret because these involved the French and Polish governments in the plot. The Ambassador was sure that Moscow wanted to keep the two countries out of the trial.

COMMUNITY OF FATE

During an interview, the Ambassador officially complained to Chicherin about the behavior of prosecutor Krylenko, particularly about his "sarcastic smile, showing polished teeth," and his general attitude in regard to the German defendants. Chicherin replied, rather irritably, that he had no control over the prosecutor's smile. Brockdorff-Rantzau then demanded an official explanation of why the German lawyer, Munte, had been rejected as a defender. Chicherin told him that it was impossible to admit Munte because there was no provision for such a contingency in any Russo-German treaty. This was technically correct, because Article X (Part I) of the Commercial Treaty provided only that nationals were entitled in the territory of the other party to the same protection from the courts and authorities in respect of their persons and property as was given to nationals of the country or the nationals of the most favored nation.

> They shall, like nationals of the country, be free to choose their lawyers and other legal advisors from among the persons admitted to exercise the legal profession under the laws of the country.[41]

When the Ambassador complained about the court's refusal to accept German witnesses, which was a serious handicap to the defendants, Chicherin disclosed that this was done to prevent a deepening of the incident, because the witnesses were involved in the crimes and, under Soviet law, could be arrested. Finally, the Count requested that the complete indictment be given to the three Germans and that the procedures pertaining to them be translated into German.

Krylenko did not modify his behavior, and it became perfectly obvious to Brockdorff-Rantzau that the trial "had been well-prepared down to the last detail, and that the verdict was a foregone conclusion." This led Brockdorff-Rantzau to look for the reasons why Germany should be maltreated, while Poland and France were handled with great reserve. He decided that this was due to the belief among the rulers of Russia that Germany's dependence on the Soviet Union was absolute and that Germany woud take any affront without breaking off relations. In order to understand this policy, one had to consider that

> the chauvinistic wire-pullers [the party leaders], the more serious their own situation becomes, the more obnoxious they act, in the delusion thereby to deceive their own people and the world about the true situation.[42]

THE END OF AN ERA

The Russian belief that relations with Germany could stand an occasional incident was due partly to the well-known attitude of Brockdorff-Rantzau against a break of diplomatic relations. The Ambassador feared that such a development would only play into the hands of the West. The mere thought of the "malicious gloating [Schadenfreude]" of Germany's opponents to know that she was once more delivered into their hands was absolutely abhorrent to the Ambassador. The prevention of such a contingency had been the object of his strategy in Russia, which was based on the possibility of a German-Russian alliance against the West. However, he did not want the Russians to make it impossible to work loyally with them.

As the trial progressed, Brockdorff-Rantzau's health began to fail rapidly. He could not sleep, he suffered from all kinds of pains, and his throat was troubling him sorely. He was in such a bad condition that he had given up drinking cognac, a most serious sacrifice,[43] for he was a great devotee of that French brandy, although he hated the French. However, he refused to leave Moscow to seek much-needed treatments.

Indications began to appear that the Russians were beginning to have second thoughts on the wisdom of having involved Germany. Izvestia pointed out that there was not a single person in the USSR who believed that the court was sitting in judgment on German-Russian relations.

> The German Reich does not sit in the dock, neither does German industry nor German firms as such, but individual German citizens who are accused of a number of unlawful acts.

President Kalinin, in a speech published by Izvestia on June 8, struck an even more conciliatory note.

> Maybe our government was a bit incautious; maybe, considering that Germany is a friendly state, a state with whom we have good-neighborly relations, we should have been more careful with the arrests and have waited.[44]

But such a course of action would not have served justice. Kalinin indicated that good relations between Germany and Russia would not be destroyed by the acts of a few private citizens. He declared emphatically that allegations by the German press that the trial was a defamation of all German industry were the rankest nonsense. Quite the contrary, the leaders of the USSR had the highest regard for German industry.

Despite these obvious attempts at conciliation, another article in *Izvestia* characterized as a bundle of lies the sworn statements presented by Seebold and Köster of the Knapp firm for the defense of the three Germans. It sardonically taunted the Germans that calling

> on God and the holy Virgin Mary could be taken as proof of the complete judicial and actual helplessness of these gentlemen and of the impossibility for them to prove their innocence.

Counselor of Embassy Hey immediately went to the Foreign Commissariat and lodged a most serious objection to the article in the name of the Ambassador. The Ambassador personally repeated to Stein German objections to the *Izvestia* article. Brockdorff-Rantzau emphasized that

> it was an *impertinence,* a *blasphemy,* as well as a mockery of *the German Embassy,* which transmitted the material, of the German firms and the accused who had delivered it, and of the Foreign Commissariat, which transferred it to the court.[45]

Brockdorff-Rantzau added that he was deeply sorry that such an inflammatory article could be printed in the official organ of the Foreign Commissariat.

Stein replied that he had already expressed official regrets to Hey. The article had been written by a journalist of no consequence. Brockdorff-Rantzau retorted sarcastically that it surprised him to hear that *Izvestia* employed such an unworthy correspondent.

The Ambassador now turned to the trial, where one of the defendants had implicated not only the A.E.G. and Knapp, but also two other German firms, Eickhoff and Siemens, in the financing of the alleged sabotage. When Stein interjected that Vishinsky was really trying to leave the German firms out of the trial, Brockdorff-Rantzau told him that the intentions of the Chairman did not alter facts. The new turn in the trial constituted a refutation of "President Kalinin's very gratifying speech."

Stein insisted that the Ambassador was mistaken; the trial was of the greatest importance to the internal affairs of the USSR. Brockdorff-Rantzau put it to him whether "any place, and especially here, domestic policy could be divorced from foreign policy." Instead of using discretion, the Soviet government had chosen to make accusations against German firms and citizens which were "almost completely unfounded." German public opinion was so aroused that it could easily force the Reich government to discontinue its friendly policy toward the Soviet Union. Stein had to realize that "no government, with the possible exception of the Soviet government, could long pursue policies opposed by public opinion."

In Berlin, Krestinsky hinted to Schubert that the Germans could expect a light verdict. Schubert informed Brockdorff-Rantzau about this hint and told him that he could offer to use his influence to renew negotiations on the extension of the Commercial Treaty, should the Russians approach him about it. He should insist on definite assurances that the talks, once resumed, would be concluded successfully.

Krestinsky's hint in Berlin was echoed by *Izvestia* in Moscow. The paper also made a strenuous effort to show German industry that there was no need for it to be aroused by the trial. Using an article in the *Kölnische Zeitung*, *Izvestia* repeated an old line:

> The German public has been misled over the alleged accusations made on the part of the Soviets against German industry. There is absolutely no basis for the fear vented in Germany. When Rykov announced the sabotage organization in March and pointed to the connections of this organization with foreign countries, he emphasized even then that this concerned the criminal activities of individuals. . . . Other statesmen, including Kalinin, commented in the same vein. . . .[46]

The *Izvestia* article asked the German press to rectify the misunderstandings by printing the facts.

Izvestia failed, of course, to point out that German firms were prominently mentioned in the indictment and in testimony given in open court; or that Krylenko and the tribunal had refused to accept witnesses for the defense on the grounds that the court already had sufficient evidence. Sworn depositions by the A.E.G., in which the concern denied the alleged meeting in Bleimann's office and refuted the charge that the corporation had contributed to the fund of the alleged counterrevolutionary organization, also had been rejected, because Soviet trial procedure did not permit the presentation of unrequested testimony. Even with these odds against them, Otto and Maier defended themselves with great spirit. The latter did especially well, telling Krylenko that the examining judge had put statements into the record which he had never made. He had signed the protocol because, in his nervous state, he had felt that it was better to do so. When he was confronted with Bashkin, Maier emphasized that there was a remarkable difference between Bashkin's confessed sabotage and the great care which he had always taken with the A.E.G. turbine. After the confrontation, Bashkin suffered a severe nervous breakdown, and he subsequently retracted his testimony.

On June 29, Krylenko made his summation. In regard to the German defendants, he declared that the A.E.G. as such was not accused. He pointed out that there was, however, a distinct possibility that meetings of foreign members of the counterrevolutionary organization had taken place in the A.E.G.'s Russian Department, where many emigrants, whose ideology was well-known, had found employment. He asked that the charges against Maier be dropped because Bashkin's testimony had proved to be false. Otto belonged not only to the Stahlhelm, but also to the Freunde des Neuen Russlands (Friends of the New Russia), from which one could conclude that Otto was politically untrustworthy. This fact, as well as his dislike of the Soviet system and his knowledge of the language and Russian conditions, made it entirely plausible that he had acted as liaison between the saboteurs and the Germans. Krylenko demanded that Otto be given a six-months' sentence, "not so much on the basis of facts as on the basis of intuition." Turning to Badstieber, Krylenko pointed out that the accused had been well aware of the poor quality of the machines delivered by Knapp, but had not reported this. He had also bribed one of the Russian defendants. The prosecutor asked the court to grant Badstieber a suspended sentence. Krylenko's request for leniency was undoubtedly due to Badstieber's cooperation. He had consistently maintained that the Knapp machinery was substandard. He had also admitted the bribery charge.

From Krylenko's attitude and other indications, Brockdorff-Rantzau concluded that Moscow had definitely decided that the involvement of the Germans in the trial had been a big mistake. The various attempts that had been made to improve relations showed that the Russians realized that Germany was the only reliable friend they had in their precarious political situation. An article in *Rabotshaia Moskva* underlined the Ambassador's conclusion with the most conciliatory comment about the Germans made in the Russian press since the trial started. The article stated bluntly that the three Germans had played only an incidental and secondary role. Even if they had not been included, the trial would have lost nothing of its outstanding importance. Krylenko had been extremely objective, and there was no doubt that the court would support the requests of the Attorney General.

Brockdorff-Rantzau responded to the cue offered by *Rabotshaia Moskva* and went to the Foreign Commissariat on July 2. Official relations with the Narkomindel had lately become rather difficult for the Ambassador. His close personal friend, Chicherin, was confined to his bed with a severe case of diabetes. Litvinov was taking a cure for heart trouble, and Stein was in Geneva. In their absence, the Narkomindel was being run by a number of young people whom the Ambassador suspected of being close to the OGPU and who had shown that they did not like Germans. Therefore, Brockdorff-Rantzau called on the only man still remaining of the "old gang," the economic expert, Stomoniakov. During a two-hour late evening discussion, the Ambassador expressed his views on the summation of Krylenko and on the expected verdict. He pointed out that the involvement of Germany had been unnecessary from the start. The "grave material" against the Germans about which Chicherin had spoken had been relegated to limbo. Brockdorff-Rantzau expressed his consternation about Krylenko's request for a suspended sentence for "the scoundrel—he could not describe him otherwise—Badstieber." Emphasizing that he had absolutely no intention of influencing the decision of the court, the Ambassador warned Stomoniakov he would publish the depositions made by Seebold and others, should Otto receive the sentence asked for by the Attorney General. He then asked Stomoniakov whether Seebold would be put on trial, adding that the best procedure would be to deport the engineer. Stomoniakov had no ideas on that subject. In reporting the discussion to the Wilhelmstrasse, Brockdorff-Rantzau advised that the German press should be told to use circumspection in case of the expected acquittals.

Two days after Brockdorff-Rantzau's talk with Stomoniakov, *Izvestia*, in a lead article, informed its readers that the trial had proven that the Germans had been "correctly accused." In the same breath, *Izvestia* pointed out that members of the bourgeoisie could work peacefully in the Soviet Union.

With the Russian and German public prepared for acquittals, the oral verdict was handed down on July 7 at 1:30 A.M., exactly four months after the arrests. Eleven of the fifty-three defendants were condemned to death; Otto and Maier were acquitted, and their immediate release was ordered. Badstieber received a suspended sentence of one year for bribery. Neither the A.E.G. nor Director Bleimann was mentioned by name in the verdict. However, the verdict maintained that some of the accused Russians ordered and received machinery of poor quality from Knapp's.

Izvestia added a number of specifics which had not been included in the oral rendition of the verdict. The funds for the sabotage organization had come from capitalistic *émigré* organizations and capitalistic circles which subsidized them. During the years from 1924 to 1927, the total amount of these contributions had come to "several hundred thousand rubles." German firms, in which "White-Guardists" held important positions, had paid 1.5 to 3 percent in commissions on delivered merchandise as a contribution to the counterrevolutionary conspiracy.

Otto and Maier were released two hours after the verdict. Before Otto, who looked like a skeleton, and Maier left for Germany, they paid a call at the Ambassador's residence. Brockdorff-Rantzau urgently advised them to use discretion in talking with journalists so that they would not harm Seebold, who was under investigation. Both agreed; Maier, who was still suffering from a bad case of nerves, assured the Ambassador that he had been completely cured of his love for communism. Badstieber, who had been fired by Knapp, refused to return to Germany. He insisted that it would be impossible for him to prove the truth of his testimony in Germany because the defective machinery was in Russia. Brockdorff-Rantzau considered the verdict "satisfactory and decent." He was sure that it had dealt a severe blow to the "chauvinistic circles" in the Soviet Union. The Ambassador privately attributed the acquittals and the conciliatory attitude to his efforts.[47] But in public he gave credit to his "young coworkers."

The investigation of Seebold took about two weeks. During this period, it appeared as if the engineer would have to stand trial. After a number of strong protests by the German government, coupled with a delay in the resumption of the negotiations on the Commercial Treaty, led to the decision by the Russians on July 21 to deport the engineer and not to place him on trial.

The major objective of the Wilhelmstrasse had been accomplished. The three Germans were acquitted, and the A.E.G., since it was not named in the verdict, was *de facto* exonerated. The German press was informed by the Foreign Office not to indulge in "shouts of triumph," but to evaluate the verdict impartially. The Soviet court, in passing an objective sentence, had confirmed the German view that the accused technicians had been innocent, or, in Badstieber's case been guilty of a minor misdemeanor. The press could state that the flimsy basis on which the Germans had been involved had unnecessarily endangered good German-Russian relations. Despite attempts by the Soviet press and by Soviet officials to be conciliatory during the last part of the trial, the damage had already been done. The Soviet government should, therefore, take adequate steps to prevent a recurrence of similar incidents. Finally, the German press was asked to pave the way for a resumption of the economic negotiations by letting Moscow know that it had an obligation to restore the confidence of German industry.

Izvestia and *Pravda* lauded the verdict as an historical document which showed the objectivity of a proletarian court. *Pravda* reported that the Berlin papers admitted that there had been wrongdoings by individual Germans. The German newspapers, according to *Pravda*, repeated in varying degrees that the USSR should guarantee that the German workers and industry would not again be subjected to "Shakhty trials." *Pravda* assured its readers that this conciliatory attitude indicated that the Germans desired to restore good relations with the Soviet Union. *Izvestia* proposed that the existing commercial agreements be extended and be made more precise; the government of the USSR had already agreed to this at the beginning of 1928.

The Shakhty Trial had seriously undermined Brockdorff-Rantzau's belief that Germany and the Soviet Union were still tied together by the community of fate, which had brought him to Moscow in 1922. The Ambassador was seriously disappointed with the new trends which became daily more apparent in Russia. He felt that the old charm which he had found in the diplomatic game with the Bolsheviks was gone. The Count's close personal relationship with Chicherin had, in some measure, compensated for the recent disappointments with the other leading Russians. But Chicherin was a very sick man, and his star was on the wane. Brockdorff-Rantzau's own health, which had been poor at the start of the trial, was worn down by the end of it.[48]

An indication of the change which had taken place in Soviet politics and in the Narkomindel was the complete absence of any representatives from the Foreign Commissariat at the railroad station when Brockdorff-Rantzau left Moscow[49] on July 18. He arrived in Berlin six days later and participated in a conference during which the total relationship between Germany and the Soviet Union was thoroughly discussed. Besides the Ambassador, Schubert, Dirksen, Litvinov, and Krestinsky participated. The talks were based on an *aide-mémoire* drafted by Schlesinger. The *aide-mémoire* was handed to Litvinov, and the talks were based on its contents. The Deputy Commissar was told that recent events indicated that the attitude of the Soviet government was based on points of view detrimental to friendly relations. Every German move in international relations was considered an affront to the Soviet Union. German firms were attacked, and Germany's leaders were constantly subjected to the worst vilifications. The decoration of persons involved in attempts to overthrow the German government by force was at first considered an unfortunate mistake. However, the Shakhty Trial proved that all of the recent actions of the Soviet government were part of a well-conceived plan. Without any definite proof, German firms had been accused of participation in the fight of international capitalism against the Soviet Union. Stalin had made it abundantly clear that the Communist Party did not approve of the conditions under which German-Russian relations, dating back to

Rapallo, were conducted. This new policy was a danger to the continuation of good relations.

Today's declarations by the German government serve the exclusive purpose of warning of underestimating the growing danger which had been brought about by the systematic negation of the fundamentals of German-Russian relations, and which had been conjured up by the organs of the governing party. Should this policy of the Soviet Union proceed from the belief that the revolutionary tendency, for reasons unknown to the German government, must now be given pre-eminence over the tendency for normal relations of state to state, then this would, indeed, create a completely new situation for the German government.[50]

After the conference, Brockdorff-Rantzau left for his estate in Schleswig. He returned to Berlin on August 28, knowing that he suffered from a dangerous cancer of the throat. His physicians told him that even in the event of a successful operation he would most certainly lose the power of speech.[51] As was usual when he was in Berlin, the Ambassador stayed at Ernest Rantzau's house. There he died on September 8, 1928.

The death of Brockdorff-Rantzau occurred at a time when an era in German-Soviet relations to which he had given a particular flavor was coming to an end. His departure from Moscow coincided with the end of Lenin's NEP and the advent of Stalin's Five-Year Plan. The new experiment did nothing to assuage the reluctance of German business circles, always hesitant but more so since the Shakhty Trial, to enter into new arrangements with the Russians. The demand for a new credit made by Scheinmann during the opening negotiations for the extension of the October 12, 1925, Commercial Treaty had met determined opposition from the German banks and from businessmen. The primary reason for this refusal to grant credits was the poor result achieved by the 300 million mark loan granted in February, 1926.

The USSR had taken only 3 percent of Germany's total exports for the years 1926, 1927, and 1928. The purchases made amounted to an average of 330 million marks for each of these years. German business had expected that the conclusion of the Commercial Treaty and the extension of the 300 million mark loan would restore economic relations to prewar levels. During 1913, Russia had taken 9.7 percent of Germany's total exports, amounting to 978 million marks.[52]

With the end of the Shakhty Trial, the reason for the interruption of the economic talks had disappeared, especially since the verdict regarding the Germans could be considered as a vindication of German businessmen involved in economic relations with the Russians. The Foreign Office had sounded German industrial and financial circles during the summer on their attitude regarding resumption of negotiations. The inquiry revealed that these circles were unanimously opposed to giving new credits until the Russian harvest, expected to be poor, was gathered. There were fears that the worsening of the agricultural situation, coinciding as it did with the new political orientation in Russia, would make economic contacts with that state even more hazardous than it had been since trade had resumed. The Economics Ministry concurred with the pessimistic evaluation made by the business and financial leaders. Nevertheless, the Ministry agreed with the Wilhelmstrasse that negotiations should be resumed before the end of 1928 to avoid interference by the due dates on two payments of 80 million marks each of the 300 million mark credit on January 1 and April 1, 1929. On August 29, the Foreign Office announced that the economic negotiations with the USSR would probably resume at the end of October. *Izvestia* published the communiqué and commented that the resumption of the negotiations was a sign that Germany intended to normalize relations and remove the bad atmosphere created by the Shakhty Trial. This was, of course, part of the reason for resuming the talks. Negotiations reopened in Moscow on November 28 and led to the conclusion of a joint protocol on December 21, which improved and clarified certain parts of the Commercial Treaty.[53]

Four days before the resumption of the economic talks, Dirksen had been appointed Ambassador to the USSR. He was quite welcome in Moscow, where he was regarded as a man in the Brockdorff-Rantzau tradition, which indeed he was. Dirksen arrived at his post early in January, 1929. Litvinov was now in charge of the Narkomindel although he did not become Foreign Commissar until the following year. Dirksen succeeded in concluding an agreement with Litvinov on January 25 which provided for the establishment of a mediation commission consisting of two representatives of each country. Disagreements not amenable to resolution by normal diplomatic processes were to be submitted to the mediation commission for compromise solution. The Russians had refused to accept a neutral chairman, which would have turned the commission into a regular court of arbitration, as the Germans wanted it to be. Therefore, decisions by the mediation commission needed ratification by the governments before becoming effective. The first case presented to the commission on June 16, 1930, dealt with all kinds of difficulties which had developed during the preceding two years. In the communiqué announcing the meeting, the Germans succeeded in forcing the Russians to make a modified public renunciation of interference in Germany's domestic affairs, which had reached alarming proportions because the Comintern once again thought that the time was ripe to stir the German workers to action. The effort initiated by the *aide-mémoire* presented to Litvinov in 1928 thus bore some fruit. The sentences in question read:

> In open discussions [the two governments] have once again become clearly aware that the principal difference of the two governmental systems need be no obstacle to the fruitful development of their friendly relations. At the same time, both governments begin with the acknowledgment that no attempts to influence the internal affairs of the other country actively must be made.[54]

The announcement did not guarantee that the Comintern's interference in Germany would cease, but once again Berlin had to be satisfied with a general statement. In any event, the deepening depression, resulting widespread economic troubles, and increasing unemployment coincided with the extreme need of the USSR for money, engineers, technicians, and skilled workers to support the vast industrialization effort initiated by Stalin. Dirksen was not only willing but eager to make the most of the Russian requirements to alleviate the economic problems of his own country and at the same time to derive maximum political *quid pro quos* from Moscow. His efforts were more successful in the economic arena than in the political field. Dirksen convinced the German government to grant financial credits. This resulted in the signing of the so-called Pyatakov Agreement on April 14, 1931. The agreement provided a revolving credit of 300 million marks to the Soviet government which was guaranteed against default by the Reich government in the same way as the credit of February, 1926.

Economic relations improved spectacularly during Dirksen's tenure in Moscow, which ended in 1933. During 1931, the total value of orders placed by the USSR in Germany amounted to 919.2 million marks. During the first half of 1932, the Soviet Union purchased

> 50 per cent of all the cast iron and nickel exported by Germany, 60 per cent of all earth-moving equipment and dynamos sold abroad, 70 per cent of all metal-working machines, 80 per cent of cranes and sheet metals, and as much as 90 per cent of all steam and gas turbines and steam presses Germany exported.[55]

Dirksen estimated that "hundreds of thousands" continued to be employed in Germany only because of the orders placed by the Soviet Union. In addition, "hundreds or even thousands of German technicians and engineers" found employment in the USSR, many of them in Moscow, which necessitated the opening of a German school for their children.[56] Economic relations thus were tremendously improved, and profits for German business increased to a point where by the end of 1932 Germany's share in Russian imports was 46 percent, only 1.5 percent short of the German share during the last full year of peace.[57]

With these wonderful economic developments, even the most anti-Bolshevik business and financial interests in Germany competed eagerly for the favors of the despised regime. No longer were concerns about the Comintern voiced, as they had been by Counselor of Embassy Hey in one of his last reports, on September 30, 1928, to the Foreign Office. Hey then referred to speeches made at the Sixth Congress of the Comintern, which had called for a "battle of extermination" against the capitalists. The Red army, Hey had reported, was indoctrinated with that aim, and he saw no evidence that the Red army was on the way to becoming conservative, in the historical manner of revolutionary armies.[58]

As a matter of fact, such considerations did not face the Reichswehr, which went full steam ahead in the exploitation of the opportunities presented in the USSR for the continued experimentations in modern weapons. Just as the death of Stresemann on October 3, 1929, had not changed the German-Soviet political relationship, neither did the resignation of Gessler on St. Valentine's Day of the preceding year affect the clandestine relationship with the Red army, because General Wilhelm Groener followed the policy of his predecessor without change.

From August 19 to September 17, 1928, General von Blomberg, slated to become chief of the General Staff in January, and six officers made an extensive inspection tour of Soviet military installations. Throughout their stay, those in the party were treated by the Red Army Command as guests of honor. Blomberg found the tank school at Kazan functioning but hampered by the lack of operational tanks. After his return, the General saw to it that this lack was remedied. A first shipment of six "tractors" was ready for delivery, via Stettin, by the middle of May, 1929.

The situation was much better at the experimental station for gases at Volsk (Tomka), which had been activated during the summer. The Russians were extremely interested and supported the station splendidly. The flying school at Lipetsk was in the best of conditions, and at the troop training area, Voronezh, German pilots and a Russian battery cooperated in the most exemplary fashion. Blomberg recommended that the three undertakings be fully supported by Germany and utilized to the limits of the possible because of their "life and death importance from the point of view of military preparedness." Furthermore, the Reichswehr gained more from the experiments than did the Red army. Blomberg advised the expenditure of all necessary efforts to get the stations working at full capacity during 1929.

During their first talk, Voroshilov had played the Polish card and revived the proposal of December, 1924. He declared, "not only in the name of the Red army but also in the name of the government of the Soviet Union, that Russia is willing to extend every conceivable aid to Germany in case of a Polish attack." He asked Blomberg whether "the Soviet Union could count on Germany in case of a Polish attack?" Blomberg cagily refused to commit himself, replying that political decisions were outside his competency. Voroshilov refused to accept this evasion and emphasized, as Chicherin had in 1924, that the Polish matter "was a decisive question for the Soviet Union."[59]

The cooperation between the Red army and the Reichswehr was matched by the splendid working relationship between the Wilhelmstrasse and the Bendlerstrasse. Despite occasional concerns voiced by one or the other of the leading members of the Foreign Office, the military collaboration was not curtailed. Not even an occasional "revelation," such as the publication by the *Chicago Daily Tribune* (Paris edition) on November 11, 1929, of an interview with Gregory Bessedovsky, late chargé d'affaires at the Soviet Embassy in Paris, created much concern in Berlin or Moscow. The *Chicago Daily Tribune* shared this nonchalance and announced at the end of the article,

> It may be recalled that in the past Socialist members of the German Reichstag have on occasion accused the Reichswehr of just such relations.

Bessedovsky had "vengefully" told the *Tribune* about German-Soviet "munitions, airplanes, ordinance, and poison gas factories in Russia."[60]

The military relationship not only continued but received increased support from German industry. Only with the advent of Hitler did the collaboration come to an end, to the mutual sorrow of the Reichswehr and the Red army. The gas experiments were discontinued, the tank school at Kazan was deactivated on August 15, and Lipetsk closed on October 31, 1933.[61]

Dirksen and Litvinov were confronted with problems similar to those faced by their predecessors, but machinery had been developed by Brockdorff-Rantzau and Chicherin which made the resolution of conflicts a relatively routine matter. Certainly, the period from 1928 to

1933 did not witness any of the upheavals which had plagued German-Soviet relations during the six years after Rapallo. Brockdorff-Rantzau had conducted relations with the Soviet Union on the basis of *Realpolitik*. This attitude had sufficed for German-Soviet relations to survive Comintern attempts at revolution in Germany, and brought about the first grant of credits with the conclusion of the Grain Agreement in 1923. The penchant for *Realpolitik* convinced Brockdorff-Rantzau, Stresemann, Gessler, and successive chancellors and leading politicians that it was the better part of wisdom to condone, support, and expand the military collaboration between the Reichswehr and the Red army. Brockdorff-Rantzau's major concern, despite the political advantage, was the danger inherent in the possibility that the Russians would use the military relationship to blackmail Germany into extensive political concessions. That fear had proven groundless, as had the concern shared by all those in the Wilhelmstrasse, from Stresemann on down to Dirksen, that revelations might be made by indiscretion or because of discovery by the counterintelligence departments of foreign countries. That concern, too, had evaporated after December, 1926.

In political relations, Stresemann's policy had called the attacks by Brockdorff-Rantzau upon his head. Stresemann had proven strong-willed, and in the end the Ambassador bowed to the Foreign Minister. Schooled in the diplomacy of the nineteenth century, the Count had insisted that Germany should never align herself unilaterally with either the East or the West, and in this feeling he had found full understanding on the part of Stresemann. Every step West was balanced by another to the East: Locarno by the signature of the Commercial Treaty of October 12, 1925 (albeit without a neutrality preamble), and entry into the League of Nations by the Treaty of Berlin, strengthened by exemption of Germany from the provisions of Article 16 of the Covenant. With the Treaty of Berlin, the high point of diplomatic achievement had been reached by Brockdorff-Rantzau's efforts.

The structure which had been erected by the combined labors of Stresemann and Brockdorff-Rantzau, based on the cornerstone of Rapallo, gave Germany maximum possibilities for diplomatic maneuver. Her close relationship with Russia contained the tangible threat which forced the Western powers into one concession after another, culminating in Germany's elevation to a permanent seat on the Council of the League of Nations. After 1926 Germany was once again a major power, as power was reckoned in those days, basking in the good will of her neighbors.

The German-Soviet relationship continued on a profitable basis.

Even during the first few months after Hitler's accession it appeared as if no drastic changes were contemplated. At the end of April the Reichstag ratified the extension of the Treaty of Berlin for an indefinite period. But it soon became evident that the Nazis had no intentions of maintaining the old affiliation. Relations between the "new" Germany and the somewhat aged USSR were exposed to excruciating strains. Over the years, mutual, acrimonious recriminations reached such violent proportions that they seemed to contain the seeds of open conflict. Instead, at harvesttime, 1939, the Nazis and Bolsheviks concluded a nonaggression pact and partitioned Poland. It seemed as if nothing could keep the Germans and the Russians apart for long. Only after Hitler turned against his new ally and failed to conquer did the Soviet Union emerge dominant in Eastern Europe. A Communist regime was imported on the tanks of the Red army and installed in Berlin. Germany was divided and remains so to this day, one part allied with the West, the other controlled by Moscow. Every so often one can hear whisperings about a new Rapallo.

NOTES TO CHAPTERS

I. From Brest-Litovsk to Rapallo

1. J. Degras, *Soviet Documents on Foreign Policy* (3 vols.; New York: Oxford University Press, 1951–1953), I, 57. Hereafter, Degras.

2. National Archives Record Group 242, World War II Collection of Seized Enemy Records, Records of the German Foreign Ministry and the Reichschancellery covering the Weimar Period, Microcopy No. T–120, Note by Maltzan, August 20, 1920, Serial 2860H, roll no. 1404, frames D551 577–580. Hereafter, all documents from the above collection will be cited as follows: Specific reference, serial/roll/frames.

3. Degras, I, 85.

4. L. Fischer, *The Soviets in World Affairs* (2 vols.; Princeton: Princeton University Press, 1951), I, 127–128. Hereafter, Fischer, *Soviets*.

5. Degras, I, 111–112; 127–128.

6. The summary of the November events is based on E. Eyck, *Geschichte der Weimarer Republik* (2 vols.; Erlenbach-Zürich: Rentsch, 1956), I, 65–69. Hereafter, Eyck.

7. Degras, I, 124.

8. The following account of Brockdorff-Rantzau's career until his retirement in June, 1919, is based on: E. Stern-Rubarth, *Graf Brockdorff-Rantzau: Wanderer zwischen zwei Welten, Ein Lebensbild* (Berlin: R. Hobbing, 1929), hereafter, Stern-Rubarth; the Brandenburg Manuscript in the National Archives (Microcopy T–120); and Brockdorff-Rantzau's *Dokumente* (Charlottenburg: Deutsche Verlagsgesellschaft für Politik und Geschichte m.b.H., 1920), hereafter, *Dokumente*, unless otherwise footnoted.

9. K. F. Nowak, *Versailles* (Berlin: Verlag für Kulturpolitik, 1927), 303. Hereafter, Nowak.

10. Memorandum by Brockdorff-Rantzau, July 18, 1917, Brandenburg MS, 1690H/1013/396 937.

11. W. v. Blücher, *Deutschlands Weg nach Rapallo* (Wiesbaden: Limes Verlag, 1951), 42. Hereafter, Blücher.

12. This account of Radek's career is based on the most recent, brilliant analysis of the Communist rising by W. T. Angress, *Stillborn Revolution: The Communist Bid for Power in Germany, 1921–1923* (Princeton: Princeton Univeristy Press, 1963), 52–59.

13. *Dokumente*, 37–63.

14. Nowak, 145–163.

15. Fischer, *Soviets*, I, 323.

16. A. Luckau, *The German Delegation at the Paris Peace Conference* (New York: Columbia University Press, 1941), 61–62. Hereafter, Luckau.

17. Nowak, 256–259.

18. The Count's speech appears in *Dokumente*, 113–118; Simons' opinion in a

series of letters to his wife published in Luckau, 116–119; the recollections of the day are described in the 1925 edition of *Dokumente;* Nowak, 266.

19. P. Scheidemann, *The Making of the New Germany: The Memoirs of P. Scheidemann* (transl. J. E. Michell) (2 vols.; New York: Appleton, 1929), II, 309–311. Hereafter, Scheidemann.

20. Luckau, 419, 90.

21. G. *Stresemann, His Diaries, Letters, and Papers* (Ed. and trans. by E. Sutton) (3 vols.; New York: Macmillan, 1935–1940), II, 517. Hereafter, Stresemann.

22. Nowak, 314; Scheidemann, II, 316; Stern-Rubarth, 111–117.

23. *Dokumente* (1925), 125–126; Brockdorff-Rantzau to Simons, August 4, 1919, 1690H/1013/397 259.

24. Maltzan to Brockdorff-Rantzau, June 23, 1919, 9105H/3444/H225 706–709.

25. E. V. D'Abernon, *The Diary of an Ambassador* (3 vols.; Garden City, N.Y.: Doubleday and Doran, 1919–1931), II, 42. Hereafter, D'Abernon.

26. G. Hilger and A. G. Meyer, *The Incompatible Allies: A Memoir History of German-Soviet Relations, 1918–1941* (New York: Macmillan, 1953), 94. Hereafter, Hilger.

27. Text of the agreement, 4829H/2457/E241 391–392; L. Shapiro, *Soviet Treaty Series, 1917–1928* (2 vols.; Washington, D.C.: Georgetown University Press, 1950), I, 40–41. Hereafter, Shapiro.

28. Brockdorff-Rantzau on his talk with Ebert, March 3, 1920, Brandenburg MS, 1691H/1013/397 267–269.

29. Notes by Brockdorff-Rantzau, July, 1920, Brandenburg MS, 1691H/1013/397 293–297.

30. Letter by Simons to Chicherin, July 22, 1920, 2860H/1404/D551 564–566.

31. Maltzan to Brockdorff-Rantzau, August 6, 1920, 9105H/3445/237 050–054.

32. Chicherin to Simons, August 2, 1920, 2860H/1404/D551 574–576.

33. Maltzan to Brockdorff-Rantzau, August 14 and 18, 1920, 9105H/3445/236 822, 825–827.

34. Hilger, 56–59.

35. Minutes of Cabinet session, November 27; draft of Simons' speech, November 9, 1920, 2860H/1405/D552 001, 023–031.

36. Schlesinger to Maltzan and Behrendt, January 29 and February 7, 1921, 2860H/1405/D552 179–180, 194.

37. Hilger, 66.

38. Simons to Haniel and Behrendt, March 29 and 30, 1921, 2860H/1405/D552 213–215.

39. Notes by Schlesinger, April 1; Behrendt to Simons, April 4; notes by Brockdorff-Rantzau, April 24 and 25; excerpt of Cabinet minutes, April 26, 1921, 4829/2457/241 395; 2860H/1405/D552 194, 217, 244–246; Brandenburg MS, 1691H/1013/397 303–307, 309–313.

40. For the text of the agreements, see: 2860H/1405/D552 218–235, 255–257; Shapiro, I, 119–120.

41. X. J. Eudin and H. H. Fisher (eds.), *Soviet Russia and the West, 1920–1927: A Documentary Survey* (Stanford: Stanford University Press, 1957), 28. Hereafter, Eudin and Fisher.

42. Undated Foreign Office memorandum initialed by Maltzan on September 15, 1921, 1563H/785/378 139–144.

43. Letter of introduction for Wiedenfeld signed by Dr. Rosen, July 9, 1921. 1563H/785/378 126.

44. Blücher, 149.

45. Hilger, 71–73.

46. Wiedenfeld's report to the Foreign Office, September 19, 1921, 1563H/785/378 160–165.

47. Wiedenfeld to Foreign Office, Haniel to Wiedenfeld, October 15 and 19, 1921, 1563H/785/378 189–191, 205.

48. Wiedenfeld to Foreign Office, November 12, 1921, 1563H/785/378 217–221.

49. Notes by Simson, December 6, 1921, Hauschild to Schmidt-Rolke (Moscow), December 14, 1921, 6701H/3046/119 009, 1563H/785/378 300–303.

50. Schmidt-Rolke to Foreign Office, December 31, 1921, 1563H/785/378 276–278; 6701H/3046/119 099–104.

51. Schmidt-Rolke to Foreign Office, December 31, 1921, 2860H/1405/D552 334.

52. Eudin and Fisher, 98.

53. Maltzan to Brockdorff-Rantzau, January 9, 1922, 9105H/3445/237 141–143.

54. Brockdorff-Rantzau to Schlesinger, January 5, 1922, 9101H/3433/227 343–349.

55. D'Abernon, I, 261–264; Blücher, 154–155.

56. Wiedenfeld to Foreign Office, February 6, 1922, 1563H/785/378 315–321.

57. Rathenau to Radek, February 16, 1922, 2860H/1405/D552 375.

58. Legal opinion by Gaus, February 20, 1922, 1563H/785/378 414–416.

59. Wiedenfeld to Litvinov, February 27, 1922; Maltzan to Wiedenfeld, March 29, 1922, 1563H/785/378 223–225, 378 412.

60. Rathenau to Chicherin, April 1, *Pravda*, April 3, *New York Herald Tribune*, April 4, 1922, 2860H/1405/552 402, 1563H/785/378 430–431.

61. H. Helbig unravels the involved negotiations which took place in Berlin preliminary to the Treaty of Rapallo in his *Die Träger der Rapallo Politik* (Göttingen: Vandenhoeck and Ruprecht, 1958), 73–101. Hereafter, Helbig, *Rapallo*.

62. Fischer, *Soviets* (one-volume abridged edition, 1960), 244–251.

63. April 16, 1922, 6698H/3036/H111 746.

64. Blücher, 166; for Nadolny's background and subsequent career, see Hilger, 261; Ebert to Brockdorff-Rantzau, July 3, 1922, Brandenburg MS, 1691H/1013/397 361.

65. Notes by Brockdorff-Rantzau, May 10, 1922, 9105H/3429/H223 115–121.

66. Notes by Brockdorff-Rantzau, June 23, 1922, 9105H/3429/H223 125–127; Brandenburg MS, 1691H/1013/397 343, 357; Helbig, 106–110.

67. Hilger, 94; H. V. Dirksen, *Moscow, Tokyo, London: Twenty Years of German Foreign Policy* (Norman, Okla.: University of Oklahoma Press, 1952), p. 48; hereafter, Dirksen.

68. Notes by Brockdorff-Rantzau, 9105H/3429/223 146–149, 201–207, 210–215; Brandenburg MS, 1691H/1013/397 361–365, 386–390, 393.

69. Notes by Brockdorff-Rantzau, 9105H/3429/H223 226–230.

70. Notes by Brockdorff-Rantzau, 9105H/3430/H223 251–256; Brandenburg MS, 1691H/1013/397 421–425.

71. Complete texts of the "Politische Richtlinien" are in 9105H/3429/H223 225–232, as well as in the Brandenburg MS, 1691H/1013/397 396–402.

72. Notes by Brockdorff-Rantzau, 9105H/3429/223 257–258, 270–275; Brandenburg MS, 1691H/1013/397 429, 431–435.

73. Brandenburg MS, 1691H/1013/397 440–441; Helbig, 119–120.

74. This agrees, as far as the conversation is concerned, with a letter Seeckt wrote to his wife on May 4, 1919. F. V. Rabenau, *Seeckt: Aus Seinem Leben,*

1918–1936 (Leipzig: Hase and Koehler, 1940), p. 165; hereafter, Rabenau. Seeckt did act as advisor to the Foreign Office after his retirement in 1926.

75. Seeckt later admitted that he had deliberately accused the Count of sacrificing the nation's honor. (Rabenau, 178.)

76. Notes by Brockdorff-Rantzau, 9105H/3429/H223 283 ff; 6812H/3154/E517 771.

77. F. Ebert, *Schriften, Aufzeichnungen, Reden* (2 vols.; Dresden: Reissner Verlag, 1926), II, 247–248.

78. Brockdorff-Rantzau to Theodor Wolff, editor of the *Berliner Tageblatt,* August 4, 1922, 6812H/3154/E517 808–809.

79. For the various drafts and notes for the *Promemoria,* see 6812H/3154/E517 779–793, 799–807; 9105H/3429/H223 300–304; for the *Promemoria,* 9105H/3429/H223 327–336; H. Helbig, "Die Moskauer Mission des Grafen Brockdorff-Rantzau," *Forschungen zur Osteuropäischen Geschichte,* II (1955), 331–335, hereafter, Helbig, "Moskauer Mission"; and G. Freund, *Unholy Alliance: Russian-German Relations from the Treaty of Brest-Litovsk to the Treaty of Berlin* (London: Chatto and Windus, 1957), pp. 131–134, hereafter, Freund. Dr. Freund published a translation of the *Promemoria* based on the document appended to Prof. Helbig's article. Helbig was the first writer to point out that the misdating goes back to the abridged version of the *Promemoria* published by J. Epstein, "Der Seeckt Plan," *Der Monat,* 1. Jahrgang, no. 2 (Berlin, November, 1948).
The following cite the *Promemoria* and/or quote from it, but misdate it July 15, 1922: Hilger, 91–94; H. Holborn, "Diplomats and Diplomacy in the Early Weimar Republic," in A. G. Craig and F. Gilbert (eds.) *The Diplomats, 1919–1939* (Princeton: Princeton University Press, 1953), p. 149; L. Kochan, *Russia and the Weimar Republic* (Cambridge, Eng.: Bowes and Bowes, 1954), pp. 62–63, hereafter, Kochan; J. W. Wheeler-Bennett, *The Nemesis of Power: The German Army in Politics, 1918–1945* (New York: St. Martin's Press, 1954), pp. 132–133.

80. "Bericht des Kapitän zur See Lohmann über die Dienstreise nach Moskau vom 27. Mai bis 19. Juni 1922," 9105H/3445/237 149–178; notes by Brockdorff-Rantzau on two talks with Lohmann, August 24 and September 1, 1922, 6812H/3154/E517 811–812, 828–830, 837; with Behnke, August 26, 1922, *ibid.,* 811.

81. Notes by Brockdorff-Rantzau, September 5, 1922, 9105H/3429/H223 361–365; 6812H/3154/E517 728–732; Brockdorff-Rantzau to Maltzan, April 13 and 19, 1923, and to Stresemann, March J8, 1924, 9101H/3431/H224 853–854, 3432/H226 813, 825.

82. Notes by Brockdorff-Rantzau about his talk with Wirth, 9105H/3429/H223 366–373, 6812/3154/517 838–839, 845–846; Brandenburg MS, 1691H/1013/397 479–483; Helbig, 123–124.

83. Notes by Brockdorff-Rantzau, 9105H/3429/H223 374–379; Helbig, 123–124.

84. Notes by Brockdorff-Rantzau, 9105H/3429/H223 380–389; Brandenburg MS, 1691H/1013/397 497–498; Helbig, 124–125.

85. Rabenau, II, 315–318; Freund, 135–140.

86. Brockdorff-Rantzau's notes on his discussion with Ebert, September 13, 1922, 9105H/3429/H223 412–422; Brandenburg MS, 1691H/1013/397 505–509; Helbig, 125–126.

87. Notes by Brockdorff-Rantzau about his talk with Stresemann, September 15, 1922, 6812H/3154/E517 869–878.

88. Notes by Brockdorff-Rantzau, 6812H/3154/E517 879–880, 896–897; Helbig, *Rapallo,* 124, n. 54.

89. Brockdorff-Rantzau to Wirth, October 4, 1922, 6812H/3154/E517 913–915.

90. Brockdorff-Rantzau to Simons, October 7, 1922, 6812H/3154/E517 932–935.

91. Notes by Brockdorff-Rantzau, October 16, 1922, 6812H/3154/E517 948.

92. Waurick had told the Count on October 5 that Colonel Hasse had asked Chicherin to reconsider the Count's *agrément*. On October 19, Captain Lohmann confirmed Waurick's information, and on the following day Brockdorff-Rantzau asked Wirth to tell Gessler that the Count now had positive proof of Hasse's action. The Count considered Hasse's action high treason. Through Gessler's intercession, an appointment between the Count and Colonel Hasse was arranged. The Colonel categorically denied the truth of the charge. Hasse followed this with a letter to the Count in which he repeated his oral denial.

Notes by Brockdorff-Rantzau on the talks with Waurick, Lohmann, Wirth, Gessler, and Hasse, October 5, 19, and 20, and the letter by Hasse dated October 21, 1922, 6812H/3154/E517 927–928, 978–979, 988, 989–993, 738.

93. Notes by Brockdorff-Rantzau, October 16, 1922, 6812H/3154/E517 940–951; Helbig, *Rapallo*, 128.

94. Notes by Brockdorff-Rantzau, October 19, 1922, 6812H/3154/E517 970–971, 975–987; Brandenburg MS, 1691H/1013/397 525–527.

95. Memorandum by Brockdorff-Rantzau, October 22, 1922, 6812H/3154/E518 008–009; Brandenburg MS, 1691H/1013/397 529.

96. Simons to Brockdorff-Rantzau, October 25, 1922, 6812H/3154/E517 739; Helbig, 129, n. 68.

97. Gessler to Brockdorff-Rantzau, October 27, 1922, 6812H/3154/E517 739; Brockdorff-Rantzau to Gessler, October 28, 1922, *ibid.*, E517 718–720. Brockdorff-Rantzau had already drafted this letter on October 22, *ibid.*, E517 998–E518 001.

98. Blücher, 169–170.

99. Brockdorff-Rantzau to Maltzan, March 27, 1923, 9101H/3431/H224 907–914; Brandenburg MS, 1692H/1013/397 563; Helbig, *Rapallo*, 143–144.

II. A YEAR OF CRISIS

1. The description of Brockdorff-Rantzau's arrival and reception is based on: Hilger to Schlesinger, November 5, 1922, 4829H/2457/241 599; Brockdorff-Rantzau to Foreign Office, November 3 and 5, 1922, 2860H/1405/D552 676–678, 684; Brockdorff-Rantzau to Maltzan, November 17 and 18 and December 9, 1922, 9101H/3431/H225 170–175, 158–162, 092–097; Foreign Office notes, 1565H/911/378 758, 769; Brockdorff-Rantzau, *Dokumente* (1925 ed.), 208; Hilger, 97; Freund, 140; Stern-Rubarth, 130.

2. Brockdorff-Rantzau to Maltzan, November 4, 12, and 17, 1922; Maltzan to Brockdorff-Rantzau, November 17, 18, and 23, and December 2, 1922, 9101H/3431/H225 221, 188, 193, 178, 168–169, 152–155, 109–115.

3. Brockdorff-Rantzau to Foreign Office, to Maltzan, November 24 and December 9, 1922, Maltzan to Brockdorff-Rantzau, November 28, December 9 and 15, 1922, 1565H/911/378 750–751, 9101H/3431/H225 092–097, 087–091.

4. Brockdorff-Rantzau to Maltzan, December 6 and 11, Maltzan to Brockdorff-Rantzau, December 22, 1922, Brockdorff-Rantzau to Ernst Rantzau, January 1, 1923, 9101H/3431/H225 094, 075–082, 049–051, 9101H/3430/H224 127.

5. Maltzan to Brockdorff-Rantzau, December 15, 16, 29, 1922, and January 6, 1923; Brockdorff-Rantzau to Maltzan, December 17, 20, 26, 1922, and January 6, 1923, 9101H/3431/H225 083–084, 086, 030, 023, 068–074; 2860H/1405/D552

719; for the Tukhachevsky proposal, see H. W. Gatzke, "Russo-German Military Collaboration during the Weimar Republic," *American Historical Review*, LXIII (April, 1958), p. 571; hereafter, Gatzke.

6. *The New York Times*, January 17, 1923.

7. *Pravda*, January 11, 1923, cited in Eudin and Fisher, 210.

8. Maltzan to Brockdorff-Rantzau, January 6, 1923, 9101H/3431/H225 025; *The New York Times*, January 15, 16, and 18, 1923.

9. Gessler to Brockdorff-Rantzau, December 20, 1922, January 18, 1923, 6812H/3154/E517 716–717, 710–712; Brockdorff-Rantzau to Gessler, January 7, 1923, *ibid.*, E517 713–715; Notes by Brockdorff-Rantzau, January 29, 1923, 9101H/3446/H237 399–402; Helbig, *Rapallo*, 129, n. 68 and 151, n. 7.

10. Hentig to Foreign Office, January 26 and 28, 1923, 2860H/1405/D552 755; 4562H/2313/E154 844; Political Report No. 4, January 29, 1923, 4562H/2313/E154 846–849.

11. Brockdorff-Rantzau to Rosenberg, February 4, 1923, 4562H/2313/154 842–3; Maltzan to Brockdorff-Rantzau, February 2, 1923, 9101H/3431/H225 010–015.

12. Notes by Brockdorff-Rantzau, February 3, 1923, 4562H/2313/E154 827–835; Brockdorff-Rantzau to Foreign Office, February 10 and 11, 1923, E154 837–841.

13. Maltzan to Brockdorff-Rantzau, February 9, 1923, 9101H/3431/225 006; Brockdorff-Rantzau to Foreign Office, February 11, 1923, 4562H/2313/154 839–841.

14. Rauscher (German Ambassador in Warsaw) to Foreign Office, March 1, 1923, 2860H/1406/D552 808.

15. Brockdorff-Rantzau to Foreign Office, March 6, 1923, 2860H/1406/D552 821–822; Hauschild to Brockdorff-Rantzau, March 27, 1923, D552 870.

16. Brockdorff-Rantzau to Maltzan, March 2, 1923, 2860H/1406/D552 815.

17. Brockdorff-Rantzau to Maltzan, February, 1923, 9101H/3431/H224 972–974.

18. While in Russia, the officers who customarily dealt with the Red army and the representatives of the Soviet government used pseudonyms which began with the initial of their last names. Thus Major Fischer used the *nom de guerre* Francke, Major Tschunke was known as Teichmann, Lieutenant Colonel Mentzel as Morsbach, and Major Niedermayer as Neumann, although at least once he used the *nom de plume* Siebert. Colonel Hasse, who was in charge of the military collaboration during its early stages, went to Russia as Herr Heller.

The identity of Francke, Teichmann, Neumann, and Morsbach is revealed in the draft of a letter by Brockdorff-Rantzau to Maltzan, April 13, 1923, 9101H/3431/H224 853–854, and that of Heller in another letter to Maltzan, 9101H/3431/H225 630.

19. Brockdorff-Rantzau to Maltzan, February 15, 1923; Maltzan to Brockdorff-Rantzau, April 19, 1923, 9101H/3431/H224 975–976, 815; Brockdorff-Rantzau to Rosenberg, March 1, 1923, 2860H/1406/D552 825–831.

20. Brockdorff-Rantzau to Stresemann, September 10, 1923, 9101/3432/H226 782–783; Hilger, 200; Helbig, 151 ff.

For the reference to the memorandum, see: 9101/3431/H224 952–954, 928. A note signed by Counselor of Legation Bohnstedt, dated March 21, 1923, contains the information that a letter and two enclosures from Brockdorff-Rantzau to the Chancellor were "burned today." 2860H/1406/D552 824.

21. Brockdorff-Rantzau to Maltzan, March 7, 1923, 9101H/3431/H224 956;

Brandenburg, 1692H/1013/397 582; Helbig, "Moskauer Mission," 316; Freund, 142; Hilger, 184.

22. Schlesinger to Brockdorff-Rantzau, March 10, April 5, and April 12, 1923, 9101H/3432/H227 296, 265, 257–258, 255; Maltzan to Brockdorff-Rantzau, 9101H/3431/H224 814–815; Schlesinger to Brockdorff-Rantzau, April 19, 1923, 9101H/3433/H227 252–254; Brockdorff-Rantzau to Schlesinger, April 30, 1923, 9101H/3433/H227 241. The agreement was ratified by Moscow and Berlin on July 5, 1923. Foreign Office memorandum, 1565H/911/379 018.

23. Brockdorff-Rantzau to Maltzan, March 28, 1923, 9101H/3432/H224 892–893; Helbig, *Rapallo,* 132.

24. Brockdorff-Rantzau to Maltzan, April 18, 1923, 9101H/3432/H224 832–835; Brockdorff-Rantzau to Cuno, April 26, 1923, 4562H/2313/E154 853; Maltzan to Brockdorff-Rantzau, February 23, 1923, 9101H/3432/H224 969–971.

25. Maltzan and Wallroth to Brockdorff-Rantzau, April 21, 1923, 2860H/1406/D552 930; Brockdorff-Rantzau to Foreign Office, April 25, 1923, 2860H/1406/D552 936; Brockdorff-Rantzau to Cuno, April 26, 1923, 4562H/2313/E154 850–851, 854–857.

26. Brockdorff-Rantzau to Maltzan, April 28 and May 1, 1923, 9101/3431/224 826, 645–646.

27. Brockdorff-Rantzau to Foreign Office, *Political Report No. 10, Geheim,* May 7, 1923, 4562H/2313/154 852–861.

28. Brockdorff-Rantzau to Maltzan, May 9, 1923, 9101H/3431/H225 620; Maltzan to Brockdorff-Rantzau, May 18 and 31, 1923, *ibid.,* 596, 599, 601, 582–583.

29. Ministry of the Interior to Foreign Office, June 8, 1923; 3242H/1591/D713 473; Wallroth to Moscow, St. Petersburg (the Germans continued to refer to Petrograd by its old appellation), and Kharkov, June 13, 1923, 2860H/1406/D553 074.

30. Maltzan to Brockdorff-Rantzau, June 7, 1923, 9101H/3431/H225 556; Foreign Office notes, 1565H/911/378 831–833.

31. Brockdorff-Rantzau to Maltzan, May 31, June 6, 7, and 13, 1923, 9101H/3431/H225 577, 549–552, 559–560, 525–530; Maltzan to Brockdorff-Rantzau, June 19, 22, and 29, 1923, 9101H/3431/H225 508–520, 497.

32. Brockdorff-Rantzau to Maltzan, April 28, 1923, 9101H/3431/H224 826; Brockdorff-Rantzau to Stresemann, September 10, 1923, 9101H/3432/H226 783–784; Helbig, *Rapallo,* 151; Brockdorff-Rantzau to Cuno, June 16 and July 10, 1923, 4564H/2329/162 523–524, 529–532; Cuno to Brockdorff-Rantzau, June 20, 1923, *ibid.,* 162 525.

33. Notes by Maltzan about the meeting, July 12, 1923, 4564H/2329/162 559; Maltzan to Brockdorff-Rantzau, July 12, 1923, 9101H/3431/H225 438–439; Brockdorff-Rantzau to Maltzan, July 11, 1923, *ibid.,* 454–456.

34. Brockdorff-Rantzau to Stresemann, February 20, 1924, 9101H/3432/H226 805–806; memorandum by Brockdorff-Rantzau for Cuno, July 29, 1923, 4564H/2329/162 539–549; Brockdorff-Rantzau to Maltzan, July 5, 1923, 9101H/3431/H225 472–475; Gatzke, 572–573.

35. Notes of the meeting by Brockdorff-Rantzau, July 31, 1923, 4564H/2329/162 550–555; approved by Cuno on August 2, 1923.

36. Brockdorff-Rantzau to Stresemann, September 10, 1923, 9101H/3432/H226 785–788; Gatzke, 573–574; Helbig, 155.

37. Hilger, 194.

38. Maltzan to chargé d'affaires (Radowitz), August 13 and 22, 1923, 4564H/2329/162 731–732.

39. Gatzke, 575–576.

40. Brockdorff-Rantzau to Stresemann, September 10, 1923, and February 20, 1924, 9101H/3432/H226 781–788, 807.

In this context, it is interesting to note that the British *Morning Post* had published an article in its August 16 issue in which it was stated that "Germany has evidently decided to restore her military might on Russian territory. . . . At present, everything connected with the Soviet Air Force and poison gas sections of the Red Army is, it is stated, entirely in the hands of Germans. All munitions factories working for the Soviet Army Commissariat are staffed by German experts. . . ." Foreign Office to Moscow Embassy, August 23, 1923, 1565H/911/378 927.

41. Brockdorff-Rantzau to Stresemann, February 20, 1924, 9101H/3432/H226 807; Gatzke, 575.

42. Brockdorff-Rantzau to Stresemann, February 20, 1924, 9101H/3432/H226 807–808; Gatzke, 575; Brockdorff-Rantzau to Foreign Office, September 23, 1923, 2860H/1406/D553 225–227; Brockdorff-Rantzau to Maltzan, October 4, 1923, 9101/3431/H225 415–417.

43. Brockdorff-Rantzau to Stresemann, February 20 and April 9, 1924, 9101H/3432/H226 807–808, 822–826; Brockdorff-Rantzau to Maltzan, November 29, 1923, and April 17, 1924, 9101H/3431/H225 273–275, 943.

44. September 22, 1923, 1565H/911/378 974–975.

45. *The New York Times,* September 23, 1923, announced the arrival of the two Communists. R. Fischer, *Stalin und der deutsche Kommunismus* (Frankfurt: Verlag der Frankfurte Hefte, no date), p. 379, states that Brandler arrived at the end of August and was followed by his closest collaborators. Hereafter, R. Fischer.

46. Grosskopf (German Consul in Siberia) to Brockdorff-Rantzau, September 25, 1923, 1565/911/378 956–957.

47. Brockdorff-Rantzau to Foreign Office, October 1, 1923, 2860H/1406/553 242.

48. Degras, I, 410; Wallroth to Moscow, September 25, 1923, 2860H/1406/553 229; *The New York Times,* September 26, 1923.

49. Maltzan to Brockdorff-Rantzau, September 28, 1923, 9101H/3431/H225 427–429, 414–419; Brockdorff-Rantzau to Maltzan, October 4, 1923.

50. Degras, I, 410–412; Brockdorff-Rantzau to Foreign Office, October 6, 1923, 2860H/1406/553 247–248.

51. Brockdorff-Rantzau to Foreign Office, October 9, 1923, 2860H/1406/553 254.

52. Brockdorff-Rantzau to Maltzan, October 13, 1923, 9101H/3431/H225 400–402.

53. Ministry of the Interior to Foreign Office, October 15, 1923, 1565H/911/378 970–971.

54. Maltzan to Brockdorff-Rantzau, October 12 and 19, 1923, 9101H/3431/H225 407–408, 394; Eyck, 353–354.

55. R. Fischer, 257–258.

56. Brockdorff-Rantzau to Maltzan, October 19, 1923, 9101H/3431/H225 389–391; Maltzan to Brockdorff-Rantzau, October 23, Brockdorff-Rantzau to Foreign Office, October 23 and 25, 1923, 2860H/1406/553 285, 287, 293.

57. Brockdorff-Rantzau to Stresemann, October 26, 1923, 9101H/3432/H226 798–799; Helbig, *Rapallo,* 160.

58. Maltzan to Brockdorff-Rantzau, October 19 and December 6, 1923, 9101H/3431/H225 395–396, 398, 259–260; December 7, 1923; Brockdorff-Rantzau to

Maltzan, December 8, 1923, *ibid.*, 246; Brockdorff-Rantzau to Stresemann, March 18, 1924, *ibid.*, 812–813; Hauschild to Brockdorff-Rantzau, January 15, 1924, 1565H/911/379 043; Brockdorff-Rantzau to Ernst Rantzau, January 31, 1924, 9101H/3430/H224 227–228; Maltzan to Brockdorff-Rantzau, January 31, 1924, 9101H/3431/H226 003.

59. Brockdorff-Rantzau to Maltzan, October 26, 1923, 9101H/3431/H225 381–383; Brockdorff-Rantzau to Schlesinger, October 25, 1923, 9101H/3433/H227 287–288.

60. Maltzan to Brockdorff-Rantzau, October 27, 1923, 9101H/3431/H225 373–375.

61. Consulate General, St. Petersburg, to Foreign Office, 1565H/911/378 992–993.

62. Hilger to Schlesinger, October 27, 1923, 4829H/2457/241 799–800.

63. Telegrams from Rauscher (Warsaw), Olshausen (Kovno), Wedel (Memel), and Brockdorff-Rantzau to Foreign Office, October 29–31, 1923, 2860H/1406/D553 294–304.

64. Brockdorff-Rantzau to Maltzan, November 2, 1923, 9101H/H225/3431/351–355; Freund, 184, 186–187.

65. Brockdorff-Rantzau to Foreign Office, November 3, 1923, 2860H/1406/553 309.

66. Schlesinger to Brockdorff-Rantzau, November 8, 1923, 9101H/3429/H223 700–702; 3433/H227 280; Brockdorff-Rantzau to Schlesinger, November 14, 1923, 9101/3433/H227 278–279.

67. Maltzan to Brockdorff-Rantzau, November 8, 15, and 29, 1923, 9101H/3431/H225 319, 332–334, 263–265; Brockdorff-Rantzau to Schlesinger, November 14, Schlesinger to Brockdorff-Rantzau, November 29, 1922, 9101H/3433/H227 279, 271.

68. Stresemann, I, 255–256; Kochan, 93–94; Freund, 168.

69. Brockdorff-Rantzau to Maltzan, December 8, Maltzan to Brockdorff-Rantzau, November 29, 1923, 9101H/3431/H225 245–246, 249, 250, 265.

70. Brockdorff-Rantzau to Foreign Office, December 4 and 7, 1923, 2860H/1406/553 382–384, 396.

71. Moscow Embassy to Foreign Office, December 7, 1923, 1565H/911/379 008.

72. Brockdorff-Rantzau to Foreign Office, December 9, 13, 16, and 17, 1923, 2860H/1406/553 400–402, 411, 416–417, 419; Brockdorff-Rantzau to Maltzan, December 14, 1923, 9101H/3431/H225 228–232; Political Report No. 17, December 14, 1923, signed by Brockdorff-Rantzau, Graap, Hilger, and Hencke, 6698H/3036/H111 754–763.

73. Brockdorff-Rantzau to Stresemann, February 4, 1924, 9101H/3432/H226 799.

74. Brockdorff-Rantzau to Foreign Office, January 20 and May 3, 1924, 2860H/1406/553 537, 807–809.

75. Brockdorff-Rantzau to Stresemann, February 4, 1924, 9101H/3432/H226 797–804; Brockdorff-Rantzau to Maltzan, in a similar vein, on May 15, 1924, 9101H/3431/H225 869; Helbig, *Rapallo*, 161.

76. D'Abernon, III, 43–44.

77. Memorandum on Russian Exports and Imports through the Trade Mission in Berlin, November 27, 1923, 1565H/911/378 968–969.

III. THE BOZENHARDT INCIDENT

1. Wallroth to Brockdorff-Rantzau, May 3, 1924, Hauschild to Brockdorff-Rantzau, May 16, 1924, 2860H/1407/553 804–805, 949; Maltzan to Brockdorff-Rantzau, May 22, 1924, 9101H/3431/H225 860.

2. Prussian Ministry of the Interior, copy of the verdict in the so-called "Cheka Trial," submitted to the Foreign Office on August 12, 1925, 6698H/3028/106 544–583; notes by Bernhard, May 7, 1924, 2860H/1407/553 799–801.

3. Hauschild Memorandum, June 16, 1924, 9101H/3432/H226 486–487.

4. Foreign Office to Krestinsky, May 3, 1924, 6720H/3054/H121 235–236.

5. Brockdorff-Rantzau to Foreign Office, May 5, 1924, 2860H/1407/553 822–823.

6. Stresemann to Brockdorff-Rantzau, May 6, 1924, 2860H/1407/553 824–825; Maltzan to Brockdorff-Rantzau, May 8 and 15, 1924, 9101H/3431/H225 875–876, 879–885, 877.

7. Brockdorff-Rantzau to Ernst Rantzau, May 7 and 14/15, 1924, 9101H/3430/H224 258–259, 261–262.

8. Brockdorff-Rantzau to Maltzan, May 7, Maltzan to Brockdorff-Rantzau, May 18, 1924, 9101H/3431/H225 892–897, 877; Foreign Office to Brockdorff-Rantzau, May 8, 1924, 2860H/1407/553 849.

9. Brockdorff-Rantzau to Foreign Office, May 12, 1924, 2860H/1407/553 899.

10. Stresemann to Brockdorff-Rantzau, May 13, 1924, 2860H/1407/553 899.

11. Brockdorff-Rantzau to Foreign Office, May 13, and to Stresemann, May 15, 1924, 2860H/1407/553 915–916, 940–941; Maltzan to Brockdorff-Rantzau, May 15 and 22, Brockdorff-Rantzau to Maltzan, May 15, 1924, 9101H/3431/H225 871–874, 859, 866–869.

12. Brockdorff-Rantzau to Foreign Office, January 17, 1924, 2860H/1406/553 564.

13. Seven-page note and enclosures signed by Stresemann; marginal notation indicating that the material was dispatched airmail, special delivery, on May 20; Brockdorff-Rantzau to Foreign Office, May 22, 1924, Hauschild to Brockdorff-Rantzau, May 23, 1924, 2860H/1407/553 975–980, 554 005.

14. Brockdorff-Rantzau to Foreign Office, May 24, Hauschild to Brockdorff-Rantzau, May 25, 1924, 2860H/1407/554 020, 014, 031; Maltzan to Brockdorff-Rantzau, May 22, 1924, 9101H/3431/H225 859–860.

15. Brockdorff-Rantzau to Maltzan, May 23, 1924, 9101H/3431/H225 855–857.

16. Brockdorff-Rantzau to Ebert, May 23, 1924, 9101H/3430/H223 923–924; Brandenburg MS, 1692H/1013/397 740–742.

17. Brockdorff-Rantzau to Foreign Office, May 26, Maltzan to Brockdorff-Rantzau, May 27, Stresemann to Brockdorff-Rantzau, May 26, 2860H/1407/544 029, 042–044, 033–035; Schlesinger to Brockdorff-Rantzau, May 30, 1924, 9101/3433/227 190–193.

18. Brockdorff-Rantzau to Foreign Office, Stresemann to Brockdorff-Rantzau, May 28, 29, and 30, Hauschild to Brockdorff-Rantzau, May 29, 1924, 2860H/1407/554 047–050, 062–066.

19. Maltzan to Brockdorff-Rantzau, May 30, 1924, 9101H/3431/H225 849–850.

20. Brockdorff-Rantzau to Foreign Office, May 30, 31, June 1, 1924, 2860H/ 1407/554 074–077, 083, 095–109; Hilger, 180–181.

21. Brockdorff-Rantzau to Maltzan, June 1, Maltzan to Brockdorff-Rantzau, June 5, 1924, 9101H/3431/H225 843–845; June 4, 1924, 2860H/1407/554 093.

22. Brockdorff-Rantzau to Foreign Office, with a request to inform the President, June 3, 1924, 2860H/1407/554 110–112.

23. Schlesinger to Brockdorff-Rantzau, June 6, Brockdorff-Rantzau to Maltzan, June 6, 1924, 9101H/3433/H227 182–184, 9101H/3431/H225 830–835; Maltzan to Brockdorff-Rantzau, June 2, 1924, 2860H/1407/554 084.

24. For details on the Junkers–Special Group R–Red army relationship, see: copy of the contract, 6898H/3027/105 464–489; copy of the concession, November 7, 1922; on the negotiations for the concession, Moscow Embassy memorandum, January 31, 1924; copy of the Junkers letter to the Main Concessions Committee, March 31, 1924, 9444H/3662/H273 314–328, 309, 292–303; Junkers Moscow to Junkers Dessau (on the Russian orders), April 26; on the discussions in the Wilhelmstrasse, Hauschild to Brockdorff-Rantzau, April 27, 1924, 2860H/1407/ 553 774, 776, 4564H/2329/162 622–627; on the military negotiations in January, 1924, Brockdorff-Rantzau to Maltzan, January 21, 25, and 31, 1924, 2860H/1406/ 553 539, 557; 4564H/2329/162 566; Maltzan to Brockdorff-Rantzau, 9101/3431/ 226 002.

For the Junkers' side in these involved deals, see: 9472H/3663/H273 736–816.

25. Brockdorff-Rantzau to Maltzan, May 1, 1924, 4564H/2329/162 742; Brockdorff-Rantzau to Maltzan, April 29 and 30, 1924, 2860H/1407/553 783– 784, 6812H/3431/225 903–904; Maltzan to Brockdorff-Rantzau, April 24, May 1, 7, and 8, 1924, 6812H/3431/225 883–884, 898, 4564H/2329/162 632–633, 741; Helbig, *Rapallo*, 163, n. 38.

26. Brockdorff-Rantzau to Foreign Office, May 19, Maltzan to Brockdorff-Rantzau, May 26, 1924, 4564H/2329/162 634, 745. For the details of the relationship between the Reichswehr and the Red air force, see: K-H. Völker, *Die Entwicklung der Militärischen Luftfahrt in Deutschland, 1920–1933* (Stuttgart: Deutsche Verlags-Austalt, 1962). Hereafter, Völker, *Entwicklung der Militärischen Luftfahrt*.

27. Brockdorff-Rantzau sent a copy of his notes on the discussion with Trotsky to Stresemann on June 13, 1924, 9101H/3432/H226 883; Freund, Appendix B, pp. 254–258, gives the whole interview in English translation; Brockdorff-Rantzau to Maltzan, June 21, 1924, 9101/3431/H225 795.

28. Brockdorff-Rantzau to Foreign Office, June 20, 1924, 2860H/1407/554 117–178; Hilger to Schlesinger, June 21, 1924, 4829H/2457/241 991.

29. Brockdorff-Rantzau to Maltzan, June 14 and 21, 1924, 9101H/3431/H225 794–795, 812–813; Brockdorff-Rantzau to Ernst Rantzau, June 29/30, 1924, 9101H/3430/H224 271.

30. Maltzan to Brockdorff-Rantzau, July 3, 1924, 9101H/3431/H225 790–792; July 11, 1924, *ibid.*, H225 786–788; Stresemann to Brockdorff-Rantzau, June 30, July 1 and 3, Brockdorff-Rantzau to Stresemann, July 2, 1924, 2860H/1407/554 201, 204–205, 207–210.

31. Stresemann to Brockdorff-Rantzau, July 4 and 13, 1924, 2860H/1407/554 212–213, 239–240; Brockdorff-Rantzau to Stresemann, July 2, 6, 10, 12, and 15, 1924, 2860H/1407/554 210, 217–219, 228–230, 236, 242; Brockdorff-Rantzau to Maltzan, July 13, 1924, 9101H/3431/H225 815–817.

32. Copy of a "Memorandum regarding a confidential discussion in the People's Commissariat for Foreign Affairs on July 17/18, 1924," 2860H/1407/554 274–275.

33. Brockdorff-Rantzau to Maltzan, July 19, 1924, 9101H/3431/H225 776–772; Brockdorff-Rantzau to Stresemann, July 18, 1924, 2860H/1407/554 246; Brandenburg MS, 1692H/1013/397 729–733.

34. Maltzan to Brockdorff-Rantzau, July 18, 1924, 9101H/3431/H225 782–784; Stresemann to Brockdorff-Rantzau, July 25, 1924, 2860H/1407/554 260–263.

35. Brockdorff-Rantzau to Foreign Office, July 26, Brockdorff-Rantzau to Stresemann, July 27, 1924, 2860H/1407/554 266–267.

36. Brockdorff-Rantzau to Maltzan, July 27, 1924, 9101H/3431/H225 767–769.

37. Shapiro, I, 277; Fischer, Soviets, II, 583; Hilger, 181–182; Freund, 197–199; Helbig, 135–138.

38. Maltzan to German missions abroad, July 29, Radowitz to Foreign Office, August 12, 1924, 2860H/1407/554 277–278, 305.

39. Degras, I, 463.

IV. Alliance with the East or Alignment with the West?

1. Maltzan to Brockdorff-Rantzau, July 3, 1924, 9101H/3431/H225 793.
2. Eudin and Fisher, 262.
3. MacDonald to Marx, August 22, 1924, 9101H/3432/H226 973.
4. Kopp to Maltzan, August 23, 1924, 2860H/1407/554 323–325.
5. Foreign Office to London Embassy, August 25, Foreign Office memoranda, September 1 and 3, 1924, 9101H/3432/H226 974, 984, 986.
6. Brockdorff-Rantzau to Maltzan, April 13, 1924, 9101H/3431/H225 988–993, 956.
7. Brockdorff-Rantzau to Maltzan, Radowitz to Maltzan, Maltzan to Radowitz, September 8, 13, 17, 20, 1924, 9101H/3432/H226 978; 2860H/1407/554 356, 349–350, 553.
8. Fischer, Soviets, II, 592.
9. Radowitz to Maltzan, September 23, Stresemann to Radowitz, September 23, 1924, 2860H/1407/554 366–369.
10. Notes by Stresemann, September 26 and October 1, 1924, 2860H/1407/554 375–377, 387–389; Stresemann, I, 465–467; Freund, 215.
11. Hauschild to Moscow and Warsaw, October 15, 1924, Rauscher (Warsaw) to Foreign Office, October 16, and Radowitz to Foreign Office, October 21, Radowitz to Maltzan and Brockdorff-Rantzau, October 18, 1924, 2860H/1407/554 414–415, 426, 419–420.
12. Radowitz to Foreign Office, October 20, 1924, 2860H/1408/554 422–423; Degras, I, 464.
13. Stresemann to Radowitz, October 21, Radowitz to Maltzan, October 24, 1924, 2860H/1408/554 424–425, 433.
14. Eudin and Fisher, 220–221.
15. Notes by Hauschild, October 25 and 28, by Stresemann, October 29, 1924, 2860H/1408/554 435–438, 445–446, 452–456; Stresemann, I, 468–470.
16. Brockdorff-Rantzau to Foreign Office, November 4 and 6, Brockdorff-Rantzau to Maltzan, November 6, 1924, 2860H/1408/554 491–492, 498–500, 9101H/3431/H225 752–755.
17. Brockdorff-Rantzau to Maltzan, November 14 and 27, 1927, 9101H/3431/

H225 750–751, 713–715; Brockdorff-Rantzau to Foreign Office, November 15, 1924, 2860H/1408/554 540.

18. Chicherin to Brockdorff-Rantzau, November 26, 1924, 9101H/3432/H226 037.

19. Stresemann to Brockdorff-Rantzau, November 27, 2860H/1408/554 592; Hilger, 156.

20. Stresemann to Brockdorff-Rantzau, December 1, 2860H/1408/554 592; Maltzan to Brockdorff-Rantzau, December 4, 1924, 6812H/3431/225 699–702.

21. Notes by Ebert, 2860H/1408/554 575.

22. Maltzan to Brockdorff-Rantzau, November 13, 14, 27, and 28; Brockdorff-Rantzau to Maltzan, December 5; Brockdorff-Rantzau to Foreign Office, November 25, 1924, 6812H/3431/225 741, 734 705, 691–697; 2860H/1408/554 575, 569–570.

23. Brockdorff-Rantzau to Foreign Office, "Political Report No. 37," December 5, 1924, 4562H/2313/E154 862–865; Z. J. Gaziorowski, "The Russian Overture to Germany of December, 1924," *Journal of Modern History*, XXX (June, 1958), 100–101; hereafter, Gasiorowski; Helbig, *Rapallo*, 164–165, bases his account on Gasiorowski.

24. Maltzan to Brockdorff-Rantzau, December 13, 1924, 4562H/2313/E154 874–876; 2860H/1408/554 636–638; Gasiorowski, 101–102.

25. Brockdorff-Rantzau to Maltzan, December 5 and 12, 1924, 9101H/3431/ H225 691–697, 677–679.

26. Zechlin (Press Department, Foreign Office) to Brockdorff-Rantzau, December 19, 1924, 2860H/1408/544 648; *The New York Times*, December 20, 1924; Gasiorowski, 102. On December 30, Maltzan formally turned his job over to Schubert. He left for Washington on February 25. Maltzan to Brockdorff-Rantzau, December 30, 1924, January 31, 1925, 9101H/3431/H225 672–675.

27. Brockdorff-Rantzau to Foreign Office, December 22, 1924, Brockdorff-Rantzau's notes on the talks with Chicherin, 4562H/2313/E154 904–906, 926–930; 9101H/3432/H226 834–838. Gasiorowski, 102–104; Freund, 217–218, wrongly concludes that Brockdorff-Rantzau acted entirely on his own in proposing to push Poland back to her ethnographic frontiers, and places the talk "in January or February, 1925."

28. Brockdorff-Rantzau to Stresemann, December 29, 1924, 4562H/2313/E154 921–925; 9101H/3432/H226 829–833.

Brockdorff-Rantzau sent copies of the covering letter and the notes to Schubert on December 30, 1924, asking him not to reveal to Stresemann that he had received them; 4562H/2313/E154 919–920.

29. Schubert to Brockdorff-Rantzau, December 29, 1924, 4562H/2313/E154 907–909; this was based, almost verbatim, on a memorandum by Bülow of December 23, 1924, *ibid.*, E154 910–912; Gasiorowski, 105.

30. Brockdorff-Rantzau to Schubert, January 6, Stresemann to Brockdorff-Rantzau, January 8, Brockdorff-Rantzau to Stresemann, January 10, 1925, 4562H/ 2313/E154 932–938; Gasiorowski, 105–106.

31. Brockdorff-Rantzau to Foreign Office, January 12 and 19, 1925, 2860H/ 1408/544 707–708; 4562H/2313/E154 956–957, 963; *Izvestia*, January 14, 1924; Notes by Stresemann, January 17, 1925, Schubert to Brockdorff-Rantzau, January 22, February 12 and 23, 1925, 2860H/1408/554 736–737, 718–720, 4562H/2313/ E154 942–943, 966–969, 975–986; Gasiorowski, 106–107.

32. Brockdorff-Rantzau to Schubert, March 21, 1925, 4562H/2313/155 131.

33. Brockdorff-Rantzau to Stresemann, February 24, 1925, Political Report No. 2,

9101H/3432/H226 839–842; 4562H/2313/E155 006–009; Notes by Schubert on his talk with Ernst Rantzau, *ibid.*, 991–992; Schubert to Brockdorff-Rantzau, *ibid.*, 993; Gasiorowski, 108–109; Helbig, *Rapallo*, 168–171.

34. Notes by Schubert, February 24, 1925, 4562H/2313/E154 989–990.

35. Brockdorff-Rantzau to Foreign Office, Political Report No. 4, March 9, 1925, 4562H/2313/E155 024–028; Brockdorff-Rantzau to Ernst Rantzau, March 7, 1925, 9101H/3430/H224 338.

36. Degras, II, 17.

37. Stresemann to Brockdorff-Rantzau, March 6, Brockdorff-Rantzau to Stresemann, March 10, Notes by Stresemann about his talk with Krestinsky, sent to Brockdorff-Rantzau on March 10, 1925, 4562H/2313/E155 010–013, 046–048, 014–019; Gasiorowski, 110; Freund, 218–219; Hilger, 134.

38. Schubert's notes, March 12, 1925, 4562H/2313/E155 030–034, 056. On Michalski's subsequent contracts with the Wilhelmstrasse, see notes by Dirksen, June 6, 1932, 9187H/3486/249 248–249.

39. Schaffer to Dirksen, March 13, Brockdorff-Rantzau to Stresemann, March 13, Schubert notes on talk with Hencke, March 13, 1925, 4562H/2313/155 063–066, 049–052.

40. Schubert to Brockdorff-Rantzau, March 16, 1925, 2860H/1408/554 941–942.

41. Notes by Stresemann, March 16, 1925, 6698H/3031/108 057–060.

42. Dufour-Feronce (London) to Schubert, March 16, 1925, 4562H/2313/155 060.

43. Stresemann to Brockdorff-Rantzau, March 19, 1925, 4562H/2313/E155 068–090; Gasiorowski, 111–112; Helbig, *Rapallo*, 173.

44. Brockdorff-Rantzau to Stresemann, March 28 and April 13, 1925 (handed to the Minister on April 22 by Brockdorff-Rantzau), 4562H/2313/155 144, 211–215.

45. Simons to Luther, March 20, 1925, 9101H/3430/E224 001–004; Brandenburg MS, 1692H/1013/397 761–765; Helbig, *Rapallo*, 172.

46. Brockdorff-Rantzau set up his resignation complete but for the name of the president and the day of April; Brockdorff-Rantzau to Simons, April 5, 1925; Brockdorff-Rantzau sent Ernst Rantzau to Simons on April 15 to intercede for his policies; 9101H/3430/H224 015–018, 007–008, 359.

47. Brockdorff-Rantzau to Schubert, March 21, Schubert's notes on the talk with Krestinsky, March 25, 1925, 4562H/2313/E155 127–137, 120–125; Brockdorff-Rantzau to Ernst Rantzau, March 21, 1925, 9101H/3430/H224 342.

48. Brockdorff-Rantzau to Stresemann, March 27, Stresemann to Brockdorff-Rantzau, April 1, Brockdorff-Rantzau to Stresemann, April 8, 1925, 4562H/2313/E155 141–144, 146–151, 178–181; Gasiorowski, 112.

49. Freund, 220–221; Hilger, 135; Helbig, *Rapallo*, 319.

50. Notes by Stresemann, April 15, 1925, 4562H/2313/E155 203–208; Gasiorowski, 114.

51. H. von Stockhausen, *Sechs Jahre Reichskanzlei: Von Rapallo bis Locarno*, ed. W. Görlitz (Bonn: Athenäum Verlag, 1954), p. 151.

52. Notes by Schubert, April 25, 1925, 4562H/2313/E155 223–228; the memorandum: *ibid.*, E155 229–242; Brockdorff-Rantzau approved this procedure on April 24, 1925, to Schubert, *ibid.*, E155 220–221; Gasiorowski, 114; Helbig, *Rapallo*, 174. Gaus-Bülow memorandum circulated for internal discussion on April 17, 1925, 6698H/3031/108 117–126.

53. The sentence in question, which preceded the "Provisional Treaty of Friend-

ship and Commerce" of June, 1922, read: "desiring to establish commercial and economic relations between the two states, and considering the necessity that each of the Contracting Parties reciprocally maintain neutrality in the event of the conflict of one of them with a third power, have agreed on the following provisions. . . ." (Shapiro, I, 173).

54. Notes by Schubert and Stresemann, 4562H/2313/E155 253–259; the notes by Schubert and Stresemann were sent to Brockdorff-Rantzau on May 1, 1925, *ibid.*, E155 272; Scheffer to Dirksen, May 8, 1925, *ibid.*, 283–286.

Dirksen proposed that a German-Russian guarantee pact with Latvia, Estonia, and Lithuania should be offered to Moscow. If the Soviet government objected, the matter could stop there; if it approved, negotiations could proceed. Memorandum by Dirksen, April 24, 1925, 5462H/2785/E380 033–034, 042.

55. Stockhausen, 161; O. Meissner, *Staatssekretär unter Ebert, Hindenburg, Hitler* (3rd ed.; Hamburg: Hoffman und Campe, 1950), p. 151; Hereafter, Meissner.

56. Degras, II, 42; Hey to Foreign Office, May 16, Notes by Schubert, May 22, 1925, 4562H/2313/E155 282, 290–292; Hilger, 134, who cites *Izvestia* of May 24, 1925.

57. Stresemann to Hey, 2860H/1408/555 201–204; Hey to Foreign Office, May 28 and 29, 1925 (copy by Hey to Brockdorff-Rantzau), 4562H/2313/E155 308–310, 223–225.

58. 4562H/2313/E155 328–335; 2314/E155 336–342; Gasiorowski, 114; Freund, 224; Helbig, *Rapallo*, 174–175.

59. Brockdorff-Rantzau to Stresemann, June 8, 1925, 4562H/2314/E155 343–348.

60. Notes by Stresemann, June 10, 1925, 4562H/2314/E155 351–359; Stresemann, II, 472–473.

61. 4562H/2313/E155 369–384; Radek also talked with Gaus and Dirksen (4829H/2457/242 115); Stresemann II, 473–475; Gasiorowski, 115–116.

62. The drafts, with marginal comments, and the final Richtlinien are in 4562H/2314/320–323, 360–365, 385–400, 405–432, 449–456, 6698H/3029/107 112–117, and 2860H/1408/555 228–231.

63. Notes by Stresemann, June 22, 1925, 2860H/1408/555 311–314; Notes by Schubert, June 23, 1925, 4562H/2314/E155 444.

64. Dirksen, 55.

V. ONE STEP EAST—ONE STEP WEST

1. Karl Kindermann, *Zwei Jahre in Moskaus Totenhäusern: Der Moskauer Studentenprozess und die Arbeitsmethode der OGPU* (Berlin: Eckart-Verlag, 1931), pp. 17, 20, 176; hereafter, Kindermann; Hilger, 138–140; Wallroth to Brockdorff-Rantzau, February 16, 1925, 2860H/1408/554 804–806.

2. Brockdorff-Rantzau to Foreign Office, December 19, Brockdorff-Rantzau to Wallroth, January 25, Wallroth to Brockdorff-Rantzau, January 27, Brockdorff-Rantzau to Foreign Office, January 28, 1925, 2860H/1408/554 804–806, 754, 761, 771–772.

3. Brockdorff-Rantzau to Ernst Rantzau, February 5, Brockdorff-Rantzau to Maltzan, February 14, 1925, 9101H/3430/224 330, 9101H/3431/H225 670–671.

4. Brockdorff-Rantzau to Foreign Office, February 10 and 16, Wallroth to Brockdorff-Rantzau, February 16, 17, and 19, 1925, 2860H/1408/554 813–815, 837, 833–834, 855.

5. Hilger, 137–142.

6. P. Scheffer, *Sieben Jahre Sowjet-Union* (Leipzig: Bibliographisches Institut, 1930), p. 321. Hereafter, Scheffer.

7. *The New York Times*, February 11, 12, and 19, 1925. Wallroth to Brockdorff-Rantzau, February 12, 1925, 2860H/1408/554 822–823.

8. Brockdorff-Rantzau to Schubert, February 16, Schubert to Brockdorff-Rantzau, February 18 and 23, 1925, 2860H/1408/554 839–840, 851–852; 4562H/2313/E154 977–978.

9. Dirksen to Brockdorff-Rantzau, March 3, Brockdorff-Rantzau to Schubert, March 21, Stresemann to Brockdorff-Rantzau, March 25, 1925, 2860H/1408/554 899; 4562H/2313/E155 132–133, 119.

10. Foreign Office notes, April 22 and August 4, 1925, 6698H/B028/106 538–539; *The New York Times*, April 16 and 23, 1925; Hey to Foreign Office, April 30, 1925, 2860H/1408/555 149–150.

11. Hey to Foreign Office, June 19, 20, and 26, 1925, 2860H/1409/555 289, 300–301, 327–328; Kindermann, 133, 162.

12. Hey to Foreign Office, June 26 and 27, 1925, 2860H/1409/555 342–343, 350; Kindermann, 97, 114, wrote later that Baumann had "hypnotized him into confessing."

13. Stresemann to Brockdorff-Rantzau, June 29, 1925, 6698H/3028/H106 402–404; 4562H/2314/E155 474–476; Brockdorff-Rantzau to Ernst Rantzau, March 7, 1925, 9101H/3430/H224 337–338.

14. Brockdorff-Rantzau to Stresemann, June 30, 1925, 2860H/1409/555 366–368; Kindermann, 209; Hilger, 143.

15. Wallroth to Embassy Moscow, July 1, Brockdorff-Rantzau to Foreign Office, July 3, 1925, 2860H/1409/555 370, 396–397; Kindermann, 226–229.

16. Stresemann to Brockdorff-Rantzau, July 2, 1925, 6698H/3028/106 404–406; Ybarra in *The New York Times*, July 4, 1925.

17. Brockdorff-Rantzau to Foreign Office, July 5, 1925, 2860H/1409/55 404–405.

18. Brockdorff-Rantzau to Foreign Office (Dr. Freund's report), 2860H/1409/555 412.

19. Stresemann to Brockdorff-Rantzau, July 4, 1925, 4562H/2314/E155 537–538.

20. Schubert notes on information orally transmitted by de Margerie on June 15, 1925, 6698H/3031/108 233–237.

21. Dirksen to Schubert, June 29, 1925, 4562H/2314/E155 522–525.

22. The account of the economic negotiations is based on the correspondence between the delegation and the Wilhelmstrasse found in 6698H/3038/H112 886–893, 985, 926; H113 177, 103–107, 277, 139–140, 014–017, 024–027, 034–042; Schlesinger's attitude is best shown in a letter to Dirksen, March 25, 1925, H112 880; his memorandum is in H113 207–214.

23. Brockdorff-Rantzau to Foreign Office, July 3, 7, and 9, Stresemann to Brockdorff-Rantzau, July 11, 1925, 4562H/2314/E155 530–532, 556–560, 568–571; 2860H/1409/555 434.

24. Wallroth to Brockdorff-Rantzau, July 13, 1925, 6698H/3028/106 409; Ernst Rantzau to Brockdorff-Rantzau, July 13, 1925, 2860H/1409/555 441.

25. Stresemann to the Cabinet, June 24, 1925, 3242H/1591/113 846–849; Stresemann to *Staatssekretär, Reichskanzlei*, July 13, 1925, 2860H/1409/555 443.

26. Brockdorff-Rantzau to Stresemann, July 15, 18, and 20, 1925, 4562H/2314/155 588–592, 598–599, 609–612.

27. Notes by Schubert on a discussion with former Chancellor Wirth, July 22, 1925, 4562H/2314/E155 638.

28. Memorandum by Dirksen, July 16, Stresemann to Brockdorff-Rantzau, July 17, 1925, 6698H/3038/H113 404–415; 3028/H106 410–412.

29. Brockdorff-Rantzau to Foreign Office, July 21 and 28, 1925, 6698H/3028/H106 417–425; 4562H/2314/E155 640–642.

30. Stresemann to Brockdorff-Rantzau, July 25 and 28, 1925, 6698H/3028/H106 426–427, 439.

31. Brockdorff-Rantzau to Stresemann, July 28, 1925, 6698H/3028/H106 439–445; delivered by Dirksen to Stresemann July 31 in the afternoon; copy to Schubert August 1, to Gaus August 3, to Chancellor Luther August 4, and Dirksen August 9.

32. Brockdorff-Rantzau to Foreign Office, July 31, 1925, 6698H/3028/H106 448–451, 459–462.

33. Brockdorff-Rantzau to Stresemann, August 3, 1925, 6698H/3028/H106 452–456.

34. Brockdorff-Rantzau to Dirksen, August 3, Stresemann to Brockdorff-Rantzau, August 4, Brockdorff-Rantzau to Stresemann, August 5, 1925, 6698H/3028/H106 468–474.

35. Brockdorff-Rantzau to Stresemann, with a request to present it to the Chancellor, August 7, 1925, 6698H/3028/H106 479–481.

36. Brockdorff-Rantzau to Foreign Office, August 8, 1925, 6698H/3028/H106 491–492; Hilger, 143–145.

37. Brockdorff-Rantzau to Stresemann, August 8, 1925, 6698H/3028/H106 482–483, 493.

38. Stresemann to Brockdorff-Rantzau, August 8, 1925, 6698H/3028/H106 488–490, 106 475–478; 6698H/3029/107 167–171.

39. Brockdorff-Rantzau to Stresemann, August 10, 1925, 6698H/3028/H106 494–497.

40. Brockdorff-Rantzau to Foreign Office, August 5 and 30, 1925, 2860H/1409/555 594–598, 765–766; Schlesinger to Dirksen, August 6, Dirksen to Schlesinger and Brockdorff-Rantzau, August 28 and 29, 1925, 6698H/3039/113 482–490; 4829H/2457/242 167–168; 2860H/1409/555 761–762; Stresemann to Brockdorff-Rantzau, August 11 and 19, 1925, 6698H/3039/H113 533–537; 2860H/1409/555 691; excerpt of the notes of the cabinet session on August 25, *ibid.*, 770.

41. Gaus's report, September 19, 1925, 6698H/3031/108 430–452.

42. Brockdorff-Rantzau to Foreign Office, for Press Department and WTB, September 8, 1925, 6698H/3028/106 505–535.

43. Correspondence between Brockdorff-Rantzau and Dirksen, September 1, 2, 5, and 26, 1925, 2860H/1409/555 771–779, 788–790; 6698H/3039/113 643–645, 3032/109 045–046, 4829H/2458/242 186–188.

44. Stresemann to Brockdorff-Rantzau, Martius to Foreign Office, September 19 and 24, 1925, 6698H/3039/113 688, 707.

45. Correspondence between Stresemann and Brockdorff-Rantzau, August 14, 18, 22, and 26, 1925, 4562H/2314/145–149, 756–762, 823–827, 833–838.

46. Brockdorff-Rantzau to Foreign Office, September 4, 19, 24, 25, and 26, 1925, 2860H/1409/555 786–787; 4562H/2314/E155 844, 849–851, 858, 868; Dirksen to Brockdorff-Rantzau, September 15, Note by Schubert, September 26, 1925, 4562H/2314/155 843, 855–856.

47. Rauscher to Foreign Office, September 27, 28, and 29, Brockdorff-Rantzau to Foreign Office, September 27, 1925, 6698H/3027/105 316, 320–323, 326. Private discussion between Skrzyński and Chicherin, J. Grzymala-Grabowiecki, *Polityka Zagranicza Polski* (Warsaw, 1926), p. 146, cited in Gasiorowski, 116.

48. Hencke to Brockdorff-Rantzau, September 24, 1925, 9101H/3429/H223 736–743; Brockdorff-Rantzau to Stresemann, September 30, 1925, 6698H/3035/ H106 045.

49. Stresemann's notes on his talk with Chicherin, September 30/October 1, 1925, 6698H/3035/H111 046–058; Stresemann, II, 478–480, contains a shortened version but makes no mention of German-Russian collaboration to push Poland back to her ethnographic frontiers; Gasiorowski, 116–117; Freund, 232–233; Helbig, *Rapallo*, 177, discusses the Stresemann-Chicherin talks. Brockdorff-Rantzau received the complete notes of the discussion, which were sent to him by courier.

50. *The New York Times*, October 1 and 2, 1925.

51. Minutes of Cabinet meeting of October 1, 1925, 3242H/1591/D713 902; Wolff's Telegraphen Büro communiqué, October 2, 1925, 6698H/3039/113 854; Stresemann, II, 480–481; Fischer, *Soviets*, II, 593; *Izvestia*, October 4, 1925, cited in Degras, II, 57–58.

52. Notes by Stresemann on the talk with Chicherin on October 2, 1925, 6698H/ 3035/H111 038–044. On October 6, the notes of the second discussion were sent to Brockdorff-Rantzau.

53. *The New York Times*, October 5, 1925.

54. "Material for the conversation of the Reich President with Chicherin," Foreign Office memorandum, 6698H/3027/H105 343–348, October 1, 1925; Wallroth to Stresemann, October 8, 1925, 4562H/2314/E155 931–934; Foreign Office memorandum, 4829/2458/242 186–188, 6698H/3032/109 121; Sokolnikov's announcement, Degras, II, 59–60; Hilger, 184–185.

55. Shapiro, I, 288–289, 302–303. The complete treaty, texts of the preliminary discussions, protocols of negotiating sessions, and notes exchanged can be found in 6698H/3029/113 889–114 261; for the treaty in English, see Shapiro, I, 288–308; a brief discussion of the negotiations and of the treaty are in J. Kuczinsky and E. Wittkowski, *Die deutsch-russischen Handelsbeziehungen in den letzten 150 Jahren* (Berlin: Verlag der Wirtschaft, 1947), p. 48–49, hereafter Kuczinsky and Wittkowski; see also Helbig, *Rapallo*, 137–138.

56. D'Abernon, II, 198; Brockdorff-Rantzau to Foreign Office, October 8, to Stresemann, October 10, 1925, 4562H/2314/155 947–948.

57. Eudin and Fischer, 271.

58. Report by Stresemann and Luther to the German Cabinet, October 19, 1925, 9101H/3432/H226 748–750; details about the meeting on the *Fleur d'Orange*, 4562/2318/E158 500.

59. *The New York Times*, October 24, 1925.

VI. The Treaty of Berlin

1. Notes by Stresemann, October 29, Brockdorff-Rantzau to Foreign Office, October 30, Foreign Office notes, November 4, Brockdorff-Rantzau's memorandum to Hindenburg, November 7, 1925, Stresemann to Brockdorff-Rantzau, November

7, 1925, demanding to be told why the memorandum had been sent to Hindenburg, 4562H/2314/E156 003, 010, E155 760, 770–787, 768.

2. Wallroth's notes, November 14, 1925, for Stresemann and Schubert, 6698H/3035/H111 023–027.

3. Excerpt from the minutes of the Cabinet session, which were sent to Brockdorff-Rantzau by messenger, 9101H/3430/H224 021–022.

4. Foreign Office notes, 4562H/2315/E156 185; *The New York Times,* December 22, 1925; Hoesch (Paris) to Foreign Office, 6698H/3035/H110 953–955.

5. Foreign Office *dementi* published by WTB; January 4, 1926, 4562H/2314/E155 794–795; Hilger, 187–188.

6. Foreign Office copy of the Russian proposal; notes by Schubert, November 21 and 23, notes by Dirksen, November 28, 1925, 4562H/2315/E156 210–217, 155 783–787; 6698H/3029/107 261–262.

7. Notes by Schubert, November 28, 1925, 6698H/3029/H107 274–277.

8. Brockdorff-Rantzau's resignation, November 28, 1925, notes on his talk with Hindenburg, and the President's letter to Stresemann, 9101H/3430/H224 031–032, 015–018, 024–030.

9. Notes by Schubert, December 11, 1925, 4562H/2315/E156 111–132.

10. Dirksen, December 18, 1925, 4562H/2315/156 185; Dufour-Feronce (London), relaying information, received from Tyrell of the British Foreign Office, to the German Foreign Office, December 20 and 22, 1925, 4562H/2315/156 208; 6698H/3035/110 978–980.

11. Notes by Schubert, December 19, 1925, 4562H/2315/E156 194–206; Stresemann's notes on the talk with Chicherin, December 22, 1925, 6898H/3035/H110 969–976; Hilger, 109, 146.

12. Notes by Stresemann, December 22, 1925, 2315/E156 231–234.

13. Notes by Schubert, December 25, 1925, 4562H/2315/156 254–258, 352–353.

14. Letter dated December 24, 1925, copy of protocol, 4562H/2315/E156 264–269.

15. Notes by Schubert, January 6 and 16, 1926, 4562H/2315/156 397–399, 435–437.

16. Schubert to Hoesch (Paris), January 20, Hoesch (Paris) and Sthamer (London) to Schubert, January 23, 1926, 4562H/2315/156 469, 500–502, 509–515.

17. Dirksen to Wallroth and Schubert, January 25, 1926, 4562H/2315/156 516–520.

18. Stresemann, II, 486–488, on his talk with Brockdorff-Rantzau; Stresemann to Hindenburg, January 20, 1926, 4562H/2314/E155 796–799; Brockdorff-Rantzau's notes on his talk with Meissner, January 23; Hindenburg to Brockdorff-Rantzau and to Stresemann, January 25, 1926, 9101H/3430/H224 034–037; 4562H/3314/E155 800, 802.

On the refusal to send reports: Dirksen to Hoesch (Paris), January 22, 1926, 6698H/3035/H110 931–932; Notes by Schubert, January 27 and 28, 1926, 4562H/2315/E156 528–529; Brockdorff-Rantzau to Ernst Rantzau, March 13, 1926, 9101H/3430/H224 369.

19. For the correspondence between Hey, Brockdorff-Rantzau, and Wilhelmstrasse, see: 6698H/3028/H106 112–114, 117–119, 126, 129, 175–176, 179–182, 196–198, 201–202, 205–210, 212–216, 221–228; Chicherin to Stresemann, December 22, 1925, 6698H/3035/H110 975–976; Schubert to Brockdorff-Rantzau, February 11, 1926, 4562H/2315/E151 547.

20. Notes by Schubert, February 1, 1926, 4562H/2315/156 534–537; Foreign Office copy of the treaty, 4562H/2315/156 592–593; Shapiro, I, 313.

21. Brockdorff-Rantzau to Foreign Office, February 1, 1926, 6698H/3030/H107 422–423.

22. Notes by Schubert, February 11 and 19, 1926, 4562H/2315/156 548–549, 589.

23. Draft treaty and protocol, February 13, Stresemann to Brockdorff-Rantzau (by courier), February 26, 1926, 4562H/2315/E155 566–668; notes on the discussion between Krestinsky *et al.*, E156 599–603, 613–616.

24. Brockdorff-Rantzau to Foreign Office, February 17, 1928, 6698H/3035/H110 911–913; on the loan: Helbig, *Rapallo*, 182–183; Hilger, 186; Kuczinsky and Wittkowsky, 55–56; Fischer, *Soviets*, II, 698–704; Degras, II, 119–120; Brockdorff-Rantzau to Ernst Rantzau, March 2, 1926, 9101H/3430/224 365.

25. Brockdorff-Rantzau to Foreign Office, March 4 and 6, 1926, 2860H/1410/556 856; 4562H/2315/E156 629–630; Wallroth and Dirksen to Brockdorff-Rantzau, March 6 and 9, *ibid.*, E156 624–628, 633–634.

26. Brockdorff-Rantzau to Foreign Office, with a request for transmission to Geneva, March 14, 1926, 2860H/1410/556 893.

27. Notes by Stresemann, March 25, 1926, 4562H/2315/E156 694–698; Brockdorff-Rantzau to Foreign Office, March 26, 1926, 2860H/1410/656 936.

28. Notes by Dirksen and Schubert on the discussion, 4562H/2315/156 713–716, 735–739; copy of the treaty and notes, 156 722–729.

29. Schubert to Brockdorff-Rantzau, March 30, 1926, 4562H/2315/156 732–734.

30. Notes by Schubert, March 31 and April 1, 1926, 4562H/2315/156 751–760.

31. Correspondence between Schubert and Hoesch (Paris) and Sthamer (London), April 1, 3, and 6, 1926, 4562H/2315/156 761–774, 789–793, 813–814, 860–863; Schubert's resumé of his talks with D'Abernon and de Margerie, April 6, 1926, 4562H/2316/156 849–859; Schubert, on his concern about foreign relations, to Maltzan, April 6, 1926, *ibid.*, 156, 840–841.

32. Keller (Brussels) to Schubert, April 8, Schubert to Rome, April 9, 1926, 4562H/2316/156 902–906, 933; Circular letter to German representatives, April 7, 1926, 6698H/3030/H107 598–605.

33. Schubert notes, April 9, 1926, 4562H/2316/156 910–917, 920–922; London to Foreign Office, April 8, 1926, *ibid.*, 156 908–909.

34. Schubert to Embassies in London, Paris, Rome, Brussels, April 9, Hoesch to Schubert, April 9, 1926, 4562H/2316/156 923–924, 945–949.

35. Sthamer to Foreign Office, April 11, Maltzan to Schubert, April 12, 1926, 4562H/2316/156 973–974, 6698H/3030/107 695.

36. Notes by Dirksen, April 12, 1926, 4562H/2316/156 978–971, 997–998; Schubert to Brockdorff-Rantzau, April 12, 1926, 157 001–004; 6698H/3030/107 732.

37. Notes by Dufour-Feronce, April 13, 1926, *Times* article by Sthamer to Foreign Office, April 14, 1926, *Temps* article by Hoesch to Foreign Office, April 14, 1926, Schubert to Sthamer, April 14, 1926, 4562H/2316/157 022–023, 020, 025, 041–045.

38. Notes by Schubert, Schubert to Brockdorff-Rantzau, April 14, 1926, 4562H/2316/157 032–040; Press Conference, April 14, 1926, 4562H/2316/157 050–061.

39. Brockdorff-Rantzau to Schubert, April 14, 1926, 4562H/2316/157 069–071.

40. The documents pertaining to these talks are in 6698H/3027/H105 527–571. On the efforts by Briand, see 4562H/2316/157 078–081.

41. Warsaw to Foreign Office, April 18, 1926, 4562H/2315/156 312–313; Dieckhoff (Washington) to Foreign Office, April 21, 1926, ibid., 156 349.

42. Brockdorff-Rantzau to Schubert, April 17, 1926, 4562H/2316/157 111; Notes by Schubert on the discussion with Krestinsky, ibid., 157 154–156.

43. Stresemann to Brockdorff-Rantzau, Brockdorff-Rantzau to Schubert, April 21 and 22, 4562H/2316/157 190–192, 224–225; Schubert to Brockdorff-Rantzau; the telegram was sent on April 25 at 5:10 P.M., 6698H/3030/107 841.

44. Stresemann to Chicherin, April 24, Chicherin to Stresemann, April 25, 1926, 4562H/2316/157 250–251, 274.

45. Brockdorff-Rantzau to Foreign Ministry, April 25, 1926, 4562H/2316/157 296–297; Eudin and Fisher, 324–326; Degras, II, 106; D'Abernon, III, 252–253.

46. Brockdorff-Rantzau to Ernst Rantzau, April 26, May 1, July 9 and 24, 1926, 9101H/3430/H224 391–392, 394, 425–426, 429; Brockdorff-Rantzau to Hindenburg, July 8, Hindenburg to Brockdorff-Rantzau, July 14, 1926, 9101H/3430/H224 038–047, 053–054; Helbig, Rapallo, 187–188.

VII. THE REORGANIZATION OF MILITARY COLLABORATION

1. Brockdorff-Rantzau to Foreign Office, May 3, Stresemann notes, May 10, Stresemann to Brockdorff-Rantzau, May 22, 1926, 6698H/3035/H111 284–288.

2. Brockdorff-Rantzau to Ernst Rantzau, May 24, June 4 and 21, 1926, 9101H/3430/H224 407, 411, 415; Brockdorff-Rantzau to Wallroth, June 23 and 24, 1926, Wallroth to Brockdorff-Rantzau, June 19, 1926, 6698H/3035/H111 266–267, 270–271, 276–278.

3. Foreign Office to Brockdorff-Rantzau, Brockdorff-Rantzau to Stresemann, June 27, to Wallroth, June 30, 1926, and Cabinet decision, 6698H/3035/H111 262–264; 3430/224/419–420.

4. Memorandum by Brockdorff-Rantzau for Stresemann and telegram to Schubert, July 5, 1926, 9101H/3432/H226 861–864, 6698H/3035/H111 252–253.

5. Schubert to Brockdorff-Rantzau, July 11, 17, and 20, Brockdorff-Rantzau to Schubert, July 13 and 16, 1926, 6698H/3035/H111 252–253.

6. "Stichworte für die Kabinettsberatung über den Fall Skoblevsky," no date, 9101H/3432/H226 261–273; Hencke Memorandum on the violations of the Treaty of Versailles, i.e., support of Russian armaments, Junkers, poison gas at Ivoshenko, special military missions, July 12, 1926, "Militärische Angelegenheiten," 4562H/2330/163 630, cited in Gatzke, 583; this memorandum was incorporated in a note by Dirksen for the Cabinet session, July 12, 1926, 6698H/3035/H111 238 ff., and was obviously based on Brockdorff-Rantzau's specific instructions to Hencke; Schubert to Brockdorff-Rantzau on the Cabinet decisions, July 20, 1926, 6698H/3035/H111 210–211.

7. Brockdorff-Rantzau to Schubert, July 21, 1926, 6698H/3035/H111 206–209.

8. Schubert to Hey, August 14, Brockdorff-Rantzau to Schubert, July 31 and August 1, Hey to Foreign Office, August 22, 1926, 6698H/3035/H111 889–890, 201–202, 168–170; Foreign Office note, August 14, 1926, ibid., H111 194; Schubert's notes about a talk with Litvinov, August 5, 1926, 9101H/3432/H226 274–

285. For the details regarding the exchange, see: 6698H/3035/H111 154–288; 2860H/1409/1410/556 109–112, 122–123; 4564H/2330/163 374, 377.

9. Eyck, II, 100–107.

10. Undated and unsigned memorandum, marked "Durchschlag Rantzau," 9101H/3433/H227 142–147; Brandenburg MS, 1692H/1013/397 780–781, dated the memorandum November 7, 1925—this date is refuted by internal evidence. Helbig, *Rapallo*, 189–190, is certain that Brockdorff-Rantzau wrote the memorandum. Professor Helbig uses it as evidence that the Count had come to accept Schlesinger's idea that Germany should deal with Russia through an economic consortium made up of a number of European states. A letter to Brockdorff-Rantzau by Schlesinger, November 3, 1926, 9101H/3433/H227 148–149, establishes Schlesinger's authorship.

11. Brockdorff-Rantzau to Stresemann, November 24, 1926, 6698H/3035/H111 119–123; Brockdorff-Rantzau to Foreign Office, November 23, 1926, 4562H/2317/ E157 929. On Krestinsky's visit, Rabenau, 541, 555 n. 1.

12. Stresemann to Brockdorff-Rantzau, November 25, Schubert notes on the talk with Krestinsky and Bratman-Brodovsky, November 29, 1926, 6698H/3035/ H111 124–125, 130–138.

13. Brockdorff-Rantzau to Stresemann, November 26, 1926, 6698H/3035/H111 115–116; Schubert's notes on the talks, December 2 and 3, 1926, 6698H/3035/ H111 095–107, 073–094; guidelines, November 30, 1926, H111 112–114; Brockdorff-Rantzau was informed of the talks by Wallroth, H111 072.

14. *Manchester Guardian*, December 3, 1926.

15. *Chef der Heeresleitung* to the Chancellor, copy to Foreign Office, May 26, 1926, 6698H/3027/H105 414–416; statement by Major Fischer to Foreign Office, April 29, 1926, 6698H/3027/H105 379–380.

16. Simons to Stresemann, April 23, Major Fischer to Dirksen, April 29, 1926, 6698H/3027/105 372–374, 379–380, H105, 372–374.

17. Dirksen interview with Director Brandenburg, April 30, Dirksen's notes about the meetings, May 3, 6, and 25, 1926, 6698H/3027/H105 381–397, 402–403. For Brandenburg's role, see: Völker, *Entwicklung der Militärischen Luftfahrt*, 142–143.

18. Junkers to Waurick, August 6, *Chef der Heeresleitung* to Chancellor, May 26, Notes by Dirksen, June 3, 1926, 6698H/3027/H105 457–460, 414–416, 404–405.

19. Foreign Office memorandum, June 7, Schlieben report, June 23, 1926, certified copy to Foreign Office, July 6, 1926, 6698H/3027/H105 434–452.

20. Foreign Office to Brockdorff-Rantzau, December 5, 1926, 6698H/3028/H106 238–239; 4564H/2330/163 408–411, 414–416.

21. Stresemann to Köpke, December 5, 1926, 6698H/3035/H106 234–235; a copy was transmitted to Major Fischer on December 6, *ibid.*, H106 240–241.

22. Copy of notes by Pünder of the Chancellery, December 6, 1926, 6698H/3035/H111 069–071.

23. Notes by Dirksen, December 7 and 8, 1926, 6698H/3028/H106 246–249; 6698H/3035/H111 067–068.

24. Köpke to Stresemann, December 7, 1926, 6698H/3028/H106 242–243. Details in 6698H/3035/H110 825–867, "Schiffe in Eisnot," June–August, 1926.

25. Notes by Dirksen, December 16, 1926, 6698H/3028/H106 250–255. Dirksen to Schlesinger, December 16, 1926, 6698H/3035/H110 876.

26. *Verhandlungen des Reichstags,* vol. 391, 8577–8586; Hilger, 203–204; *The New York Times,* December 17 and 18, 1926.

27. Schubert notes, December 17, 1926, 6698H/3028/H106 258–259; Kochan, 122.

28. Maltzan's telegram of the news item to Foreign Office, December 18, 1926, 6698H/3028/H106 267.

29. Confidential Foreign Office memorandum, December 11, 1926, 6698H/ 3027/H105 499–500; Junkers-Reich Agreement, December 20, 1926, 6698H/ 3027/H105 507–511; Brockdorff-Rantzau to Foreign Office, December 28, 1926, 6698H/3027/H105 502–503; Wallroth to Brockdorff-Rantzau, December 30, 1926, *ibid.,* H105 304; Dirksen to Brockdorff-Rantzau, December 31, 1926, *ibid.,* H105 506.

30. *The New York Times,* January 10, 1927; for the whole Künstler interview, see: C. F. Melville, *The Russian Face of Germany: An Account of the Secret Military Relations Between the German and Soviet Governments* (London: Wishart and Co., 1932), pp. 181–185. The *Manchester Guardian* reprinted the Künstler article from the *Leipziger Volkszeitung* (SPD); Sthamer to Foreign Office, February 18, 1927, 6698H/3027/H106 314.

31. Foreign Office notes, January 10, 1927, 6698H/3027/H106 281–283.

32. Memorandum by Dirksen, for a talk with General Hasse on December 18, 1926; Foreign Office notes, January 6, 24, and February 9, and by Schubert, February 23, 1927, 6698H/3028/H106 240–244, 275–277, 291–297, 343–353; Gatzke, 587; Helbig, *Rapallo,* 195.

33. Foreign Office notes, Schubert to Brockdorff-Rantzau for Colonel Thomsen, January 26, 1927, 6698H/3027/H105 505, 3028/H106 296.

34. Translation of the article sent to Dirksen by Fischer, February 12, Paris to Foreign Office, February 14, Schubert's note on the talk with Bratman-Brodovsky, February 18, 1927, 6698H/3028/H106 302, 311–313.

35. Correspondence between Brockdorff-Rantzau and Schubert, February 18, 19, 21, 23, 1927, 6698H/3028/106 318–322, 332–333, 343; Fischer to Dirksen, February 19, 1927, 6698H/3028/H106 326–327; Foreign Office notes for Gessler's talk, 6698H/3028/H106 315–317, 334–341; Notes and various preliminary drafts, dated February 21, 1927, 6698H/3028/H106 315–317, 334–341.

36. Notes by Kemper about the meeting with Unshlikht, April 1, 1926, 9101H/ 3432/H226 849–857; *ibid.,* H226 848; Gatzke, 581–582; Helbig, *Rapallo,* 180–181; Hilger, 195–202; Notes by Schubert that the collaboration had not been discussed, February 26, 1927, 6698H/3028/106 362.

37. Excerpts from the minutes of the Ministers' Conference, February 26, 1927, 4564H/2331/164 073–083.

38. Protocol, dated February 26, 1927, and minutes of the May 18, 1927 meeting, 4564H/2330/163 527–528, 880–885.

39. Notes by Dirksen, May 21, 1927, 6698H/3036/H111 736–737; Brockdorff-Rantzau to Stresemann, August 15, 1927, 9480H/3668/276 406; Notes by Schubert about the Unshlikt meeting, July 26, 1927, 4564H/2331/163 899–901, discussions with Brockdorff-Rantzau on August 4 and 6, 1927, *ibid.,* 163 906; Notes by Dirksen, July 28, 1927, 9480H/3668/276 417–418.

40. For the details of the continuing military collaboration, see "Militärische Angelegenheiten mit Russland," 4564H/2329/2330, 2331/162 516–163 318–163 585–164 069; 9480H/3668/276 061–276 236; 9481H/3668/276 238–276 508.

41. Notes by Stroben for Dirksen, July 22, 1927, 9481H/3668/276 433.
42. *Parliamentary Debates*, House of Commons, 5th Series (1927), vol. 208, p. 383; WTB dispatch, June 29, 1927, 9481H/3668/276 425.

VIII. THE END OF AN ERA

1. Sthamer (London) to Foreign Office, February 24, 1927, 4562H/2317/E158 226–229; Schubert to Brockdorff-Rantzau, February 19, Notes about a talk between Wallroth and Bratman-Brodovsky, March 3, 1927, 6698H/3027/H105 701–708; 3028/106 274–276.
2. Brockdorff-Rantzau to Schubert, March 4 and 5, 1927, and February 25, 1927, 6698H/3027/H105 715–730.
3. Dirksen to Schubert, March 10, 1927, 6698H/3027/H105 761–765; Helbig, *Rapallo*, 196–197.
4. The account of the tempest over the *Excelsior* interview is based on "Dementis betreffend Schubert-Interview an Exzelsior, Stresemann Rede für die ausländischen Presse," 6698H/3035/H111 289–387; Notes by Schubert, 4562H/2317/E158 352–357, 368; Hoesch (Paris) to Foreign Office, March 17, 1927, 4562H/2318/E158 384–385; Brockdorff-Rantzau to Ernst Rantzau, March 6, April 15 and 30, 1927, 9101H/3430/H224 497–498, 547, 552, 559–560.
5. Degras, II, 182, 189; Eudin and Fischer, 365.
6. Sthamer to Foreign Office, May 13, Hey, chargé d'affaires in Moscow, to Foreign Office, May 14, 1927, 6698H/3027/105 903, 905.
7. Copy of notes taken by Gregory on his conversation with Dieckhoff on May 25, handed to Köpke by the English Ambassador in Berlin on June 4, 1927. Dieckhoff's own report had been received before that date, 6698H/3027/H105 676–678.
8. Sthamer to Foreign Office, May 27, Dirksen to the German Ambassador in Washington, May 27, Stresemann to German Diplomatic Missions, May 28, 1927, 6698H/3027/105 680–681, 636, 601–603.
9. Foreign Office notes, May 27, 1927, 6698H/3027/H105 624–625.
10. Dirksen memorandum for Wallroth, June 3, 1927, 6698H/3028/H106 612–618; shortened, to Stresemann on June 12, *ibid.*, H106 641–643.
11. Hey to Foreign Office, May 27 and 31, notes by Dirksen, June 2, 1927, 6698H/3027/H105 628–630, 658, 670; Hey to Brockdorff-Rantzau, May 28, 1927, 9101H/3429/H223 659–662.
12. Stresemann notes, June 7, 1927, 6698H/3027/H105 358–365; *The New York Times*, June 8, 1927.
13. Excerpts from the Stresemann-Briand talks, June 13, 1927, 6698H/3027/H105 927.
14. Stresemann to Foreign Office, June 15, 1927, Cues (*Stichworte*) for the Foreign Minister's speech, no date, 6698H/3028/H106 645, 658.
15. Hey to Foreign Office, June 23 and 26, 1927, 6698H/3028/H106 672–673.
16. Sthamer to Foreign Office, July 5, Foreign Office notes about a discussion with the 1st Counselor of the Soviet Embassy in Berlin, Arens, June 27, 1927, 6698H/3027/H105 979, 953–958.
17. Brockdorff-Rantzau to Ernst Rantzau, August 12, 1927, 9101H/3430/H224 568–569; Brockdorff-Rantzau, August 8, 1927, 6698H/3028/H106 689.
18. Degras, II, 233–235; L. Fischer, 240.

19. Brockdorff-Rantzau to Foreign Office, August 23 and September 5, 1927, 6698H/3027/H106 012–013, 018–019; Chicherin to Brockdorff-Rantzau, September 2, Brockdorff-Rantzau to Chicherin, September 3, 1927, 9101H/3432/H226 104, 101–102.

20. Brockdorff-Rantzau to Ernst Rantzau, September 10, 20, and 23, 1927, 9101H/3430/H224 591, 594, 460.

21. Foreign Office memorandum, July 20, 1927, 5462H/2785/380 312–314; Brockdorff-Rantzau to Ernst Rantzau, November 5, 1927, *ibid.*, H224 630–631; Schlesinger to Hilger and Hencke, October 22, 1927, cited in Helbig, *Rapallo,* 197–198.

22. Brockdorff-Rantzau's speech, November 4, Chicherin's speech sent by him to Brockdorff-Rantzau, November 5, 1927, 9101H/3432/H226 087–091. The "sceptical poet" Brockdorff-Rantzau quoted was Goethe, and the translation of the quote from Goethe's *Faust* is by B. Taylor (New York: Modern Library, 1950), p. 11; excerpts from the Ambassador's speech in Stern-Rubarth, 130; Brockdorff-Rantzau to Ernst Rantzau on his feeling about the speech, November 12, 1927, 9101H/3430/H224 632; Brockdorff-Rantzau to Chicherin, November 6, 1927, 9101H/3432/H226 081–082.

23. Brockdorff-Rantzau to Stresemann, November 16, 1927, 4562H/2319/E159 476–478; Hilger, 157; Brockdorff-Rantzau to Ernst Rantzau, November 22, 1927; 9101H/3430/H224 641; Brockdorff-Rantzau to Stresemann, April 12, 1928, 9101H/3432/H226 872.

24. Stresemann to Brockdorff-Rantzau, November 17, 20, and 27, Brockdorff-Rantzau to Stresemann, November 23, 1927, 4562H/2319/E159 480–483, 495–497, 486–490; Brockdorff-Rantzau to Ernst Rantzau, November 22, 1927, 9101H/3430/H224 637–638, 641–642; Notes by Schubert, November 25 and December 23, 1927, 4562H/2319/E159 491–493, 527–529; Foreign Office notes, 4562H/2319/E159 498, 504, 535–537; Schlesinger to Brockdorff-Rantzau, December 23, 1927, 9101H/3433/H227 123; Hilger, 158.

25. Notes by Schubert, February 20, 1928, 9101H/3432/H226 329–340; Helbig, *Rapallo,* 199–200.

26. Brockdorff-Rantzau to Ernst Rantzau, February 6 and 16/17, 1928, 9101H/3430/H224 687–693.

27. Hilger, 217–218.

28. The account of the events related to the trial are based on "AEG-Donez Prozess" and "Schachty-Prozess und Schachty Nachklänge," 6698H/3034/H110 050–201, 527–735, unless otherwise noted.

29. Deposition by F. Goldstein, April 7, 1928, 6698H/3034/H110 121–126.

30. Brockdorff-Rantzau to Ernst Rantzau, March 24, 1928, 9101H/3430/H224 719–721.

31. Foreign Office memorandum, no date, 5462H/2785/E380 298.

32. Shapiro, I, 290, 300.

33. Brockdorff-Rantzau to Foreign Office, March 30, 1928, 6698H/3034/H110 085–086.

34. *The New York Times,* April 1, 1928.

35. Stresemann to Brockdorff-Rantzau, April 7, 1928, 6698H/3034/H110 126–127.

36. Brockdorff-Rantzau to Stresemann, April 8, 1928, 6698H/3034/H110 176.

37. Brockdorff-Rantzau to Ernst Rantzau, April 7, 1928, 9101H/3430/H224 727.

38. Hencke to Brockdorff-Rantzau, April 28, 1928, 9101H/3429/H223 630–635.

39. Brockdorff-Rantzau to Foreign Office, May 8 and 12, 1928, 6698H/3034/ H110 531–532, 533.

40. Walter Duranty, *The New York Times*, May 19, 1928.

41. Shapiro, I, 290.

42. Brockdorff-Rantzau to Foreign Office, May 22, 1928, 6698H/3034/H110 572–573.

43. Brockdorff-Rantzau to Ernst Rantzau, June 2 and 11, 1928, 9101H/3430/ H224 772–, 777, 786.

44. Brockdorff-Rantzau to Foreign Office, May 29 and June 8, 1928, 6698H/ 3034/H110 581, 592.

45. Brockdorff-Rantzau to Foreign Office, June 19 and 22, 1928, 6698H/3034/ H110 595–597, 598–599.

46. Brockdorff-Rantzau to Foreign Office, June 28, 1928, 6698H/3034/H110 621–623.

47. Brockdorff-Rantzau to Ernst Rantzau, July 14, 1928, 9101H/3430/H224 793.

48. Brockdorff-Rantzau to Ernst Rantzau, July 14, 1928, 9101H/3430/H224 793–794; Stern-Rubarth, 149–150; Hilger, 220.

49. Scheffer, 323.

50. Schlesinger, to Dirksen, July 14 and 20, 1928, 6698H/3034/H110 696–706, 686–687.

51. Stern-Rubarth, 159; Helbig, *Rapallo*, 148.

52. For the statistics, see: Kuczinsky and Wittkowski, 32–33, 58–59.

53. Schubert to Brockdorff-Rantzau, June 22, 1928, 6698H/3034/110 613–616; on the resumption of the negotiations, see 6698H/3041/114 974–985, 115 014, and Hilger, 235–236.

54. Hilger, 235.

55. Hilger, 240.

56. Dirksen, 96; Hilger, 240–241.

57. M. Beloff, *The Foreign Policy of Soviet Russia, 1929–1941* (2 vols.; London: Oxford University Press, 1947), I, 41.

58. Hey to Foreign Office, September 30, 1928, 6699H/3058/118 239–246.

59. "Reise des Chefs des Truppenamts nach Russland, August/September, 1928," 9480H/3668/276 183–236; on the tanks, 4562H/2331/163 954–966.

60. Hoesch (Paris) to Foreign Office, November 11, 1929, 9480H/3668/276 133–135.

61. Details about the final years of collaboration can be found in "Handakten Dirksen," 9480H/3668/276 238–508; J. Erickson, *The Soviet High Command* (London: St. Martin's Press, 1962), pp. 343–349; regarding Lipetsk in Völker, *Entwicklung der Militärischen Luftfahrt, passim*.

BIBLIOGRAPHICAL ESSAY

After the voluminous publication of Tsarist documents, the government of the USSR has been extremely reluctant to publish additional materials. The absence of substantial Soviet documentary collections has been alleviated by the opening to research of the captured files of the German Foreign Office. The vast amount of material for the Weimar period has been sifted by a number of researchers who have published the results of their labors in a number of excellent monographs and articles.

The present study is based on the thorough exploration of over 100 rolls of microfilmed German Foreign Office files. Events are reconstructed on the basis of that documentary evidence. Here, of course, is also the major difficulty. Relations with Moscow are seen primarily through German eyes. Fortunately, the reporters were astute, intelligent, well-trained diplomats, determined to be as objective in their evaluation of Soviet motives as possible. Nevertheless, the author frequently had to make an educated guess at the reasons behind the reason for a particular Kremlin policy. The historian determined to let both sides have their day in court would find it easier if the boast that "Communists disdain to conceal their views and aims" were true. Despite the obvious pitfalls, the German documents are the major source for an evaluation of German-Soviet diplomatic relations. This situation will continue until similar collections are made available by the USSR.

I. UNPUBLISHED DOCUMENTS.

The evidence used in the preparation of this monograph is almost exclusively drawn from the captured German Foreign Office Documents available on microfilm from the National Archives, Washington, D.C. A convenient guide to the films here used is provided by E. Schwandt's *Index of Microfilmed Records of the German Foreign Ministry and the Reich's Chancellery Covering the Weimar Period,* Washington: The National Archives, 1958. The 100 rolls listed below have been actually read, page by page, while numerous more not listed had to be perused for relevant material. Obviously, the "Nachlass des Reichsministers Dr. Gustav Stresemann" had to be checked. Most of the collection covered domestic affairs, personal correspondence, and political writings. The documents of interest to this monograph were found in the files of the "Büro des Reichsministers," Serial 2860H, rolls 1343, 1404–1417, 1455, and the Cabinet protocols dealing with German-Russian relations in Serial 3242H, rolls 1591–1592. An excellent evaluation of the "Nachlass" was made by H. W. Gatzke in "The Stresemann Papers," *Journal of Modern History,* XXVI, No. 1 (March, 1954), 49–59.

310 COMMUNITY OF FATE

The "Nachlass Brockdorff-Rantzau" contains a veritable goldmine of information. Serial 9101H, roll 3429 covers the period from 1922 to 1928; it deals with the appointment to Moscow and private business affairs. Roll 3430 reproduces letters from Brockdorff-Rantzau to Ebert, Simons, Hindenburg, and their replies, as well as letters to Ernst Rantzau. Roll 3431 holds the very important correspondence with Maltzan, which began on November 3, 1922, and ended on February 14, 1925. Rolls 3432–3433 contain letters and reports from the Wilhelmstrasse, the correspondence between the Ambassador and Moritz Schlesinger, and letters from Ernst Rantzau to his brother. Rolls 3434–3436, 3438–3441, 3443–3444 deal with the period from 1918 to Brockdorff-Rantzau's appointment to Moscow. Serial 9105H, rolls 3445–3446 shed light on the controversy with von Seeckt. Most of the material in these rolls is also reproduced in Serial 6812H, roll 3154. Finally, Serials 1690H, 1691H, 1692H, roll 1013, contain the manuscript for a biography of Brockdorff-Rantzau by the noted German historian Erich Brandenburg. The Wilhelmstrasse, to which the manuscript was submitted, refused permission to publish it.

Copies of the documents used by Brandenburg were found in the cellar of the historian's bombed house by Dr. Herbert Helbig, who based his article, "Die Moskauer Mission des Grafen Brockdorff-Rantzau," in *Forschungen zur Osteuropäischen Geschichte*, II (Berlin, 1955) on these materials. In 1958, Dr. Helbig published an expanded version of his article as one of three chapters in *Die Träger des Rapallo-Politik,* published by Vandenhoeck and Rupprecht of Göttingen. In the first chapter of his book, Professor Helbig unravels the involved preliminaries which led to Rapallo in a thorough and competent manner. The third chapter deals with the military collaboration between the Reichswehr and the Red army. Dr. Gatzke's article, "Russo-German Military Collaboration during the Weimar Republic," in the *American Historical Review*, LXIII, No. 3 (April, 1958), 565–597, superseded all previous works on the subject until the publication of John Erickson's excellent narrative and analytical account of the collaboration in his *The Soviet High Command: A Military-Political History, 1918–1940* (London: St. Martin's Press, 1962).

Reports and similar materials from the German Embassy in Moscow are contained in Serial 1565H, roll 795, Serial 1565H, roll 911, Serial 1843H, 1844H, roll 1053, Serial 9444H, roll 3662, and Serial 9472H, roll 3663. Information dealing primarily with the economic relations between the two countries for the years 1920–1928 can be found in "Handakten Schlesinger," Serial 4892H, rolls 2457–2458, as well as in the "Handakten" of Direktor Wallroth, Serial 5265H, rolls 2568–2573. The "Nachlass Maltzan" covers the Ruhr invasion, the Bozenhardt incident, and the preliminaries to Locarno in rolls 3048 and 3059, Serial 6702H.

The extensive collection "Russland" in the files of the "Büro des Staatssekretärs," Serial 4562H, rolls 2313–2323, contains the kind of material which is passed up from the departments for final decision before transmission to the Foreign Minister, as well as notes by the Undersecretary, copies of policy statements, and similar matter. This, of necessity, means that quite a bit of the material appears in other collections as well. In general, I traced a given document from the lower echelon to the Foreign Minister in order to discover the origin of an idea, the start of a policy, and the comments by the officers consulted. Serial 4561H, rolls 2310–2312 deals with the Baltic States, while Serial 4564H, rolls 2329–2331 covers "Militärische Angelegenheiten mit Russland" from March 13, 1923, to May 18, 1930. Serial 4484H, roll 2226 contains papers dealing with German-Russian economic negotiations for the period 1925–1929. Serial 4556H, rolls 2299–2302, covers relations with Russia, Poland, Danzig, and general problems with Eastern Europe.

The "Handakten" of Dirksen are of particular interest for political matters because he, not Wallroth, his nominal superior, dealt directly with Brockdorff-Rantzau and Stresemann. Serial 5462H, roll 2785, contains "Geheim-Berichte Graf Rantzau, sowie sonstige Dienste, 1925, 1926, 1927," and reports by secret agents; not much of value is included. Serial 9480H, 9481H, roll 3668 deals with the military collaboration and contains copies of papers also filed in the Office of the Undersecretary, as well as newspaper clippings, letters, and similar peripheral materials.

Secret documents are collected in "Geheimakten, 1920–1936." Those pertaining to relations with Russia are contained in Serial 6698H, rolls 3027–3044, Serial 6699H, roll 3058, Serial 6700H, roll 3045, and Serial 6701H, rolls 3046–3047.

Unfortunately, documentary publications by the USSR for the period 1922–1928 are extremely scarce, leaving the historian no choice but to deduce Russian motives and policy from the German materials. In this connection, chroniclers of diplomatic relations owe a debt of gratitude to Louis Fischer for his two-volume *The Soviets in World Affairs: A History of the Relations between the Soviet Union and the rest of the World, 1917–1929*, the second edition of which was published in 1951 by Princeton University Press. Mr. Fischer had the confidence of Chicherin, who revealed considerable information, as a study of the German documents proves. In 1957 the Soviet Foreign Ministry began the publication of *Dokumenty vneshnei politiki SSR* (Documents on the Foreign Policy of the USSR), nine volumes of which have now appeared covering the period from 1917 to 1926. The new series supersedes the three-volume *Istoriya diplomatii* published in 1941–1945 and edited by a committee of Soviet scholars under V. P. Potiemkin. I have used volume 3 of the French edition, *Historie de la Diplomatie*, which deals with the years 1919–1939. Because of its peculiar bias, this volume adds little to an objective evaluation of German-Russian relations. In 1959 the Soviet Foreign Ministry published selected documents bearing on the Locarno Conference, *Lokarnskaya konferentsia 1925g. Dokumenty*. In addition, there is available a 1927 publication by the People's Commissariat for Foreign Affairs, *Desiat let Sovetskoi diplomatii: Akty i dokumenty* (Ten Years of Soviet Diplomacy: Reports and Documents).

II. Published Documents.

For published Soviet documentary materials in English, one has to turn to the collections edited by Jane Degras and published by the Oxford University Press: *Soviet Documents on Foreign Policy*, which covers the period 1917–1941, and the first two volumes on *The Communist International*, which cover the years 1919–1928. Evidence drawn from the official publications of the Russian Communist party and the Comintern are made available by X. Eudin and H. H. Fisher in *Soviet Russia and the West: A Documentary Survey*, published by the Stanford University Press in 1957. Dr. Leonard Shapiro compiled and edited *Soviet Treaty Series: A Collection of Bilateral Treaties, Agreements, and Conventions, etc., Concluded Between the Soviet Union and Foreign Powers*, vol. I, 1917–1928 (Washington: Georgetown University Press, 1950). *A Calendar of Soviet Treaties, 1917–1957*, compiled by R. M. Slusser and J. F. Triska, published by Stanford University Press in 1954, provides a listing of all "Secret Soviet-German Military Agreements, 1923–1933," which, according to the authors, have been accepted as authentic by historians. Diligent search in the documents has failed thus far to produce actual evidence of some of the agreements.

III. Memoirs, Autobiographies, and Biographies.

Many of the major actors on the Weimar stage have published their memoirs; most of these proved disappointing, and few added anything of real substance, when compared to the documentary evidence, to the understanding of German-Russian diplomatic relations. An exception is the remarkable book produced by G. Hilger and A. G. Meyer, *The Incompatible Allies: A Memoir History of German-Soviet Relations, 1918–1941*, published by Macmillan in 1953. Hilger, one of Brockdorff-Rantzau's close collaborators, produced a highly factual account. Herbert von Dirksen's *Moscow, Tokyo, London: Twenty Years of German Foreign Policy* (Norman; University of Oklahoma Press, 1952), which was written from memory, is rather disappointing as a source for German-Russian relations. Stresemann's *Vermächtnis*, edited by H. Bernhard (3 vols.; Berlin: Ullstein, 1932–1934), has been superseded by the "Nachlass."

Otto Gessler's *Reichswehrpolitik in der Weimarer Zeit*, edited by K. Sendtner (Stuttgart: Deutsche Verlags-Anstalt, 1960), contains some interesting material, but nothing of real significance. Gessler maintains that the military collaboration was really completely inconsequential. Hans Luther's memoir, *Politiker ohne Partei: Erinnerungen* (Stuttgart: Deutsche Verlags-Anstalt, 1960), is marred by his attempt to justify his actions and place himself into the proper historical perspective. His account of the Locarno Conference is pedestrian, as is his quarrelsome attitude on the well-deserved praise Stresemann received for this accomplishment. Friedrich Ebert's two volumes of *Schriften, Aufzeichungen, Reden* (Dresden: Reissner Verlag, 1926), deal primarily with domestic politics.

Otto Meissner's *Staatssekretär unter Ebert, Hindenburg, Hitler: Der Schicksalsweg des deutschen Volkes von 1918–1945, wie ich ihn erlebte* (3rd edition; Hamburg: Hoffman und Campe, 1950), promises much more in the title than it delivers. As an apologia, it falls into the same genre as Wipert von Blücher's *Deutschland's Weg nach Rapallo: Erinnerungen eines Mannes aus dem zweiten Gliede* (Wiesbaden: Limes Verlag, 1951), although Blücher remembered a great deal of interesting material. Much more important is Edgar Vincent Viscount D'Abernon's *The Diary of an Ambassador* (3 vols.; Garden City: Doubleday and Doran, 1929–1931), which provides a number of insights, particularly on his part in the preparation of the Locarno Treaties. Brockdorff-Rantzau published only a defense of his position at and on Versailles, which appeared in three editions, the last one entitled *Dokumente und Gedanken um Versailles* (Berlin: Verlag für Kulturpolitik, 1925). The only available biography of the Ambassador is still Edgar Stern-Rubarth's panegyric, *Graf Brockdorff-Rantzau: Wanderer zwischen zwei Welten: Ein Lebensbild,* published by Hobbing of Berlin eight months after the Count's death. The author was provided with material by Ernst Rantzau, but much of it, for obvious reasons, could not be utilized.

Karl Kindermann described his experience in *Zwei Jahre in Moskaus Totenhäusern: Der Moskauer Studentenprozess* (Berlin: Eckart Verlag, 1931). He does not succeed in removing the aura of naive innocence which surrounded the whole affair. Paul Scheffer, the Moscow correspondent of the *Berliner Tageblatt* from 1921 to 1929, describes the Soviet Union quite well, but reveals little of any importance in his *Sieben Jahre Sowjet-Union* (Leipzig: Bibliographisches Institut, 1930). M. von Stockhausen's *Sechs Jahre Reichskanzlei: von Rapallo bis Locarno. Erinnerungen und Tagebuchnotizen, 1922–1927,* edited by W. Görlitz (Bonn: Atheneum Verlag, 1954), contains only peripheral information. The same is true of W. Zechlin's *Pressechef bei Ebert, Hindenburg, und Kopf. Erlebnisse eines Pressechefs und Diplomaten* (Hanover: Schlüter, 1956). Louis Fischer provides excellent vignettes of European life and politicians from the twenties to the forties in *Men and Politics: An Autobiography* (New York: Duell, Sloan, and Pearce, 1941).

Articles and books on Stresemann have proliferated to a point where a separate essay could easily be written, covering many pages. Fortunately, the task has been well accomplished by Dr. Gatzke in "Gustav Stresemann: A Bibliographical Article, " *Journal of Modern History,* XXXVI (March, 1964), 1–13. There is, to the best of my knowledge, no biography of Maltzan, Schubert, or Schlesinger, all of whom appear prominently in this work. General v. Rabenau edited two volumes of Seeckt's paper, one of which is of interest here, namely, *Seeckt: Aus Seinem Leben, 1918–1936* (Leipzig: Hase und Koehler, 1940).

On the Russian side, Chicherin still awaits a full-length biography, although a vignette appears in Fischer's *Autobiography* and a somewhat longer treatment in *The Diplomats, 1919–1939*, edited by G. A. Craig and F. Gilbert and published by Princeton University Press in 1953. A. V. Pope's *Maxim Litvinoff* (New York: Fischer, 1943), is a very sympathetic study of the Deputy and, later, Commissar for Foreign Affairs.

IV. GENERAL STUDIES, MONOGRAPHS, AND ARTICLES.

Numerous secondary works have appeared over the years dealing with the Weimar Republic. Dated but still very useful are the following: A. Rosenberg, *Geschichte der deutschen Republik* (Karlsbad: Graphia, 1935); S. W. Halperin, *Germany Tried Democracy: A Political History of the Reich from 1918 to 1933* (New York: Crowell, 1946); W. M. Knight-Patterson (W. W. Kulski), *Germany from Defeat to Conquest, 1913–1933* (London: Allen and Unwin, 1945); E. Luehr, *The New German Republic: The Reich in Transition* (New York: Minton, Balch, 1929); H. Quigley and R. T. Clark, *Republican Germany: A Political and Economic Study* (London: Methuen, 1928); G. Scheele, *The Weimar Republic: Overture to the Third Reich* (London: Faber, 1946); and F. L. Schuman, *Germany since 1918* (New York: Holt, 1937).

Among the more recent works, the following are of special interest: G. A. Craig, *From Bismarck to Adenauer: Aspects of German Statecraft* (Baltimore: Johns Hopkins Press, 1958); M. Göhring, *Bismarck's Erben, 1890–1954. Deuschland's Weg von Wilhelm II bis Adolf Hitler* (Wiesbaden: Steiner, 1959); R. N. Hunt, *German Social Democracy, 1918–1933* (New Haven: Yale University Press, 1964); E. Matthias, *Die deutsche Social demokratie und der Osten, 1914–1945. Eine Übersicht* (Tübingen: Arbeitsgemeinschaft für Osteuropaforschung, 1954); T. Schieder, *Die Probleme des Rapallo Vertrags: Eine Studie über die deutsch-russischen Beziehungen, 1922–1926* (Köln: Westdeutscher Verlag, 1956); E. Vermeil, *L'Allemagne Contemporaire: Sociale, Politique, Culturelle, 1890–1950* (2 vols.; Paris: Aubier, 1952); F. Stampfer, *Die Vierzehne Jahre der ersten deutschen Republik* (Hamburg: Auerdruck, 1953); E. Eyck, *Geschichte der Weimarer Republik* (2 vols.; Erlenbach-Zürich: Hentsch, 1956). (An English translation by H. Hansen and R. White was published by Harvard University Press in 1963.)

A fine view of foreign relations during the Weimar period is afforded by L. Zimmerman in *Deutsche Aussenpolitik in der Ära der Weimarer Republik* (Göttingen: Musterschmidt Verlag, 1958). Among the studies dealing with German-Russian relations, the following are particularly noteworthy: G. Freund, *Unholy Alliance: German Russian Relations from the Treaty of Brest-Litovsk to the Treaty of Berlin* (London: Chatto and Windus, 1957); L. Kochan, *Russia and the Weimar Republic* (Cambridge: Bowes, 1954); E. H. Carr, *German-Soviet Relations between the Two World Wars, 1919–1939* (Baltimore: Johns Hopkins Press, 1951); and J. Korbel, *Poland Between East and West: Soviet and German Diplomacy Towards Poland, 1919–1939* (Princeton: Princeton University Press, 1963); and the analysis of the December proposals by Z. J. Gasiorowski in an article in the *Journal of Modern History*, XXX, No. 2 (June, 1958), 99–117, entitled "The Russian Overture to Germany of December 1924."

Two books published in East Berlin interpret German-Russian relations along approved Communist lines, which detracts considerably from their scholarly value. These are F. Klein, *Die Diplomatischen Beziehungen Deutschlands zur Sovietunion, 1917–1932* (2nd ed.: Rütten und Loening, 1953), and A. Norden, *Zwischen Berlin und Moskau. Zur Geschichte der deutsch-sowietischen Beziehungen* (Dietz Verlag, 1954).

Werner T. Angress analyzes the *Stillborn Revolution: The Communist Bid for Power in Germany, 1921–1923* (Princeton: Princeton University Press, 1963), with great virtuosity and brilliant scholarship. His bibliographical essay is a service to historians interested in the role played by the KPD during the Weimar Republic's early years. His evaluation of Ruth Fischer's *Stalin and German Communism: A Study in the Origins of the State Party* (Cambridge, Mass.: Harvard University Press, 1948), is excellent. What Dr. Angress does for 1921–1923, Ossip K. Flechtheim did in 1948 for the history of the KPD in *Die Kommunistische Partei Deutschlands in der Weimarer Republik* (Offenbach: Bollwerk Verlag K. Drott).

The military collaboration between the Reichswehr and the Red army has come in for its fair share of attention. The most recent studies are Erickson's mentioned above, and Karl-Heinz Völker, "Die Entwicklung der Militärischen Luftfahrt in Deutschland, 1920–1933: Planung und Massnahmen zur Schaffung einer Fliegertruppe in der Reichswehr," in *Beiträge zur Militär- und Kriegsgeschichte*, vol. 3 (Stuttgart: Deutsche Verlagsanstalt, 1962); the same volume also includes a study of the German General Staff during the years 1871 to 1945. In 1932 C. F. Melville published *The Russian Face of Germany: An Account of the Secret Military Relations between the German and Soviet-Russian Governments* (London: Wishart, 1932); this was followed by T. H. Morgan's *Assize of Arms: The Disarmament of Germany and her Rearmament, 1919–1939*, published in 1945 by Oxford University Press. In the second issue of its first volume, *Der Monat* (Berlin, November, 1948) published Julius Epstein's "Der Seeckt Plan," which was followed by G. W. F. Hallgarten's article, "General Hans von Seeckt and Russia, 1920–1922," *Journal of Modern History*, XXXI, No. 1 (March, 1949), 28–34; in 1954 two more detailed accounts appeared: G. Castellan's "Reichswehr et Armée Rouge, *1920–1939*," in *Les Relations Germano-Soviètiques de 1933–1939*, edited by J. B. Duroselle and published in Paris by Libraire Colin, and H. W. Gatzke's *Stresemann and the Rearmament of Germany*, published by the Johns Hopkins Press in 1958. Dr. Gatzke presented further evidence about the involvement of the civilian authorities, including Stresemann, in his article.

General works dealing with the German army are those by W. Goerlitz, *Der Deutsche Generalstab* (Frankfurt: *Verlag der Frankfurter Hefte*, 1951); by W. Erfurth, *Die Geschichte des deutschen Generalstabes, 1918–1945* (Göttingen: Musterschmidt Verlag, 1957); by H. J. Gordon, *The Reichswehr and the German Republic, 1919–1926* (Princeton: Princeton University Press, 1957); and by G. A. Craig, *The Politics of the Prussian Army, 1640–1945* (Oxford: Clarendon Press, 1955).

Newspaper accounts have been used only when they appeared in the documents, thus indicating direct interest by the Wilhelmstrasse in the particular article, or when reference was made to a report.

INDEX

Agreement on the Repatriation of Prisoners of War: 14; Supplementary Agreement, 20–22, 88–89, 99, 101
Albert, Heinrich, 65
Allgemeine Elektrizitätsgesellschaft (A.E.G.), 26, 254, 256, 265, 273
All-Russian Central Executive Committee. *See* Russia
All-Russian (Union) Communist Party (B): Congresses, 18, 95; Bozenhardt incident, 94
American Relief Administration, 21–22
Arcos raid, 246

Baden, Prince Max von, 2, 3
Badstieber, Wilhelm, 254, 259, 263, 264, 266, 272, 273
Baltruschaitis, Jurgis K., 266
Bashkin (brothers), 265, 267, 271, 272
Baumann (OGPU), 154
Behncke, Admiral Paul, 39, 46
Behrendt, Gustav, 18
Behrens, Admiral, 59
Berliner Tageblatt, 133
Bersol, poison gas, 239
Berthelot, Philippe, 212
Bessedovsky, Gregory, 280
Bleimann (A.E.G. Director), 254, 267, 271, 273
Blomberg, Colonel (later General) Werner von, 239, 279–80
Boldt, J. C., 148
Borah, Senator William E., 133
Bozenhardt, Johannes, 87–88, 96
Brandenburg (Director for Aviation), 229
Brandler, Heinrich, 72, 74, 77
Bratman-Brodovsky, Stepan J. (Counselor of Soviet Embassy, Berlin, 1922–1931): Bozenhardt incident, 91–92; League of Nations, 116; Chicherin visit to Poland, 177; Treaty of Berlin, 188, 190; Thoiry, 227; military collaboration, 238
Brest-Litovsk, Treaty of, 1, 3
Briand, Aristide: 185, 248; discussion with Chicherin, 195; Treaty of Berlin, 214; German admission to League, 225; Thoiry, 225

Brockdorff-Rantzau, Count Ulrich K. C. von: biographical sketch, 3–5; early appointments, 5, 15; policy on peace treaty, 6; Brest-Litovsk, 6–7; program speech, 7–8; Versailles, 9–12, 13, 35, 38, 48, 126, 127, 129, 137, 166; resumption of relations with Russia, 19; Rapallo, 26, 30; political instructions for the ambassador to Moscow, 34; Bolsheviks, 35; military collaboration, 35, 38–41, 57–58, 64–71, 222–23, 235, 237, 239–40, 261; *agrément*, 36, 287n92; *Promemoria*, 36–38, 62, 97; arrival and reception in Moscow, 49–50; Russo-French *rapprochement*, 50, 55, 59–60, 63, 83–84; Comintern, 51, 59–60, 70, 75–76, 80–85, 119, 130–31; Russian relations with West, 61–62, 136–37; Petrov case, 72–73; Bozenhardt incident, 90–92, 98, 101, 107; Dawes Plan, 114; League of Nations, 115, 119, 121, 137, 188–89, 226, 250; Locarno, 129, 132, 168, 178, 245; Student Trial, 147, 148, 150, 153–54, 159, 165; Cheka Trial, 150; Hilger exoneration, 159, 164, 165; resignations, 168, 192; Chicherin trip to Poland, 176–77; direct access to the president, 200; consular agents, 202; Treaty of Berlin, 200, 218; Skoblevsky exchange, 221, 224–25; Thoiry, 226; Russo-British relations, 249; war scare in Russia, 250; fifth anniversary in Moscow, 250–52; Hölz, 252; Deutsch (A.E.G.) ultimatum, 259–60; industrial conditions, 255; Shakhty arrests, 264–65, trial, 267; death, 276
—relations with diplomats: Stresemann, 12, 43–44, 166–67, 169–72, 253, 260–61; Chicherin, 30–32, 251–52; Ebert, 30, 32, 96–97; Wirth, 32, 34, 40, 45–47; Seeckt, 35–36, 54–55, 130, 286n75; Schlesinger, 78–79; Maltzan, 124; Hindenburg, 188–89; Schubert, 245
—German relations with nations: Great Britain, 20, 128; France, 95; Russia, 52, 58, 60, 75, 122–23, 126, 164–67, 177, 242, 250, 268–73 *passim;* and

317

Brockdorff-Rantzau (*continued*)
Russian proposals for treaties, 122–26, 130–31, 134, 138, 142, 144–45, 155, 158, 162, 163, 174–75, 187
Brown, Walter L., 22
Bülow, Bernhard W. von, 119, 121, 139
Bukharin, Nikolai I.: 78; Ruhr occupation, 52; Bozenhardt incident, 101; Shakhty arrests, 261–62
Butyrka jail, 263

Chamberlain, Sir Austen: 126, 185; Treaty of Berlin, 211; note on articles 16, 17 of League Covenant, 213–14; break of diplomatic relations with Russia, 242
Cheka, 2. *See* OGPU
Cheka Trial, 149–51, 165
Chicago Daily Tribune (Paris), 280
Chicherin, Georgi V.: 7, 41, 50, 53, 113, 272, 280; relations with Germany, 16, 28, 117–18, 120, 132, 141–42, 178–81, 182–84, 227; Rapallo, 29; Brockdorff-Rantzau, 30–32; League of Nations, 51, 116, 119, 122, 124–26, 142, 158–59, 182–83, 196, 251; Ruhr occupation, 57; economic negotiations, 60, 157; Russo-French *rapprochement*, 59, 128, 195, 203; Comintern, 59, 63, 80–85, 178; military collaboration, 70, 109, 231, 240; Communist Party, 70; Petrov incident, 73; Bozenhardt incident, 90, 96, 100, 111; candidate for Chairman of Council of People's Commissars, 95; Treaty of Berlin, 124–26, 158–59, 161–63, 183, 198–99; Poland, 124–26, 162, 176–77, 185, 204–05; reports to Central Executive Committee, 131; Student Trial, 147–49, 151–55 *passim*; Cheka Trial, 149; Hilger exoneration, 153, 159–60, 167–68; meeting with Skrzyński, 177; Great Britain, 182–83; Hindenburg, 184; discussion with Briand, 195; Seeckt, 190; Thoiry, 226–27; discussion with Stresemann on British break of relations, 248
Clemenceau, G. E. B., 9
Comintern: 130, 147, 248, 249, 278; attempts to revolutionize Germany, 21, 22, 77; relation to Soviet government, 51, 63, 80–85; anti-British propaganda, 242
Commercial Treaty: negotiations, 156–58, 174, 184–85; ratification, 203; Article XI (Part I), 255, 256–57, 268;

extension, 253, 277. *See also* Germany, Russia (treaty negotiations)
Communist Party Congress, 1, 18, 95
Communist Party of Germany (KPD): 51, 79, 82; attempt at revolution, 6; rising in the Ruhr, 14, 63; armed rising in Central Germany (March action), 18; German October, 74, 81, 85; Reichstag elections, 97; Bozenhardt incident, 109; Comintern aid, 111; Student Trial, 146; Cheka Trial, 149. *See also* Petrov, Stalin, Zinoviev
Consular agents, arrest of, 200–02
Cuno, Wilhelm (Chancellor, November, 1922–August, 1923): 51; Ruhr occupation, 53; military collaboration, 57, 65–71; Poland, 67
Czechoslovakia: Russo-Czech treaty, 140, 159, 191, 193, 196; Treaty of Berlin, 216; German arbitration treaty, 185–86

D'Abernon, Lord Edgar Vincent (British Ambassador to Germany, 1920–1926): evaluation of Maltzan, 13; relations with Schubert, 124; Treaty of Berlin, 210–14; German-Russian relations, 218
Dawes Plan, 112, 114, 227
Derutra, 232
Deutsch, Felix (A.E.G.): Bozenhardt incident, 99; ultimatum, 254; arrest of technicians, 258
Deutsche Diplomatische-Politische Korrespondenz, 267
Deutsche Volkspartei (DVP), 12
Deutschnationale Volkspartei (DNVP), 78, 79, 95
Dirksen, Herbert von: 133; Commercial Treaty, 156, 161, 163, 178; Treaty of Berlin, 144, 158, 191, 199–200; military collaboration, 233, 235, 238; Shakhty, 259, 275; Ambassador to USSR, 277; economic relations, 278
Ditmar, Max von, 146, 152, 154
Dittmar, L. W. F., 148
Domatovsky (lawyer), 264
Druffel, Consul, 89
Drummond, Sir Eric, 180
Duchovskoi (lawyer), 151
Dufour-Feronce, Baron Albert: opposes German-Russian treaty, 135; Treaty of Berlin, 215
Duranty, Walter, 54
Dzerzhinsky, Felix, 2, 99, 154